CLASSICAL COUNTY HISTORIES
GENERAL EDITOR: PROFESSOR JACK SIMMONS

THE
HISTORY AND ANTIQUITIES
OF THE
COUNTY OF RUTLAND

THE
HISTORY
AND
ANTIQUITIES
OF THE COUNTY OF
RUTLAND

JAMES WRIGHT

With a new introduction by Jack Simmons

This edition originally printed for B. Griffin, London 1684–1714 with additions printed by W. Harrod, 1788.

Republished 1973 by EP Publishing Limited in collaboration with Rutland County Council.

Copyright © in reprint 1973 EP Publishing Limited
East Ardsley, Wakefield
Yorkshire, England

Copyright © in introduction 1973
Jack Simmons

Second impression 1973

ISBN 0 85409 853 4

Reprinted in Great Britain by Scolar Press Ltd., Menston, Yorkshire, U.K.

INTRODUCTION

T his is the shortest of all the chief county histories; appropriately, since Rutland is the smallest English county. But if the book is short, it is not inconsiderable. It stands very early in the succession of works of its kind, preceded only by Dugdale and Thoroton, and it is in some respects a pioneer. Bibliographically, the book is a standing challenge. Among the national libraries, the Bodleian alone possesses copies of all its original elements, as they have been brought together in this reprinted edition. And James Wright himself is an engaging creature, different in character, in outlook and tastes, from any of the other county historians, earlier or later. Let us begin with him.

I

His father was Abraham Wright (1611-90), Fellow of St John's College, Oxford; his mother Jane, daughter of James Stone, of the neighbouring village of Yarnton. It seems to have been at Yarnton that he was born, in 1643.[1] Abraham Wright had made his way forward as a scholar and Laudian divine, under the particular patronage of Juxon, Bishop of London, but his promising career was blighted by the Civil War. Juxon presented him to the vicarage of Oakham, Rutland, in 1645. In order to take possession of it, however, he was required by the victorious Parliamentarians to subscribe the Covenant, which he refused to do; and he was ejected from his Fellowship at the same time. For the next fifteen years he lived at Peckham, just outside London, and then in London itself. At the Restoration in 1660 he was able to claim the living of Oakham. He stayed there for the rest of his life.

We hear nothing of James Wright's boyhood and youth. He may have followed his father to Merchant Taylors' School; but, for some unexplained reason, he does not seem to have proceeded to a university.[2] He read law, and in 1666 became a student of New Inn, migrating thence three years later to the Middle Temple, from which he was called to the bar in 1672. He practised, or at least continued to study, the law for the rest of his life.[3] He was living in the Middle Temple in 1678, when a fire occurred there, in which he lost his library. It was evidently a good one, including an early manuscript of Leland's *Itinerary*.[4]

We may infer that he lived chiefly in London for the rest of his life, but that he paid frequent visits to Rutland — not only to Oakham, to see his father, but also perhaps to

[1] Stapleton, *Three Oxfordshire Parishes* (1893), 277.
[2] A. Wood, *Athenae Oxonienses*, ed. P. Bliss, iv (1820), 277.
[3] Two volumes of his notes of cases, and other legal matters, dated 1694-1716, are in the British Museum: Add. MSS. 22609-10.
[4] T. Hearne, *Remarks and Collections* (1885-1921), ii.227.

INTRODUCTION

Manton, of which he acquired the manor in 1683.[1] He tells us that he enjoyed "angling, and such like diversions of a country retreat".[2] His first published work seems to have been an anonymous poem on the ruins of St Paul's after the Great Fire. That appeared in 1668, and was followed by nothing else that we know of until 1684, when he produced his *History of Rutland*.[3] We do not hear anything of his life during these years – apart from his misfortune in 1678. Some of his time must have been spent in collecting the materials for this, his one work of learning. He may well have been making a good income from the law. Anthony Wood said sneeringly that he produced "little trival things of history and poetry, merely to get a little money, which he will not own";[4] but we have no other indication that Wright was poor, and those words were published in 1692, when he had not printed much. No doubt he inherited whatever his father had to leave when he died in 1690.

The whole tenor of Wright's work is that of a London Tory of the middle class. There was never any doubt about the Toryism: he was a Church-and-King man through and through. He displays his political feelings most clearly in a little book he published in 1685: *A Compendious View of the Late Troubles and Tumults in this Kingdom*. It is a piece of contemporary history, an account of the past eight years – the years of the Popish Plot, of the Whigs' attempt to curb the powers of the Crown, and of Charles II's adroit achievement in turning the tables on them. In it Wright displays a fervent admiration for the King, and he ends (Charles having died suddenly, as the book was passing through the press) with an exhortation to his countrymen to give James II the support that his brother had earned. Yet Wright's Toryism was sensible, after all. Just as his father, a staunch Anglican, accepted the Revolution when it came in 1688 and took the oaths to William and Mary, so he himself did not become a Jacobite, though Hearne seems to have had some reason to suppose that he joined the Roman Catholic church secretly in Charles II's time and remained there till his death.[5]

Wright never touched on politics again in anything he published. For the moment, indeed, he forsook original authorship altogether. In 1687 he produced a translation of a guide-book to Paris, and in 1693 an abridged English version of Dugdale's *Monasticon*. Then in that same year came *The Humours and Conversations of the Town* – almost certainly his – followed by *Country Conversations* in 1694.[6]

Country Conversations is a slight performance, but charming. It purports to recount the talk of three friends, two Londoners and their host in the country. The subject of the first conversation is "the modern comedies", and it is here that Wright reveals his interest in the stage, which had become one of the chief pleasures of his life. He inherited it from his father, the clergyman, who had acted before Charles I when he was young and had written plays, such as "a comical entertainment called *The Reformation*" and *Love's Hospital*, which was performed at St John's when the King and Queen visited Laud there in 1636.[7] The elder Wright kept a commonplace book, which includes passages from Shakespeare, Ben Jonson, and a number of their contemporaries.[8] In the preface to his version of the *Monasticon* James Wright observed: "Warwickshire has produced two of the most famous and deserving writers in their several ways that England can boast of – a Dugdale and a Shakespeare". Now he was more specific. "There is hardly a scene in Shakespeare (tho' he writ near 100 years since)", he wrote, "but we have it still in admiration, for the vivacity of the wit, the justness of the character, and the true, natural, and proper expression".[9] The balance of the argument between the three friends in the book is, as we might expect, in favour of the older comedies, together with a few of those written shortly after the Restoration. The modern ones are dismissed, in a way that clearly reflects their author's preferences, for their stale repetition of stock characters and for their lewdness, tedious and unvaried.

[1] *V. C. H. Rutland*, ii.79.
[2] Preface to *Country Conversations* (1694).
[3] After a fashion common to men of his time and class, Wright usually published anonymously. The *History of Rutland* is the only one of his publications that bears his name. The antiquary Hearne, who knew him personally, is our main contemporary authority for the ascription of Wright's other works. Wright gave him a list of them himself.
[4] *Athenae Oxonienses*, iv.278.
[5] *Remarks and Collections*, iv.252.
[6] *The Humours and Conversations* was reprinted at Gainsville, Florida, in 1961. In tone and subject matter it is very like *Country Conversations*, and the reference in the preface of the later book to a slight work by the same author, written in the preceding summer, fits this pamphlet well.
[7] Wood, iv.277; W. C. Costin, *History of St John's College, Oxford* (1958), 46.
[8] British Museum: Add. MS. 22608. It bears James Wright's signature on fol. 1.
[9] *Country Conversations*, 4.

INTRODUCTION

So we come to Wright's last work of any importance, the *Historia Histrionica* of 1699. Again, it is no more than a little book; Wright was always a short-winded author. But it is an urbane and well-informed review of the history of the English drama in the early part of the seventeenth century. It was reprinted, as an historical document, by Dodsley (on Bishop Warburton's recommendation) in the eighteenth century, and by Edward Arber in the nineteenth, who remarked that "so far as it goes, this is one of the most authentic accounts in existence of the English stage in the later years of Ben Jonson and during the Commonwealth".[1] An eminent modern scholar, Professor Bentley, finds the little book "surprisingly well informed" and makes repeated use of it in his history of the stage.[2]

Wright now felt he had said what he had to say, in prose. He published two more poems on St Paul's in 1697 and 1709, and the *Farther Additions* to this history of Rutland – almost wholly in verse – in 1714. That was all. He corresponded with Hearne amicably enough (apart from a little coolness about an order for one of Hearne's books in 1712)[3] and gave him a list of his writings, which he had refused to the "injudicious and partial" Anthony Wood.[4] He had indeed a very low opinion of Wood's *Athenae*, set down in measured terms when he first perused it: "The many falsities positively affirmed by this author, his nonsensical way of expressing himself, improper, ungrammatical and obscured English, and above all his magisterial and ill-natured censuring of those who are infinitely above him both for learning and quality, has blasted the performance".[5]

Wright died – unmarried, as it seems – in 1716. He bequeathed his printed books to a Mr Midleton, his manuscripts to his friend William Bromley (a former Tory Speaker of the House of Commons, and Secretary of State at the close of Queen Anne's reign).[6] Hearne noted, with surprise, that he left behind him the comfortable sum of £1,600.[7]

II

Wright begins his book on Rutland with a generous tribute to his predecessors in the study of English local history. Towards the close of the sixteenth century a number of people had written historical descriptions of counties. William Lambarde was the pioneer, in Kent, followed quickly by others. The finest artist among them was Richard Carew, whose *Survey of Cornwall* was a work of literature, as fresh today as when it was first published in 1602. Carew's neighbours in Devon were naturally led to emulate him. No less than three – Tristram Risdon, Thomas Westcote, and Sir William Pole – made the attempt, though their work remained in manuscript, not printed until much later. That is also true of other studies written at the same time – of Dorset, for example, of Staffordshire and Suffolk.

Meanwhile, two other important contributions were being made to the same end. The cartographers Saxton, Norden, and Speed, not to mention the numerous compilers of estate maps, sometimes very precise and elaborate, laid the foundations essential for good topographical work; and the heralds, by their visitations, were stimulating an interest in genealogy and family history.

The next steps in bringing all these inquiries together were taken in the Midlands. William Burton (whose brother wrote *The Anatomy of Melancholy*) set to work on his own county. His *Description of Leicestershire* was published in 1622, but against his will, since he knew it was not complete and wished to improve it. We must regret that the second edition, which he finished in 1638, was never printed (it was one of the casualties of the Civil War), for the book as we have it is a rather unsatisfactory sketch. But it remains important through the example it set, and especially through Burton's friendship with his Warwickshire neighbour William Dugdale. Dugdale avowedly went on where Burton had left off, and in his *Antiquities of Warwickshire* (1656) produced what must be regarded as the first of the fully-developed county histories. It is still, three hundred years later, one of the most impressive of them all. Dugdale was at once learned, well connected, enthusiastic, and

[1] *An English Garner*, ii (1879), 272.
[2] G. E. Bentley, *The Jacobean and Caroline Stage*, vi (1968), 53.
[3] *Remarks and Collections*, iii.500, iv.35.
[4] *Ibid.*, ii.372.
[5] Bodleian MS. Eng. misc. e.82, fol. 43v.
[6] Hearne, *Remarks and Collections*, vi.103. The MSS. included a continuation of his *Compendious View* from 1685 to the time of his death: *ibid.*, vi.175. Hardly any of Wright's own letters seem to be extant. There is one dated "Ewston Hall, 29 Sept. 1696", to Peter le Neve: Bodleian MS. Don. d.90, fol. 331.
[7] *V. C. H. Rutland*, ii.79; Hearne, *Remarks and Collections*, vi.18.

energetic beyond fatigue. As a work of scholarship his book was, both in range and in depth, much more considerable than any of its predecessors. It set a model that influenced all such studies for a century to come.

Dugdale soon found a worthy successor, and declared imitator, in Robert Thoroton, whose *Antiquities of Nottinghamshire* was published in 1677. The next county history was this one of Rutland, which appeared seven years later. In his preface Wright freely acknowledges the supremacy of Dugdale, but states that he has taken Burton's *Leicestershire* as his pattern. Reading between the lines of what he says, one may guess that he wished to prepare the reader for a slighter work than Dugdale's. He could not claim a tithe of Dugdale's scholarship, nor was he willing to go so far in pursuit of his materials. Burton supplied a much-respected precedent. Both were dealing with small counties, for which the same method was appropriate : a brief general description, followed by the treatment of each parish, in alphabetical order. Both were lawyers, and paid attention occasionally to cases of importance in the courts – one here, for example, about a will (p. 33), another involving the ecclesiastical jurisdiction of the Crown (p. 78), a third the existence of a forgotten market at Lyddington (p. 81); and Wright took the trouble to include a substantial glossary of the terms used in Domesday Book, for the assistance of laymen unacquainted with them. He also followed Burton in paying careful attention to "the antiquity of a church window" and to the inscriptions on funeral monuments. With this sad difference, however : that whereas in Burton's time most of them were still intact, they had since suffered the horrible iconoclasm of the Civil War, when windows were smashed and inscriptions defaced by the Parliamentarians "as if they had a mind thereby to exterminate the memory of their forefathers, and do what in them lay, that posterity should not know that there ever was a better generation of people than themselves".[1] Wright made no secret of his political and religious convictions.

He enjoyed another advantage, the extent of which we cannot now assess. In his preface he speaks of his debt to Sir Wingfield Bodenham of Ryhall, who made his collections for the history of Rutland available to him. In part these derived from Roger Dodsworth, one of the most notable antiquaries of his time, a voracious and intelligent inquirer to whom Dugdale was greatly beholden. They also came from another source. Bodenham was a tough Royalist, who was imprisoned in the Tower during the Civil War; and he beguiled his weary confinement by scouring the public records (many of which were then kept there) for references to his own county. Wright built on his foundations, with additional research of his own, as he tells us, in the Tower, the Rolls Chapel, and the records of the Exchequer.

When his book came to be published it showed two innovations, which were important for the future. He called it *The History and Antiquities of the County of Rutland*. That formula, which he devised, became the standard adopted by most county historians, throughout the eighteenth century. Indeed when Thomas Blore produced the first part of what was intended to be a new history of Rutland, displacing Wright's, in 1811, the title he adopted was exactly the same.

The conclusion of Wright's preface is given to acknowledging the liberality of those who had defrayed the cost of the plates – noblemen and country gentry, the Dean and Chapter of Westminster, the author's father, still alive at Oakham when the book was published. The works of his predecessors, Dugdale and Thoroton, had also included some plates that were due, as they indicated, to the generosity of friends. With Wright the emphasis changes. His pictures number twenty in all (excluding the map and the shields of arms used to illustrate pedigrees). Three-quarters of them show country houses and church monuments. Every one was paid for in this way. Here we see the full and frank emergence of a sensible convention that eased the financial difficulties of publishing county histories and was freely adopted by most of Wright's successors for the next 150 years. As we should now phrase it, the author bore the cost of his research and of production, the county paid for the illustrations. Wright pleasantly remarked that the names of these contributors "ought to be remembered while this book shall last".

We have cause to be grateful to them, for several of the plates depict buildings that have since been altered or destroyed: Martinsthorpe (p. 90), Tolethorpe (p. 128), Brooke (*Additions*, p. 6), South Luffenham (*Additions*, p. 7). Normanton (p. 94) gives one a sharp pang : for not only has this house gone, but its successor too, and the lonely church with its

[1] Preface, para. 6.

elegant classical tower is now about to be submerged by the waters of a reservoir.

The character of the plates deserves attention. The monuments are very well depicted, as any one can see who goes to Exton today with Wright's book in his hand. The two churches that are illustrated, Ketton and Oakham, come out less successfully, for the draughtsman has not solved his problems of perspective and proportion. But the small pictures of country houses, modest and quite unpretending, have all the value of a plain record. Neat and simple, they get as near perhaps as any work of the kind could to the matter-of-fact photography of our own day. Only in the plate of Burley-on-the-Hill, included in the *Farther Additions*, is there an attempt to produce an atmospheric effect. By the time that supplement was published, in 1714, the fashion was changing, towards the amplitude and grandeur of the Georgian age.

The map is a workmanlike performance, perhaps by Robert Morden. It includes two minute town plans, of Oakham and Uppingham, and it follows the example set by Dugdale in showing the sites of deserted villages.

The text of the book is for the most part brief, formal and dry. The lawyer is uppermost in Wright here, not the lively essayist. He starts with three explanations of the etymology of Rutland and with an account of the shire in general and its government, plunging quickly then into his entries for the parishes and places separately, numbering sixty-two in all. He makes no effort to describe them in any physical sense. He usually confines himself to indicating the ownership and descent of the manor and the state of the church, with any monuments and windows of heraldic interest that it contains. His manorial history has been wholly superseded today; but he records some things that have disappeared — deserted villages like Gunthorpe (p. 67) and Pickworth (p. 106); monuments that have gone, at Ketton for example (p. 73) and Langham (p. 75). At Exton (p. 53) he preserves an Old French inscription that is now defaced beyond repair. Exton indeed takes up more room here than any other parish, even the county town of Oakham. That is understandable by us still, for its church contains one of the richest collections of post-Reformation monuments in England. Happily, those he depicts and describes here are still extant, though the Hall near by (shown on p. 49) was burnt down in 1810 and survives only as a ruined shell.

Wright was no rigidly accurate scholar, and there are evident carelessnesses in his work.[1] The pagination goes wrong here and there, and he more than once allows an entry about a church to end with the words: "The present patron is   ". It is no reflection on him that he should have spelt place-names in various fashions, for that was the practice of his time; but it is, all the same, a little startling to find Essendine spelt in seven different ways, without comment (pp. 62-4). Occasionally his spellings are useful indicators of current pronunciation: Barleytharp (p. 19), Edyweston (p. 41).

He may have felt a certain dissatisfaction with his book after it was published, for in 1687 he produced sixteen pages of *Additions* to it, which include an index. They comprise some *corrigenda* (p. 12), some fresh documents, and four more plates. Twenty-seven years later, near the end of his life, he issued a set of *Farther Additions* devoted solely to Burley-on-the-Hill. Since the book was first published, that estate had passed from the Villiers to the Finch family, and Daniel Earl of Nottingham had built the immense house that we still see today. Among the modest houses of Rutland this was indeed a leviathan; as Sir Nikolaus Pevsner observes, "many a ruler of a minor state in Germany would have been proud of such a palace".[2] Even Macaulay, who did not care for the builder, allowed that it stood on "one of the noblest terraces in the island".[3] It was completed in 1705. Wright must have been a supporter of Nottingham, as a moderate Tory. He evidently felt compelled to depict this stupendous new adornment to his county. His tribute to it runs beyond the plain prose of the rest of the book. Here the literary man takes over at last, to give us a set of more than 200 verses — conventional enough, for Wright was no poet, yet not without the faint gaiety and charm that exhale from his work elsewhere.

Looking at James Wright in the context of his life, so far as we can see it, and considering him as an early member of the company of county historians, it becomes clear that he stands well apart from all the rest. He was a lawyer and a man of letters, who resided chiefly in London, away from the county of his choice. Though well read, he was not a trained scholar. He was capable of assembling and ordering his materials competently and

[1] A good many corrections, particularly of the pedigrees, are to be found in Richard Gough's copy of the book in the Bodleian (Gough Rutland 2).
[2] *The Buildings of England: Leicestershire and Rutland* (1960), 289.
[3] *History of England*, iv (1858), 545.

of carrying his task through to a conclusion : for he had the constructive sense and the tenacity to make a book. Among county historians, those are not qualities to be taken for granted. So many of his successors went to their graves with the tasks they had set themselves unfinished, leaving no more than the torso of a book or – worse still – nothing but a pile of notes. Quietly and without any fuss, Wright won through. He completed his task ; and then he turned to other matters, public and private, on which he also had something to say.

III

Nevertheless, it could not be contended that he had written a definitive history of Rutland. Stimulated by such examples as he had set, the historical scholarship of the eighteenth century advanced, notably in the field of local studies. Even Dugdale's *Warwickshire*, a much more considerable work than Wright's, was found in need of revision and was corrected and genuinely improved by William Thomas in 1730. In the 1770s John Nichols, a London printer and publisher, began to work on the adjacent county of Leicester, with a view to superseding Burton's book. It was natural that others should think of doing the same for Nottinghamshire and Rutland. Both tasks were attempted more or less simultaneously. We do not know which effort began first, or whether either of the editors was influenced by the other. Perhaps they were working in quiet rivalry. The two were John Throsby, parish clerk of St Martin's in Leicester, who revised Thoroton's *Nottinghamshire*,[1] and William Harrod, bookseller of Stamford, who undertook Wright. Both worked to exactly the same pattern, reprinting the original text section by section and interspersing it with additions and corrections contributed by themselves. Since Harrod's work appeared in 1788 and the first volume of Throsby's not until 1790, it might seem plain that Harrod set the example. But Throsby's work was much the more extensive, and he probably embarked on it first. As for the method, it was hardly recondite ; each may have determined to adopt it independently of the other.

There was however one great difference between them. Harrod's work was never completed. It was evidently a financial failure, and abandoned when two parts only had been published ; whereas Throsby held on – valiantly, through great financial difficulties – to finish his task in 1796. Moreover, comparing what the two men actually published, it must be said that Throsby's contribution is a good deal better than Harrod's. Though neither of them was really well qualified for his task, Throsby had the virtues of enthusiasm and tenacity, whereas Harrod clearly looked on his work very much as a publisher. It does not rise above the level of what his age called book-making.

Still, it is not without interest. It shows us something of the progress that was being made in historical studies during the century after Wright's book appeared. Harrod was no scholar, but he was equally no fool. He had already proved himself capable of useful work in a history of Stamford, and went on to produce little books on Mansfield in 1801 and Market Harborough in 1808. As a bookseller he had some means of judging the public demand. Here, at the ordinary man's level, was what was now coming to be expected over and above what Wright had offered.

This was the last effort made to supplement the original work of 1684. When the history of Rutland was next attempted, by Thomas Blore, it was on different lines (though as it happened he too, like Wright, was a lawyer, of the Middle Temple). In 1811 he produced an instalment of a new history of the county, an elaborate piece of research based on a far fuller investigation of the national records than Wright had – or could have – undertaken in the seventeenth century, and enriched with engravings after the exquisite drawings made by his son Edward, one of the finest antiquarian draughtsmen this country has produced. Though the work as it stands contains no preface, no statement of intentions, it was clearly designed to supplant Wright's altogether. But it was never completed. This one fragment (comprising Vol. I, Part 2) was all that appeared. It treated the East Hundred alone, leaving the other four and the general history of the county untouched.

So things remained, for another hundred years. Then, at the beginning of the twentieth century, under the daemonic drive of William Page the *Victoria History* got going, for Rutland as for most other English counties. The first volume, devoted to the history of the

[1] His edition was reprinted in this series of "Classical County Histories" in 1972.

county in general, was published in 1908 ; the second, treating it parish by parish, followed in 1935 ; and the whole was rounded off with a separate slim index volume in 1936. At last the history of Rutland had been written on a large scale, not by one man however but by a group of competent scholars.

Anybody who wishes to inform himself about the county's past turns today, as a matter of course, to the *Victoria History*. But the true lover of Rutland will wish to have Wright by him too. It is appropriate that the book should be reprinted now, complete with all its supplements, at the very moment when Rutland itself, as an autonomous unit of local government, is to disappear. For here is the little county, modestly described in a short book, which was written at another striking juncture in its history : the moment when it produced the two oddities who are its most celebrated sons – Jeffery Hudson, the royal dwarf, and Titus Oates ; when its greatest house was despoiled in the Civil War and then rebuilt in overtopping splendour. The author was very much a man of his age, suffering in it, participating in its passion, savouring its pleasures. He had a strong sense of both past and present, and he brought them together in this book, which gives him his place in the vanguard of the English county historians.

JACK SIMMONS

PUBLISHERS' NOTE

The present edition of Wright's *Rutland* comprises the following elements, all reprinted photographically and complete:

1. The original book of 1684, reprinted from Leicestershire County Library, copy no. 426774.
2. The *Additions* of 1687, from the same copy.
3. The *Farther Additions* of 1714 (including Wright's plate of Burley-on-the-Hill). This and item 4 are reprinted from copies in the possession of Mr J. Chandler of Stamford.
4. William Harrod's new edition (two parts only issued, 1788).
5. Harrod's advertisement of 1790, listing the contents of his edition and adding the plate of the arms of the nobility and gentry. Reprinted from a copy in the Bodleian Library, Oxford.

The following errors of pagination seem to be found in all copies of the work: page 90 of the *History* is numbered page 92, followed correctly by page 91; and page 3 of the *Farther Additions* is numbered as page 5, followed correctly by pages numbered 4 and 5. The publishers are particularly grateful to Mr Chandler and to the Bodleian Library for the assistance they have afforded.

THE
HISTORY
AND
ANTIQUITIES
Of the COUNTY of
RUTLAND:

COLLECTED
From RECORDS, Ancient MANUSCRIPTS,
MONUMENTS on the Place, and
other AUTHORITIES.

Illuſtrated with SCULPTURES.

By JAMES WRIGHT of the Middle Temple.
Barriſter at Law.

Ne parva averſeris ; ineſt ſua gratia parvis.

Printed for *Bennet Griffin* at the Griffin in the Great *Old Baily*, and
are to be ſold by *Chriſt. Wilkinſon* at the *Black Boy*, and by *Sam.
Keble* at the *Turks-Head* in *Fleetſtreet*, 1684.

TO THE

NOBILITY

AND

GENTRY,

Inhabiting within, or otherwise relating to,

The COUNTY of

RUTLAND,

JAMES WRIGHT

Presents and Dedicates

This WORK.

THE
PREFACE
TO THE
READER.

I Suppose there needs no Appology for a Work of this Argument, or that I should set forth the usefullness of this sort of Learning in any long Discourse, it being already sufficiently known to all Gentlemen and Schollers. Let me however borrow a few lines extreamly pertinent to this subject, out of an Epistle formerly writ by Thomas Wotton Esquire, Father of the first Lord Wotton, and printed before the Perambulation of Kent, composed by the Learned John Lambert Esquire, formerly a Bencher of Lincolns Inne. Mr. Wottons words are these : I must needs say, that (the sacred Word of Almighty God always excepted) there is nothing either for our Instruction more profitable, or to our minds more delectable, or within the Compass of common understanding more easie or facile, than the study of Histories, nor that study for none Estate more meet than for the Estate of Gentlemen ; nor for the Gentlemen of England, no History so meet as the History of England. For the dexterity that men have either in providing for themselves, or in comforting their friends (two very good things) or in serving their King and Country (of all outward things the best thing) doth rest cheifly upon their own and other folks experience.

Since Mr. Lambert writ his abovementioned Perambulation of Kent, it hath been much desired by several worthy Persons, that all the Counties of England might be accordingly described by others ; which perhaps may be in time : some are done already, as Kent, Cornwal, Leicestershire, Cheshire, Nottinghamshire, but above all Warwickshire, several Cities and Towns also, as London, Canterbury, Oxford, Cambridge, Windsor, Exeter, Stamford, Feversham, all which have been treated of in several distinct Vollumes, writ by several Authors. Other Counties I hear are now in hand as Yorkshire, Staffordshire, and Hartfordshire.

As to this undertaking of mine, I must acquaint the Reader, that having been above twenty years past, for the most part, resident in the County of Rutland (tho' no Native of the same) I collected many years ago something of this nature for my own private satisfaction. Which Notes, tho' few and those imperfect, I have since been encouraged by several Persons of Honour and Quality to compleat into a just Vollume as it is now publisht. In the performing of which I have had some help from certain Papers collected by Sir Wingfeild Bodenham Knight ; formerly, while he lived, of Ryhall in this County ; who in the late times of Anarchy being a Prisoner in the Tower for his faith and Loyalty to his King, had there sufficient Leisure to make several Collections of Antiquity, which he did cheifly from the Labours of that Industrious and Famous Antiquary Mr. Roger Dodsworth ; among which miscellaneous Papers of his, I found diverse Notes relating to this County, as will appear by my Citations. Also through the favour of the right worthy Sir John Cotton, Baronet, I have had the perusal of his famous and incomparable Library of Manuscripts at Westminster, tho' in truth my affairs would not permit me to spend so much time there, as I might have done, had I had no other Avocations. Nor ought I to forget to acknowledg the assistance which I have found ; as well from the Learned Works as personal friendship and incouragement of the highly deserving Sir William Dugdale Knight, Garter King at Arms ; Sir Henry St. George Knight, Clarentieux ; with other Gentlemen belonging to the Office

of

of Arms, to whose Civilities I am obliged. Yet all this I thought not sufficient till I made an actual search among the Records themselves remaining in the Tower, at the Chappel of the Roles, and in the Exchequer at Westminster, especially the Augmentation Office.

The Pedigrees, which I have inserted in this Treatise, are some transcribed from the Authentick Roles of descent remaining in the possession of the respective Families; but the most of them are copied out of the Visitation Books made for this County, and remaining in the Office of Armes. Several of which Pedigrees may possibly be reduced much higher, if the parties concern'd will give themselves the trouble and charge to search further. For my part I have set down only such things as have arrived to my knowledg without Importuning any for intelligence; some Gentlemen being unwilling (for reasons best known to themselves) to have the Evidences of their Families or Estates viewed by any Stranger. For this reason cheifly, I have been cautious and sparing in treating of the modern Proprietors and present Possessors of the Estates mention'd in this Book. For whereas the antient Titles are to be found in publick Records, or to be gathered from printed Authors, or other authentick Writings. On the contrary he that treats exactly of the present must be of necessity beholding to report and personal Information, which will betray him that relyes thereon to Error, in regard of those many dormant Conveyances upon condition, and Settlements in trust, &c. which abound now a days more than ever. But if not withstanding all my endeavors to the contrary, I have been guilty of any mistakes, I am very willing and ready, upon better evidence to annex the Errata in a Supplement or Appendix.

As to the Method in my Description of this County, I have in several particulars followed that which hath been heretofore used by the industrious William Burton Esquire, formerly a member of the Inner Temple, in his Description of Leicestershire. Which President being drawn by the hand of an antient and learned Barrister, seems most proper for me to observe; not only placing the Towns alphabetically, and such other slighter matters, but cheifly in the concise, yet satisfactory account of the subject. The said Mr. Burton, as a Lawyer, tells us in his Preface to his Reader, That those Cases of Law which of later times have happen'd within his Shire, he hath breifly remember'd, in some shewing the Arguments and Reasons of the Judgments. And so have I in like manner here in Rutland. And that such Antiquities as these are not inconsistent with a Lawyers Observation, he tells us further in the same Preface, that for his own part, he of his knowledg can affirm, that the Antiquity of a Church Window, for the proof of a match and issue had, hath been delivered in evidence to a Jury at the Assizes, and been accepted. And therefore he hath set down the Arms in Church Windows, and the Inscriptions of Tombs; for that perhaps they may rectifie Armories and Genealogies, and may give testimony, proof, and end to many differences. These are his Words, which I think I may not improperly apply also to my own undertaking.

This was, I confess, a subject much more facile and delightsome to be writ of by those who lived before the late civil Wars, that is before the Rebells had tore up so many brass Inscriptions in Churches, and broke the windows of Gods house, where they saw any memorial of Antiquity; as if they had a mind thereby to exterminate the memory of their forefathers, and do what in them lay, that Posterity should not know that there ever was a better Generation of People than themselves.

The violation of funeral Rites was formerly esteem'd a thing abhorrant not only to Christian Religion, but also to the bare humanity of the antient Romans and all the civilized parts of the World, tho Heathen. And tho the old common Laws of England have given an action to the Widdows, and to the Heirs of those whose Monuments are defaced, as may be seen in Sir Edward Cokes 3d. Institutes. p. 202. and in other Books there cited, yet in the Reign of E. 6. some covetous and ill principled People began to be mighty busie at this work, and so also in the beginning of the Reign of Queen Elizabeth, till that wise Queen put a stop to their Career, by her Proclamation dated 19. Sept. in the 2d. year of her Reign, and by another in the 14th. year of her Reign, forbidding under severe Penalties, that any should break or deface any Monument of Antiquity or Inscription set up in Churches, or other publick Places, for the memory of the deceased to their Posterity, only, and not for any religious honour. The said Proclamation of Sept. 19. (too long to be here transcribed) may be seen at large in Weavers Funeral Monuments, fol 50. But the causes that procured the Prohibition of such actions are extreamly worthy note : And they are thus exprest in the words of that Proclamation.——— By which
means

means not only the Churches remain at this day fpoiled, broken, and ruinated, to the offence of all noble and gentle Hearts, and the extinguifhing of the honorable and good memory of fundry vertuous and noble Perfons deceafed, but alfo the true underftanding of divers Families in this Realm (who have defcended of the Bloud of the fame perfons deceafed) is thereby fo darken'd, as the true courfe of their Inheritance may be hereafter interrupted contrary to Juftice, befides many other offences that do hereof infue.

Thus much I thought not improper to infert in this place, to fhew not only the impiety but alfo the illegality of fuch actions, which tend only to the difornament of Churches, and to blind the truth of Hiftory.

I begin my account of every Town with the ftate and condition that it was in at the Norman *Conqueft, above* 600. *years ago. This I have out of the old Record in the Exchequer call'd* Domefday-Book : *which is the oldeft publick Record in* England ; *begun to be made in the year* 1081 (14. W. 1.) *by the command of that King ; to ferve for a punctual and certain information of all the Lands in* England, *who were at that time the prefent Owners thereof, and who had been, before the Conqueft ; how much the feveral Lordfhips were worth yearly, and of what contents the fame were. At the time of the compofing it was a meer* Liber cenfualis *or* Tax Book; *but of later time it is become the moft facred and unqueftionable Evidence that is in matters of Tenure.*

And in regard the Rights of Advowfon and Prefentation to Churches hath been always efteem'd a material part of a Lordfhip, I have inferted the antient Patrons *of the feveral Churches in this County, with the Endowments of feveral Vicarages, as they remain of Record in the Regiftry of* Lincoln ; *and thefe Notes I have had, I muft confefs, from an abftract of that Regifter, formerly tranfcribed by the abovementioned Mr.* Roger Dodf-worth.

In reading what I cite, out of Domefday-book *efpecially, you will meet with feveral obfolete and uncommon words, as* Berwica, Bordarii, Sockmen, Villain, Saca and Soca, &c. *Of all which I will here in the beginning of this Work give an Expofition, cheifly, out of our Law-Books, as the moft proper Interpreters, they being all old Words relating to Tenures and Eftates.*

Berwica, *in Englifh a* Berew *or* Berwit, *in* Domefday-book *fignifyeth, a Hamlet or Village appurtenant to fome other* Town *or* Mannour. *And Sir* Henry Spelmen *in his Gloffary, defcribes it to be* Manerium minus, ad majus pertinens, non in gremio Manerii fed vel in confinio, vel disjunctius interdum fitum eft : *And according to this fignification is Sir* Edward Cokes *citation out of* Domefday *in* Gloucefterfh. Hæ Berwicæ pertinent ad *Berchley,* & fit recitat plus quam viginti Villas. *Co.* 1. *Inft* 116. *a.*

Bordarii, *fays Sir* Edward Coke, *is derived of the French word* Borde, *a Cottage: and fignifyeth the fame with* Cotarii, *that is* Bores *holding a little houfe with fome land of husbandry, bigger than a Cottage. And* Coterelli *are meer* Cottagers qui Cotagia & Curtilagia tenent. *Thefe* Bordarii *were ever named after the* Villani *in* Domefday-book *Co. Lit. fo.* 5. *b.*

Bovata terræ, *a Bovate or Oxgange of Land, is as much as an Ox can till, and may contain, Meadow, pafture, and Wood, neceffary for fuch tillage, Co. Lit. fo.* 5. *a.* Octo Bovatæ faciunt Carucatam terræ, & 18. acræ faciunt Bovatam terræ.

Carucata, *a* Carucate *or* Carve *of Land, otherwife called a Plowland, may contain houfes, mills, pafture, meadow, Wood &c. Co. Lit. fo.* 86. *b. and it is Sir* Edw. Cokes *opinion, that a Carucate, or Plowland, is not of any certain content, but as much as one plow can by courfe of husbandry plow in a year, which in fome Countries is more than in other, and therefore a Plowland may contain leffe in one place than in another ; yet fays the fame Author, of antient time every Plowland was of the yearly value of* 5. *nobles per an. and this was the living of a Plowman or Yeoman.* Et ex duodecim Carucatis conftabat unum feodum militis. *Co. Lit. fo.* 69. *a.*

Demefne, *or* Demain, (Dominicum) *hath divers fignifications. But the moft common acceptation of Demefne Lands is to fignifie the Lords cheif feat or Manfion with the Lands thereunto belonging, which he and his Anceftors have from time to time kept in their own manual occupation. Yet in Law all the parts of a Mannour, except what is in the hands of Freeholders, are faid to be Demains. Co. Lit. fo.* 17. *a.*

Geldum, *in* Domefday-Book *is generally written for the* Danegeld, *and fo to be underftood.*

derſtood. *Which was a Tax or Tribute impoſed by a certain Law in the* Saxons *time, upon every Town and Village in* England. Spelm. Gloſſ. verb. Geldum. *The Rate was at firſt* 12. d. *and afterwards rais'd to* 2. s. *per an. for every Hide of Land. This Impoſition began Anno* Domini 1007. *in the time of King* Etheldred, *who was forced by vaſt ſums of mony to buy a peace with the* Danes, *tho it laſted but for a time. However this Tax being once ſet on foot was continued, till releaſed in part by King* Edward *the Confeſſor, and totally by King* Steven *in the beginning of his Reign. After which the word was never more uſed, but the like Impoſitions were in after Ages called* Tallages *and* Taxes. Vid. Spelm. Gloſſ. verb. Danegeldus. Selden, Mare Clauſum lib. 2. ca. 11.

Hida. *Some hold a Hide of Land to contain four yard Land, ſome one hundred acres. But Sir* Edward Coke *is of opinion, that a Hide is all one with a Carucate or Plowland: and that neither is of any certain content, but as much as a plow can till in a year, with good Husbandry.* Co. Lit. f. 69. a.

Knights Fee. *It is agreed by all good Authors that a Knights fee ought to be eſtimated not according to the quantity of Land, but the value of the Eſtate: and that* 20 l. *per an. was antiently call'd a Knights fee, be the number of acres he held more or leſſe.* Mr. Selden *cites the antient Record call'd* Modus tenendi Parliamentum, *and ſhews that the Knights fee is there computed* ad vigenti Libratas terræ. Seld. Tit. Hon. part. 2. ch. 7. *which is land worth* 20. l. *per an. vide* Lows caſe. Co. Rep. lib. 9. f. 124. *theſe Knights fees at ſome times were liable to a kind of Tax call'd* Eſcuage, *aſſeſt by Parliament higher or lower: and the Tenants in Chivalry paid the ſame proportionably as they held their eſtates, ſome for one Knights fee, ſome for half, and ſome for the* 20th. *and ſome for the* 100th. *part of a Knights fee. I have ſeen a Record in the Exchequer; It is* Paſch. 29. E. 3. Inter communia, ex parte Rememoratoris Theſaurarii, Tit. Fines &c. Rotulo quarto in dorſo. *In which it appears that* John Son of Richard le Wright de Horneſburton, *gave one penny for his Releif for one Meſſuage, and the third part of one Bovate of Land in* Horneſburton *in* Holderneſſe *in the County of* York, *which he held of the King, as of his honour of* Albemarle, *by the ſervice of the one thouſand one hundred and fiftieth part of a Knights fee. And the Releif in Chivalry being always a fourth part, his eſtate was it ſeems valued at* 4. d. *per an. now according to this computation the whole Knights fee did amount to* 19 l. 3 s. 4 d. *Yet hath the value of theſe Knights fees been very differently eſtimated in ſeveral Kings Reigns, ſometimes at* 20 l. *per an. ſometimes at* 40 l. *ſometimes at* 15 l. *and ſometimes at* 10 l. *per an. as may be ſeen in the* Second Inſtitutes, p. 596.

Leuca, *or* Leuga. *Signifies in* Domeſday book, *a Mile, as then computed; and did contain twelve* Quarantenes *or* Furlongs. Monaſ. Ang. 1. Vol. f. 313. *which according to our preſent meaſure, makes a mile and a half.*

Librata terræ. *Is land of* 20 s. *per an. value. In old time Lands were granted according to their value, as* Centum Libratas terræ, *a hundred pound of Land; or* centum Solidatas terræ, *a hundred ſhillings of land; as may be ſeen in the* Firſt Inſtitutes fo. 5. b. *and in* Fitzh. N. B. fo. 87. f. *where we read of* viginti Libratas, terræ, vel reditus, *as two things of the ſame ſignification.*

Quarantena, *is a furlong of Land, conteining* 40. *perches, each perche* 16. *foot, Twelve of theſe* Quarantenes *or* Furlongs *at the time of the* Norman Survey, *were accounted to a mile; tho' at this day but eight.* Spelm. Gloſſ. verb. Quarantena.

Saca & Soca. Sac, *or* Sak *is an old word ſignifying Coniſans of pleas in a Court belonging to a Mannour, with a Liberty of amercing the Tenants for offences, and levying the ſaid Amerciaments to his own uſe.* Seld. Tit. hon. part. 2. c. 7. *The word* Sac (*ſays Sir* Henry Spelman *in his Gloſſ.) ſignifies in the* Saxon *as much as* Cauſa, Lis, Certamen, *in the* Latine. *And I cannot find any different ſignification of the word* Soca.

Sockmen. Socmanni, *ſo often mention'd in* Domeſday-book, *were tenants of Freehold of inheritance, who held their Lands of the Lord in Free Soccage, and not by Knights ſervice, paying yearly to their Lords a certain free Rent.* Co. Lit. fol. 5. b. *Yet did theſe* Socmanni *or Freeholders perform certain ſervices beſide their Rents. As for Inſtance: in the Mannour of* Stonely *in the County of* Warwick, *the cuſtome was, that each of them at his death ſhould give to the Lord an intire Heriot, i. e. his horſe and Armes if he had any, otherwiſe his beſt beaſt. That his heir ſhould be admitted to the inheritance at* 15. *years of age paying his Rent doubled for a Releif. That in harveſt they ſhould upon notice and requeſt*

come

come to help the Lord, with every of their Tenants, themselves to ride up and down on horse back to see that the others work well, and both they and their Tenants to have at Noon meat and and drink provided by the Lord, &c. Antiquities of Warwicksh. p. 170. The Successors of these Sockmen, in such Mannours where the King was Lord at the time of Domesday Survey, are now called Tenants in Antient Demesne, and Capable of several priviledges and Immunities. Co. 4. Inst. p. 269. Which Priviledges and the original cause of them, you may read of, in Co. 2. Inst. fol. 542.

Villains, were of two sorts : Villains of Bloud, and Villains of Tenure. The first of these were themselves and their issue Bondmen, and bound to do such services as the Lord should command, ubi sciri non poterit vespere quale servitium fieri debet mane. These had no property in any Estate, they could purchase but the Lord might enter and hold it to his own use. Yet were these Villains free against all men but only their Lords : Neither could the Lord himself kill or maim his villain, for that would be an Infranchisement to him and his posterity. The other Villains were only by Tenure; and they were free men themselves, but only they were obliged to do certain customary services yearly, as to plow and manure the Lords Land, or bring in his harvest &c. The first sort of these are now quite worn out, and in process of time become free like other men. The second sort are now called Coppyholders, which sayes Fitzh. N. B. fol. 12. c. is but a new invented name, for of old time they were called Tenants in Villainage, or of Base tenure. These sort of Tenants in Villainage were before the Conquest, Tenants of Freehold and held by free services; but when they were ejected from their Estates by the Conquering Normans, they afterwards obtain'd back again their old Lands to hold at the will of their new Lords in Villainage, by servile offices, but certain and expresse; yet did their persons remain free tho' their Tenure was servile. Co. Lit. fol. 172. b. Villani, in Domesday book, as Sir Edward Coke thinks, are not taken for Bondmen; but such are there called Servi. Co. Lit. fol. 5. b. This we ought to understand of the Villains of Bloud, and that the word Villani is appliable in that old Record to the Villains by tenure only; so call'd de Villis, where they inhabited upon Farmes of husbandry, and did their Lords work.

Virgata Terræ, a Yard land; Is a quantity of land of different computation in divers places, in some Countries 10, in some 20, in some 24, in some 30 acres. Co. Lit. fol. 5. a.

The Ornamental part of this Book, which is the Cuts and Sculpture, hath been performed at the Charges of several Persons of honour, and Gentlemen of Worship; whose names ought to be remembred while this Book shall last, for the Love they bear to this County, where the Divine, Providence has given them a pleasant Heritage, and to the Memory of their Ancestors, whose ashes remain here. And they are as follows,

His Grace the Duke of Buckingham, gave the plate of Burly Stables, page 32.

The Right honorable William Earl of Denbigh, gave the plate of Martinsthorp house. p. 90.

The Right honorable Robert Earl of Aylesbury, gave four plates of four curious Monuments of his Lordships Ancestors in Exton Church, viz. Of John Harington Esq; and Alice his Wife, of Sir James Harington Knight, and Dame Lucy his Wife, of John Lord Harington, and of Anne Lady Bruce, f. 54, 55, 57, 59.

The Right honorable Edward Earl of Gainsborough, gave the plate of Exton house. p. 49.

The Right honorable Bennet Lord Sherard, gave the plate of the County Map.

The honorable John Noel Esq; gave the plate of the Monument lately erected in Exton Church to the memory of his Brother James Noel Esquire, p. 61.

Sir Thomas Mackworth Baronet, gave the plate of Normanton house, p. 94.

Christopher Brown of Tolethorp Esq; gave the plate of Tolethorp house. p. 28.

Edward Brown of Ryhall Gentleman, second Son of the said Christopher, gave the plate of the County hall within the Castle of Okeham, p. 104.

And of the Clergy, these,

The Reverend the Dean and Chapter of Westminster, Impropriators of the Church of Okeham in this County, gave the plate of the said Church, p. 99.

Abraham Wright Clerk, Vicar of the said Church, and one of the Governours of the old Hospital at Okeham, gave two plates of Arms and Antiquities in the windows of the said Church and Hospital, p. 101, 102.

George Topham Clerk, Prebendary of the Prebend of Ketton founded in the Church of Lincoln, gave the plate of Ketton Church, p. 72.

THE

THE
HISTORY
AND
ANTIQUITIES
OF
RUTLANDSHIRE.

Of the COUNTY in General.

THE County of **Rutland**, or (as it is latinized) *Rotelandia*, is sufficiently known to be the least County in this Kingdom: Its form round: Its dimensions not above some twelve miles over in any place: Its situation is on the North parts of **Northamptonshire**, (from which it is divided by the River **Welland**), on the East of **Leicestershire**, and South of **Lincolnshire**: By which three Counties this is enclosed from the rest of **England**.

Concerning the Etymology of the Name; there goes a Tale of one *Rut*, who rid round this County in a day: In memorial of which act, the space of ground so encircled, was from him called **Rutland.** Another opinion (a little, and but a little, more probable) is, that it took that name from the ruddy complexion of the Soil. Which notwithstanding I never perceived, but in one part of the County, and that about **Glaiston.** And no doubt there is few Shires in **England**, but produce a Mould of the same colour in some parts or other. To these therefore let me add one Etymology more, which is, that *Rotelandia* may possibly be so named from its Circular form, *quasi Rotunda-landia*, or *Rotundlandia*, which by contraction, leaving out the Consonants, *n* and *d*, for the more easie pronunciation, makes *Rotulandia*.

And this the rather, because the word *Rotunda*, signifying not only round, but well fashioned, handsom, and perfect, may in all its significations be justly applied to this County.

Touching the Original of this County, it is to be noted, that **Rutland**, as it is now limited, was not a County of it self at the time of the **Norman** Conquest, and that a great part of the Towns, those especially, which lie on the South limits of this Shire, did at that time belong to the County of **Northampton**; and as part of that County, they are to be found under the Title of **Northamptonshire**, in the General Survey taken in the Reign of King *William* the first, commonly call'd *Domesday Book.* In which Book, and under the said Title of **Northahmptonshire**, hath been (of later times) incerted the following Note;

Inquisitio coram VVillielmo *de* Saham *& Sociis suis, inter* Rageman *de* An. 4. E. 1.

Com **Northant** *Hundr. de* **Sutton** *Juratores Inquisit.*) *quot Hundred. &c. sint in Com.* **Northant** *dicunt quod Comitat.* **Roteland** *quondam fuit pertinens ad Com. istum quousq; Dominus* H. *rex pater Domini regis nunc illum dedit Domino regi Alman. sed nesciunt de modo,* (*huic concordat Hundred. de* **Spelho** *& plura alia Hundreda ibidem.*)

A   Which

VVhich part of this County, then belonging to 𝕹𝖔𝖗𝖙𝖍𝖆𝖒𝖕𝖙𝖔𝖓𝖘𝖍𝖎𝖗𝖊, was at that time known by the name of 𝕮𝖚𝖎𝖈𝖊𝖑=𝖘𝖊𝖆 VVapentake.

The other Towns, now belonging to this County were at that time (as I conceive) in some sort appertaining to the County of 𝕹𝖔𝖙𝖙𝖎𝖓𝖌𝖍𝖆𝖒, in regard they are to be found adjoyning to that Title in the abovementioned Survey of *Domesday*. And the authority of the Sheriff of 𝕹𝖔𝖙𝖙𝖎𝖓𝖌𝖍𝖆𝖒𝖘𝖍𝖎𝖗𝖊 did remain a long time after in 𝕽𝖚𝖙𝖑𝖆𝖓𝖉; for by a Statute made 51 *H.* 3. That Sheriff is appointed to be Escheator for this Country.

Stat. de Scaccario 51. H. 3.

And here we must note, that at the Conquest, the name 𝕽𝖔𝖙𝖊𝖑𝖆𝖓𝖉 was proper to those few Towns only, last abovementioned, as part of 𝕹𝖔𝖙𝖙𝖎𝖓𝖌𝖍𝖆𝖒=𝖘𝖍𝖎𝖗𝖊.

VVhich were these, *Viz.*

𝕲𝖗𝖊𝖙𝖍𝖆𝖒
𝕮𝖔𝖙𝖊𝖘𝖒𝖔𝖗𝖊
𝕺𝖛𝖊𝖗𝖙𝖚𝖓𝖊
and 𝕾𝖙𝖗𝖆𝖙𝖔𝖓
𝕿𝖎𝖘𝖙𝖊𝖗𝖙𝖚𝖓𝖊
𝕿𝖎𝖊
𝖀𝖚𝖎𝖈𝖍𝖎𝖓𝖌𝖊𝕯𝖊𝖓𝖊 } In 𝕬𝖑𝖋𝖓𝖔𝖉𝖊𝖘𝖙𝖔𝖚 VVapentac.
𝕰𝖗𝖊𝖓𝖙𝖚𝖓𝖊
𝖀𝖚𝖎𝖙𝖊𝖜𝖊𝖑𝖑𝖊
𝕬𝖑𝖊𝖘𝖙𝖆𝖓𝖊𝖘𝖙𝖔𝖗𝖕
𝕭𝖚𝖗𝖌𝖊𝖑𝖆𝖎
𝕰𝖗𝖜𝖊𝖑𝖑𝖊

𝕺𝖈𝖍𝖊𝖍𝖆𝖒 Cherchesoch *cum* v. *Berewicis.* } In 𝕸𝖆𝖗𝖙𝖎𝖓𝖊=𝖘𝖑𝖊𝖎𝖊 VVapentac.
𝕳𝖆𝖒𝖊𝖑𝖉𝖚𝖓𝖊 Cherchesoch *cum* vii. *Berew.*
𝕽𝖊𝖉𝖑𝖎𝖓𝖈𝖙𝖚𝖓𝖊 Cherchesoch *cum* vii. *Berew.*

VVhich two VVapentacs, at the time of the Conquerors Survey, did belong to the Sheriffdom, or charge of the Sheriff of 𝕹𝖔𝖙𝖙𝖎𝖓𝖌𝖍𝖆𝖒 for the gathering of the Kings Tax or Revenue, which in those days did amount to a hundred and fifty pounds of silver *per Ann.* from 𝕽𝖔𝖙𝖊𝖑𝖆𝖓𝖉:

The VVords of the Record are, *Hæc duo Wapent. adjacent Vicecomitatui* 𝕾𝖓𝖔𝖙𝖎𝖓𝖌𝖍𝖆𝖒 *ad geld. Regis.* 𝕽𝖔𝖙𝖊=𝖑𝖆𝖓𝖉 *reddit regi* C L. *libras albas.*

Domesd. Tit. Rotel.

However tho 𝕽𝖔𝖙𝖊𝖑𝖆𝖓𝖉 was formerly no County of it self; yet was it to some purposes, even at that time, an entire parcel of Land, or Soak, as appears by *Domesday Book,* where speaking of the Estate which *Gislebert de Gant* held in 𝕰𝖒𝖕𝖎𝖓𝖌𝖍𝖆𝖒, we may read these words,

Ipse ten. in ead. Villa vii. *hid. & dim. & unam Bovatam terre de Soca regis de* 𝕽𝖔𝖙𝖊𝖑𝖆𝖓𝖉, *& dicit Regem suum Advocatum esse.*

Domes. Tit. Northamp. No. 46.

To this may be added what we read in *Cambden, viz.* That King *Edward* the Confessor by his last VVill and Testament bequeathed this little County (*i. e.* so much of it, as then bore the name of 𝕽𝖔𝖙𝖊𝖑𝖆𝖓𝖉) to his wife *Eadith* for her life, and after her death to St. *Peters* at 𝖀𝖚𝖊𝖘𝖙=𝖒𝖎𝖘𝖙𝖊𝖗: In these words,

Camb. Brit: Rut.

Volo quod post mortem Eadgithæ *Reginæ Conjugis meæ* 𝕽𝖔𝖙𝖊𝖑𝖆𝖓𝖉 *cum omnibus ad se pertinentibus detur Monasterio meo Beatissimi* Petri, *& reddatur sine tardatione Abbati & Monachis ibidem Deo servientibus in perpetuum.*

Besides this VVill mentioned by Mr. *Cambden,* there is a large Charter of the said King *Edwards* to be seen in Sir *William Dugdales Monasticon,* whereby that pious King, confirming to the said Church divers Lands formerly given by other Kings his Predecessors:
It follows,

——*Postremò ego ipse pro spe retributionis æternæ & pro remissione delictorum meorum & pro animabus patris mei, & matris meæ, & omnium parentum meorum, & ad laudem omnipotentis Dei, posui in Dotalitium, & in perpetuam hæreditatem super Altare, varia ornamentorum Genera quibus Ecclesiæ serviretur, vel in quotidianis vel solennibus ministeriis: & ad usus fratrum inibi Deo servientium, de meo jure, quod mihi soli competebat absq; ullius reclamatione vel contradictione, Ista (inter alia)* 𝕽𝖔𝖙𝖊𝖑𝖆𝖓𝖉 *cum omnibus ad se pertinentibus, post mortem* Edgithæ *Reginæ.*

Monas. Ang. 1 Vol. 61.

Which Charter was dated at 𝖀𝖚𝖊𝖘𝖙=𝖒𝖎𝖓𝖘𝖙𝖊𝖗 on the day of the Holy Innocents, *Ann. Dom.* 1064. and in the 25*th.* year of that Kings Reign.

But this Donation was soon after cancelled, and made void by King *William* the Conquerour upon his arrival in this Nation, allowing only to the Church of 𝖀𝖚𝖊𝖘𝖙𝖒𝖎𝖓𝖘𝖙𝖊𝖗 the Tithes of 𝕽𝖔𝖙𝖊𝖑𝖆𝖓𝖉, which Tyths, in process of time, were also diminisht

Camb. Brit. Rut.

diminisht to those only of the Church of **Okeham** and parcels thereunto appertaining; but as to the Lands, he reserving a great part of them to himself, divided the rest among *Robert Mallet* a Norman, Lord Chamberlain of **England**; *Gilbert de Gant* who came into **England** in his Army, and was his Wives Brothers Son; Earl *Hugh*; *Albertus*, or *Aubrey*, the Clerk; and divers others : But in a more special manner, he exprest his bounty to his Neice *Ju-*

Bar Eng. 1 Vol. 55.

dith daughter of *Lambert de Leins*, and *Maud* Countess of *Albemarle*, the Conquerors sister by the Mothers side : To which *Judith*, her said Uncle gave eighty six Lordships in **Northamptonshire** and **Rutland**. She became the Wife of *Waltheof* Earl of **Northumberland**, a Saxon of great account, whom the Conqueror made also Earl of **Northampton** and **Huntington**; but the said *Waltheof* being afterwards (*viz. Anno* 1073.) beheaded, for conspiring against the King;

Id. 56.

and this Countess *Judith*, being suspected of promoting her Husbands death, she lived a penitent Widdow all the rest of her life. She founded the Priory of **Helenstow** in **Barkshire**, and procured from King *William* a Charter of divers immunities for the Monks of **Saltry** in **Huntingtonshire**, which Religious House she much frequented in her time.

But to return from this digression, It seems that **Rutland** was a County before *Henry* the Third's time : For in the Fifth of King *John*, *Isabel* his new Queen had, at her Coronation, assigned her in Parliament, for her Dower, among other

Rot. Cart. 17. Johan. pars 2. m. 3. n. 29.

Lands, *Com.* **Roteland**. *& villam de* **Rokingham**, *in Com.* **Northampt**. *de communi assensu & concordi voluntate Archiepiscoporum, Episcoporum, Comitum, Baronum, Cleri, & populi totius Regni.*

Rot. Pip.

Also in the twelfth year of the said King *John*, *Robert de Braibroc*, as Custos or Sheriff of this County, did account for the

Videsis etiam, Origen. Juridiciales, cap. 5. pag. 16.

Profits of the same, in the Exchequer. Of which *Custodes*, being, I suppose, neither more nor less in effect than Sheriffs, there is to be found a large Catalogue, even from the tenth year of *Henry* the Second : Some of which held the Office for life, as may appear by the List hereafter inserted. By all which it appears, that **Rutland**, tho not a County at the time of the Norman Conquest, yet was made such long before the time of King *Henry* the Third.

Of the Wapentakes or Hundreds at the Conquest.

Domesday Titt Rotel.

AT the time of the Survey made by *William* the Conqueror, commonly called *Domesday* Book; There were in **Roteland**, (I mean so much of the present County, as then bore that name) only two Wapentakes; **Alfnodestow**, and **Martinesleie**.

In **Alfnodestou** Wapentac were two Hundrets, in each of which were reckon'd twelve Carucates, as they were taxed or rated to the Geld, but in each of the said two Hundrets there was really tweny and four Carucates. This Wapentac (saith the Record) is half in **Turgastune** Wapentac, and half in **Brochelou** Wapentac. That is, it was at that day accounted as part of those two Wapentakes in **Nottinghamshire**.

In **Martinesleie** Wapentac was one Hundret, in which was reckon'd twelve Carucates, as taxed or rated to the Geld; and forty eight Plows might possibly be going therein, besides the three demesne Mannours of the King, in which there might be fourteen Plows.

These two Wapentacs (as I observed before) did in those dayes belong to the Vice County or Sheriffdom of **Snotingham** for the collection of the Kings Tax or Geld.

Thus far out of the ancient Record called Domesday *Book.*

Of the Hundreds, 9. E. 2.

Nomina Vill. in Scacc. ex parte Rem Thes. Fol. 106.

IT was found by inquisition taken at **Okeham** on Tuesday next before the Feast of S S. *Tiburtius* and *Valerian* (which is *Apr.* 14.) in 9 E. 2. before *Gilbert Holme* the Sheriff (or under Sheriff) of *Rutland*, that there was at that time in this County four Hundreds, *Viz.*

1. **Martinesle**. 3. **Est** Hundred.
2. **Alnestowe**. 4. **Wrondedyke**.

Of

Of the three firſt of which, the King was Lord, and received the profits of the ſame, (as in the Sheriffs turns, and Suit of Courts) except in certain Liberties ; all which profits of the ſaid Hundreds were at that time aſſigned to the Lady *Margaret de Gaveſton* Counteſs of **Cornwall** to hold at the Kings will.

The Fourth, *viz.* **Wrondedyke** was found to be late the Eſtate of *Guy de Bellocampo* Earl of **Warwick**, and was at that time in the Kings hands by reaſon of the Nonage of *Thomas* Son and Heir of the ſaid Earl : In which Hundred the Biſhop of *Lincoln* had his Liberty in the Soke of **Lydinton**.

And note, That then the preſent Hundred of **Okeham** Soke was included in that of **Martinſle**, which are now two diſtinct Hundreds.

Of the Hundreds at this day.

THe County of **Rutland** is at this day divided into five Hundreds, *viz.* **Okeham** *Soke*, **Alſtoe**, *Eaſt* Hundred, **Wrangdyke**, and **Martinſly**.

1. **Okeham** *Soke* lies on the edge of **Leiceſterſhire**, and contains cheifly the Weſt parts of this Shire, except one Town call'd **Clipſham**, lying in the utmoſt limits Northwards on the borders of **Lincolnſhire**, the whole Hundred of **Alſtoe** being interpoſed. In this Hundred are contain'd about nine Towns, among which one Market, **Okeham**.

2. **Alſtoe** Hundred takes up the North Parts, and borders on part of **Leiceſter** and **Lincoln** Shires, and contains in its diviſion twelve Towns.

3. The *Eaſt* Hundred lies (as its name imports) on the Eaſt Limits of this County, towards **Stamford** ; and hath in its diviſion about thirteen Towns and Villages.

4. **Wrangedyke** or **Barowden** Hundred takes up the South parts of this County, and is bounded by the River **Weland**, parting this and **Northamptonſhire**, this Hundred contains about fourteen Towns and Villages.

5. The Hundred of **Martinſley** lies in the middle of the County, encloſed with the other four, and has formerly contain'd in its diviſion twelve Towns

and Villages, among which one Market, **Uppingham**.

There is alſo another Hundred (tho not commonly ſo accounted in the ordinary computation) and that is the Hundred of **Caſterton** *parva*, lying wholly within the Eaſt Hundred, and contains eight Towns and Villages, part of Eaſt Hundred, as commonly reputed : *viz. Little* **Caſterton**, **Ryal**, **Belmeſthorp**, **Eſenden**, **Tinwel**, **Inthorp**, **Tickencote**, and **Tolethorp**. Which ſaid Hundred of Little **Caſterton** together with many large Priviledges and Liberties to the ſame belonging, King *Henry* the Seventh on the fourteenth day of *May* in the nineteenth year of his Reign, granted to *Chriſtopher Brown*, Eſq; whoſe Heir of the ſame name, enjoys the ſame at this day.

Ex Antogr. penes Chr. Brown Armig.

COncerning the Eccleſiaſtical Government, this County was alwayes under the Archdeacon of **Northampton**, and part of the Dioceſs of **Lincoln**, till the year 1541. At which time King *Henry* the eighth, erecting a new Biſhopwrick at **Peterborough**, made *John Chambers* (the laſt Abbot there) the firſt Biſhop of that See, and aſſigned to his Juriſdiction, the Archdeaconry of **Northampton** and **Rutland**, which laſt is now one of the Rural Deanery's of that Dioceſs , having within its limits forty nine Pariſh Churches , or Chappels Parochial ; five of which, *viz.* **Empingham** ; **Ketton** *cum* **Tixover** ; and **Lydington** *cum* **Caldecot**, being three Prebends belonging to the Church of **Lincoln**, are of peculiar Juriſdiction, and exempt from the Ordinary.

In the Kings Book of valuations.

There are
{ Rectories ——————— 31
{ Vicarages ——————— 12

In 45 *E.* 3. (1371.) this County did contain forty four Pariſhes, out of all which , was paid to the Aid then granted in Parliament for the Wars in **France** the Sum of 255 *l.*4 *s. viz.* the Sum of 5. *l.*16.*s.* from every Pariſh one with another.

Stows Anals Fol. 268.

I

I Will now proceed to give an account of the General Officers which have been belonging to this County, so far as I can recover their names. And first for the noble Earls of **Rutland**.

But before I mention the History of their persons, I conceive it not improper to say something of their Title, and Office, or Jurisdiction.

Earls in Latin *Comites,* were so called (as all good Authors do agree) *à Comitatu five à Societate Principis qui etiam dici possunt Consules à consulendo.* These were Persons of the greatest eminency, and were in continual attendance upon their Princes, for matters of Council and Authority. Some think the Name and Office came to us as also to the French, from the Roman Emperors, who when that Empire was grown to the full strength, begun to have about them a certain Privy Council, which was called *Cæsaris Comitatus,* and then those whose counsel they used in War and Peace were termed *Comites* : Or rather, (as I find it in another Author) those Emperours stiled them in War *Commilitones,* in the Court *Comites.*

By the Saxons they are called *Eoldormen,* or *Eorles,* from whence cometh our word *Earls,* in whose disposition and Government (saith Mr. *Selden*) upon delegation from the King, the County was; the Title of Earl being then Officiary and not Hereditary, except in some particular Shires. These Earls sate in the *Scyre mote* with the Bishop of the Diocess twice every year, where Charge was given touching God's Right and the World's Right. (Or as in another Author, *Agantur itaque primò debita veræ Christianitatis jura; secundò Regis placita; postremò causæ singulorum dignis satisfactionibus expleantur.*) But by the Conquerour this medling of the Bishop in *Turnes* was prohibited.

These Earls were the Cheif Governors or Justices of the Respective Counties under the King, and they received the third part of the Profits of the County to themselves, the other two parts going to the King. (I speak not of

Camb Brit. pag. 167.

Seld. Notes on Poly-olbion pag. 193.

Antiq. Warw. pag. 299.

those Earldomes that were Palatinate, as **Chester** after, and **Mercland** before the Conquest; for they had the whole profit.) These Earls, who were the Kings Officers, did exercise in old time very great power, in granting, releasing, and imposing Liberties and Exactions, which since only the Crown hath as unseperably annext unto it.

But this power whatsoever it was, together with their third part of the profit of the County is now ceas'd, and by time quite worn away. The Sheriff being now the Kings immediate Officer in the several Counties, who in former times was only a Deputy to the Earl ; as the name imports, *Vice Comes,* or Vicount, (of latter times made a Title of Honour, tho formerly Officiary only) subordinate to the Earl, as the Earl was to the King.

One Remarkable instance of the ancient power of these Earls is given by the Learned *Selden* in these words, *I have seen Original Letters of Protection (a perfect and uncommunicable power Royal) by that great Prince* Richard *Earl of* **Poiters** *and* **Cornwal**, *Brother to* Henry 3. *sent to the Sheriff of* **Rutland**, *for and in behalf of a Nunnery about* **Stamford**.

From this Authority of Mr. *Selden,* I think, I may safely make this further Observation ; that tho this County of **Rutland**, did not give Title to any Earl before the thirteenth of *Richard* the Second, yet it had vertually an Earl long before, who was Superior to the Sheriff in **Rutland**, as the Earls were in other Counties : and that those whose Names we find in the following list of Sheriffs, during the latter part of the Reign of *H.* 3. and the beginning of *E.* 1. were but his Deputies.

And this seems the more probable, in regard that King *H.* 3. in the thirty sixth year of his Reign, granted the Mannour and Castle of **Okeham** in this County to the said *Richard* Earl of **Cornwal**, (who was also King of the Romans) in Tail, whose Son and Successor *Edmund* Earl of **Cornwal**, in 28 *E.* 1. died seised of the said Castle and Mannour with several Members thereunto belonging, as also of the Bailywick or Shrievalty of the County of **Rutland**, without Issue.

Seld. Notes on Polyolb. p. 224.

Seld. ubi supr.

Bar. Engl. 1 *Vol.* 764, 766.

Earls

Earls of *RUTLAND*.

1. *Edward.*

Bar. Eng.
2 Vol. 156.

THE firſt Earl, entitled from this County that I read of, was *Edward* Eldeſt Son to *Edmund* ſurnamed of *Langele* Earl of **Cambridge**, and Duke of **York**, fifth Son of King *Edward* the third. Which *Edward* was Created Earl of **Rutland**, *Feb.* 25. in the thirteenth year of King *Richard* the ſecond, but to enjoy that Title no longer than his Fathers life. In the fourteenth year of *Richard* the ſecond, he was Conſtituted Lord Admiral, in the next year he was made Juſtice of all the Kings Foreſts South of **Trent.** In the twentieth year of *Richard* the ſecond he was Conſtituted Governour of the Iſles of **Garneſey, Jereſey,** and **Wiht,** Warden of **Newforeſt,** Conſtable of **Dover** Caſtle, and Warden of the Cinque Ports : And in the one and twentieth year of *Richard* the ſecond, Conſtable of **England,** and in the ſame year advanced to the Title of Duke of **Albemarle.** Soon after which, upon King *Richards* depoſal in Parliament, held the firſt year of *Henry* the fourth, his Title of Duke was taken from him. Yet afterwards he obtain'd ſuch favour with the King, that in the Parliament held the ſeventh year of *Henry* the fourth he was reſtored to his Hereditary Title of Duke of **York.** This *Edward* built and endowed the Colledge of **Fotheringhay,** in which Church he was buryed, being kill'd in the Battle of **Agincourt,** the third year of *Henry* the fifth. He dying without Iſſue, his Nephew *Richard*, Eldeſt Son of his younger Brother *Richard* of **Coningſborough** Earl of **Cambridge**, was found to be his next heir. This *Richard* was alſo heir on his Mothers ſide to *Edmund Mortimer* Earl of **March,** *viz.* Son of *Ann* Daughter of *Roger* de *Mortimer*, Earl of **March,** and Siſter of the ſaid *Edmund*, who dyed without Iſſue, the third year of *Henry* the fifth. This great Prince, great by his Father, but greater by his Mothers ſide, as being deſcended from *Lionel* Duke of **Clarence,** third Son of King *Edward* the third, Marryed *Cecyly* Daughter of *Ralph Nevil* Earl of **Weſtmorland,**

and by her had ſeveral Sons; among others, *Edward* Earl of **March,** (afterwards King by the name of *Edward* the fourth) and *Edmund* ; **Id. 151.**

Which *Edmund* was Created Earl of **Rutland** ; but little enjoy'd that Title, being barbarouſly ſtab'd by the Lord *Clifford*, preſently after the Battle of **Wakefeild,** (in which Battle his Father loſt his life) this *Edmund* being then but twelve years of age, *Anno Dom.* 1460. **2. *Edmund.***

The Title of Earl of **Rutland** being thus determined in the Males of this Royal Family, we ſhall find it however continued to the preſent poſſeſſor by a Female. For the aboveſaid *Richard* Duke of **York,** Father to King *Edward* the fourth, had ſeveral Daughters ; of which *Ann*, the Eldeſt, was married firſt to *Henry Holland* Duke of **Exeter,** from whom being divorced (the twelfth year of *Edward* the fourth) and having no iſſue by him, ſhe afterwards became the Wife of Sir *Thomas* St. *Leger*, Knight, by whom ſhe had one ſole Daughter and heir, *Ann*, Married to *George Maners*, Lord *Roos* in right of his Mother, Siſter and Coheir to *Edmund* Lord *Roos* ; which *George* Lord *Roos* dying in the fifth year of *Henry* the eighth left iſſue by the ſaid *Ann*, *Thomas Maners* Lord *Roos*, who in conſideration of his high deſcent, as above ſpecified, was on the twenty eighth of *June* in the ſeventeenth year of King *Henry* the eighth, advanced to the Title and Dignity of Earl of **Rutland,** intail to him and his heirs Males of his body. **Id. 295.**

Which ſaid Earl *Thomas* Married *Alianore* Daughter of Sir *William Paſton* Knight, by whom he had iſſue *Henry* his next Succeſſor, *John* who took to Wife one of the Daughters and Coheirs of Sir *George Vernon* of **Haddon** in *Com.* **Derby**, *Roger*, *Thomas*, and *Oliver*: And departed this life, *September* the twentieth, in the five and thirteth year of *Henry* the eighth. **3. *Thomas.***

Henry

4. *Henry.*   *Henry* Earl of **Rutland**, Son and heir of the said Earl *Thomas*, was in the second year of *Edward* the sixth, made Constable of **Nottingham** Castle, and cheif Justice of the Forest of **Shirewood**. In the third and fourth of *Phillip* and *Mary*, he was made Captain general of all the forces then designed against *France*. In the first of *Elizabeth* he was constituted Leiutenant of the Counties of **Nottingham** and **Rutland**; and in the third year of that Queen, Lord President of the Council in the North, and installed Knight of the most Noble Order of the Garter, and dyed the seventeenth of *September* 1563. (5. *Eliz.*)

5. *Edward.*   *Edward*, Son and heir of the said *Henry*, succeeded; who among divers other honours, was in the year 1582, Constituted Lieutenant of the County of **Lincoln**, and in the year 1584. Install'd Knight of the Garter; and departed this life the fourteenth of *April*, 1587. without issue Male.

6. *John.*   Whereupon *John* his Brother, as heir Male succeeded to the honour and Dignity of Earl of **Rutland**, who, in the nine and twentieth of *Elizabeth*, was made Constable of **Nottingham** Castle, and soon after Lieutenant of **Nottinghamshire**, and died 21 *February* 1587. Leaving issue *Roger*, *Francis*, and *George*.

7. *Roger.*   Which *Roger*, succeeding his Father, was in the first year of King *James* made Lord Leiutenant of **Lincolnshire**, and sent Embassador into **Denmark** with the Order of the Garter to that King, and dying without issue the 26 *June*, 1912.

8. *Francis.*   *Francis* his Brother and heir, succeeded, who among divers other honours, was Justice in Eire of all the Forests North of **Trent**, and Knight of the most Noble Order of the Garter. But

died without issue male, the 17 *December*, 1632. (8. *Car* i.)

To whom succeeded Sir *George Maners*, his Brother and next heir Male, but he dying without issue the nine and twentieth of *March*, 1641. The Title of Earl of **Rutland** did thereupon resort to   9. *George.*

John Maners Esquire, then seated at **Haddon** in the County of **Derby**, as next heir Male, *viz.* Son and heir of Sir *George Maners*, Son of *John Maners* Esquire, second Son of *Thomas* first Earl of **Rutland** of this Family. Which said Earl *John* departing this life the nine and twentieth of *September* 1679 full of years and honour;   10. *John.*

His only Son, *John*, then commonly called Lord *Ros* (who had been summon'd by special writ to the House of Lords in his Fathers life time, by the Title of *John* Lord *Maners* of **Haddon**) succeeded: And is the present Earl of **Rutland**, and Lord Leiutenant of **Leicestershire**. Which Noble Lord hath been thrice Married, first to the Lady *Ann Pierpont* Eldest Daughter to *Henry* Marquess of **Dorchester**; but from her being lawfully divorced by Sentence of the Court Christian, and her issue disabled by Act of Parliament to inherit to any of his Lands or Honours, and he also inabled to Marry again, he next Wedded the Lady *Diana* Daughter to *Robert* Earl of *Aylesbury*, Widdow of Sir *Seamour Shirley* Baronet, and surviving her, took to Wife *Catherine* Daughter to *Baptist* Viscount *Campden*, by whom he hath issue.   11. *John.*   *Bar. Eng.* 2. *Vol. p.* 299.

The Lineal descent of which noble Family from *Robert de Todeni*, a Noble *Norman*, who built **Belvoir** Castle, *Com.* **Leicest.** and seated himself there, in the Reign of King *William* the Conquerour, I have here inserted, as follows.

Robertus

Robertus de Todeni —— Adela.
Temp. W. C.

Willielmus *vocat. de* Albi- —— Maltilda *f.* Simonis *de St.*
ni, Brito, *ob. in prin.* Hen. 2.   Liz *Com.* Hunt. *primi.*

Willielmus *de* Albini *fecundus* —— Adeliza.
al. Meſchines, *ob.* 14 H. 2.

Robertus Ros *cognomine* Furſan, —— Iſabella *f.* Willielm.   Willielmus *de* Albini *ter-* —— Margeria
ſtruxit *Caſtellam de* Hamlake *in*   *cognomine* Leo Regis   tius Vic. Rotel. War. Leic.
Com. Eborum, *ob.* 11 H. 3.   Scotiæ.   Buck. Bed. *temp.* R, 1. *ob.*
                                                   20 H. 3.

Robertus *fil.* 2.   Willielmus *f. & h. cui pa-* —— Lucia *f.* Re-   Willielmus *de* Al- —— Albreda
Baro in Scotia.   ter *dedit* Caſtellam *de*   ginaldi *de*   bini, *quartus, ob.*   Biſeth.
                  Hamlake.   Fitz Piers.   32 H. 3.

Robertus *Dom.* Ros *de* —— Iſabella *f. & h.* Willielmi
Hamlake, *ob.* 13 E. 1.   *de* Albini *Dom. de* Belvoir.

Willielmus *Dom.* Ros —— Maltilda *f. & coh.*
ob. 10. E. 2.   Joh. *de* Vaux.

Willielmus *Dom.* Ros, —— Margeria *Sor & coh.* Egi-   Johannes *Dom.* Ros,
ob. 17. E. 3.   dii *Dom.* Badleſmere.   *ob.* 11 E. 3. *ſ. p.*

Willielmus *Dom.* Ros —— Margareta *f.* Ra-   Thomas *Dom.* Ros, —— Beatrix, *ob.*
ob. 26 E. 3. *ſ. p.*   dulfi *Dom.* Nevil.   *ob.* 7 R. 2.   3 H. 5.

Johannes *Dom.* Ros,   Margareta *f.* Johan. —— Willielm. *Dom.* Ros *Dom. The-*
ob. 17 R. 2. *ſ. p.*   Arundel, *Mil.*   ſaurarius Angliæ, *ob.* 2 H. 5.

Johannes *Dom.* Ros.   Willielmus   Thomas *Dom.* Ros, *fra-* —— Alianor *f.* Richardi
occiſus 1421. *ſ. p.*   cæſus, *ſ. p.*   ter *& h. ob.* 9 H. 6.   Beauchamp, *Co.* War.

Thomas *Dom.* Ros, *attinctus* —— Philippa *f.* Joh. *Dom.* Tiptoft,
in Parliamento, 1 E. 4.   *& ſor. & coh.* Joh. *Co.* Worceſt.

Robertus Maners *de* Etal —— Eleanora   Edmundus *Dom.* Ros,   Johannes   Iſabella, *Ux.* Tho.   Margareta.
Caſtle in Com. Northumb *m.*   ſor. *& coh.*   *ob.* 24 H. 7. *ſ. p.*   *ob. ſ. p.*   Gray, *Ar.*

Georgius *Dom.* Ros —— Anna *f.* Thomæ St. Leger, *mil.*   Edvardus   Elizabeth *Uxor*   Cecilia *Uxor*
jure Matris, *ob.* 5 H. 8.   *& Annæ f.* Richardi *D.* Eborum.   Maners.   Wil. Fairfax, *Ar.*   Tho. Fairfax.

Thomas Maners *Comes* —— Alianora *f.* Willielmi
Rutland. *ob.* 35 H. 8.   Paſton, *m.*

Henricus *Comes* —— Margareta *f.* Radulfi   Johannes Ma- —— Dorothea *f. & h.* Geor. Ver-   Rogerus
Rutland. *ob.* 5 El.   *Com.* Weſtmoreland.   ners, *Armig.*   non *de* Haddon *in Co.* Derb. *m.*   Thomas
                                                                           Oliverus

Edvardus *Com.* —— Iſabella *f.* Tho.   Johannes *Com.* —— Elizabeth *f.* Fran-   Georgius Ma- ——
Rutl. *ob.* 29 Eli.   Holcroft, *mil.*   Rutl. *ob.* 29 El.   ciſci Charlton, *Ar.*   ners, *mil.*

Elizabetha   Rogerus, *Comes*   Franciſcus *Com.* —— Franciſca *f. & h.*   Georgius,   Johannes *Comes* —— Franciſca *f.* Edvar.
Ux. Will.   Rut. *ob.* 26 Jac. *ſ. p.*   Rutl. *ob.* 8. Car. 1.   Hen. Knivet, *M.*   *Com.* Rutl.   Rut. *ob.* 31 Car. 2.   *Dom.* Montague.
Cecil *Dom.*   *ob.* 17 Car.
Burghley.   1. *ſ. p.*   Johannes *nunc* —— Catherina *filia* Baptiſtæ
               Catherina *Ux.* Georg.   *Com.* Rut. 1680.   Vicecom. Campden *Ux.* 3.
Willielmus   Duc. Buck.
Dom. Ros *ob.*
18 Jac. *ſ. p.*   Johannes *vocat.* Dom. Ros.   Thomas-Baptiſt.   Catherina.

Sheriffs of RUTLAND.

THE first Sheriff of this County, of whom I find any mention, is *Richard de Humet*, Conftable of *Normandy*, in the time of King *Henry* 2. to whom that King granted the Cuftody of this County, in the 10*th*. year of his Reign, and therefore it is to be prefum'd that 𝕽𝖚𝖙𝖑𝖆𝖓𝖉 was made a County of it felf about that year.

HENR. 2.

An. Dom.	A.R.	
1164	10	Richard. de Humet.
1165	11	
1166	12	
1167	13	
Al.Wil.Baffet. 1168	14*	
1169	15	
1170	16	
1171	17	Idem.
1172	18	
1173	19	
1174	20	
1175	21	
1176	22	
1177	23	
1178	24	
1179	25	
1180	26	Willielm. Molduit.
1181	27	
1182	28	
1183	29	
1184	30	Idem.
1185	31	
1186	32	
1187	33	
Al. Almericus 1188	34*	
Difpenfer.		

RICH. I.

Al. Almericus 1190	1*	Anna Brigg.
Difpenfer. 1191	2	Will. Albeney & Will. Frefney.
1192	3	
1193	4	
1194	5	Iidem.
1195	6	
1196	7	
1197	8	
1198	9	Williel. Albeuine, vel Albini.

JOH.

1200	1	Benedic. de Haverfam.
1201	2	Robertus Malduit.
1202	3	Idem.
1203	4	
1204	5	Radulp. Normanvil.
1205	6	Idem.
1206	7	

An. Dom.	A.R.	
1207	8	
1208	9	Idem.
1209	10	
1210	11	
1211	12	Rober. & Hen. de Brabro.
1212	13	
1213	14	
1214	15	Iidem.
1215	16	
1216	17	

HENR. 3.

1217	1	Robert. & Hen. de Brabro.
1218	2	Alan. Baffet.
1219	3	
1220	4	
1221	5	
1222	6	
1223	7	Idem.
1224	8	
1225	9	
1226	10	
1227	11	
1228	12	Galfrid. de Rockingham.
1229	13	
1230	14	
1231	15	
1232	16	
1233	17	
1234	18	
1235	19	
1236	20	
1237	21	
1238	22	
1239	23	
1240	24	Idem.
1241	25	
1242	26	
1243	27	
1244	28	
1245	29	
1246	30	
1247	31	
1248	32	
1249	33	
1250	34	
1251	35	
1252	36	
1253	37	
1254	38	Radulph. de Greneham.
1255	39	
1256	40	Idem.
1257	41	
1258	42	
1259	43	Anketyn de Markinal.

C

An. Dom.	A.R.	
1260	44	
1261	45	
1262	46	
1263	47	
1264	48	
1265	49	
1266	50	Idem.
1267	51	
1268	52	
1269	53	
1270	54	
1271	55	
1272	56	

EDWARD. 1.

An. Dom.	A.R.	
1273	1	Pet. Wakervil, & Wil. Bouile.
1274	2	
1275	3	
1276	4	
1277	5	Idem.
1278	6	
1279	7	
1280	8	
1281	9	Alberic. de Whitleler,
1382	10	
1283	11	
1284	12	
1285	13	Idem.
1286	14	
1287	15	
1288	16	
1289	17	Edmund Cones Cornubiæ.
1290	18	
1291	19	
1292	20	
1293	21	
1294	22	
1295	23	Idem.
1296	24	
1297	25	
1298	26	
1299	27	
1300	28	
1301	29	
1302	30	Marg. Vidua Edm. Com. Corn.
1303	31	
1364	32	Eadem.
1305	33	
1206	34	

EDWARD. 2.

An. Dom.	A.R.	
1308	1	Marg. Vid. Edm. Com. Corn.
1309	2	
1310	3	Eadem.
1311	4	

An. Dom.	A.R.	
1312	5	Eadem.
1313	6	Marg. Vidua Pierce Gaveston
1314	7	Eadem.
1315	8	
1316	9	Hugo de Audeley, qui duxit in
1317	10	uxorem prædictam Marga.
1318	11	
1319	12	Idem.
1320	13	
1321	14	
1322	15	John de Aldeburgh.
1323	16	Idem.
1324	17	Edmund Comes Cantii.
1325	18	Idem.
1326	19	

EDWARD. 3.

An. Dom.	A.R.	
1327	1	Hugo de Audeley Comes. Glouc.
1328	2	
1329	3	
1330	4	
1331	5	
1332	6	
1333	7	
1334	8	
1335	9	
1336	10	
1337	11	Idem.
1338	12	
1339	13	
1340	14	
1341	15	
1342	16	
1343	17	
1344	18	
1345	19	
1346	20	
1347	21	
1348	22	Wil. de Bohun Com. Northam.
1349	23	
1350	24	
1351	25	
1352	26	
1353	27	Idem.
1354	28	
1355	29	
1356	30	
1357	31	
1358	32	
1359	33	Willielmus Wade.
1360	34	
1361	35	Idem.
1362	36	
1363	37	
1364	38	Humph. de Bohun.
1365	39	Idem.

An. Dom.	A.R.	
1366	40	
1367	41	
1368	42	
1369	43	Idem.
1370	44	
1371	45	
1372	46	
1373	47	Johannes de Whitlesbrough.
1374	48	Idem.
1375	49	Simon Ward.
1376	50	Idem.

RICH. 2.

An. Dom.	A.R.	
1378	1	Johannes Whittlebury.
1379	2	Thomas de Burton.
1380	3	Johannes Basings.
1381	4	Willielmus Morwood.
1382	5	Johannes de Whittlesbury.
1383	6	Willielmus Flore.
1384	7	Walterus Scarle.
1385	8	Johannes de Calverley.
1386	9	Robertus de Veer,
1387	10	Idem.
1388	11	Johannes Whittebury.
1389	12	Walterus Skarles.
1390	13	Edwardus Com. Rutland.
1391	14	
1392	15	
1393	16	
1394	17	Idem.
1395	18	
1396	19	
1397	20	
1398	21	Thomas Ondeley.
1399	22	Idem.

HEN. 4.

Recorda manca per totum hujus Regnum.

HEN. 5.

An. Dom.	A.R.	
1413	1	Thomas Ondeby.
1414	2	Jacobus Bellers.
1415	3	Johannes Boyvill.
1416	4	Thomas Burton, Mil.
1417	5	Robertus Brown.
1418	6	Robertus Chisleden.
1419	7	Johannes Pensax.
1420	8	Thomas Burton, Mil.
1421	9	Idem.

HEN. 6.

An. Dom.	A.R.	
1422	1	Thomas Burton.

An. Dom.	A.R.	
1423	2	Johannes Ondeby.
1424	3	Johannes Davis, Mil.
1425	4	Johannes Colepeper.
1426	5	Henr. Plessington, Mil.
1427	6	Thomas Burton, Mil.
1428	7	Johannes Denys.
1429	8	Johannes Colepeper.
1430	9	Thomas Flore.
1431	10	Henr. Plessington, Mil.
1432	11	Johannes Boyvile.
1433	12	Willielmus Beaufo.
1434	13	Rob. Davis & Joha. Pilton.
1435	14	Johannes Branspath.
1436	15	Hugo Boyvile.
1437	16	Laurentius Sherard.
1438	17	Willelmus Beaufo.
1439	18	Thomas Burton.
1440	19	Henr. Plessington, Mil.
1441	20	Thomas Flore.
1442	21	Willielmus Beaufo.
1443	22	Thomas Barkeley.
1444	23	Johannes Basings, Mil.
1445	24	Willielmus Walker.
1446	25	Johannes Boyvile.
1447	26	Willelmus Haselden.
1448	27	Hugo Boyvile.
1449	28	Robertus Fenne.
1450	29	Thomas Floure.
1451	30	Willielmus Heton.
1452	31	Robertus Sherard.
1453	32	Robertus Fenne.
1454	33	Willielmus Beaufo.
1455	34	Willielmus Haselden.
1456	35	Thomas Flore.
1457	36	Thomas Dale.
1458	37	Robertus Fenne.
1459	38	Everardus Digby.
1460	39	

EDW. 4.

An. Dom.	A.R.	
1461	1	Johannes Francis.
1462	2	Thomas Palmer.
1463	3	Idem.
1464	4	Willielmus Greenham.
1465	5	Thomas Flore.
1466	6	Richardus Sapcots, Mil.
1467	7	Willielmus Brown.
1468	8	Galfridus Sherard.
1469	9	Johannes Dale.
1470	10	Thomas Flore.
1471	11	Brian Talbot.
1472	12	Thomas Barkley, Mil.
1473	13	Willielmus Haselden.
1474	14	Johannes Pilton.
1475	15	Willielmus Brown.

C 2

An. Dom	A.R.	
1476	16	Johannes Sapcote.
1477	17	David Malpas.
1478	18	Henry Mackworth.
1479	19	Johannes Pilton.
1480	20	Galfredus Sherard.
1481	21	Willielmus Palmer.
1482	22	David Malpas.

EDWARD. 5.

1483	1	Willielmus Brown.

RICHARD. 3.

1484	1	Galfredus Sherard.
1485	2	Johannes Pilton.

HENER. 7.

1486	1	Everardus Digby.
1487	2	Willielmus Brown.
1488	3	David Malpas.
1489	4	Maurice Barkley.
1490	5	Thomas Sapcots.
1491	6	Johannes Digby, Mil.
1492	7	Robertus Harington.
1493	8	Christopher Brown.
1494	9	Johannes Pilton.
1495	10	Thomas Sherard.
1496	11	Thomas Sapcots.
1497	12	George Mackworth.
1498	13	Robertus Harington.
1499	14	Everardus Digby.
1500	15	Johannes Chisleden.
1501	16	Christopher Brown.
1502	17	Johannes Digby.
1503	18	Johannes Harington.
1504	19	Mauritius Berkely.
1505	20	Willielmus Pole.
1506	21	Thomas Sherard.
1507	22	Richard Flowr.
1508	23	Johannes Coly.
1509	24	Everardus Feilding, Mil.

HENER. 8.

1509	1	Christopher Brown.
1510	2	Edward Sapcote.
1511	3	George Mackworth.
1512	4	Johannes Harington.
1513	5	Everardus Digby.
1514	6	Thomas Brookesby.
1515	7	Johannes Caldecot.
1516	8	Johannes Harington.
1517	9	Johannes Digby, M.
1518	10	Everardus Digby.
1519	11	Willielmus Fielding.

An Dom	A.R.	
1520	12	Johannes Harrington, Jun.
1521	13	Johannes Harrington, Sen.
1522	14	George Mackworth.
1523	15	Johannes Digby, M.
1524	16	Franciscus Brown.
1525	17	Johannes Caldecot.
1526	18	Willielmus Fielding.
1527	19	Edwardus Sapcots.
1528	20	Everardus Digby, M.
1529	21	Edwardus Catesby.
1530	22	Georgius Mackworth.
1531	23	Edwardus Sapcots.
1432	24	Everardus Digby, M.
1533	25	Johannes Harington, M.
1534	26	Georgius Mackworth.
1535	27	Edwardus Sapcots.
1536	28	Andreas Noel, Ar.
1537	29	Thomas Brudnel, Ar.
1538	30	Franciscus Mackworth, Ar.
1539	31	Richardus Cecil, Ar.
1540	32	Johannes Harington, M.
1541	33	Kenelmus Digby, Ar.
1542	34	Edwardus Sapcots, Ar.
1543	35	Franciscus Mackworth, Ar.
1544	36	Georgius Sherard, Ar.
1545	37	Anthonius Brown.
1546	38	

EDWARD. 6.

1547	1	Anthonius Colly, Ar.
1548	2	Simon Digby, Ar.
1549	3	Kenelmus Digby, Ar.
1550	4	Andreas Noel, Ar.
1551	5	Anthonius Colly, Ar.
1552	6	Johannes Harington, M.
1553	7	

MAR.

1554	1	Kenelmus Digby, Ar.
1555	2	Simon Digby, Ar.
1556	3	Franciscus Mackworth, Ar.
1557	4	Andreas Noel, Ar.
1558	5	Anthonius Brown, Ar.

ELIZAB.

1559	1	Anthonius Colly, Ar.
1560	2	Jacobus Harington, M.
1561	3	Kenelmus Digby, Ar.
1562	4	Georgius Sherard, Ar.
1563	5	Willielmus Caldecot, Ar.
1564	6	Georgius Mackworth, Ar.
1565	7	Johannes Floure, Ar.
1566	8	Jacobus Harington, M.
1567	9	Kenelmus Digby, Ar.

An. Dom.	A.R.	
1568	10	*Anthon. Colly,* Ar.
1569	11	*Johannes Floure,* Ar.
1570	12	*Maurice Berkley,* Ar.
1571	13	*Anthon. Brown,* Ar.
1572	14	*George Mackworth,* Ar.
1573	15	*Thomas Cony,* Ar.
1574	16	*Robertus Sapcots,* Ar.
1575	17	*Willielmus Caldecot,* Ar.
1576	18	*Anthon. Colly,* Ar.
1577	19	*Johannes Floure,* Ar.
1578	20	*Jacobus Harrington,* Mil.
1579	21	*Michael Catesby,* Ar.
1580	22	*George Mackworth,* Ar.
1581	23	*Willielmus Feilding,* Ar.
1582	24	*Rogerus Smith,* Ar.
1583	25	*Anthon. Colly,* Ar.
1584	26	*Thomas Cony,* Ar.
1585	27	*Kenelmus Digby,* Ar.
1586	28	*Jacobus Harrington,* Mil.
1587	29	*Andreas Noel,* Mil.
1588	30	*George Sheffeild,* Ar.
1589	31	*Robertus Sapcots,* Ar.
1590	32	*Henry Herenden,* Ar.
1591	33	*Willielmus Feilding,* Ar.
1592	34	*Rogerus Smith,* Ar.
1593	35	*Jacobus Harrington,* Mil.
1594	36	*Johannes Harrington,* Mil.
1595	37	*Andreas Noel,* Mil.
1596	38	*Willielmus Feilding,* Ar.
1597	39	*Henry Ferrers,* Ar.
1598	40	*Johannes Harrington,* Mil.
1599	41	*Thomas Mackworth,* Ar.
1600	42	*Andreas Noel,* Mil.
1601	43	*Jacobus Harrington,* Mil.
1602	44	*Johannes Harrington,* Mil.

JACOBUS.

An. Dom.	A.R.	
1603	1	*Willielmus Bodendine,* Ar.
1604	2	*Willielmus Bulstred,* Mil.
1605	3	*Basil Feilding,* Ar.
1606	4	*Henry Berkley,* Ar.
1607	5	*Guido Palmes,* Ar.
1608	6	*Edwardus Noel,* Mil.
1609	7	*Thomas Mackworth,* Ar.
1610	8	*Willelmus Halford,* Ar.
1611	9	*Johannes Elmes,* Ar.
1612	10	*Robertus Lane,* Mil.
1613	11	*Anthon. Andrews,* Ar.
1614	12	*Franciscus Bodinden,* Ar.
1615	13	*Edwardus Noel,* Mil. & Bar.
1616	14	*Richardus Cony,* Mil.
1617	15	*Guido Palmes,* Mil.
1618	16	*Abraham. Johnson,* Ar.
1619	17	*Richardus Halford,* Ar.
1620	18	*Anthon. Colly,* Ar.
1621	19	*Edwar. Harington,* Mil. & B.

An. Dom.	A.R.	
1622	20	*Robertus Lane,* Mil.
1623	21	*Robertus Tredway,* Ar.
1624	22	*Johannes Osborne,* Ar.

CAROLUS 1.

An. Dom.	A.R.	
1625	1	*Guido Palmes,* Mil.
1626	2	*Willelmus Gibson,* Ar.
1927	3	*Henr. Mackworth,* Ar.
1628	4	*Everardus Falkener,* Ar.
1629	5	*Johannes Huggeford,* Ar.
1630	6	*Johannes Wingfeild,* Mil.
1631	7	*Richardus Halford,* Ar.
1632	8	*Anthon. Colly,* Mil.
1633	9	*Richardus Hickson,* Ar.
1634	10	*Franciscus Bodington,* Mil.
1625	11	*Henr. Mynne,* Mil.
1936	12	*Edwar. Harington,* Mil. & B.
1637	13	*Edwardus Andrews,* Ar.
1638	14	*Johannes Barker,* Ar.
1639	15	*Thomas Leuit,* Ar.
1640	16	*Robertus Horsman,* Ar.
1641	17	*Thomas Wait,* Ar.
1642	18	
1643	19	
1644	20	
1645	21	
1646	22	*Abel Barker,* Ar.
1647	23	*Christoph. Brown,* Ar.
1648	24	

CAROLUS 2.

An. Dom.	A.R.	
1649	1	
1650	2	
1651	3	
1652	4	Temporis hoc spatium detur
1653	5	
1654	6	Oblivioni
1655	7	
1656	8	
1657	9	
1658	10	
1659	11	
1660	12	*Eusebius Pelsant,* Mil.
1661	13	*Thomas Hartop,* Mil.
1662	14	*Richardus Wingfeild,* Mil.
1663	15	{ *Hug. Ducy,* Mil. Baln. { *Willielmus Palms,* Ar.
1664	16	*Thomas Mackworth,* Bar.
1665	17	*Richardus Rouse,* Ar.
1666	18	*Carolus Halford,* Ar.
1667	19	*Beaumont Bodenham,* Ar.
1668	20	*Walter Moor,* Ar.
1669	21	*Edwardus Horsman,* Ar.
1670	22	*Andreas Broughton,* Ar.
1671	23	*Thomas Pilkington,* Ar.

1672

An.Dom	A.R.		An.Dom	A.R.	
1672	24	*Thomas Barker*, Ar.	1679	31	*Johannes Wingfield*, Ar.
1673	25	*Johannes Newland.* Ar.	1680	32	*Chriſtopher. Brown*, Ar.
1674	26	*Willielmus Atkins.* Ar.	1681	33	*Thomas Barker*, Bar.
1675	27	*Richardus Fancourt*, Ar.	1682	34	*Richard Verney*, Ar.
1676	28	*Johannes Wallet*, Ar.	1683	35	*Andreas Noel*, Mil.
1677	29	*Samuel Brown*, Ar.	1684	36	*Edwardus Coney*, Ar.
1678	30	*Anthonius Palmer*, Ar.	1685		

Knights of the Shire in Parliament.

This little County having never had any City, Borough, or Corporation within its limits, ſends only two Knights for the Shire, to the Houſe of Commons in Parliament. A Liſt of whom I have here Collected from the 23 *Ed.* 1. to this day: So far as any Records are extent.

Regn. E D W. 1.

A.R.	
23	*Ro. de Flikeſthorp*, & *Sim. de Bokminſter.*
26	*Johan de Foleville*, *Williel. de Berks.*
28	*Williel. de Blunt*, *Joha. de Foleville.*
29	*Iidem.*
30	*Joha. de Sexton*, *Rober. de Flythorp.*
33	*Theobaldus de Nevil.*
34	*Rob. de Flixthorp*, *Tho. de Buckland.*
35	*Williel. le Blunt*, *Bernardus de Brus.*

Regn. E D W. 2.

	A.R.	
	2	*Williel. de Baſiggs*, *Symon de Lyndon.*
	4	*Radulf. de Bellaſago*, *Nicol. de Burton.*
London.	5	*Richardus de Bouton.*
Weſtminſt.	5	*Bernardus de Brus*, *Rober. de la Sale.*
Weſtminſt.	6	*Willi. de Sancto Lucio*, *Bricius le Danes.*
Windſor.	6	*Willi. de Helewell*, *Alanus de Frankton.*
Woodſt.	6	*Johan. de Wynil*, *Walterus Poul.*
	8	{ *Reginaldus de Warley*, { *Haſculphus de Whitewell.*
Linclon.	9	*Nich. de Burton*, *Rogerus Pucoſt.*
Weſtminſt.	9	*Aſculphus de Whitewell*, *Joh. Baſſet.*
	10	*Joha. Baſſet*, *Aſculphus de Whitwell.*
	15	*Johan. de Hakelyne*, *Rober. Birom*,
	16	*Rober. de Luſwyks*, *Rich. de Seyton.*
	17	*Willi. Haward*, *Williel. de Alesbury.*
	19	{ *Haſculphus de Whitewell*, { *Stephanus de Wytleford.*

Regn. E D W. 3.

	A.R.	
Weſtminſt.	1	*Johan. de Boivyle*, *Steph. de Wittelisford.*

A.R.		
1	*Johan. de Wittelisbur*, *Johan. de Bellafogo.*	Linc.
2	*Rich. de Sancto Licio*, *Willi. de Aylesbury.*	Sarum.
2	*Rich. de Sancto Licio*, *Johan. de Bellafago.*	Ebor.
2	*Johan. de Wittlebury*, *Rich. de Sancto Licio*	Northamp.
2	*Johan. de Beaufou*, *Johan. de Wevyle.*	Ebor.
4	*Johannes de Weynil*, *Walterus Poul.*	Weſtminſt.
4	*Rich. de Sancto Licio*, *Tho. de Grenham.*	Winton.
5	*Clem. de Caſterton*, *Johan. de Wevyl.*	
6	*Johan. de Wyvil*, *Walterus Poul.*	
6	*Rogerus de Denford*, *Richard. de Seyton.*	
7	*Johan. le Hunt*, *Thomas de Wenge.*	
8	*Johan. de Wittilbury*, *Johan. Hakelut.*	Weſtminſt.
8	*Johan. Hakelut*, *Johan. de Weyvil.*	Ebor.
9	{ *Rich. de Sancto Licio*, { *Haſculph. de VVhitewell.*	
10	*Rich. de Sancto Licio*, *Thomas de VVenton.*	Notting.
10	*Iidem.*	Weſtminſt.
11	*Johan. de Seyton*, *Johan. Baſſet.*	
11	*Tho. de Wympton*, *Sim. de Lyndon.*	
12	*Johan. Haklut*, *Thomas de Grenham.*	Weſtminſt.
12	*Joha. Hakeluit*, *Reginaldus de la More.*	Northam.
13	*Joha. de Haklut*, *Rogerus de Bellofago.*	
13	*Joha. Hackeluyt*, *VValterus Poul.*	
14	*Tho. de Grenham*, *Rogerus de Deneford.*	Weſtminſt.
14	*Joha. de VVyville*, *VValterus Poule.*	
14	*Robertus de Holewell.*	
15	*Willi. VVade*, *Rogerus de Beafo.*	
17	*Haſculphus de VVhitewel*, *VVil. VVade.*	
18	*Iidem.*	
20	*VVil. VVade*, *Reginaldus de Tykeſovere.*	
22	*Iidem.*	
22	*Joha. Hakelut*, *VVilli. VVade.*	
25	*VVill. VVade*, *Reginaldus de Tykeſovere.*	
26	*Galfridus de la Mare*, *Rolandus Daveys.*	
26	*Rolandus Daveys.*	
27	*VVillielmus de Burton.*	
28	*VVill. de Burton*, *Rolandus Deneys.*	
29	*VVll. Beaufen*, *Rob. de Luffenham.*	
31	*Iidem.*	
35	*Rolan. Daveys*, *Wil. Wade de Stokefaſton.*	
36	*Joha. de Boyvil*, *Rober. de Luffenham.*	
37	*VVilliel. Beaufon*, *VVilliel. VVade.*	

39

A.R.	
39	*Rob. de Luffenham, VVill. Beaufo.*
42	*Will. Beaufo, Walterus de Scayle.*
43	*Joha. Boyvile, Will. Beaufou.*
Weftminft. 45	*Laurentius Hauberk, Nichol. Grene.*
Winton. 45	*Laurentius Hauberk.*
46	*Nichol. Grene, Johan. VVittlesbury.*
47	*Ric. Nevylle, Joha. Knotte de Gretham.*
50	*Joh. Bafyngs, Tho. de Burton,* Chivalers.
51	*Nichol: Grene, Lurentius Hauberk.*

Regn. RIC. 2.

1	*Thomas de Burton,* Chivaler.
Glouc. 2	*Walterus Scarle, Nichol. Morwood.*
Weftminft. 2	*Joh. Hellewel, Chiva. Lauren. Hauberk*
3	*Tho. de Burton, Chiv. Walterus Scarle.*
4	*Joh. Wittlebury, VVill. Norwood.*
5	*Tho. de Burton, Johan: VVittelbury.*
5	*Joh. Daveys, Will. Morewod.*
6	*Joh. Daveys, Will. Flore.*
6	*Joha. Helwell, Williel. Morewode.*
Weftminft. 7	*Joh. de Calverly, Joh. VVitlebury,* Chiva.
Sarum 7	*Rober. de Harryngton, Nichol. Grenham.*
8	*VVilliel. Flore, VVilliel, Marwod.*
9	*Hugo de Calmley, Johan. Knot.*
10	*Johan. VVitlebury, VValterus Scarle.*
11	*Hugo Browe, Oliverus Maleverer,* Chiva.
12	*Joh. Daneys,* Chivaler *VValterus Scarle.*
13	*Hugo de Calvele, Oliverus de Maleverer.*
14	*Hugo Browe, Johan. de Calveley.*
15	*Hugo Grenham, Johan. Bufhe.*
16	*VValterus Scarle, Johan. Elme.*
17	*Johan. Daveys,* Chivaler*; Johan. Elme.*
18	*Joh. VVitelbury Senior, Walterus Scarle.*
20	*Rob. Pleffington, Rogerus de Flore.*
21	*Oliver. Maleverer,* Chiva. *Tho. de Outeby.*

Regn. HEN. 4.

1	*Rogerus Flore, Johan. Durant.*
2	*Johan. Durante, Williel. Outeby.*
4	*Tho. Ondeby, Rogerus Flore.*
5	*Tho. Thorp, Joh. Penfax.*
6	*Tho. Ondeby, Johan. Flore.*
8	*Johan. Penfax, Rober. Scarle.*
9	*Rober. Brewe, VVilliel. Sheffeld.*

The Records are wanting during the Refidue of this Kings Reign, and in like manner are they imperfect as to feveral years in the Reigns of *H. 5. H. 6.* and *E. 4.*

Regn. HEN. 5.

1	*Johan. Penfax, Johan. de Burgh.*
2	*Rogerus Flore, Rober. Brewe.*

This *Roger Flore,* Efq; was Speaker

of the Houfe of Commons, in the **4, 5,** and **7th.** years of this King.

A.R.	
8	*Rober. Brewe, Williel. Sheffeld.*
9	*Johan. Culpepir,* Ar. *Tho. Grenham,* Ar.

Regn. HEN. 6.

1	*Hen. Plefington,* Mil, *Roger. Flore,* Ar.
3	*Tho. Burton, Henr. Plefington.*
5	*Tho. Burton,* Mil. *Johan. Colepepir,* Ar.
7	*Rober. Browe, Johan. Boyvile.*
13	*Johan. Browe, Williel. Beaufo.*
20	*Joha. Braunfpath,* Ar. *Will. Heyton,* Ar.
25	*Hugo Boyvile, Everard Digby.*
27	*Everardus Digby, Joh. Browarnig.*
28	{ *Everardus Digby de Stokedri,* { *Robertus Frene de Exton.*
29	*Tho. Palmer, Everardus Digby,* Armi.
38	*Johan. Browe, Johan. Boyville.*
38	*Everardus Digby,* Ar. *Radu. Beaufo,* Ar.

Regn. EDW. 4.

6	*Johan. Browe,* Ar. *Joha. ....* Ar.
12	*Brian Talbot,* Ar. *Joha. Pilton.*

The Writs, Returns, and Indentures from the 12th. of *E. 4.* to the firft of Queen *Mary,* are all thought to be loft. *Prin. Bre. Parl. rediviva.* p. 203.

The following Names I have Collected from the Records remaining in the Chappel of the *Roles.* But the Returns for feveral Parliaments are wanting. Such as are to be found, are,

Regn. EDW. 6.

1	*Kenel. Digby,* Ar. *Anthon. Colly,* Ar.

Regn. MAR.

1	*Andre. Nowell,* Ar. *Kenelm. Digby,* Ar.	Weftminft.
1	*Anthon. Colly,* Ar. *Johan. Hunt,* Ar.	Oxon.

Regn. PH. & MA.

1,2	*Jaco. Harrington,* Ar. *Anthon. Colly,* Ar.
2,3	*Jaco. Harrington,* Mil. *Kenel. Digby,* Mil.
4,5	*Jaco. Harrington,* Mil. *Kenel. Digby,* Mil.

Regn. ELIZ.

14	*Jaco. Harrington,* Mil. *Kenel. Digby,* Ar.
28	*Jaco. Harrington,* Mil. *Andre. Nowell,* Mil.
30	*Jaco. Harrington,* Mil. *Andre. Nowell,* Mil.
43	*Joh. Harrington,* Mil. *Andre. Nowell,* Mil.

Regn:

The Returns, for the whole Reign of King *James*, are wanting.

Regn. C A R. 1.

A.R.

1	*Will. Bulftrode*, Mil. *Fran. Bodenham*, Mil.
3	*Guido Palmes*, Mil. *Will. Bulftrode*, Mil.
15	*Baptifta Noell*, Ar. *Guido Palmes*, Mil.
16	*Baptifta Noel*, Ar. *Guido Palmes*, Mil.

Regn. C A R. 2.

A.R.

12	*Phil. Sherard*, Ar. *Sam. Brown*, Ar.
13	*Edward. Noel*, Ar. *Phil. Sherard*, Ar.
30	*Phil. Sherard*, Ar. *Tho. Mackworth*, Bar.
31	*Phil. Sherard*, Ar. *Abellus Barker*, Bar.
32	*Tho. Mackworth*, Bar. in loco *Abelli Barker*, defunct.
33	*Phil. Sherard*, Ar. *Edwar. Fawkener*, Ar. *Oxon.*

Lords Lieutenants of this County.

Bar. Eng. 2. Vol. 297

IN the firft year of Queen *Elizabeth*, *Henry* Earl of 𝔯𝔲𝔱𝔩𝔞𝔫𝔡, was conftituted Lord Lieutenant for the Counties of 𝔑𝔬𝔱𝔱𝔦𝔫𝔤𝔥𝔞𝔪 and 𝔯𝔲𝔱𝔩𝔞𝔫𝔡.

Bar. Eng. 1. Vol. 589.

In the Twelfth of the faid Queen, *Henry* Earl of 𝔥𝔲𝔫𝔱𝔦𝔫𝔤𝔡𝔬𝔫 was conftituted Leiutenant of the Counties of 𝔩𝔢𝔦𝔠𝔢𝔰𝔱𝔢𝔯 and 𝔯𝔲𝔱𝔩𝔞𝔫𝔡. And again in the 17*th.* of the faid Queen:

Id. ib.

In the Thirty eighth year of the faid Queen, *George* Earl of 𝔥𝔲𝔫𝔱𝔦𝔫𝔤𝔡𝔬𝔫, fecond Brother and Heir to the former Earl, was conftituted Lieutenant of the faid Counties. And again in the firft year of King *James*.

Id. ib.

In the Twelfth year of King *James* *Henry* Earl of 𝔥𝔲𝔫𝔱𝔦𝔫𝔤𝔱𝔬𝔫 Grandfon, and Heir to the aforefaid Earl *George*, was conftituted Lieutenant of the faid Counties. So alfo in the firft of King *Charles* I.

In the 14. *Car.* 1. *Ferdinando* Lord *Haftings*, Eldeft Son to the laft mentioned Earl *Henry* was joyned with his Father in the Lieutenancy of the faid Counties.

Id. ib.

In the twelfth year of our now Soveraign, King *Charles* 2. *Baptift* Lord Vicount *Campden*, was conftituted Lord Lieutenant of the County of 𝔯𝔲𝔱𝔩𝔞𝔫𝔡; being the firft Lord Leiutenant of this County apart by it felf.

In the Thirty fourth year of our now Soveraign, upon the death of the faid Lord, his Son and Heir, the Right Honourable *Edward* then Vicount *Campden*, and foon after created Earl of 𝔊𝔞𝔦𝔫𝔰𝔟𝔬𝔯𝔬𝔲𝔤𝔥, was conftituted Lord Lieutenant of this County of 𝔯𝔲𝔱𝔩𝔞𝔫𝔡, and *Cuftos Rotulorum* of the fame.

Thus far of the COUNTY in General: I come now to treat of the feveral Towns, Villages, and Places of Note, perticularly; And Firft of

ASHWELL.

ASHWELL.

Domesday tit. **Rotel.**

THIS Town lies in the hundred of **Alſtoe**. At the time of the *Norman* Conqueſt it was called **Exwelle**, at which time Earl *Haroldus* held here two Carucates of Land, as it was rated (*ad geldam*) to the Tax. The Arable Land was ſix Carucates, afterwards at the time of *Domeſday* Survey one *Gozelinus* (whom the Record call *Homo Hugonis Comitis*) held here two Carucates, and thirteen Villains, and three *Bordarii* (or Cottagers) all which had amongſt them five Carucates and ſixteen Acres of Meadow. In the time of King *Edward* the Confeſſor, this Town was valued at 100 ſhillings, but at the time of the aforeſaid Survey, at 6 *l.*

The Mannour of **Aſhwell** was in the time of *Ed.* 2. Poſſeſt by the *Touchets*, from whom diſcends the now Earl of **Caſtle-Haven**. The firſt of which family, that I read of, to die ſeized of this
Rot. fin. 8 *E.*2. *m.* 1.   Lordſhip, was *Thomas Touchet*; after whoſe death, Sir *Robert Touchet* Knight, his Son and Heir, doing his Homage, had Livery of his Lands, in the eighth year of King *E.* 2. and left iſſue *Thomas*, which *Thomas* Married *Joan* one of the Daughters and Coheirs of *Nicholas* Lord *Audley* of **Heleigh**, and by her

had iſſue Sir *John Touchet*, Knighted in the 33 of *E.* 3. And in the ſame year,
H. 33. *E.* 3. *Rot.* 2. *ex parte Rem. Theſ.*   the ſame Sir *John* acknowledged himſelf to hold of *Edward* Prince of **Wales**, the Mannor of **Aſhwell**, with the Appurtenances in the County of **Rutland** being parcel of the Lands of *Robert de Brus* Attaint of Treaſon, by the ſervice of the third part of a Knights fee. The ſame Sir *John* being in the 15 *R.*2. found to be one of the Heirs of the
Bar. Eng. 2 *Vol.* 28.   foreſaid *Nicholas* Lord **Audley**, did thereupon aſſume the Title of Lord **Audley**, and his Deſcendents have been ever ſince ſummon'd to the Parliament by that Title: This Lord *John* departed this life on the 19*th.* of *December* 10 *H.* 4. being then ſeized among ſeveral other Lordſhips elſewhere, of two parts of the Mannor of **Aſhwell** in *Com. Roteland.* and left *James* his Son and Heir then ten years of age.

In the 7*th.* of *H.* 8. It was found by Office that *Brian Palmes* held the Mannour of **Aſhwell** with its Appurtenan-
Eſc. 7 *H.* 8.   ces, in the County of **Rutland** of our Lord the King, but by what ſervices the Inquiſitors knew not; and that *Francis Palmes* was his Son and Heir, From whom is deſcended *William Palmes*, Eſq, the preſent Lord of this Mannour.

Willielm. Palmes *de* Nabourn *Com.* Ebor. ——— .... *Soror* Briani Roucliff *Baronis Scaccarii,* 1 *H.* 7.

Bryan Palmes, *fil. & Heres.*	Guido Palmes, *Servient* ——— Jana *fil. & coh. de* .... *ad Legem,* 20 *H.*7. *fil.* 2. Drew *de* Briſtou.

Brianus Palmes *de* Aſhwell. —— Iſabella *f. & h.* .... Lindley *de* Lindely *Com.* Ebor.   Jana *Uxor* Nicholai Farefax *de* Walton, *Mil.*

Franciſcus Palmes *de* Aſhwell. —— Margareta *ſoror* Andreæ Corbet, *Mil.*

Franciſcus Palmes *de* Aſhwell. —— Anna *f.* Stephani Hadnal *de* Shervil *in Com.* Hamptonæ.

Guido Palmes *de* Aſhwell, *M. nat.* 1580. —— Miria *f. & coh.* Edw. Stafford, *M.*   *Soror & h.* Willielmi Stafford.

Brianus Palmes, *M.* —— Miria *f. & coh.* Gervaſii Tevery *de* Stapilford *in Com.* Not.

Tevery Palmes, *ob. ſ. p. fil.* 2.	Franciſcus Palmes, Ar. *ob. ſ. p.* —— Maria *f.* Mildmay *Com.* Weſtmer. *poſtea nupta* Johanni *Com.* Exeter.	Willielmus Palmes, Ar. —— Maria *conſanguinea & coh.* Willel. *Dom.* Eure.

Guido.	Willielmus.	Margareta.	Eliſabetha.	Maria.	Anna.

D   *Ih*

Of the ADVOWSON.

Reg: Linc.

In the 27 H. 3. (which was in the time of *Robert Grosted* Bishop of *Lincoln*) the Lady *Elizabeth de Tuchet*, presented to the Church of *Ashwell*.

The Rectory of *Ashwell* is valued in the Kings Book at 20 *l*. 16 *s*. 1 *d*.

The present Patron is *William Palmes*, Esq; Lord of the Mannour.

In the Church.

About the Verge of an Ancient Tomb in the Chancel.

✠ **H**ic jacent Johannes Vernam & Rosa **uxoz ejus parentes Magistri** Johannis Vernam **Canonici Ecclesiaz Cath. Saz & Here, qui quid,** Johannes **obiit** xx. **die** Januarii **Anno Dom. M. CCCC. octogesimo. Et** Rosa **memorata obiit decimo septimo die mensis** Decembris **Anno Domini M. CCCC. septuagesimo nono, quoz animabus ppicietur Deus,** Amen.

Elizabeth Wilcocks *born in this Town, but living in* Derbyshire *in the condition of a Servant, in the year* 1648. *gave the Rent of a Tenement scituate in the Parish of St.* Peter *at* Derby, *of the value of seven pounds* per Annum, *to the Poor for ever ; One Moiety whereof to the Poor of this Town, the other Moiety to be equally divided between the Poor of St.* Peters Parish *in* Derby, *and the Poor of* Elverston *in that County, yearly. As appears by a Memorial graved on a Plate of Brass, and set up in this Church.*

AYSTON.

M.S.Wingfeildi
Bodenham, Mil.
f. 101. b.

LYes in the Hundred of **Martinsly**. Of this Town there is no mention in *Domesday Book*, it being no doubt, one of those seven Berews or Hamlets, surveyed at that time under the Title of **Ridlinctune** *Cherchesoch*. In the 14 E. 1. Sir *William Murdoc*, Kt. gave **Astoneston**, otherwise called **Aston** near **Uppingham** in the County of **Rutland** to his Son *Hugh*. Which *Hugh* not long after dying without issue his Estate came to *Alice* his Sister, the Wife of *Thomas de Boyville*, in whose Posterity it continued until the 8*th.* year of King *Edw.* 4. in the which year *John Boyville* then Lord of **Aston** and **Wardly** in this County, and of **Stockerson** and **Cranoe** in **Leicestershire**, died, leaving three Daughters his Coheirs; how, making Partition among themselves in the same year, this Town and **Wardly** were assigned to the purparty of *Thomas Restwold*, who had married *Margaret* one of the three Sisters ; and **Cranoe** and **Stockerson**, to *Cockaine* and *Sothill*, who had married the other two.

The present Lord of **Ayston** is the Right honourable the Earl of **Cardigan**.

Of the ADVOWSON.

In the 13 H. 3. Sir *Henry Murdoc*, Kt. presented to the Church of **Astaneston**, *seu* **Aston**.

The Rectory of **Ayston** is valued in the Kings Books, at 8 *l*. 7 *s*. 7 *d*.

The present Patron is

BARLY-

BARLYTHORP.

Barlytharp is a small Village in the Parish of **Okeham**, which with some part of that Town, belongs to the Dean and Chapter of *Westminster*, by the name of the Mannour of **Okeham** *cum* **Barlytharp**. Which Mannour may be the more observable on this account, that it, only, in all this County remains at this day to the Church of St. *Peters* at *Westminster*, which Church was formerly (as is before observed) intituled to all **Roteland**. And while the Neighbouring Lands have run through many Possessors, this Lordship alone hath been constant to its old Lords ever since the Reign of *Edward* the Confessour, to our age (except a small time that it was in the Crown upon the desolution, 31 *H*. 8.) Tho in truth those Lords have not alwayes retain'd the same name. For before *Anno* 1539. they were the Abbot and Covent of *Westminster*, at which time King *Hen*. 8. dissolved the Abby, and erected a Dean and Chapter, making *William Benson*, then Abbot, the first Dean: Two years after he made it a Bishoprick, and placed *Thomas Thilby* the first (and last) Bishop there; who being removed to **Norwich**, 1550. the Bishoprick was suppress by King *Edward* 6th. and that Church became once more under the absolute Government of a Dean and Chapter : Afterwards in the year, 1557. Queen *Mary* restored it again to an Abby and Covent. But Queen *Elizabeth* soon after coming to the Crown, suppress the Abby a second time, and a third time restored the Jurisdiction of a Dean and Chapter.

Upon the desolution of the Monastery of St. *Peters* at *Westminster*, which was surrendred in *December* 31 *H*. 8. The Annual profits of this Mannour were as follows, *viz.*

	l.	s.	d.
Rent of Assize. ——	27.	2.9.	*ob.*
Perquisites of Court, that year,	1.	3.11.	

Viz. Common fine 3 *s*. 8 *d*. other fines of Lands 9 *s*. Amercements 11 *s*. 3 *d*. *Comp. pro Com. Rutland. in offic. Augm. 32 H. 8.*

As appears by the Accompt of *Thomas Busbye*, Collector of the said Revenues at that time.

Upon the suppression of the Abby, after the Death of Queen *Mary*, as abovesaid, Queen *Elizabeth* by her Letters Patents, dated 21 of *May* in the 2 year of her Reign, granted among other things, this Mannour, together with the Tithes of **Okeham, Langham, Egleton, Brooke, Gunthorpe**, and **Barlythorpe**, to the Dean and Chapter of St. *Peters* at *Westminster*, and to their Successors for ever. *Pat. 2. Eliz. p. 11.*

BARROW *or* BERK.

Barow is a small Village in the Hundred of **Alstoe**, part of the Parish and Mannour of **Cotsmore**.

Nom. Vil. in Scacc.

In the 5th. year of *E*. 2. *Rob. de Colvile*, at that time within age and the Kings Ward, was Lord of **Berk** and **Wenton**.

Rot. fin. 7 El.

In the 7th. year of Queen *Elizabeth*, *John Wyssan* past a Fine of the Grange and Tenements of **Barrow** in the Parish of **Cottesmore**, then in the Tenure of *John Nicolas*, to Sir *James Harrington*, to hold of the King *in Capite*.

It was found by Office taken at **Okeham** 22 *March* Anno 13 *Jac*. after the Death of *John* Lord *Harrington* the Elder, that the said Lord dyed seized (*inter alia*) of the abovementioned **Barrow** Grange, and of the Lordship of **Barrow**, which he held of *Thomas* Earl of **Exeter** in Soccage, as of his Mannour of **Bourne**, by suit of Court and the yearly Rent of 3 *s*. 4 *d*. for all services. *Esc. 14 Jac. p. 2. n. 116.*

BARROWDEN.

BARROWDEN.

Domesd. in Northampt n. 1.

Barrowden, lies in the Hundred of 𝔚𝔯𝔞𝔫𝔤𝔬𝔦𝔨𝔢, and is the cheif Town of that Hundred. At the time of the Survey Recorded in *Domesday Book*, the King held this Mannour, then called 𝔅𝔢𝔯𝔠𝔥𝔢𝔡𝔬𝔫𝔢, and therein four Hides bating one yard Land ; the Arable Land was ten Carucates, there were at that time nine Villains, and ten Sockmen (or Tenants in Soccage) with three *Bordarii* (or Cottagers) all which possest six Carucates of Land and a half, there were also six Acres of Meadow, and six Acres of Thorns ; And to this Mannor did Appurtain at that time certain Lands in 𝔖𝔢𝔞𝔱𝔬𝔫, 𝔗𝔥𝔬𝔯𝔭𝔢, 𝔐𝔬𝔯𝔠𝔬𝔱𝔢, 𝔅𝔦𝔰𝔟𝔯𝔬𝔬𝔨, 𝔊𝔩𝔞𝔦𝔰𝔱𝔬𝔫, and 𝔏𝔲𝔣𝔣𝔢𝔫𝔥𝔞𝔪.

Bar. Eng. 1 Vol. 398.

Henry Duke of 𝔑𝔬𝔯𝔪𝔞𝔫𝔡𝔶 (soon after King of 𝔈𝔫𝔤𝔩𝔞𝔫𝔡, by the name of *Henry* 2.) gave to *William*, Son of *William Maduit*, who had been Chamberlain to *H.* 1. his Grandfather, among other Lands, 𝔅𝔢𝔯𝔤𝔢𝔡𝔬𝔫𝔢 in *Com.* 𝔞𝔲𝔱𝔩𝔞𝔫𝔡, with the whole Soak or Hundred thereunto belonging ; and after he came to be King, confirmed the said gift. After this in the 26 *H.* 2. the said *William* was made Sheriff of 𝔞𝔲𝔱𝔩𝔞𝔫𝔡, in which Office he continued till the 33 of that King. After him succeeded *Robert* whose Son and heir *William Maduit*

Id. 199.

was one of the Rebellious Barons against King *John*, and in the 41 *H.* 3. died seized of the Mannour of 𝔅𝔢𝔯𝔴𝔢𝔡𝔢𝔫 and Hundred of 𝔚𝔯𝔞𝔫𝔤𝔢𝔡𝔶𝔨𝔢, with certain Lands of 30 *l. per an.* value lying in 𝔠𝔬𝔱𝔱𝔢𝔰𝔪𝔬𝔯𝔢 and 𝔊𝔯𝔢𝔱𝔥𝔞𝔪, all in *Com.* 𝔞𝔲𝔱𝔩𝔞𝔫𝔡; whose Son and heir *William Maduit*, became Earl of 𝔴𝔞𝔯𝔴𝔦𝔠𝔨 in 47 *H.* 3. and dyed without issue 52 *H.* 3.

Bar. Eng. 1. Vol. 626.

In the time of *E.* 2. *Edmund Colvile*, who Married *Margaret* the Daughter of *Robert de Ufford*, was seized of the Mannor of 𝔅𝔢𝔯𝔤𝔥𝔡𝔬𝔫, and died so seized in the 9*th.* year of that Kings Reign. In which said 9 *E.* 2. *Thomas*, Son and heir of the Earl of 𝔴𝔞𝔯𝔴𝔦𝔠𝔨, at that time the Kings Ward, was certified to be Lord of this Mannour.

Nom. Villar.

Ter. Mic. 14 *E.* 3. *Thomas de Bellocampo* Earl of 𝔚𝔞𝔯𝔴𝔦𝔠𝔨, Son and heir of *Guy*, Son and heir of *William de Bellocampo* late Earl of 𝔚𝔞𝔯𝔴𝔦𝔠𝔨, Son and heir of *Isabel*, Sister and heir of the abovementioned *William Maduit* Earl of 𝔴𝔞𝔯𝔴𝔦𝔠𝔨, paid to the King a Releif of 100 Marks, for the Mannour of 𝔅𝔢𝔯𝔤𝔥𝔡𝔬𝔫 in *Com. Rotel.* with the Hamlets of South 𝔏𝔬𝔣𝔣𝔢𝔫𝔤𝔥𝔞𝔪, 𝔐𝔬𝔯𝔠𝔬𝔱𝔢 and 𝔐𝔞𝔫𝔱𝔬𝔫 in the said County, held of the King in Capite by the service of being the Kings Chamberlain of his Exchequer, and *per Baroniam.* The said Earl paid also a Releif of 100 𝔰. for certain Lands in 𝔊𝔯𝔢𝔱𝔥𝔞𝔪 and 𝔠𝔬𝔱𝔱𝔢𝔰𝔪𝔢𝔯𝔢 in the said County, held of the King by the service of one Knights Fee.

Abs. Rel. pen. W. D'ewes Bar.

This Estate being afterwards forfeited by *Thomas Beauchamp* the second of that name, Earl of 𝔚𝔞𝔯𝔴𝔦𝔠𝔨, was by King *R.* 2. granted to *Thomas Mowbray*, Earl of 𝔑𝔬𝔱𝔱𝔦𝔫𝔤𝔥𝔞𝔪 and Duke of 𝔑𝔬𝔯𝔣𝔬𝔩𝔨. This *Thomas* the second, was Son and Successor in the honour to the above mentioned *Thomas de Bellocampo*, who falling into the displeasure of King *R.* 2. was by him banished and confined to the Isle of 𝔐𝔞𝔫, and all his Estate seized and granted away, some to *Thomas Holland* Earl of 𝔨𝔢𝔫𝔱, and some to the abovesaid *Mowbrey* Duke of 𝔑𝔬𝔯𝔣𝔬𝔩𝔨; but upon *H.* 4*ths.* coming to the Crown the said Earl of 𝔚𝔞𝔯𝔴𝔦𝔠𝔨 was restored to his Liberty and Estate.

Bar. Eng. 1. Vol. 307.

Id. 235.

Afterwards in the Reign of King *H.* 7. This Estate coming into the Crown again, in such manner as I have set forth under the Title of 𝔘𝔭𝔭𝔦𝔫𝔤𝔥𝔞𝔪, *infra*; King *Edward* 6. in the begining of his Reign, granted this Lordship (then valued at 31 *l.* 8 *s.* 5 *d. ob.*) together with several other Towns then called 𝔚𝔞𝔯𝔴𝔦𝔠𝔨 Lands, to his Sister the Lady *Elizabeth* ('afterwards Queen) to hold from *Mic.* 38 *H.* 8. *Durante bene placito*, which demise, it seems, continued not long ; for within five years after, the said King *Edward* 6*th.* in the 5*th.* year of

Comp. pro Com. Rutl. in offic. Augm. 3 E. 6.

Pat. 5. *E.* 6. *pars.* 7.
of his Reign granted all that the Mannor and Hundred of 𝕭𝖆𝖗𝖔𝖜𝖉𝖊𝖓 *alias* 𝖂𝖗𝖆𝖓𝖌𝖉𝖎𝖐𝖊 in the County of 𝕽𝖚𝖙𝖑𝖆𝖓𝖉, to *William Cecyl* (afterwards Lord *Burly*) and his heirs , to hold of the King *in Capite* by Knights service. From which *William* Lord *Burly* is lineally descended the Right honourable *John*, now Earl of 𝕰𝖝𝖊𝖙𝖊𝖗, the present Lord of this Mannour.

Car. 23. *E.* 3. *n.* 9.
King *Edward* 3. by his Charter dated at *Westminster* 12 *March* in the 23 year of his Reign, granted to *Thomas de Bellocampo* Earl of 𝖂𝖆𝖗𝖜𝖎𝖈𝖐, and his heirs, one Mercate weekly on the *Saturday* at his Mannour of 𝕭𝖊𝖗𝖌𝖉𝖊𝖓 in *Com. Rotel.* and one Fair there yearly for four dayes, *viz.* on the Vigil, and Feast day of St. *John* Baptist and two days after. *Nisi Mercatum illud & feria illa sint ad nocumentum vicinorum mercatorum & vicinarum feriarum.*

Of the ADVOWSON.

Reg. Linc.
In the 30th. year of *H.* 3. (which was in the time of *Robert Grosted* Bishop of 𝕷𝖎𝖓𝖈𝖔𝖑𝖓) Sir *William Maduit* Knight presented to the Church of 𝕭𝖊𝖗𝖊𝖜𝖉𝖊𝖓.

Reg. Linc.
In the 40th. year of *E.* 1. (which was in the time of *John Dalderby* Bishop of 𝕷𝖎𝖓𝖈𝖔𝖑𝖓) *Guy de Beauchamp* Earl of 𝖂𝖆𝖗𝖜𝖎𝖈𝖐 presented to the said Church.

Certif. pro Com. Rutl. in offic. Augm. 2 *E.* 6.
Here was formerly within our Lady Chappel in this Church, one Chantry founded and endowed with Lands, partly by King *Edward* 2. in the 7 year of his Reign, and partly by *Richard Smyth* and *Thomas Nichols.* The particulars of which foundation were in the 2 *E.* 6. Surveyed and certified by *Richard Cecyl* Esq; and *Thomas Hays,* Commissioners for that purpose, as followeth, *viz.*

Founded for the maintenance of one Priest to sing Mass there for ever : Hath of Lands and Tenements lying in 𝕭𝖆𝖗𝖔𝖜𝖉𝖊𝖓, *to the value of* 56 s. 8 d. *per An. whereof in Rents resolute* 7 s. *remains clear for the Portion of the Chauntry Priest there, named Sir* Raffe Himan *of the age of* 43 *years, being of good report, who also serveth the Cure there,* 49 s. 8 d. *inde pro Decima Regi* 8 s. *per An.*

The Rectory of 𝕭𝖆𝖗𝖗𝖔𝖚𝖌𝖍𝖉𝖊𝖓 is valued in the Kings Books at 14 *l.* 13 *s.* 1 *d.*
The Present Patron is

BELMESTHORP.

Domesd. Northamp. *no.* 56.
𝕭𝖊𝖑𝖒𝖊𝖘𝖙𝖍𝖔𝖗𝖕 lies in the East hundred : and did at the time of the 𝕹𝖔𝖗𝖒𝖆𝖓 Conquest appertain to the Mannour of 𝕽𝖞𝖍𝖆𝖑𝖑 as a Member of the same, and was at that time held of the King by Countess *Judith,* who had here one hide and a half, in Demesne two Carucates, with fourteen Villains, and six *Bordarii* possessing four Carucates,

here was at that time one Mill of 10 *s.* and 8 *d.* and sixteen Acres of Meadow, the whole then valued at 6 *l.*

Nom. Vill. in Scacc.
In the Reign of *Ed.* 2. it had also the same Lord with 𝕽𝖞𝖍𝖆𝖑𝖑, *Hugo le Dispencer.*

The present Lord of this Town is the Right Honourable *John* Earl of 𝕰𝖝𝖊𝖙𝖊𝖗.

BELTON.

𝕷ies in the Hundred of 𝕺𝖐𝖊𝖍𝖆𝖒 Soak, and within the Limits of the old Forrest of 𝕷𝖞𝖋𝖊𝖎𝖑𝖉. Of this Town I find no mention in *Domes-*

day, it being no doubt included amongst the seven Berews or Hamlets belonging to 𝕽𝖊𝖉𝖑𝖎𝖓𝖈𝖙𝖚𝖓𝖊 *Cherchesoch.*

In the Reign of *E.* 2. *William le Blount*

Blount was **Lord** of this Mannor. In whose Posterity it continued, as it seems, a long time: for

In the first year of *Henry* 5. Sir *Walter le Blount*, Son and heir of Sir *Thomas le Blount* Treasurer of 𝕹𝖔𝖟𝖒𝖆𝖓𝖉𝖞, settled the Mannour of 𝕭𝖊𝖑𝖙𝖔𝖓 (*Com. Rutl.*) with other Lands elsewhere on *Thomas Langley* Bishop of 𝕯𝖚𝖗𝖍𝖆𝖒, and *John Bayssham* Clerk, to the use of *Senchia* his Wife (a Spanish Lady) during her life; and to the heirs Males of his Body: The remainder to *Thomas* his second Son, and the issue Male of his Body: And so to *James* his third Son, and *Peter* his fourth Son, with remainder to his right heirs.

In the 28*th.* of *H.* 8. the then Lord 𝕸𝖔𝖓𝖙𝖏𝖔𝖞 held this Mannour with the Appurtenances of the King *in Capite* by Knight service, and dying so seized, left *Charles Blount* Lord 𝕸𝖔𝖓𝖙𝖏𝖔𝖞 his Son and heir.

Afterwards this Mannour came to the Family of *Hasilwood*, and in that name continued, till in the Reign of King *James*, *Thomas Hasilwood* Esq; by his Deed of bargain and sail, conveyed the same to *George Butler* and *Thomas Phillips*, which Deed is inrolled in the Common Pleas, *Mic.* 11. *Jac. rot.* 19.

King *E.* 3. in the sixth year of his Reign, granted to *William le Blount* then Lord of this Mannour, that he and his heirs for ever should have and enjoy at their Mannour of 𝕭𝖊𝖑𝖙𝖔𝖓 in *Com. Rotel.* yearly, one Fair for three days, *viz.* The Eve, day, and Morrow of St. *James* the Apostle: *Nisi feria illa sit ad nocumentum vicinarum feriarum.* And this was twice granted, first by Charter dated at 𝕹𝖔𝖙𝖙𝖎𝖓𝖌𝖍𝖆𝖒, 24 *Apr.* 6 *E.* 3. and after by another Charter dated at 𝖂𝖔𝖔𝖉𝖘𝖙𝖔𝖈𝖐 20 *July* in the same year.

𝕭𝖊𝖑𝖙𝖔𝖓 is at present the Seat of *Richard Verney* Esq; a true Lover of Antiquities, and a worthy *Mecænas*; whose descent form that eminent Family of this name, long time seated at 𝕮𝖔𝖒𝖕𝖙𝖔𝖓-𝕸𝖚𝖗𝖉𝖆𝖈𝖐 in *Com.* 𝖂𝖆𝖗𝖜𝖎𝖈𝖐, appears in the following Pedigree.

Johan. Verney.

Richard. Verney, —— Alianora *f. & h.*
mil. ob. 5 H. 7.   Joh. Loutham.

Edmundus Verney, —— Elizabetha *f.* Williel.
ar. ob. 10 H. 7.   Feilding, *mil.*

Richard. Verney, —— Anna *f.* Williel. Davers *unius*
ar. ob. 18 H. 8.   *Justic. de Banco. temp.* H. 7.

Thomas Verney, —— Alicia *Sor. & coh.*
mil. 28 H. 8.   Edmun. Tame *mil.*

Richard. Verney, —— Francisca *f.* Georg.
mil. 3.4. P.M.   Raleigh, *ar.*

Georg. Verney, —— Jana *f.* Williel.
ob. 16 El.   Lucy, *ar.*

Richard. Verney, —— Margareta *Sor. & h.* Fulconis
mil. ob. 1630.   Grevil *Dom.* Brook.

Grevillius Verney, —— Catherina *f.* Roberti
ar. ob. 1642.   Southwell, *mil.*

Grevillius Verney *de* Compton-Murdack *in Com.* Warwick, *ar. fil. & hæres.*	Maria *f.* Joh. Prettyman *de* Lodington *Com.* Leic. Baronet. *Ux.* 1.	Richard. Verney *de* Belton *in Com.* Rotel. *ar. fil.* 2.	Francisca *fil.* Thomas Dove *de* Upton *in Com.* Northampton, *ar. Ux.* 2.

Johan. Verney *de* Mid. Temp. Lond. *Jurisconsultus.*	Georg. Verney, No. Coll. Ox. Socius & Affin. Fund.	Thomas Verney,	Maria *Ux.* ...... Davenport *de* Colvely *Com.* Cest. *ar.*	Richardus.	Diana.

com. pro com.
Rutl. in Offic.
Augm. 3. *E.* 6.

I find in the account of *John Doddington* the Kings Receiver in this County 3. *E.* 6. mention of a certain small Estate in 𝕭𝖊𝖑𝖙𝖔𝖓 belonging to the late desolved Monastery of 𝕺𝖚𝖑𝖚𝖊𝖘𝖙𝖔𝖓 in *Com. Leicester. Viz.* One Cottage and certain Lands there with the appurtenances, then demised to *William Clerke* to hold at the Will of the Lord from year to year, paying the yearly Rent of 4 *s.* at the Feasts of the Annunciation of our Lady and St. *Michael* equally.

Comp. ut sup.

Here was also belonging to the late desolved Monastery of 𝕷𝖆𝖚𝖓𝖉 in *Com. Leicest.* One Tenement with certain Lands of the yearly Rent of 20 *s.* demised by the said Monastery to *Thomas Drake:* Also the Tithes with one piece of Land or Meadow call'd 𝕰𝖘𝖙-𝕳𝖎𝖐𝖑𝖊𝖓𝖌𝖘 demised by the said Covent to *Thomas Woodhouse, alias Webster* at the yearly rent of 6 *l.* 10 *s.* All which was granted by King *Edward* 6. 25. *May* in the 2*d.* year of his Reign to *Gregory* Lord *Cromwell,* and *Elizabeth* his Wife, for their two Lives.

Here was also belonging to the said Monastery of 𝕷𝖆𝖚𝖓𝖉, one other Tenement with Lands thereunto belonging of the yearly Rent of 10 *s.* Demised by the said Monastery to *Thomas Woodhouse alias Webster* for the term of sixty one years by Deed dated 22 *May* 30. *H.* 8.

Comp. ut sup.

In the Church of Belton.

About the Verge of a fair Tomb adjoyning to the North East Angle of the Chancel.

✠ 𝕳𝕰𝖗𝖊 𝖑𝖞𝖊𝖙𝖍 𝖙𝖍𝖊 𝕭𝖔𝖉𝖞 of Thomas Haselwood 𝕰𝖘𝖖𝖚𝖎𝖗𝖊 𝖆𝖓𝖉 Clemence 𝖍𝖞𝖘 𝖂𝖞𝖋𝖋𝖊, 𝖜𝖍𝖎𝖈𝖍 Thomas 𝖉𝖊𝖕𝖆𝖗𝖙𝖊𝖉 𝖝𝖝 𝖉𝖆𝖞 𝖔𝖋 December 𝖎𝖓 𝖙𝖍𝖊 𝖞𝖊𝖆𝖗 𝖔𝖋 𝖔𝖚𝖗 𝕷𝖔𝖗𝖉 𝕲𝖔𝖉 M. D. LIX. 𝖆𝖓𝖉 𝖙𝖍𝖊 𝖘𝖆𝖎𝖉 Clemence 𝖉𝖊𝖕𝖆𝖗𝖙𝖊𝖉 𝖙𝖍𝖊 .... 𝖉𝖆𝖞 𝖔𝖋 ...... 𝖎𝖓 𝖙𝖍𝖊 𝖞𝖊𝖆𝖗 𝖔𝖋 𝖔𝖚𝖗 𝕷𝖔𝖗𝖉 𝕲𝖔𝖉 M. D............ 𝖚𝖕𝖔𝖓 𝖜𝖍𝖔𝖘𝖊 𝕾𝖔𝖚𝖑𝖘 𝕲𝖔𝖉 𝖍𝖆𝖛𝖊 𝖒𝖊𝖗𝖈𝖞, Amen

BRAUNSTON.

Lies in the Hundred of 𝕺𝖐𝖊𝖍𝖆𝖒-Soak: And borders on the skirts of 𝕷𝖊𝖎𝖈𝖊𝖘𝖙𝖊𝖗𝖘𝖍𝖎𝖗𝖊, having been formerly part of the forest of 𝕷𝖞𝖋𝖊𝖎𝖑𝖉. Of 𝕭𝖗𝖆𝖚𝖓𝖘𝖙𝖔𝖓 there is no mention in *Domesday*-Book, it being at that time, no doubt, included in the Survey of 𝕳𝖆𝖒𝖊𝖑𝖉𝖚𝖓𝖊 *Cherchesoch* to which Town of 𝕳𝖆𝖒𝖇𝖑𝖊𝖙𝖔𝖓, 𝕭𝖗𝖆𝖚𝖓𝖘𝖙𝖔𝖓 continues a Chappel of ease to this day.

Clauf. 6. *Joh:*
m. 16.

King *John* in the 6. year of his reign, directed his precept to the Sheriff of 𝕽𝖚𝖙𝖑𝖆𝖓𝖉, commanding him to deliver to *Hamon Falconer* 8 *l.* of Land in the Mannour of 𝕭𝖗𝖆𝖚𝖓𝖘𝖙𝖔𝖓 formerly belonging to *Nicholas de Menil.* in the 17*th.* year of the same King the like precept was directed to the Sheriff of 𝕽𝖚𝖙-

19.*Joh. m.*
17.

𝖑𝖆𝖓𝖉 to deliver to *William Ferrars* the Land which the King had formerly given to *Hamon Falconer. Robert le Fauconer* (who descended I suppose from this *Hamon,*) was one of those eminent Persons in this County, who in 29. *E.* 1. received the Kings writ of Summons to attend him well fitted with horse and Armes on the Feast of the Nativity of St. *John Baptist* next ensuing, at 𝕭𝖊𝖗𝖜𝖎𝖈𝖐 upon 𝕿𝖜𝖊𝖊𝖉, in order to a War against the Scots.

In the 9. *E.* 2 The Prior of 𝕶𝖊𝖓𝖊𝖑-𝖜𝖔𝖗𝖙𝖍, and 𝕿𝖍𝖊𝖔𝖇𝖆𝖑𝖉 *de* 𝕹𝖊𝖞𝖛𝖎𝖑𝖊 were Lords of 𝕭𝖗𝖆𝖚𝖓𝖘𝖙𝖔𝖓.

Nom. Vill. in
Scacc.

Afterwards the *Chiseldines* became Lords of 𝕭𝖗𝖆𝖚𝖓𝖘𝖙𝖔𝖓 (somuch as did formerly belong to *Theobald de Neyuyle.*)

which

which came into that Family by match with *Anne* Daughter and heir of *William de Burghe*; which *Anne* dyed seized in her demean as of fee of the Mannour of 𝕭𝖗𝖆𝖚𝖓𝖘𝖙𝖔𝖓, and other Lands and Hereditaments in this County 7. *Martij*, 23. *H.* 6. Leaving *John Chisildine*, Son of *John Chisildine*, Son of the said *Anne*, her next heir; as ap-

pears by Inquisition taken at 𝕺𝖐𝖊𝖍𝖆𝖒 23. *April*, next following; by which Inquisition it also appears that she held the said Mannour by knights service of *Humphrey* Duke of 𝕭𝖚𝖈𝖐𝖎𝖓𝖌𝖍𝖆𝖒, as of his Castle of 𝕺𝖐𝖊𝖍𝖆𝖒, and that the said Mannour was then valued at 12. marks *per An.* over and above all Reprizes. *Esc.* 23 *H.* 6. *n.* 14.

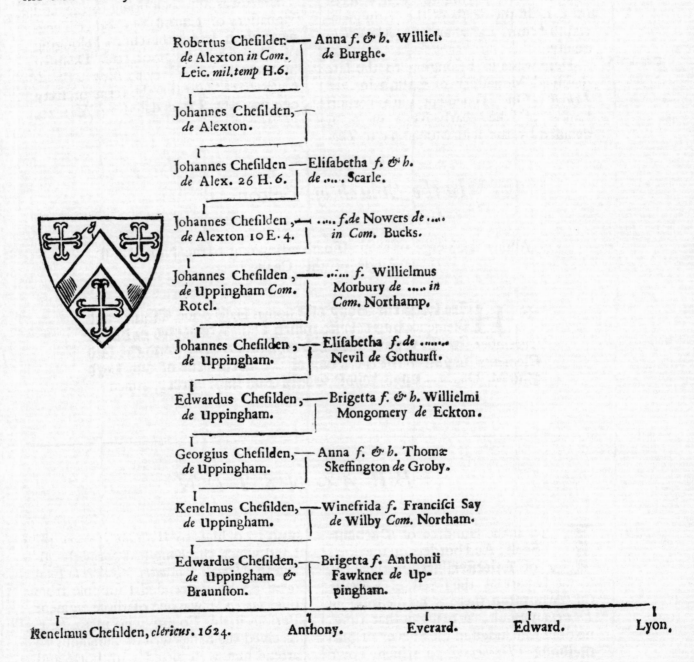

Robertus Chesilden, *de* Alexton *in Com.* Leic. *mil. temp* H.6. ——— Anna *f. & h.* Williel. de Burghe.

Johannes Chesilden, *de* Alexton.

Johannes Chesilden *de* Alex. 26 H. 6. ——— Elisabetha *f. & h.* de ..... Scarle.

Johannes Chesilden, *de* Alexton 10 E. 4. ——— ..... *f. de* Nowers *de* ..... *in Com.* Bucks.

Johannes Chesilden, *de* Uppingham *Com.* Rotel. ——— ..... *f.* Willielmus Morbury *de* ..... *in Com.* Northamp.

Johannes Chesilden, *de* Uppingham. ——— Elisabetha *f. de* .... Nevil *de* Gothurst.

Edwardus Chesilden, *de* Uppingham. ——— Brigetta *f. & h.* Willielmi Mongomery *de* Eckton.

Georgius Chesilden, *de* Uppingham. ——— Anna *f. & h.* Thomæ Skeffington *de* Groby.

Kenelmus Chesilden, *de* Uppingham. ——— Winefrida *f.* Francisci Say *de* Wilby *Com.* Northam.

Edwardus Chesilden, *de* Uppingham & Braunston. ——— Brigetta *f.* Anthonii Fawkner *de* Uppingham.

Kenelmus Chesilden, *clericus.* 1624.   Anthony.   Everard.   Edward.   Lyon.

In the first of Queen *Mary*, *John Burton*, was found to die seized of one Messuage in the tenure of *John Holly*, two Cottages, two Gardens, two Tofts and 9 *s.* rent in 𝕭𝖗𝖆𝖚𝖓𝖘𝖙𝖔𝖓, which he *Esc.* 1. *Mar.*

held of the Queen *in Capite* by Knights service, and that *William Burton* was his Son and heir: which *William* had issue as appears in the following Scheme.

William

William Burton, *of* Braunston *in Com.* Rut.		Alice *d. of* Richard Peck.				
John Burton *of* Stockerson *Com.* Leiceſt.	Bartin Burton, *of* Okeham *Com.* Rutland.	Simon Burton, *of* Braunſton. —— Mary *d. of* John Welſh.		Auguſtin Burton.	Suſan *Ux.* Geoffrey Wilcocks *de* Knoſſington.	
William Burton, —— Jane *d. of* Richard Halford *of* Ediweſton. *of* Braunſton.			Bartin Burton, *of* Braunſton.	Auguſtin Burton, *of* London.	Alice.	

Ex autographis. Queen *Elizabeth* in the 26th year of her reign did, by her Letters Patents bearing date 12. of *June*, in the ſaid year, give and grant unto *Edward Wymarke* of **London** Gent. a parcel of Land in this field, partly Wood ground and partly Paſture, containing by eſtimation fourteen acres more or leſſe, commonly call'd the **wiſpe**, with all the appurtenances, profits and commodities thereunto belonging, with all and ſingular the Woods, underwoods, and Trees growing or being in or upon the ſame; The like grant was afterwards made of the Premiſes by King *James* on · the 13th. day of *June* in the 9th. year of his reign, to *Thomas Eely*, and *George Merreils*; afterwards the ſaid Eſtate was by ſeveral Deeds and Conveyances from the aboveſaid *Wymarke*, *Eely*, and *Merreils*, ſettled on *Bartin Burton* of **Okeham** (*Com.* **Rutl.**)his Heirs and Aſſignes for ever, in Truſt that the rents, iſſues, revenues and profits of the ſame ſhould from time to time for ever be employ'd to and for the common good of the Freeholders of **Braunſton** having common in the ſaid Town, and for and towards the maintenance of a Preacher to preach in the Chappel of **Braunſton**, or in default thereof, for and towards the repair of the ſaid Chappel and the Bells therein, and for the repair and amendment of decayed bridges and highways, and releif of ſuch poor as to the Truſtees ſhould ſeem moſt convenient. Which ſaid *Bartin Burton* dying, *Andrew Burton* of **Okeham** Eſq; his Son and heir, die by indenture bearing date the 19th. of *Ap.* 1636. convey the ſaid Eſtate over to ſeveral Truſtees, ſome of which are now living, under the Truſts above ſpecified.

In the Church.

In Braſs, on a handſome Tomb.

HEre lyeth Kenelme Cheſeldyn *of* **Uppingham** *Eſquire, who lineally deſcended from* Anne Broogh *Daughter and Heir to the Lord* Broogh, *who married* Winefrid *Daughter of* Francis Say *of* **Wilby** *in the County of* **Northampton** *Gent. and had by her a* xi. *Sons and three Daughters, who deceaſed the 2. of* Auguſt 1596. *leaving* Edward *his Son and Heir Succeeding.*

  As I was ſoe are ye,
  As I am ſoe ſhall ye be.

On a Grave Stone.

HIC *jacet Corpus* Edwardi Cheſeldyn *de* **Braunſton** *in Com.* **Rotel.** *Armigeri, qui obiit* 13. *die* Junij *Anno Domini.* 1642.

E

BROOK.

THis Town lyes in the Hundred of Okeham Soak : And within the limits of the old Forest of Lyfeid. It had formerly the same Lord with Okeham, viz. *Walkeline de Ferrers:* (of whom see more in Okeham.) Of Brook there is no mention in *Domesday* book, it being at that time survey'd as one of the five Berews or Hamlets belonging to Okeham *Cherchesoch.*

In the 9. E. 2. The Prior of Kenilworth was Lord of Brook, and part of Braunston.

Neer this Town was scituated a small Priory, yet the onely Monastery of either Sex in this County. They were call'd Canons regular of S. *Augustine;* in regard their order is said to be first instituted by that famous Doctor of Christs Church, S. *Augustine;* who being born in Africa, and betaking himself to the study of Philosophy grew so excellent a Scholar, and so famous a Rhetorician, that being sent for to Millain in Italy, there to teach Rhetorique, by the preaching of S. *Ambrose* then Bp. of Millain, he was reclaimed from the Heresie of the *Manickees* wherewith he had been tainted : And afterwards coming to Hippo, he was by *Valerius* then Bishop of that place ordained a Priest, in which City he shortly instituted a Covent of Clerks, and lived according to the rule constituted by the holy Apostles, instructing them in the Evangelical perfection, viz. love of Poverty, Obedience, and Chastity. Upon the Death of *Valerius* he was chosen Bp. of Hippo, but notwithstanding being desirous to continue his religious course of Life, he founded a Monastery of Clerks within the Precincts of his Church.

The habit of these Canons, was a white Coat and a Linnen Surplice, under a black Cloak, with a hood covering their head and neck, which reached to the shoulders; having under it, doublet, Breeches, white and stockings,

and shooes or slippers; and when they walk out, a black corner'd cap, or a broad hat : their Crowns being shaven, but not so much as other Monks.

This House was formerly a Cell belonging to the Canons Regular of S. *Augustine* at Kenilworth in Warwickshire, given to that Monastery by *Hugh de Ferrers*, Son of *Walkeline* the first Baron of Okeham, which gift was confirmed by *William* brother of the said *Hugh*, in these words,

Ego W. de Ferrariis meos homines atque meos Amicos saluto. Vobis viventibus atque venientibus notifico, quatenus ex mea parte, Elemosinam, quam Hugo *frater meus Priori & Canonicis de* Kiningword *dedit, libenter concedo.*

This was also ratified by King H. 2. by his charter containing (*inter alia*) *Concedo etiam & in Elemosinam confirmo supradictis Canonicis, terram de* Broch, *cum Bosco, & exsartis sicut* Hugo de Ferraris *eis divisit & concessit, assensu* Walchelini *nepotis sui &* Willielmi *fratris sui, sicut in eorum Cartis continetur.*

In the 19th. year of H. 3. on the Friday next before the Feast of Penticost, the Prior of Kenilworth presented Frier *Richard de Ludington* one of the Canons of Kenilworth, to be Prior of the house of Broc; which *Richard*, the then Bp. of Lincoln invested into the said Office, by delivering into his hands the Book of the said Priory.

At the time of the desolution of this House *Roger Harwel* was Prior of Broke, and had a grant from the King of 10 *l.* per *An.* for his maintenance, until he should be otherwise provided of some Ecclesiastical preferment, which grant bears date 2. *July.* 28. H. 8. But it seems that this *Roger Harwel* did not behave himself well and prudently in the surrender of the same as appears by the following Letter writ to Secretary *Cromwel*, and dated 17. *June* 1536. from the Abbot of Kenelworth.

Ryght

Bib. Cotton
Cleopatra. E. 4.
f. 244.

Ryght honorable and my singular good Master, my covenable duety with condigne Recommendacyons humbly unto your Mastership remembryd : may it please you to be further advertissd of such matter as at this day I and my pore house are much perplexed and unquietid in, concerning our mannor or Cell of Bjoke in the County of Rotteland which by the injust and untrue demeanor and behaviour of such my Chanon as I sent thider for to have the Governance and rule thereof and for that he had not such profitable and commodyous pencyon assigned and made sure unto him during his life as he and his counsel wold and could devyse and aske hath intytled the Kings hyghness in his Court of augmentatyons unto the hoole tytle and interest thereof, which woll and shall be onles your merciful favour be ministrid and shewed therein a utter undoyng and distruction of my house and Monastery for ever, for it is not unremembred I dowte not unto you that when I first receiv- ed your Letters concerning the said house at my next sending after the said your Letters I offrid the ferme and lesse of the same unto ony friend of yours that it please you to nam thereunto and so entred into bargeyn and lesse and dimisid it after such forme and facion as ye knowe, with bond of a M. mark unto the lesse for his surety and state therein, accordingly, wych if it cannot be performed by us we be dangred in the said sum by the Laws of this Realme, wherefore it may please you of your goodness and profit charite to be a mean unto the Kings highnes and to or- der of his Counsel that shall have the he- ryng ordring and determination of the said matter that our just trewe and persit in- terest of the said Manner of Bjoke with the appurtenancies which war perpetually and freghly given unto our Monastery of Kenellwojth, in pure Almesse as it is most evidently apparent in evidenc may stille be- longe and apperteyn unto our said house ac- cording as thys Law is and right doth re- quire and aske, and for that it shall not becom me to stand in contention and traverse with his highnes or to defend or prosecute any thing that his Grace and Counsel do suppose and deme to be his right and title by his Lawis newly made and ordened it may please your Mastershippe for and in my name to be solicitour and mediatour that I and my house may have and enjoye of the Lesse of our said Sovereyghne Lord the Residue of all the Landis and Tenements at this day belonging unto the said Cell of Bjoke for such resonable Rent as they now be demysed by me and for like yerys in fee ferme to thentent that such my Lesse as now hath them by me may enjoy and con- tinue such dimyssion as is dymised unto them in salvation of the Bond of the said M. mark wherunto I and my house stand charged. And where it pleased the Kings highnes for my good and true service done to his grace at the Insurrection at Coventre to my great charge, to promise me his fa- vour in ony my reasonable suyte concern- yng ryght of my house, I shall for his goodnes to me in this case shewed accept my selfe well recompensid, and what end soever your Mastershippe shall take I shall at all oures abyde, for in you nowe is all my trust as God knoweth who ever prosper you in honour. At Kenellwojth the xvii. day of Junij,

Your humble Orator
WILLIAM *Albat ther.*

This Priory was in the 26th. H. 8. valued at 40. *l. per an.* as appears by a Catalogue then taken of the values of all Religious houses, which Cata- logue was afterwards inserted in the Book of first Fruits and Tenths. But in **Speeds** Catalogue, which was made at the time of the Suppression (later than the other) it is valued at 43. *l.* 13. *s.* 4. *d.* *Speed hist. p.* 1090.

After the dissolution of this house (which happened, which the other lesser Monesstaries in the year 1536. (28. H. 8.) that King granted to *Anthony Cope* Esq; the late Priory of Canons of the blessed virgin *Mary* of Bjoke, in Bjoke, in the County of Rutland: As also the Mannor of Bjoke with the Appurtenances in the said County of Rutland, to hold *in Capite* by Knights service, reserving out of the premises the yearly rent of 4. *l.* 13. *s.* 11. *d.* payable at *Michaelmas*, which Grant bears date the 9. of *Sept.* in the 28. H. 8. *Pat.* 28. H. 8. *pars.* 2.

In the 2. year of *Edw.* 6. Sr. *An- thony Cope* Knight, obtain'd Licence of the King to alienate the said Mannor of Bjoke in *Com.* Rutland, to *Andrew Noel* Esq; and his heirs for ever. In which honourable family this Mannour continues at this day. *Pat.* 2. E. 6. *pars.* 3.

See Biddington.

In the Church.

On a fair Monument in the Chancel,
the following Inscriptions.

CArolus Andræi *proles generosa* Noeli
  Incolit hunc Tumulum corpore, mente Polum.
In quo certârunt totas exprimere Dotes
  Natura & Virtus, Marsque Minerva, *suas:*
Esse pium tribuit Virtus, Natura Decorum,
  Mars *fortem, ingenium clara* Minerva *dedit.*
Hic tamen eripitur primævo flore Juventæ,
  Ut soleant rapido gemma perire Noto.

If Gifts of mind and Body might
Make *Death* forbear to claim his Right,
This compleat Knight had not by fate
Enjoy'd on Earth so short a date:
But Death, impartial in his Power,
Untimely cropt this Blooming Flower;
Whose hopeful Youth, scarce in her Prime,
Did Promise much for future time.

Obiit Anno Do. 1619.
Ætatis suæ 28.

BURLEY.

Domesday tit. Rotel.

BUrly on the Hill stands a mile North east from **Okeham**, in the hundred of **Alsto** : most dauntily seated (says *Cambden*) and over-looking the Vale. Before the time of the Conquerours survey one *Ulf* a *Saxon* did hold in **Burgelai** 2. Carucates as rated to the Geld or Tax, which land was indeed seven Carucates. Afterwards *Goisfridus* the Man, or *Fermour*, of *Gislebert de Gand* held here two Carucates, and thirty Villains, and eight *Bordarii* having four Caruca-tes and thirty acres of Meadow. A wood (*pro loca pastilis*) of one mile in length and three furlongs in breadth. In the time of King *Edward*, this was valued at 4. *l.* but at the time of the said survey at 5. *l.*

Nom. Vill. in Scacc.

In the 9. E. 2. *Nicholas de Segrave* was Lord of **Burly** and **Alesthorpe** (a small Village hereunto adjoyning) of which last there is nothing now re-maining. Yet was the said Village at the Conquerours survey valued at 40. *s.* and held of the King by one *Ogerus* Son of *Ungemar.* Here were then in-habiting eleven Villains and four *Bor-darii* possessing four Carucates and six-teen acres of meadow. Here was also a Wood of three furlongs in length and two in Breadth,

Domesday tit. Rotel

In the 27 E. 3. *Warenus de Insula* Son and heir of *Gerard de Insula* Knight, did release to *Anne* late wife of *Edward* le *Despenser* Knight, and to the heirs of the said *Anne* all his Right in the Mannour of **Burghlet**. In the same year also *William de Ferrariis*, relea-sing to the King all his right in the Castle and Mannour of **Morend** and other Lands, the King was pleased to grant in exchange to *Thomas le Dis-penser* and his heirs Mails, a Moiety of the Mannour of **Burghlet**.

Clauf. 27. E. 3. M. 11.

I read in Bp. *Godwins* Catalogue of
En-

English Bishops, under the Title of *Henry Spencer* Bp. of 𝕹𝖔𝖗𝖜𝖎𝖈𝖍, that the said martial Bp. in the year 1381. when he first heard of the Commotions then newly rais'd by *Wat Tyler* and *Jack Straw, &c.* was at his Mannour of 𝕭𝖚𝖗𝖑𝖊 neer 𝕺𝖈𝖐𝖆𝖒 Castle, from whence he marcht directly with such force as he could suddainly gather, and suppreſt the Rebels in his Dioceſſe, headed by one *John Lifter* a Dyer of 𝕹𝖔𝖗𝖜𝖎𝖈𝖍. But we muſt obſerve that as he did this more as a valiant *Spencer*, than a Biſhop, ſo alſo he enjoy'd this Mannour not as belonging to his Biſhopwrick but as his paternal Inheritance, or Lay fee : For I find an old Rent of 12. *s.* 4. *d.* ariſing to the Crown from *Thomas le Diſpencer* for a Leet *cum pertinenciis* in 𝕭𝖚𝖗𝖑𝖊𝖞 which the ſaid *Thomas* held *in Capite*, and this is ſtill charg'd upon the Sheriff of 𝕽𝖚𝖙𝖑𝖆𝖓𝖉𝖘 accounts in the Pipe Office, at this day.

In the 18. year of *R.* 2. *Robert de Pleſſington* Son and Heir of *Robert de Pleſſington* Knight held the Mannour of 𝕭𝖚𝖗𝖌𝖍𝖑𝖊 with the Appurtenances in the County of 𝕽𝖚𝖙𝖑𝖆𝖓𝖉, and one yard Land with the Appurtenances in 𝕬𝖑𝖊𝖘=𝖙𝖍𝖔𝖗𝖕 in the ſaidCounty parcel of the ſaid

Godw.Cat. Bps. Nor.

Stows Annals fo. 291.

H. 18. *R.* 2. *ex parte Rem. Thes. Rot.* 2.

Mannour, of the King *in Capite* by the ſervice of half a Knights fee.

In the 27 *H.* 6. *John Fraunceys* Eſq; and *Iſabel* his wife, Couſin and heir of *William Pleſſington* Son and heir of *Henry Pleſſington* Knight, held the Manour of 𝕭𝖚𝖗𝖑𝖊𝖞 of the King *in Capite* by the ſervice of half a Knights Fee.

Afterwards this Mannour coming into the family of the *Sapcotes*, by reaſon that *Thomas Sapcotes* 2d. Son of Sr. *Richard Sapcotes* of 𝕰𝖑𝖙𝖔𝖓 (*in com.* 𝕳𝖚𝖓𝖙.) had married *Jane* daughter and coheir of the aboveſaid *John Francis*, it continued in that name and family till the 3. of *Ed.* 6. in which year it was found that *Edward Sapcotes* dyed ſeized of the Mannour of 𝕭𝖚𝖗𝖑𝖊𝖞 which he held of the King *in Capite* by knights ſervice, and that *Dorothy Durant* wife of *John Durant, Thomas Wake,* and *Robert Brooksby,* were his next heirs. Which ſaid *Thomas Wake* in the ſame year obtain'd the Kings Licence to alienate his purparty, *viz.* the 3d. part of the ſaid Mannour of 𝕭𝖚𝖗𝖑𝖞 to Sr *John Harington* Knight and his Heirs. Alſo in the 4th. year of Queen *Elizabeth* the foreſaid *Robert Brooksby* obtain'd Licence to alienate his 3d. part to Sr. *James Harrington* Son of the ſaid Sr. *John.*

Ib. M. 27. *H.* 6.

Eſc. 3.E. 6.

3 *E.* 6. *p.* 2.

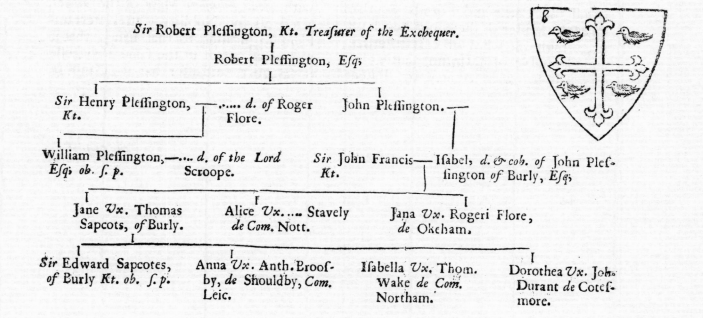

Sir *Robert Pleſſington, Kt. Treaſurer of the Exchequer.*

Robert Pleſſington, *Eſq;*

Sir Henry Pleſſington, ——..... *d. of* Roger Flore.   Kt.

John Pleſſington. ——

William Pleſſington, ——.... *d. of the* Lord Scroope.   *Eſq; ob. ſ. p.*

Sir John Francis— Iſabel, *d. & coh.* of John Pleſſington of Burly, *Eſq;*   Kt.

Jane *Vx.* Thomas Sapcots, *of* Burly.

Alice *Vx.*.... Stavely *de Com.* Nott.

Jana *Vx.* Rogeri Flore, *de Okeham.*

Sir Edward Sapcotes, *of* Burly Kt. *ob. ſ. p.*

Anna *Vx.* Anth. Brooſby, *de* Shouldby, *Com.* Leic.

Iſabella *Vx.* Thom. Wake *de Com.* Northam.

Dorothea *Vx.* John Durant *de* Coteſmore.

Esc. 14. Jac. pars 2 n. 116.

It was found by Office taken 22 *Martii,* 13 *Jacobi,* that *John* Lord *Harrington* the Elder died seized (*inter alia*) of the Mannour of **Burly** and **Allesthorp** Lands *alias* **Awstroppe**-Field, which he held in *Capite* by the 4th. part of a Knights Fee.

Rot. fin. m. 14. Jac.

In the Family of the *Haringtons* of **Exton**, this Lordship continued, till purchased from the heirs general of that Family, by the eminently great Sr. *George Villers,* whom (for the extraordinary merits of his person) King *James* created, first, Gentleman of his Bedchamber, then Master of the Horse, after which on the 24. of *Apr.* 1615. He was elected into the society of the Companions of the most Noble Order of the Garter, soon after general Warden and chief Justice of all the Forests North of **Trent**, then on the 27. *Aug.* following

Bar. Eng. 2 Vol. 429, 430.

advanced to the Title of Lord **Whaddon**, of **Whaddon** (in *Com.* **Bucks**,) soon after Vicount *Villers,* on the 5th. *Jan.* 1616. created Earl of **Buckingham**, on the 1 *Jan.* 1617. Marquess of **Buckingham**, on the 13. *Jan.* 1618. Lord high Admiral of **England**, **Ireland**, and **Wales**, on the 4. *Feb.* Sworn of the Privy-Council, and about the same time, made Justice in **Eyre** of all the Parks and Forests South of **Trent**, Master of the Kings Bench Office, high Steward of **Westminster**, and Constable of **Windsor** Castle; afterwards he was created by Patent

bearing date, *May* 18. 2 1. *Jac.* Earl of **Coventry**, and Duke of **Buckingham**. He was also Lord high Steward of **England** at the Coronation of King *Charles* the First, and Chancellour of the University of **Cambridge**: And what is more than all, the Mignion of two great and good Kings.

After the Duke of **Buckingham** had purchased this Lordship as aforesaid, he made it one of the finest Seats in these parts of **England**; improving the house to that advantage, that it became a second **Belvoir**, and in some respects superior to that famous Seat of the Earls of **Rutland**: scituate on a hill, a princely Park and Woods adjoyning, overlooking the little, but rich, Vale of **Catmus**, and several fair Lordships belonging to the same Owner.

Here it was that that Duke entertained King *James* and all his Court, in a manner worthy the gratitude of so beloved a favorite. And among the famous Bishop *Andrews* his printed Sermons, we find several preacht before the King at **Burley** by **Okeham**.

Here it was that the King, Prince *Charles,* and Court, were first presented with *Ben. Johnsons* Mask of the *Gipsies,* acted all by Nobility; an Entertainment so pleasing to that King, that it was acted again in the same Progresse at **Beaver**, and after that at **Windsor**.

Alexander

Alexander *de* Villiers, *Ortus*
è stemmate Normannorum.

Nicholaus *de* Villiers, *miles*
vixit tempore E. 1.

Galfridus *de* Villiers, *Dominus de*
Brokesby *in Com.* Leic. 20 E. 3.

Johannes *de* Villiers, —— Johanna *Sor. & coh.* Simonis
de Brokesby.   Pakeman.

Richardus *de* Villiers,——
ob. 15 R. 2.

Johannes *de* Villiers,——
ob. 4 H. 5.

Johannes *de* Villiers,   Willielmus *de* Villers, —— Johanna *Sor. & coh.*
ob. f. p.   *fil.* 2. *ob.* 20. E. 4.   Johannis Bellere.

Johannes Villers,—— Elizabetha *fil.* .... Southill
ob. in vit. pat.   *de* Everingham.

Johannes Villers,—— Agnes *fil.* Johannes
miles 22 H. 7.   Digby.

Willielmus Villers,—— Collet *fil. & h.* Richardi
ob. 6 Mariæ.   Clark, *vidua* Richardi Beaumcut *de*
                          Cole Orton.

Audrey *fil.* Willielmi —— Georgius Villers, —— Maria *fil.* Anthonii
Saunders *de* Harring-   *de* Brokesby *mil.*   Beaumont *de* Cole-
ton *Com.* North. *Arm.*   *ob.* 1605.   orton, *Com.* Leic. *ar.*
Vx. 1.   *Vx.* 2.

Willielmus   Edwardus Vil-—— Barbara *neptis*   Johannes Vice- Georgius *Dux*   Catherina   Christo-   Maria *Vxor*
Villers, *de*   lers, *m. Pre-*   Olivarii *Vic.*   comes *Pur-*   Buckingha-   *fil. & h.* phorus   Willielmi
Brokesby   *sidens de* Mun- Grandison.   *bec.*   miæ *assisina-*   *Comitis*   *Comes de*   *Comitis de*
mil. & bar.   *ster.*   *tus* 1628.   Rutlan   Anglesy.   Denbigh.

         Willielmus—— Jacobus *ob.*   Georgius *Dux*   Franciscus *Dominus*   Maria, *vidua* —— Jacobus *Dux*
         Villers,   infans.   Buckiagha-   Villers, *occisus f. p.*   Caroli *Dom.*   Richmondiæ
         Vicecomes   miæ *natus*,   1648.   Herbert.   *Mar.* 2.
         Grandison.   1627.

         Barbara   Esme *Dux*   Maria *Vxor*
         Ducissa   Richmond.   Richardi
         de Cle-   *ob.* 1660.   *Comitis De*
         veland.   *f. p.*   Arran.

But during the late Rebellion, in the year 1645. the Parliament Army prevailing in thefe parts, they placed a fmall Garrifon in this Houfe, juft enough to guard their Committy, and to harraffe the Country; but being too weak to defend themfelves from any attempt that might be made by the Royalifts, they fet fire to the Houfe and Furniture, and left it. Yet the Stables 'fcaped the effect of their malice, which remain to this day the nobleft (or at leaft equal to any) Building of this kind in 𝕰𝖓𝖌𝖑𝖆𝖓𝖉.

Burley Stables on the East-side.

Of the Church there.

I'N the 2 E. 1. (1274) The Priorefs of 𝕰𝖆𝖙𝖔𝖓 (*viz*, Nun. 𝕰𝖆𝖙𝖔𝖓 in *Com.* 𝖂𝖆𝖗𝖜𝖎𝖈𝖐) prefented to the Vicarage of the Church of 𝕭𝖚𝖗𝖌𝖑𝖊. To which Houfe the Rectory of 𝕭𝖚𝖗𝖑𝖞 was found to belong, at the time of the fuppreffion.

Here was formerly in our Lady Chappel in this Church one Chantry founded by Dame *Elizabeth Sapcots*: The particulars of which Foundation were in the 2 *E.* 6. Surveyed and thus certified by *Richard Cecyl*, Efq; and *Thomas Hays*, Commiffioners for that purpofe, *viz.*

Founded for one Prieft to fing Mafs there for ever, and hath one Penfion out of the Lands of the late Monaftery of 𝕻𝖎𝖕𝖜𝖊𝖑𝖑 *in the County of* 𝕹𝖔𝖗𝖙𝖍𝖆𝖒𝖕- 𝖙𝖔𝖓, *per Annum* 110 s. *whereof in Almes diftributed to poor people at the day of the Obit of the faid Lady* Sapcotts, *per An.* 3 s. 4 d. *Remains for the Penfion of the Chantry Prieft, named Sir* Thomas Wat-fon,

Esc. 14. Jac. p. 2. m. 116.

son, *aged 42 years, of good report among his Neighbours there, per* An. 106 s. 8 d.
inde pro decima Regi, *per* An. 9 s. 4 d.

Plate belonging to the said Chantry, one Chalice of 11 *oun. delivered to the Jewel House.*

Ornaments valued at ——— 9 s. 8 d.

It was found by Office in the 14 of King *James*, that *John* Lord *Harrington* the elder, dyed seized of the Rectory of **Burly**, which he held in Soccage of the Mannour of East **Greenwich**, by Fealty only.

The Vicarage of **Burly** is valued in the Kings Books at 10 *l.* 13 *s.*

The present Patron is the Duke of **Buckingham**.

BYSBROOK, or PISBROOK.

BIsbrook lies in the Hundred of **Wrangdyke**. It appears in the Conquerours Survey, that at that time, the King held in this Town and **Glaiston** (as parcel of his Mannour of **Berchedone**) one Hide of Land and a half, of Arable four Carucates, and eight Acres of Meadow.

Domesd. Nort. n. 1.

At the same time, one *Robertus* held of *Judith* the Countess, in this Town (then writ **Bitlesbroch**) two Hides and one yard Land, three Carucates and a half of Arable, in demesne one Carucate, two Servants, and twelve Villains, with four *Bordarii*, possessing two Carucates and a half. Here were twenty Acres of Meadow, and a Wood one furlong and a half long, and as much in breadth, formerly valued at 20 *s.* but then at 30 *s. Edwardus tenuit cum* Saca & Soca.

Ib. n. 56.

In the Reign of *E.* 2. *John de Nevile* of **Wymondewold**, and *Thomas de Midleton* were Lords of **Bitlesbroke**.

No. Vil. in Scacc.

In the 36 *E.* 3. *William de Burton* Lord of **Tolethorp** granted to *Richard de Bajocis* Knight, and *Robert de Bajocis* his Son, and to their heirs, all his Lands and Tenements in **Bitelesbroke** (*Com. Rutl.*) late belonging to *John Midleton*, and by him purchased of *John de Wempton*.

Clauf. 36. E. 3. m. 19.

King *Edward* the 6th. in the first year of his reign, granted to *Richard Lee* (among other things) the Mannour of **Bysbroke** with its appurtenances in the County of **Rutland**, with all and singular Messuages, Lands and Tenements in **Bysbroke** formerly belonging to the Colledge of **Fodrynghey** in the County of **Northampton**, to

1 E. 6. p. 1.

hold of the King in *Capite* by Knights Service.

In the second year of King *E.* 6. the said *Richard Lee* obtain'd Licence to alienate the said Mannour to *Anthony Andrews* and his Heirs. Which *Anthony* dyed seized of the said Mannor in the 1. *El.* leaving *Edward Andrews* his Son and heir. But part of this Estate the said *Anthony* devised to *Anthony* his second Son. Upon which devise there afterwards arose a notable Case, which was adjudged in the Court of Wards *Ter. Mic.* 32. and 33. *Eliz.* and is thus reported by Serjeant *Moor.*

2 E. 6. p. 4.

Esc. 1. El.

Anthony Andrews having Issue three Sons *Edward.*, *Anthony*, and *Fabian*, and being seized in Fee simple of Land, in **Pisbroke** in the County **Rutland**, by his last Will in writing, *An.* 1557, devised the said Lands to remain after the Death of his Wife, to *Anthony* his Son and his heirs, and in case *Fabian* lived till the said Lands come to *Anthony*, then that *Anthony* pay to *Fabian* 10. *l.* per *An.* so long as the said *Fabian* liveth. *Anthony* the Father dyes : *Anthony* the Son cometh to the Lands, payeth the Rent, hath issue, and dyes. The question was whether the Land be charged by Law with this Rent, as a Rent Seck to be paid by the issue of *Anthony* to *Fabian* still living, or whether it was determined by the Death of *Anthony.* And it was resolved upon advice with *Wray* and *Anderson* chief Justices, that the Land remain'd still charged with the said Rent as a Rent Seck, and that the heirs or Assignes of *Anthony* were obliged to pay it during the Life of *Fabian.*

Moors Rep. f. 721.

F

Anthony

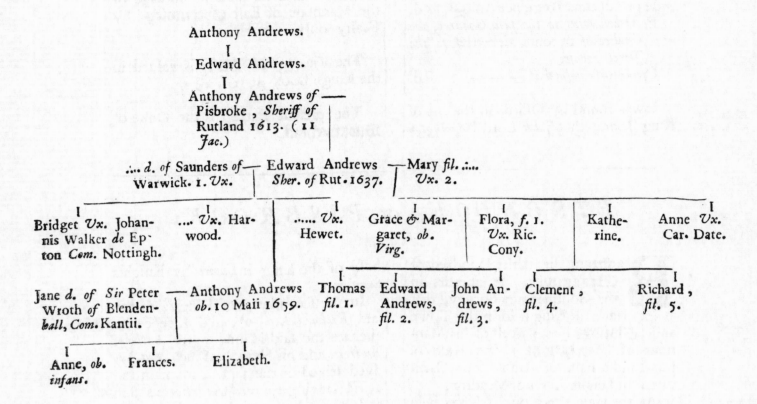

Anthony Andrews.
|
Edward Andrews.
|
Anthony Andrews of —
Pisbroke , *Sheriff of*
Rutland 1613. (11
Jac.)

....*d. of* Saunders *of*—— Edward Andrews ——Mary *fil.* ....
Warwick. 1. *Vx.*   Sher. *of* Rut. 1637.   *Vx.* 2.

| Bridget *Vx.* Johannis Walker *de* Epton *Com.* Nottingh. | .... *Vx.* Harwood. | ...... *Vx.* Hewet. | Grace & Margaret, *ob.* Virg. | Flora, *f.* 1. *Vx.* Ric. Cony. | Katherine. | Anne *Vx.* Car. Date. |

Jane *d. of Sir* Peter —— Anthony Andrews   Thomas   Edward   John An-   Clement ,   Richard ,
Wroth *of* Blenden-   *ob.* 10 Maii 1659.   *fil.* 1.   Andrews,   drews ,   *fil.* 4.   *fil.* 5.
ball, *Com.* Kantii.   *fil.* 2.   *fil.* 3.

Anne, *ob.*   Frances.   Elizabeth.
infans.

The laſt of this Family who own'd this Lordſhip was *Edward Andrews* Eſq; who had been Sheriff of this County in the year 1637. and not long after ſold his Eſtate in this Town. The Preſent Lord of this Mannour is the Right Honourable *John* Earl of **Rutland.**

Of the Church there.

Bib. Cot. Sub cap. Cleopatræ E. 4. *f.* 273.

THE Church of **Biſbrooke** , did formerly belong to the Monaſtery of **Daventry**, and upon the Diſſolution of that Houſe , it was deſigned to be Impropriated to *Cardinal* Colledge (now called Chriſt Church) in the Univerſity of **Oxford** ; As I find in a Liſt of all thoſe Parſonages intended to be annext to that Colledge.

Comp. pro Com. Rutland. in offic. Augm, 3 E. 6.

But it ſeems that Colledge enjoyed it not long, if at all : For King *E.* 6. by Letters Patents dated 8 *Maii* in the third year of his Reign granted the ſaid Rectory to Sir *Edward Montague* Knight, Cheif Juſtice, and to *John Cam-* *pinet,* their Heirs and Aſſignes for ever, to hold in Soccage, as of the Mannour of **Geddington** in *Com.* **Northampton** by whom it was ſoon after, *viz.* 6 *July* 3 E. 6. conveyed to *Anthony Andrews* and *Dorothy* his Wife, and to the heirs and Aſſignes of the ſaid *Anthony* for ever.

The Vicarage of **Byſbrooke** is valued in the Kings Books at , 6 *l.* 4 *d.*

The preſent Patron is

CALDECOT

CALDECOT:

Caldecot is a small Village in the hundred of **Wrangdike**, and Borders on part of **Northamptonshire**. It hath had a dependence on the Mannour of **Lydington**, ever since the Conquest.

See **Lydington**.

The Present Lord of this Town, as also of **Lydington**, is the Right Honourable *John* Earl of **Exeter**.

I find in the account of *John Doddington* the Kings Receiver in this County, in 3 *E*. 6. mention of certain Lands in this Town parcel of the late dissolved Monastery of **Pipwell** in the County of **Northampton**.

Comp. pro com:
Rutl. in Offic.
Augm. 3 *E*. 6.

CASTERTON *Magna*, or BRIG-CASTERTON.

Camb. Brit.
in Lincolnsh.
p. 534.

THis Town lies in the East hundred.

Mr. *Cambden* is of opinion, that the Antient Roman Station, mentioned in *Antoninus*, and called *Gausennæ*, stood in this Place, and that the great Town of **Stamford** in **Lincolnshire**, distant about a mile from hence, grew out of the Ruins of this; the affinity of the name of the Rivulet that runs here, called *Guash* (the only River proper to this County) conduces to this purpose. So also do the great number of old Roman Coins, which have been, and still are found in Plowing and Diging in the adjoyning fields and Grounds.

Descrip. Leic.
p. 132.

Of which many Roman Coins found in and about this Lordship, I must here observe to the Reader, what Mr. *William Burton* notes in his description of **Leicestershire**. That it was the Custom of the Romans under the foundation of their Altars, or any other Building, Monument, or peice of work of note, to cast or lay some of their Emperors Coyns in whose time the said Foundation was laid, to signifie the beginning, and preserve the memory of the said Work to Posterity. For the same reason also they used to put into their Urns among the ashes of the deceased, some Coins of the Emperour then Reigning, and so bury the same.

It is supposed (saith Mr. *Cambden*) that this *Gausennæ* was overthrown when the Picts and Scots had spoiled all the Country, as far Southwards as to **Stamford**, where *Hengist*, and his English Saxons with their unwearied force and singular prowess, hindred the passage of those furious Nations, so that after many of them were slain, and more taken prisoners, the rest betook themselves to flight.

Camb. ub. sup.

Before the Conquest Earl *Morcar* held **Castertone**, but at the time of *Domesday* Survey, *Hugo* the Son of *Baldric* held it in farm of the King. There were at that time three hides and a half, of arable nine Carucates, in Demesne one Carucate, twenty four Villains, two Socmen, two *Bordarii*, with a Preist and two Servants, having seven Carucates. Here was also express in the same Survey a Mill of 16 *s*. and sixteen acres of Meadow, with a *Spinetum* (or ground over run with thorns) of three furlongs in length, and two in breadth, all formerly valued at 6 *l*. but then at 10 *l*.

Domesday
North. No. 1

In the Reign of *E*. 2. *John de la Ware* was Lord of **Brig-Casterton**. *Henry* Lord *Scroop* of **Bolton** in the Reign of *H*. 6. was seized of the Manner

Nom. Vill. in
Scac.

Bar. Eng.
1 Vol. 656.

Mannour of **Casterton** in *Com. Rotel.* and died so seized in the 47 year of that King.

Afterwards this Town became part of the Possessions of Sir *John Hussy* Knight, the first and last Baron of that name created by King *Henry* the 8*th.* Which said Lord *Hussy* was beheaded in *June* 1537. (29 *H. 8.*) for being ingaged with the Commons in **Lincolnshire**, who in the foregoing year made a tumultuous Commotion, on the account of the alteration of Religion. After which this Estate came to the Crown; and accordingly I find, that *William Astewood*, the Kings Bayly in these parts 3 *E.* 6. accounted for the Rents and profits of **Bridge-Casterton** parcel of the Lands of *John* Lord *Hussy* attaint of High Treason, the sum of 23 *l.* 1 *s.* 8 *d.* Also for the Farm of the Mannour or Capital House of **Woodhead** parcel of the Lands of the said Lord *Hussy* then in demise to *Richard*

Comp. in offic.
Augment. pro
Com. Rut.
3 E. 6.

Norley for one and twenty years by Indenture dated 14 *Apr.* 34 *H.* 8. the sum of ———— 14 *l.*

The present Lord of **Casterton Magna** and of **Woodhead**, is the Right Honourable *John* Earl of **Exeter.**

Of the ADVOWSON.

In the 46 *H.* 3. The then Queen of **England**, as Leiutenant or Agent for the Lord *Edmund* her Son, who was then absent in parts beyond the Seas, presented to the Church of **Casterton.**

In the 40 *E.* 1. Sir *John la Ware* Kt. presented to the Church of Great **Casterton.**

Reg. Linc.

Ib.

The Rectory of **Casterton Magna** is valued in the Kings Books, at 11 *l.* 2 *s.* 9 *d.*

The present Patron is

Woodhead.

Within the Parish of **Big Casterton** lies **Woodhead**, formerly a Village and Chapelry, now only one house, and that in Ruins.

In the 17*th.* of *Edw.* 1. the Lady *Hawisia*, Widdow of *Robert de Greley* Lord of this Mannor, by vertue of her Dower of the Lands belonging to the

Regist. Linc.

said *Robert*, presented to the Chappel of **Woodhead**; The profits of which were at that time found to consist in the tithes of Corn, Hay, Wool, Lamb, Calves, and Pigs, arising out of the Demesnes of the Mannour of **Woodhead**, and in all the Oblations of the Family of the Lord of **Woodhead**, together with one Bovate of Land.

C ASTERTON *Parva.*

Little **Casterton** lies in the East Hundred. Of this Town there is no mention in *Domesday* Book, it being no doubt at the time of that Survey, included either under the title of the other **Casterton**, or **Tolethorp**.

In the Reign of *E.* 2. The Prior *de*

Nom. Vill.

novo Loco (or **Newsted**) was Lord of little **Casterton**.

In the 50*th.* year of *E.* 3. Sir *Thomas de Burton* Kt. did by his Deed dated on the *Saturday* next after the Feast of St. *Martin* the Bishop, convey unto *John Brown* of **Stamford** Esq; all his Lands, Tenements, Rents and Services

in

Ex Stem. pen.
Chr. Brown
Ar.

in the Village of little **Casterton**, with the Reversion of the Patronage of the Church there. From which *John Brown* is descended *Christopher Brown* , Esq; Lord of this Mannour. Of which Family *vide* **Colethorp**, *infra*.

Comp. pro com.
Rutl. in Offic.
Aug. 3. *E.* 6.

In the 3. *E.* 6. *Robert Hickin*, the Kings Bayly in these parts, accounted in the Court of Augmentations for the Sum of 40. *s.* for the yearly Rent, or farm, of one Message with the Lands thereunto belonging in **Casterton** *parva*, then in the Tenure of *Francis Brown* Esq; late parcel of the possessions of the foresaid Priory of **Newsted**, and 60. *s.* more for the farm of one other Messuage with the Lands thereunto belonging then in the Tenure of *Robert Johnson*, parcel of the possessions of the said Priory, in all 100. *s.*

Of the ADVOWSON.

Reg. Linc.

In the time of *Oliver Sutton* Bishop of Lincoln (which was, in the reign of King *Edward* 1.) Sir *John de Oketon*, and *Alice* his Wife, presented *William de Empingham* Clerk to the Church of little **Casterton**, and recovered their presentation to the said Church from the Prior *de novo loco* in **Stamford**.

The Rectory of **Casterton=Parva** is valued in the Kings Books at, 6 *l.* 15 *s.* 3 *d.*

The present Patron is *Christopher Brown* Esq;

In the Church of Little Casterton.

Graved in Brass about the Verge of a Gravestone.

✠ **Hic jacet Dominus** Thomas Burton **miles quondam Dominus de** Colthorp **ac Ecclesie istius Patronus qui obiit** .... **Et Domina** Margarita **Uxor sua in ejus sinistris quorum animabus propitietur Deus**, Amen.

CLIPSHAM.

Nom. Vil. in
Scacc.

Bar. Eng. 1.
Vol. 691.

CLipsham belongs to the hundred of **Okeham** Soak, notwithstanding it lyes on the utmost Limits of this County, adjoyning to **Lincolnshire**, and hath the whole hundred of **Alstoe** interposed between this Town and **Okeham**.

Of this Town I find no mention in *Domesday* Book.

In the 9. *E.* 2. the then Lord *de la South* was Lord of this Town, at that time written **Kilpesham**.

In the 26. *E.* 3. *William* Lord *Zouche* of **Harringworth** dyed seized of the Mannour of **Kilpsham** (the same with **Clipsham**) in the County of **Rutland**, leaving *William* his Grandson his heir, who died seized of the said Estate 5. *R.* 2. and in the same Family it continued till the 3. *H.* 5. in which year another *William* dyed seized of the said Estate, after which I find no more mention of this Town in that Family.

Hil. 5. *H.* 4.
ex parte Rem.
Thesaur.

As to the Tenure, it appears by Office found in the 5*th.* year of *H.* 4. That *William le Zouche* (or *Souche*) Son and heir of *William le Souche* held of the King at the day of his Death, among other lands in diverse Counties, the Mannor of **Clipsham**, with the Advowson of the Church of the same, with all the appurtenances in the County of **Rutland**, as of the Castle of **Hokham** by the service of the 20*th.* part of a Knights fee.

And thus we may see how it comes that this Town lying so far distant, doth notwithstanding belong to the hundred of **Okeham=Soak**; *viz.* by reason of the Tenure and relation in point of Estate to **Okeham** Castle, and possibly they both had in former times the same Owner, the Estates of great men being

in

in old time taxt and assest together, tho lying in divers hundreds, sometimes in divers Counties; and therefore in process of time a Town in one hundred has been reckon'd belonging to an other, and a Town in one County belonging to an other, divers Examples of which may be seen in the Antiquities of **Warwick-shire**, *p.* 588. *b.* and *p.* 481.

1. H. 7. p. 3.   King *H.* 7. in the first year of his reign granted to *David Phillips* (among other things) the Mannour of

Clipsham, to hold by the same services, by which it had been formerly held.

It was found by inquisistion taken at **Okeham** 22. *Mar.* 13. *Jac.* after the decease of *John* Lord *Harrington*, that the said Lord dyed seized (*inter alia*) of the Mannour of **Clipsham** in this County.
Esc. 14. *Jac. p. 2. n.* 116:

The present Lord of this Mannour is *Ezechiel Johnson* Clerk, Grand-Son of *Robert Johnson* Archdeacon of **Leicester.**

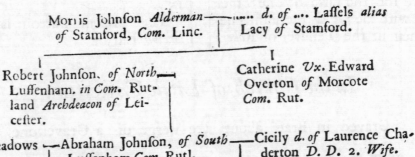

Morris Johnson *Alderman of* Stamford, *Com.* Linc. ———— ..... *d. of* .... Lassels *alias* Lacy *of* Stamford.

Robert Johnson. *of North* Luffenham. *in Com.* Rutland *Archdeacon of* Leicester. ———— Catherine *Ux.* Edward Overton *of* Morcote *Com.* Rut.

..... *d. of* ..... Meadows 1. *Wife.* ——— Abraham Johnson, *of South* Luffenham *Com.* Rutl. ——— Cicily *d. of* Laurence Chaderton *D. D.* 2. *Wife.*

Isaak Johnson,   Samuel *ob. s. p.* 1658.   Daniel *ob.* 1670.   James.   Nathaniel.   Francis.   Elizabeth.

Anne *da. of* John Boate *of North* Kilworth *Com.* Leic. *clerk Ux.* 1. *ob.* 1635. ——— Ezechiel Johnson, *natus,* 1607. ——— Thalia *da. of Sir* Edw. Heron *of* Cressy-hall *Com.* Linc. *Ux.* 2. *ob. s. p.*

Margaret *Ux.* Thomæ Marsh, *Gen.*   Anne *Ux.* Thomæ Johnson, *ar.*

Of the Church there.

Reg. Linc.   IN the 4. *H.* 3. *John de Fraxineto* presented to the Church of **Kilpesham**.

Ib.   In the 2 *E.* 1. Sir *Eudo la Zouch* Knight presented to the said Church.

Certif. pro com. Rutl. in Office Augm. An. 2. E. 6.   Here was formerly within the Chappel of St. *Nicholas* in this Church one Chauntry founded by *William la Zouche.* The particulars of which Foundation were surveyed, and thus certified by *Richard Cicyl* Esq; and *Thomas Hays* Commissioners for that purpose 2. *E.* 6. *viz.*

Founded for the maintenance of one Priest to sing there for ever. Hath of

Lands and Tenements in the Counties of **Rutland** *and* **Lincoln** ----- 106. *s.* 8. *d. Whereof Rents Resolute,* 4. *d. remains cleer for the portion of the Chauntry Priest Sir* Richard Tayler, *aged* 46. *years and is impotent but of very honest Report, and hath nothing to live upon but this Chauntry,* 106 *s.* 4 *d. per An.* Inde pro Decima Regi per An. 9 *s.* 8 *d.*

One Challice parcel gilt, delivered to the Jewel-house.

Ornaments valued at 1 2 *s.* 4 *d.*

The Rectory of **Kilpesham** is valued in the Kings Books at, 10 *l.* 0 *s.* 3 *d.*

The present Patron is

COTSMORE.

LYes in the hundred of **Alſtoe.** In the Conquerors ſurvey it is recorded that one *Goda* a Saxon did formerly hold here 3 Carucates of Land, as taxt to the Geld; The Land was 12 Carucates. Here the King held 3 Carucates in Demeſne, and 3 Sock=men, with 40 Villains, and 6 *Bordarii* having 20 Carucates, here was 40 Acres of Meadow, and a Wood of one Mile in length and 7 furlongs broad, Valued in the time of King *Edward* at 7 *l.* and at the time of that Survey at 10 *l.*

Domeſday tit. Rotel.

Ib. Of the Land of this Mannour one *Goiſfridus* held half a Carucate, he had one Plow and 8 Villains, valued at the time of the aforeſaid Survey at 20 *s.*

Cotſmoze and **Greetham** were heretofore part of the poſſeſſions of *Waleran* Earl of **Warwick,** who diḍd in the 6*th.* year of King *John,* which *Waleran* in his life time gave the ſaid Mannors to a younger Son of his call'd by his own name *Waleran,* but he died iſſuleſs.

Bar. Eng. 1. *Vol.* 7 l.

In the reign of *Edw.* 2. *Thomas Beauchamp* Earl of **Warwick** (deſcended from the aforeſaid *Waleran*) was Lord of **Coteſmoze.** Which deſcent was as follows.

Nom. Vill.

Margareta *f.* Humph. *de Bohun Com.* Heref. ── Walerannus *Comes* War. *ob.* 6 John. ── Alicia, *Vx.* 2.

Henricus *Comes* Warw. *ob.* 13 H. 3. ── Margeria *fil.* Hen. D'oily.

Willielmus *de* Mauduit, *Regis Camerarius.* ── Alicia.

Thomas *Comes* Warw. *ob.* 26 H. 3. *ſ. p.*

Margeria *Soror & Hær. Vx.* Joh. *de* Pleſſetis *Com.* War. *ob.* 47 H. 3. *ſ. p.*

Willielmus Mauduit *Comes* Warw. *ob.* 52 H. 3. *ſ. p.*

Iſabella *Sor. & H.* ── Willielmus *de* Bellocampo, *ob.* 53 H. 3.

Willielmus *de* Bello campo, *Comes* War. *ob.* 26 E. 1. ── Matilda *f.* Johannis Fitz-Jeoffrey.

Guido *de* Bellocampo, *Comes* Warw. *ob.* 9 E. 2. ── Alicia *S. & h.* Roberti Tony.

Thomas *de* Bellocampo, *Comes* Warw. *ob.* 43 E. 3. ── Catherina *f.* Rogeri Mortimer *Com.* March.

Thomas *de* Bellocampo, *Comes* War. *ob.* 2 H. 4. ── Margareta *fil.* Williel. *de* Ferrars *de* Groby.

Richardus *de* Bellocampo, *Com.* War. *& Alber. ob.* 17 H. 6. ── Iſabella *f. & h.* Thom. *Dom.* Diſpencer, *Vx* 2.

Anna *Vx.* Richardi Nevil, *Com.* War. *& Sarum.*

Henricus *de* Bellocampo, *Dux* Warw. *ob.* 23 H. 6. *ſ. p. ſuperſtite.*

It

Esc. 2. El.

It was found by office taken in the 2d. of Queen *Eliz.* that *John Durant* held two parts of the Mannour of **Cottesmore**, with the Appurtenances in **Gretham**, **Wempton**, and **Barrow**, of the Queen, by Fealty, and the Rent of one pair of Spurs. Which Family of the *Durants* had been a long time seated here ; whose descent so far as it relates to this Branch, I have here incerted, in respect to so ancient and honourable a Name, tho now quite worn out in **Rutland.**

Sir Walter Durant *Kt. Bayliff of* Archendown *Forest, in Com.* Sussex.

John Durant.——Evelina *d. & coh. of* William Placetis, *qui ob.* 2 E. 1.

Richard Durant *f.* 1. *ob.* 7 E. 3.   John Durant *fil.* 2.——....*d. of Sir* Charles Lupus, 2. *W.*   Simon.   Michael.

Sir John Durant, *of* Cotsmore *& Barrow, Com.* Rutl.——Isabel *d. of Sir* John Lacy.   Thomas Durant.   Isabel *Vx.* Thomæ Peers.

Sir Hen. Durant, *of* Cotsmore.——Margaret *da. of* Rouland *St.* Liz.

Sir Robert Durant, *of* Cotismore.——Elizabeth *d. of* .... Sherard.   John Durant.

John Durant *of* Cottismore *& Bar.*——Anne *d. of* William Fitzwilliams.   Sir Jeoffrey Durant *Knighted by* H. 7. *ob. s. p.*

Cicily *d. of* Augustine Freeston, 1. *W.*——Thomas Durant, *of* Cottismore.—— Jane *d. of* .... Harington, 2. *W.*

Margaret *d. of* John Holcroft, 1. *W.*——John Durant, *of* Cotsmore.——Margaret, 2. *W.*——Dorothy *d. & coheir of* ...... Sapcot, 3. *W.*

Margaret *d. of* John Lane *of* Kettering *Com.* North. 1. *W.*——William Durant, *of* Cottsmore , *ob.* 20. El.——Margaret *d. of* George Sherard 2. *W.*   John Durant.   Jane, *Vx:* Rob. Nichols.   Dorothy , *Vx.* Williel. Bringhurst.

John Durant, *of* Yarnton. *Com.* Oxon.——Catherine *d. of* John Lane *of* Walgrave *Com.* Northamp.   Rose, *Vx.* Arthur Langworth *of the* Bril *in Com.* Sussex.

Esc. 14. Jac. *p.* 2. *n.* 116.

It was found by Office taken at **Okeham** in this County, 22 *March,* in the 13 year of the reign of King *James ,* after the death of *John* Lord *Harrington* the Elder, that the said Lord *Harrington* dyed seized (*inter alia*) of this Mannor of **Cottesmore**, which he held of *Thomas* Earl of **Exeter**, as of his Mannour of **Preston**, by Fealty, and the Rent of one pair of Gilt Spurs, or 6 *d.* for the same, at the Feast of **St.** *Michael* yearly.

Of later times, this Town and **Barrow**, came by purchase to *Ambrose Crook* Esq; (a younger brother of Sir *George Crook* Knight, the Judge) by whose Daughter and Heir it was conveyed in Marriage to Sir *Edward Heath* Knight of the Bath , (eldest Son and Heir of Sir *Robert Heath* Attorney general , and Lord chief Justice of the Kings Bench, under King *Charles* 1st. of blessed Memory) which Sir *Edward* dying, left issue *Margaret* his only Daughter and Heir , marryed to Sir *Thomas Fanshaw* Knight, by whom she

left

left iſſue _Suſanna_ her Daughter and ſole Heir, now married to the honourable _Baptiſt Noel_ Eſq; ſecond Son (now living) of the Right honourable _Baptiſt_ Lord Vicount _Campden_.

Of the ADVOWSON.

Reg. Linc. In the 13. _H._ 3 _William Mauduit_ the Kings Chamberlain (who had married _Alice_ Daughter of _Waleran_ Earl of _Warw._) gave his conſent to the preſentation to the Vicarage in the Church of **Coteſmoʒe**. _Quæ Vicaria conſiſtit in toto Alteragio qucd valet v. marc. & in decimis garbarum de toto Dominico Parſonæ, & in minutis decimis, & in nutrimentis animalium ipſius, & in decimis ſeni de_ **Wenton**, _& in una Virgata terræ vicario aſſignata in_ **Coteſmoʒe** _de terra pertinente ad Eccleſiam._

In the 23. _H._ 3. the ſaid _William Mauduit_ and _Alice_ his Wife preſented _Ib._ to the Church of **Coteſmoʒe**, which they recovered from the Prior of the holy Sepulcher at **Warwick**, in an Aſſize of Darrain preſentment.

In the 40. _E._ 1. _Guy de Beaucamp_ Earl of **Warwick** preſented to the ſaid Church.

In the 11. year of King _James_, _John_ _Ib._ Lord _Harrington_ the Elder dyed ſeized of the Advowſon of this Church appendent to the Mannour.

The Rectory of **Coteſmoʒe** is valued in the Kings Books at, 25 _l._ 16 _s._ 1 _d._

The preſent Patron is.

EDYWESTON.

Edyweſton lyes in the hundred of **Martinſley**. Of this Town there is no mention in _Domeſday_ book, it being no doubt, included in the Survey of **Hameldune** _Cherchſoch_, as one of the ſeven Berews or Hamlets thereunto belonging.

Mon. Ang. 2. Vol. 951. In the reign of King _H._ 2. _William de Tankerville_ the Kings Chamberlain, confirming his Father _Ralphs_ dotation, gave to God and the Abby of St. _George_ of **Bauquerville** in **Noʒmandy** in the dioceſs of **Roan**, among divers other Lands in **France** and **England**, the Town and Church of **Weſton** (_Com._ **Rotel.**) The ſaid King _Henry_ alſo gave leave to the ſaid Monks to plow up and convert into Tillage all _Id. 952._ their Lands, which of the ſaid _Williams_ gift they held in the Foreſt of **Rutland**; confirming all their Eſtates as well here as beyond ſea, with the grants of Priviledges and immunities re-_Nom. Vil._ lating to their Tenure. The Abbot of which Abby was Lord of this mannour in the reign of _E._ 2.

Mon. Ang. 1. Vol. 965. King _Richard_ 2. in the 14_th._ year of his reign gave leave to the Abbot and Covent of St. _George_ of **Bauquerville** in **Noʒmandy** of the Order of St. _Benedict_, to give the Mannour, Houſe or Priory of **Edyweſton** with the Appurtenances in the County of **Rutalnd** (which they then poſſeſt) to the Prior and Covent of Carthuſians adjoyning to the City of **Coventry**, and to their Succeſſors for ever.

And in that Houſe this Eſtate conti-_Comp. pro com. Rutl. in Offic: Augm. 3 E. 6._ nued till the diſſolution, which was in the 30. _H._ 8. (1539) at which time _Francis Conyers_ Eſq; held this Mannour of **Edyweſton** _cum pertinentiis_, together with the Advowſon of the Church here, by leaſe from the ſaid Priory, dated 3. _October_. 13. _H._ 8. for the term of 50. years, at the yearly Rent of 13 _s._ 4 _d._ payable at _Michaelmas_. Paying moreover to the Gardian of the Hoſpital of St. _John_ and St. _Anne_ of **Dikeham** 26 _l._ 13 _s_ 4 _d._ quarterly according to a Compoſition made between the ſaid Gardian, and the aboveſaid Prior and Covent.

After which this Eſtate being in the Crown, upon the Diſſolution of the ſaid Priory as aboveſaid,

King _Edward_, 6_ih._ in the 4_th._ year of his reign, granted all that the Man-_4. E. 6. purs 7._ nour of **Edyweſton** with its Appurtenances in the County of **Rutland**, and the Advowſon of the Church there, to _William_ Lord Par of **Kendale**, then Marquiſs of **Noʒthampton**, to hold of the King in _Capite_, by Knights Service.

The preſent Lord of this Mannour is _Charles Halford_ Eſq;

G   _William_

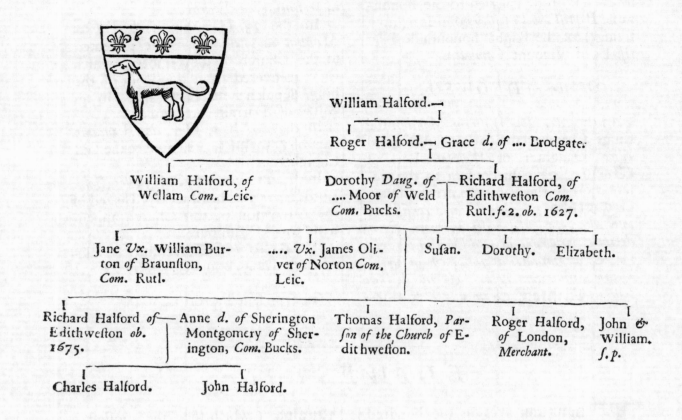

William Halford.—

Roger Halford.— Grace *d. of* .... Brodgate.

| William Halford, *of* Wellam *Com. Leic.* | Dorothy *Daug. of* .... Moor *of* Weld *Com.* Bucks. | Richard Halford, *of* Edithweston *Com.* Rutl. *f.* 2. *ob.* 1627. |

| Jane *Vx.* William Burton *of* Braunston, *Com.* Rutl. | ..... *Vx.* James Oliver *of* Norton *Com.* Leic. | Susan. | Dorothy. | Elizabeth. |

| Richard Halford *of* Edithweston *ob.* 1675.— Anne *d. of* Sherington Montgomery *of* Sherington, *Com.* Bucks. | Thomas Halford, *Parson of the Church of* Edithweston. | Roger Halford, *of* London, *Merchant.* | John & William. *s. p.* |

| Charles Halford. | John Halford. |

Of the ADVOWSON.

Reg. Linc.

In the 17. *H.* 3. the Abbot of 𝕭𝖆𝖚𝖘𝖐𝖊𝖗𝖛𝖎𝖑𝖑𝖊 presented to the Church of St. *Mary* at 𝖂𝖊𝖘𝖙𝖔𝖓. The Rectory of 𝕰𝖉𝖞𝖜𝖊𝖘𝖙𝖔𝖓 is valued in the Kings Books, at 14 *l.* 7 *s.* 4 *d*

The present Patron is *Charles Halford* Esq;

In the Church.

On a handsome Monument, in the North Wall of the Chancel.

Hic situs est Ricardus, Halford *Armiger,* Pacis fautor, ideoque non immerito ei tribueretur non solum nomen sed etiam Locus *justiciarii* Pacis. Sepultus Vicessimo quinto die Decembris, *Anno Domini,* 1627.

Richardus Halford *Armiger, Filius* Richardi, *Justiciarius pacis,* & bis Vicecomes Comitatus 𝕽𝖚𝖙𝖑𝖆𝖓𝖉𝖎𝖊, duas sibi adjunxit uxores, Annam filiam Sheringtonis Mongomery de 𝖘𝖍𝖊𝖗𝖎𝖓𝖌𝖙𝖔𝖓 in Comitatu 𝕭𝖚𝖈𝖐𝖘 per quam duos habuit Filios, Carolum, & Johannem; & Janam *Filiam* Johannis Day de 𝕮𝖍𝖆𝖗𝖉 in Comitatu 𝕾𝖔𝖒𝖊𝖗𝖘𝖊𝖙. obiit 28 die Octobris Anno Ætatis suæ 81. Annoque *Domini,* 1675

𝕰𝖌𝖑𝖊𝖙𝖔𝖓

EGLETON.

Egleton lies in the hundred of **Okeham** *Soak.* Of this Town there is no mention in *Domefday* Book, it being included in **Okeham** *Cherchefoch.*

In the time of *Edw.* 1. this Town, together with **Okeham** and **Langham** in this County, was part of the Poffeffions of *Edmund* Earl of **Cornwall**, Son of *Richard* Earl of **Cornwall** (a younger Son of King *John* by *Senclia* his Wife,) which *Edmund* had the Cuftody of this County from the 16th. year of the faid King *E.* 1. till the 28th. in which year he died without iffue. After whofe death that King being pleafed to allow 500 *l. per An.* to *Margaret* his Widdow during her life, affigned her for the payment of the fame, this Town, and feveral other profits in this County. Which *Margaret* married for her fecond Husband *Piers de Gavefton.*

In the 9 *E.* 2. The faid Lady *Margaret de Gavefton*, was Lady of this Town.

Of later time, this Mannor did belong to Sir *Anthony Brown* Knight, from whom it was conveyed to the Crown. And accordingly I find that *Robert Harbottell* the Kings Receiver in thefe parts did account in the Court of Augmentations, *Mic* 2 *E.* 6. for the fum of 30 *l.* 15 *s.* 10 *d.* for the Rents and profits of **Egleton**, *perquifit de* Anthonio Brown *milne,* viz.

Rents of Affize, from *William* l. s. d.
 Feilding, Thomas Barforth, } 0. 3. 8.
 Cler. and *Emme Procter,* Wid.
Rents of Tenants at Will.   29. 19. 6.
Profits of two Courts, that year. 0. 12. 8.

The Prefent Lord of this Mannour is the Right Noble *George* Duke of **Buckingham.**

HEre was formerly in the Church of **Egleton** (which is a Chappel of Eafe belonging to **Okeham**) a Guild or Fraternity, fo called from the Saxon word ᵹelꝺ and ᵹilꝺ, which fignifieth mony : becaufe that fuch as were either for Charity, Religion, or Merchandize fake affociated, did caft their monies, goods, yea and fometimes Lands together, for the publick fupport of their own common charge. Thefe *Guilds* had their Annual Feafts and Neighbourly meetings, they chofe yearly Officers, and maintained a Prieft to fay Maffes for the living and dead of the Fraternity. which cuftom was very antiently ufed, and is ftill continued by the *Germans,* who call the frequent yearly Banquets of the Country people made at their common charge, *Gilden.*

From thefe *Gilds,* or Fraternities, divers Companies in the Citys and Corporations of *England* took their firft Patterns.

Concerning which *Guild* here at **Egleton** it was thus certified by *Richard Cicyl* Efq; and *Thomas Hays* Commiffioners to enquire of, and Survey the fame, in the 2 *E.* 6. *viz.*

It was founded for the maintenance of one Prieft to fing there for ever, and hath of Lands and Tenements thereunto appurtaining in divers places within the County of **Rutland** *to the yearly value of* 108 *s.* 6 *d. Whereof in Rent refolute to fundry perfons* 29 *s. and fo remaineth cleer by the year for the portion of the Guylde Prieft there named Sir Thomas Kelfo of the age of feventy years, who is a very poor man of good report emonge his Neighbours but unable to ferve a cure, and hath no other living* 79 *s.* 6 *d. never charged with any Tenths.*

Memorandum, The number of Houfling people (i. e. Communicants) *in* **Egleton** *under the Cure of the Parfon there, are four, and in* **Okeham** *under the Cure of the Vicar there four hundred; in all, where the Lands of the faid Guild do lie, four hundred and four.*

Another Prieft of neceffity is to be appointed to help in the Miniftration of the Cure

Cure of **Okeham**, which is a great Town, and the cheeffe Merkett Town of the Shere of **Rutland**, and hath but one Curate to minister there, who in time of Gods visitation is unable to discharge the same.

There remaineth in the hands of Redmayle of **Egleton** husbandman, and Nowel Lloyde of **Burley**, late Wardens of the said Gylde of **Egleton**, in stock of redy mony to them delivered by the hands of Sir Edward Sapcotts *Knight*, Robert Harbottel, Thomas Malson, and Thomas King, late Wardens of the said Gylde, as of such Mony as they had collected and gathered of the Devotion of the people of several Townships adjoyning to the house of the said Gylde, in An. 31. Regis nuper H. 8. which they before this Certificate taken, meant to have distributed to the poor Folks Boxes in the Parish Churches of the said Towns where it was before Collected, 72 s.

Comp. in offic. Augment. pro Com. Rut. 3 E. 6.

Thus far the abovesaid Certificate. But a more exact particular of the Estate formerly belonging to this *Guild* appears in the account of *Thomas Astwoode* the Kings Receiver in the 3. E. 6. *viz.*

One Cottage with a small pightel of Land scituated over against the Cross in the high street of **Egleton** aforesaid, then in the Tenure of Thomas Kelsoo, per An. 8 s.

One Cottage scituated in the high street of the said Town of **Egleton** neer the Bridge there, then in the Tenure of Thomas Seyton, per An. 4 s.

One Tenement new built scituated upon Smythe Green, call'd the Slate house then in the Tenure of Robert Harbottel, per An. 6 s. 10 d.

One Messuage with a Pightel scituate in the high street of **Egleton** with certain Lands in the Field there, then in the Tenure of Robert Brown, per An. 40 s.

One Messuage in **Okeham** in the West street there, with two yard Land in the Common Fields there, then in the Tenure of Thomas Symer, per An. 33 s. 4 d.

One Cottage scituate opposite to the Cross in the Market there, then in the Tenure of Miles King, per An. 14 s.

One Void peice of ground containing by estimation half a Rod, adjoyning to the east end of the Stone Wall of the said Tenement of Miles King, then in the Tenure of VVilliam Halbie, per An. 2 s.

One small piece of ground in **Okeham** aforesaid containing by estimation in breadth 6. foot, and in length 30. foot, adjoyning to the east end of the Orchard of the Tenement of the said Miles King, then in the Tenure of Richard Cutte, per An. 4 d.

In all 108 s. 6 d.

Comp. ut sup.

All which Estate King *Edward* the 6th. granted by his Letters patents under the great Seal of **England** dated 16. Feb. in the 3. year of his reign, to *Edward Warner*, and *John Gosnolde*, Esquires, their Heirs and Assignes for ever, to hold of his honour of **Eye** in *Com.* **Suffolk**, in free Soccage and not in *Capite*, without any tenth reserved; who by their Deed dated 20 *Feb.* in the said 3*d.* year of that King, conveyed over all and singular the premises to *Robert Harbottel* Gent. his Heirs and Assignes for ever.

EMPINGHAM.

Empingham is scituated in the East hundred, and was at the taking of the General Survey in the Conquerers time held by *Gislebert de Gand*. Here were then reckond 4. hides of Land, of which 3. were held in Demesne. The arable Land contain'd eight Carucates or Plowlands, in Demesne four Carucates, together with eight Servants, and twenty five

Domesd. in Northampt. n. 46.

Villains, who held four Carucates: here were at that time five Mills of the Rent of 42 s. and 8 d. and ten Acres of Meadow. Here was also at that that time a Wood containing one Quarantene (or furlong) in length, and ten Perches in breadth. All which was at that time valued at 10 l. The same *Gislebert* held also in this Town seven Hides and a half, and one Bovate of Land

Land of the Kings *Soak* of **Rutland** *& dicit Regem suum advocatum esse.* The arable land was fifteen Carucates which were held at that time by fourteen Sockmen, and fifty one Villains, there were also in the same Tenure five Mills of the Rent of 24 *s.* also ten Acres of Meadow, and ten Acres of Wood, all then valued at 8 *l.*

Id. n. 30.

At the same time *Salfredus* held of *William Peurel* two Hides and a half in **Empingham**. The arable Land was four Carucates, in Demesne one Carucate, with one Servant and eight Villains, and eight *Bordarii* (or Cottagers) who had a Carucate, also one Mill and a half, of the Rent of 12 *s.* with four acres of meadow and six acres of Wood, all then valued at 20 *s. Edwardus & Fregis tenuerunt cum* Saca *&* Soca.

By all which it appears that this Town was in that age much bigger and more confiderable than of late years.

Not long after the Conquest the *Normanvilles* became Lords of this Town and **Normanton** in this County. A Family of eminent note in those days for millitary affairs. For I find that about the later end of King *John's* reign *Ralf de Normanvill* was sent by the King with forces to the defence of **Kenilworth** Castle, in *Com.* **Warwick**, against the Rebellious Barons of those times.

Antiquit. of Warwickfh. *p.* 160.

In the reign of King *John, Ralf de Normanvile* paid 60 marks, one *Dextrarium* (*i.e.* a horse for the great Saddle) and one Palfrey, for the farm of the County of **Rutland**, and for enjoying free Warren in his lands of **Empingham**.

Ex collec. Wingf. Bodenham *m. f.* 16.

In the 5 *H.* 3. the King directed his precept to *Hugh de Nevile* commanding him without delay to deliver to *Ralf de Normanvill* in his Baliwicke of of the forest **Clive**, six Oaks, and six *Furchias* (*i.e.* Forks,) for the building of a certain Hall by him designed to be built at **Amplingham**. This last mention'd *Ralf* dyed in the 43 *H.* 3. and left issue *Thomas de Normanvill*, whose Daughter and heir, *Margaret*, became the wife of *William de Basings*, who died Lord of this Mannour in 9 *E.* 2. The same *William* appears to be one of those eminent persons in this County who in the 29 *E.* 1. received the Kings

Clauf. 5. *H.* 3. *m.* 15.

Nom. Vil.

writ of Summons to attend him at **Barwick** upon **Tweed**, well fitted with Horse and Armes, from thence to march against the Scots.

Clauf. 29. *E.* 1. *m.* 13.

In the reign of King *Edward* the 1. the then Lord of this Mannour had a grant from the King to hold a Market in this Town every *Thursday*, and one Fair every year on the Eve, day, and morrow of St. *Botolph* (*i. e. May* 17.) which grant runs in these Words.

Edwardus dei gratia Rex Angliæ, Dom. Hiberniæ *& Dux* Aquitaniæ *Archiepiscopis, Episcopis, Abbatibus, Prioribus, Comitibus, Baronibus Jufticiariis, præpofitis Miniftris & omnibus Ballivis & fidelibus fuis falutem. Sciatis nos de gratia noftra fpeciali conceffiffe & hac carta noftra confirmaffe dilecto & fideli noftro* Edmundo de Paffeleye *&* Margarete *Uxori ejus, quod ipfi & heredes ipfius* Margarete *imperpetuum habeant unum mercatum fingulis feptimanis per diem* Jovis *apud manerium fuum de* **Empingham** *in Com.* **Rotel**. *& unam feriam ibidem fingulis annis pro tres dies duraturam, videlicet in Vigilia, in die, & in Craftino Sancti* Botulphi, *nifi mercatum illud & feria illa fint ad nocumentum vicinorum mercatorum & vicinarum feriarum. Quare volumus & firmiter precipimus pro nobis & heredibus noftris quod predicti* Edmundus *&* Margareta *& Heredes ipfius* Margarete *in perpetuum habeant prædicta mercatum & feriam apud Manerium fuum prædictum cum omnibus libertatibus & Liberis confuetudinibus adhujufmodi mercatum & feriam pertinentibus, Nifi mercatum illud & feria illa fint ad nocumentum vicinorum mercatorum & vicinarum feriarum ficut predictum eft. Hiis teftibus venerabilibus patribus* W. *Archiepifcopo* Eborum *Angliæ primate,* ff. Elien. *Epifcopo Chancellario noftro,* ff. Winton *Epifcopo,* Johannis de Britanum *Comite* **Richemund**. Edomaro de Valentia *Comite* **Pembroch**, Hugone de Curteney. Willielmo Martyn *& aliis. Dat per manum noftram apud* Ebor. 25. *die* Novembris *Anno regni noftri* 12.

Per breve de privato figillo.

Penes Tho. Markworth Brronet.

The above mention'd *Margaret* Wife of *Edmund de Paffelye* was, no doubt, the same who was Daughter and Heir to *Thomas de Normanville.* She had it seems two Husbands, this *Edmund de*

Paffeley

Paſſeley, and *William de Baſings*, but ſhe left no iſſue male, but only by *Baſings*, whoſe Son *Thomas de Baſirgs* was heir to his Mother, and enjoyed this Lordſhip by Inheritance.

Ex autog.
penes Tho.
Mackworth
Bar.

The beforementioned Sir *Thomas de Normanville* had a Grant to have Divine Service Celebrated in his own private Chappel here at **Empingham**, which Grant appears, by computation, to be made by *Benedict de Graveſend* Biſhop of **Lincoln**, and bears date at **Liding-ton** in the 14*th.* year of his Conſecration, which was *An. Dom.* 1272. (56 *H.* 3.) Which Deed being too prolix to be here inſerted, I ſhall only take notice of the chief heads, from whence we may obſerve the nature of ſuch Grants and Licenſes for Oratories in private Chappels, and with what reſtrictions they were made in antient times, *viz.*

1. The ſaid Grant was made with the conſent and aſſent of the Incumbent of the Pariſh Church.

2. It was for the uſe only of the ſaid Sir *Thomas de Normanville*, his heirs, their Wives, and their own Family, without the ringing of a Bell, *cum ſola panis & aquæ benedictione.*

3. That the Chaplain of the ſaid Chappel before ever he entred upon his Office, ſhould make his corporal Oath to the Incumbant of the Pariſh Church, faithfully and truly to deliver over to the ſaid Incumbant, his Vicar or Subſtitute, all ſuch oblations, and obventions, and other profits that ſhould come to his hands, within three days after he received the ſame. And alſo

4. That the ſaid Chaplain ſhould make like Oath not to adminiſter the Euchariſt, or any other Sacrament, in the ſaid Chappel, to the prejudice of the Mother Church, or any other Neighbouring Church, but that he ſhould ſend all ſuch as deſire the ſame, as well thoſe of the ſaid Knights Family as others (except ſuch as lie at the point of Death) to their Mother Church to receive.

5. That the ſaid Knight, his heirs and Family, during their reſidence at **Empingham**, ſhall be bound to reſort to the Mother Church to hear Divine Offices there, in like manner as the other Pariſhioners, on certain days, *viz.* Chriſtmaſs, Purification, Aſhwedneſday, Palm Sunday, Eaſter Eve, Eaſter-day, Aſcen-

tion day, Whitſunday, Allſaints, the Aſſumption of the Virgin, and the Dedication of that Church, unleſs hindred by ſickneſs or ill weather.

6. If the ſaid Knight or his heirs be abſent from his Mannour for the ſpace of one month, Divine Offices to ceaſe in the ſaid Chappel during abſence.

7. That the ſaid Offices be celebrated in the ſaid Chappel ſooner than in the Mother Church.

8. That the ſaid Knight his heirs and ſucceſſors, for themſelves and their Wives, ſhall be ſworn to obſerve the ſaid Injunctions, ſo long as they enjoy the ſaid Chappel, renouncing all Royal prohibitions and priviledges to the contrary; and that they and their Chaplain ſhall alwaies ſubmit themſelves to the Juriſdiction of the Biſhop of **Lincoln**, the Dean and Chapter of **Lincoln**, and the Prebend of **Empingham**, for the time being.

Eſc. 2. El.

It was found by Office in the 2*d.* year of Queen *Elizabeth*, that *Francis Mackworth*, *Eſq;* held certain Lands in **Empingham** and **Hardwick**, of the yearly value of 43 *l.* of the Lord *Barkley*, by Knights ſervice; and that *George Mackworth* is his Son and heir. Which *George* was the Great Grandfather of Sir *Thomas Mackworth* Baronet, the preſent Lord of this Mannour, which he enjoys by Inheritance from the beforementioned *Ralph de Normanville*, who died 43 *H.* 3. This eſtate having now continued in the ſame blood, though not in the ſame name, above four hundred years.

See more in **Normanton**, *infra.*

Comp.pro com
Rutl. in Offic:
Augm. 3 E. 6.

I find in the account of *Thomas Aſtwood* the Kings Receiver in theſe parts 3 E. 6. That the ſaid accountant, among other Rents and profits, accounted for 2 *s.* 8 *d.* of the Rent of two Acres of Land called *Coblers Croft*, *vel le Chappel Croft*, lying in the ſouth field of **Empingham** given to the Maintenance of one Lamp in the Pariſh Church there, then in the Tenure of *Ann Mackworth* Widdow. Alſo for 2 *s.* of Rent iſſuing out of the Tenement of *Francis Mackworth*, Eſq; ſcituate in the middle of the ſaid Town, then in the tenure of *Thomas Exſton*, which ſaid tenement in times paſt by cuſtom uſed to find at the ſecond Maſs in the morning on Chriſt-maſsmafsday one Torch and five pence in Money, which by confent of the Parifhioners there, was afterward changed into the abovefaid Rent of 2 s.

Of the Church.

KIng *Henry* 1. gave and confirm'd the Tithes of this Town, and certain Lands here, to the Church of **Lincoln**, as appears by the following Charter.

Mon. Ang. p. 3. f. 254.

Henricus *Rex* Anglorum , S. *Comiti* & Hugoni *Vice-comiti* & *omnibus Baronibus fuis de* **Nozhantona fcira** *Salutem: Sciatis me conceffiffe Ecclefiæ Sanctæ Mariæ* **Lincolie** & Roberto *Epifcopo* **Linc.** *Ecclefiam de* **Hempingeham** & *illas tres Bovatas Terræ quas Giffebertus de Gant crevit in Elemofina,* & *volo* & *præcipio ut honorifice teneat cum om-*

nibus confuetudinibus, & *fi Comes de Auco diffaifivit eum tunc præcipio ut Abb. Camer. cito reffaifiat. Tefte* Osberto *Vice-comite apud* **Bzantonam.**

In the 29. *H.* 3. The then Archdeacon of **Nozthampton** prefented to the Vicarage of the Prebend of **Empingham.**

Reg. Linc.

The Prebend of **Empingham**, belonging to the Church of **Lincoln** is valued in the Kings Books at 25 *l.* 6 *s.* 5 *d.*

And the Vicarage at 7 *l.* 14 *s.* 8 *d.* The Patron of which laft is the Prebendary for the time being.

E X T O N.

Exton is fcituate in the hundred of **Alftoe.** At the time of the Norman Conqueft, Earl *Wallef* held in **Exentune** two Carucates of Land as it was rated to the Tax or Geld. The arable Land was twelve Carucates. Afterwards at *Domefday* Survey, Countefs *Judith* held here three Carucates and thirty feven Villains, having eight Carucates, and two Mills of the value of thirteen fhillings. A Meadow of fix Furlongs in length. A Wood (*Silva per loca paftilis*) of five furlongs in length and five in breadth. All which was valued in the time of King *Edward* at 8 *l.* but at the time of that Survey at 10 *l.*

Domefday tit. Rotel.

From which *Wallef* (or *Waltheof*) Earl of **Nozthumberland** and **Huntington**, and *Judith* his Countefs, this Eftate defcended by *Matilda* their Daughter and heirefs, to *David* King of the Scots, who was alfo in right of his wife Earl of **Huntington.** From whofe iffue it went again by a female, to the Noble family of *Brus,* and from that name to the *Greens*, from them to the *Culpeppers*, and from them to the *Haringtons*, by whofe heir General it was in the laft age fold: Having con-

tinued in the fame Line and blood for near 600. years; as may appear more particularly by the following ftory, and Pedigree.

Bar. Erg. Vol. 379.

Yet we muft obferve that part of this Town formerly belong'd to the *Baffets* of **Dzapton** in **Staffozdfhire.** For I find that when *Ralf Baffet* engaging on the part of the Rebellious Barons againft King *H.* 3. was kill'd at the Battel of *Evefham, Anno Domini* 1265. Yet that King foon after tendering the Condition of *Margaret* his VVife, and at the fpecial inftance of Prince *Edward*, affigned her feveral Lands belonging to her Husband, and among others, **Exton** in **Rutland**, for her fupport, during pleafure. The ancient Arms of thefe *Baffets* are ftill (or very lately) remaining in a VVindow, on the South fide of this Church. O. 3 Piles, g.

In the 9 *E.* 2. there were three Lords in this Town, *viz. Bernardus de Brus*, *Ralf Baffet*, and *Jeoffrey de la Mare*, each of which had here a Mannor.

No. Vil. in Scacc.

VVhich faid *Bernardus de Brus* was Grandfon to *Bernard de Brus* a younger Brother to *Robert de Brus* Earl of **Carrick** from whom the Royal Line

of

of **Scotland** deſcends. Of this younger Branch of this moſt Noble Family deſcended two Daughters Coheirs, *Joan* and *Agnes*; from *Agnes* deſcends the Right Worſhipful and Eminent Family of the *Cottons*, who by reaſon of that deſcent enjoy at this day the fair and antient Lordſhip of **Connington** in the County of **Huntington**. The other Siſter and Coheir, *Joan*, was married to Sir *Nicholas Green*, Kt. and continued in poſſeſſion of this Mannour; whoſe only Daughter and heir, *Jane*, became the wife of *Thomas Culpepper*, whoſe Son and heir Sir *Thomas Culpepper*, Kt. left iſſue *Catherine* his only Daughter and heir, who took to Husband *John de Harrington* (deſcended by a younger Branch from the antient Barons of that name, who were Lords of **Haverington** in the County of **Cumberland**) whoſe Son and heir *Robert Harrington*, died ſeized of the Mannour of **Exton** with the appurtenances in **Greetham**, **Cotſmore**, **Whitwell**, and **Barnardſhill**, 12 *Feb.* 16 *H.* 7. after whoſe death all the ſaid Lands deſcended to *John Harrington* his Son and heir, at that time thirty years of age, which *John* by his Will dated 13 *April* 15 *H.* 8. deviſed all his Lands and Tenements in **Cotſmore**, and **Greetham** to *Robert* his Younger Son, and died 5 *Nov.* 15 *H.* 8. leaving iſſue *John Harrington* his Son and heir, afterwards Knighted. Which Sir *John* departed this life in the firſt year of Queen *Mary*, having been High Sheriff of this County the year immediately before his death; after whoſe deceaſe, It was found by Office in the ſaid firſt of Queen *Mary*, that Sir *John Harington* Kt. held the Mannor of **Exton** of the Queen, as of her honour of **Huntington**, by Knights ſervice, and the Rectory of **Exton** of the Queen *in Capite*, by Knights ſervice.

This Sir *John* left iſſue Sir *James Harrington* his Son and heir, who by *Lucy* his Wife, Daughter of Sir *William Sidney*, had three Sons, *John*, *Henry* and *James*: Of which *John* the eldeſt was in the firſt year of King *James* advanced to the Dignity of a Baron of this Realm, by the title of Lord *Harington* of **Exton** in *Com.* **Rutland.** To

Eſc. 16 *H.* 8. *in Scac. ex parte Fanſhaw.*

M.S. Wingf. Bodenham. m.

Eſc. i. M.

Bar. Eng. 2 Vol. 416.

whoſe tuition the ſaid King *James* committed his only Daughter, the Princeſs *Elizabeth*, till her Marriage with *Frederick* Count Palatin of the **Rhine**; after which attending her into that Country, he died in his return homewards at **Wormes** in **Germany**, on the 24 day of *Auguſt*, 1613. leaving iſſue by *Anne* his Wife (Daughter and ſole heir to *Robert Kelway*, Eſq;) *John* Lord *Harrington* his only Son ſurviving; who dying without iſſue at **Kewe** in *Com.* **Surry**, 27 of *February* following,

This Lordſhip was ſoon after ſold to Sir *Baptiſt Hicks*, Kt. in purſuance of a ſettlement made by Indenture dated, 18 *Feb.* 11 *Jac.* between the laſt mention'd *John* Lord *Harrington*, and the Lady *Anne Harrington* Widdow, his Mother, whereby the Mannours of **Exton**, **Horn**, **Pickworth** *alias* **Pickworth-Stockinge**, **Stretton**, **Cottſmore**, **Ridlington**, **Clipſham**, **Barrow**, **Lee** *alias* **Leighfeild**, **Market-Overton**, North-**Luffenham**, **Whitwell**, and **Greetham**, all in this County, were ſettled on the ſaid *John* Lord *Harrington* in tail, the Remainder to the ſaid Lady *Anne* her heirs and Aſſignes for ever, in truſt and confidence, that ſhe, her heirs and Aſſignes or ſome of them, ſhall within convenient time after his deceaſe, ſell ſuch or ſo much of the ſaid Mannours as ſhall be thought meet for the payment of all and every the Debts of the ſaid Lord, and the Lord his Father: The overplus of the ſaid Eſtate to remain after the deceaſe of the Lady *Anne* above-ſaid, to his two ſiſters and Coheirs, *Lucy* then wife of *Edward* Earl of **Bedford**, and *Frances* who became the wife of Sir *Robert Chicheſter* of **Raleigh** in *Com.* **Devon**, Knight of the Bath, *viz.* Two third parts of the ſaid overplus Eſtate to the Lady **Bedford**, and one third part to the Lady *Chicheſter*.

This Eſtate being thus purchaſed as aboveſaid, it deſcended to the Right Honourable *Baptiſt* Lord Viſcount *Cambden* Lord Leiutenant of this County late deceaſed, this Town having been the uſual ſeat of his Reſidence, when in theſe parts.

Eſc. 14. *Jac. P. 2. n.* 116.

Eſc. 14. *Jac. P. 2. n.* 116.

The

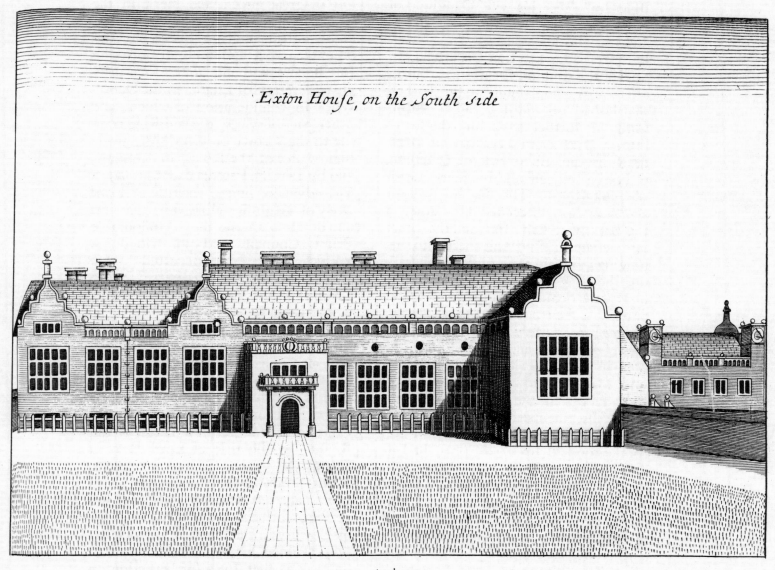

Exton House, on the South side

The said Lady *Lucy* Counteſs of 𝔅𝔢𝔡𝔣𝔬𝔷𝔡 having in her life time ſold all that vaſt Eſtate in this County, which formerly belonged to the *Ha-ringtons*, died without Iſſue, *Anno* 1628. But her memory ſtill ſurvives, highly Celebrated in Dr. *Donnes* Poems.

Inſcrip.Tum. uli apud Exton.

Her ſiſter *Francis* aboveſaid left iſſue by her ſaid Husband Sir *Robert Chicheſter*, only one Daughter, *Anne*, who being married to *Thomas* Lord *Bruce*, left iſſue the Right Honourable and truly Noble *Robert* now Earl of 𝔄𝔶𝔩𝔢𝔰𝔟𝔲𝔯𝔶, who by deſcent from his ſaid Grandmother, enjoys at this day, the fair Lordſhip of 𝔇𝔲𝔩𝔱𝔬𝔫 in *Com.* 𝔏𝔢𝔦𝔠𝔢𝔩𝔱𝔢𝔯𝔩𝔥 with its members of 𝔑𝔢𝔴𝔟𝔬𝔩𝔡, 𝔐𝔞𝔯𝔨𝔢𝔦𝔩𝔡, and 𝔐𝔞𝔯𝔩𝔱𝔬𝔫, formerly belonging to the *Haringtons*.

Of which moſt noble and antient Family of *Brus*, I muſt obſerve that they have been doubly related to this Family

of *Harrington*; the *Harringtons* at firſt deriving this Eſtate from the *Bruces*, and being at laſt determined in the male line, the ſole heir of that Family is, as above expreſt, the aforeſaid Noble Lord the Earl of 𝔄𝔶𝔩𝔢𝔰𝔟𝔲𝔯𝔶. Whoſe Common Anceſter was *Robert de Brus*, a 𝔑𝔬𝔷𝔪𝔞𝔫 Knight, who came into 𝔈𝔫𝔤𝔩𝔞𝔫𝔡 in the Conquerors Army, and was of ſuch eminency that he obtained to himſelf, through the favour of his Prince, and his own merits, no leſs then forty three Lordſhips in 𝔜𝔬𝔷𝔨𝔩𝔥𝔦𝔯𝔢 and thoſe parts; together with the Territory of 𝔄𝔫𝔞𝔫𝔡𝔞𝔩𝔢 in 𝔖𝔠𝔬𝔱𝔩𝔞𝔫𝔡. The principal ſeat of whoſe Barony was at 𝔖𝔨𝔢𝔩𝔱𝔬𝔫 Caſtle in the Northriding of 𝔜𝔬𝔷𝔨𝔩𝔥𝔦𝔯𝔢. This *Robert* founded and Endowed a Monaſtery of Canons Regular of St. *Auguſtin*, at 𝔊𝔦𝔰𝔟𝔲𝔯𝔫𝔢 in 𝔠𝔩𝔢𝔞𝔳𝔢𝔩𝔞𝔫𝔡, in the ſaid County of 𝔜𝔬𝔷𝔨, and departed this life in the 6. *Steph.* (1141.) leaving iſſue

Monaſ. Ang.
2 *Voll.* 148.
Bar. Eng.
1 *Vol.* 447.

H

issue by *Agnes* his wife, Daughter of Sir *Fulc Paynel*, two Sons, *Adam* and *Robert*. To his younger *Son Robert* he gave in his life time 𝔄𝔫𝔞𝔫𝔡𝔞𝔩𝔢, to hold of the King of 𝔖𝔠𝔬𝔱𝔩𝔞𝔫𝔡 , but he afterwards complaining to his Father, that he had no wheat bread in 𝔖𝔠𝔬𝔱𝔩𝔞𝔫𝔡, he further gave him the Lordship of ℌ𝔢𝔯𝔱 , and Territory of ℌ𝔢𝔯𝔱𝔫𝔢𝔰𝔰 in the Bishoprick of 𝔇𝔲𝔯𝔥𝔞𝔪, to hold of himself and his heirs, Lords of 𝔖𝔨𝔢𝔩𝔱𝔬𝔫. The Elder Brother *Adam de Brus* succeeded his Father in the Barony of 𝔖𝔨𝔢𝔩𝔱𝔬𝔫, and the other large estate in 𝔈𝔫𝔤𝔩𝔞𝔫𝔡 thereunto belonging; but after the fourth Generation, the issue male of that line failing, his Estate became divided among four Sisters, Coheirs, married to *Walter de Fauconberge*, *Marmaduke de Thweng*, *Robert de Ros*, and *John de Bellew*, men in that age of great eminency, and from whom most of the principal Families in the North are descended. In the mean time *Robert* Lord *Brus* of 𝔄𝔫𝔞𝔫𝔡𝔞𝔩𝔢 , the second Son of the foresaid *Robert de Brus*, had issue *William de Brus*, who left issue *Robert de Brus* the second, who married *Isabel* one of the Daughters and Coheirs of *David* Earl of *Angos* and ℌ𝔲𝔫𝔱𝔦𝔫𝔤𝔱𝔬𝔫 , third Son of *Henry* Prince of 𝔖𝔠𝔬𝔱𝔩𝔞𝔫𝔡, by whom he had issue *Robert* the third ; and *Bernard de Brus* : from which *Bernard* did descend the *Bruces* of 𝔈𝔵𝔱𝔬𝔫, of whom I have already spoken. But *Robert* the eldest Son (who was called the Noble) married *Martha* Daughter and heir of *Adam* Earl of 𝔠𝔞𝔯𝔯𝔦𝔠𝔨, and had issue *Robert le Brus* Earl of 𝔠𝔞𝔯𝔯𝔦𝔠𝔨, who in right of his Grandmother *Isabel* became King of 𝔖𝔠𝔬𝔱𝔩𝔞𝔫𝔡, *An. Dom.* 1306. From this original did descend the Noble *Edward Bruce* of 𝔨𝔦𝔫𝔩𝔬𝔰𝔰𝔢 in the Kingdom of 𝔖𝔠𝔬𝔱𝔩𝔞𝔫𝔡: A per-

son of great esteem and merit in the Court of King *James* the sixth , and highly instrumental in the peacable Union of the two Kingdoms, by reason of his Intelligence with Sir *Robert Cecil* principal Secretary of Estate, in the Queens time: In consideration of which, and other good services, the said King coming to the Crown of 𝔈𝔫𝔤𝔩𝔞𝔫𝔡, made him Master of the Roles, in 𝔏𝔬𝔫𝔡𝔬𝔫, and by Letters Patents dated 8 *July* 2 *Jac.* advanced him to the title of Lord *Bruce* of 𝔨𝔦𝔫𝔩𝔬𝔰𝔰𝔢, aforesaid. He was also of his Majesties most Honourable Privy Council in both Kingdoms. VVhich Noble Lord departed this life 14 *Jan.* 8 *Jac.* and was buried in the Chappel of the Roles in *Chancery*-lane, where there is to be seen a very fair Monument Erected to his memory. VVhose Son *Thomas* Lord *Bruce* (abovementioned) was by Letters Patents dated 21 *Junii* 9 *Jac.* Created Earl of 𝔈𝔩𝔤𝔦𝔫 in the Kingdom of 𝔖𝔠𝔬𝔱𝔩𝔞𝔫𝔡 ; and on 1 *Aug.* 17 *Car.* 1. advanced to the degree of a Baron of this Realm, by the title of Lord *Bruce* of 𝔚𝔥𝔞𝔯𝔩𝔱𝔬𝔫 in the County of 𝔓𝔬𝔯𝔨. VVhose Son and heir *Robert* Lord *Bruce* (abovementioned) was and is a person of such eminent merits, as well for his Loyalty in the late times of defection , as since his Majesties happy Restauration, that for a further addition of honour, he was by Letters Patents dated 18 *March*, 16 *Car.* 2. advanced to the Titles of Lord *Bruce* of 𝔖𝔨𝔢𝔩𝔱𝔬𝔫, in the County of 𝔓𝔬𝔯𝔨, Viscount *Bruce* of 𝔄𝔪𝔭𝔱𝔥𝔦𝔩𝔩, in the County of 𝔅𝔢𝔡𝔣𝔬𝔯𝔡, and Earl of 𝔄𝔶𝔩𝔢𝔰𝔟𝔲𝔯𝔶 in the County of 𝔅𝔲𝔠𝔦𝔨𝔫𝔤𝔥𝔞𝔪. He is also hereditary High Steward of the Honour of 𝔄𝔪𝔭𝔱𝔥𝔦𝔩𝔩, Lord Leiutenant of the County of 𝔅𝔢𝔡𝔣𝔬𝔯𝔡, and one of the Lords of his Majesties most honourable Privy Council.

Bar. Eng. 2 *Vol.* 466.

Id. p. 467.

Waltheof

Waltheof *Comes de* Huntington & Northumb. *decap.* 1075. — Juditha *Comitissa, Neptis* Williel. Conq.

David *Rex* Scotorum & *Comes* Huntington *jure vxoris.* — Matilda, *relicta* Simonis *de St.* Liz *Comitis* Hunt.

Henricus Scotorum Princ. *ob. in vit. pat.* 1152. — Ada *f. Comitis* Warren.

Robertus *de* Harington, *Dominus dè* Haverington *in Com.* Cumbriæ. — Agnes *Sor. & h.* Williel. *de* Cancfeld *de* Aldingham *in Com.* Lanc.

David *Comes* Angos & Huntington. *fil.* 3. — Matilda *f. & coh.* Hugonis Co. Cestriæ.

Robertus *de* Brus. — Isabella.

Johannes de Harington, *mil. baln.* & *Dom.* Harington *temp.* E. 1. — ... *f.* Richardi Barlingham. *mil.*

Robertus *cognomine nobilis, a quo Reges Scotiæ.* | *Dom.* Bernardus *de* Brus. *fil.* 2. — Constantia *de* Morton.

Robertus *de* Harington, *mil. ob. ant. pat.* — Elizabeth *fil. & coh.* Johan. *de* Molton, *de* Egremond.

Dom. Bernardus *de* Brus *ob.* 29 E. 2. — Agatha.

Johannes *Dominus* Harington. *ob.* 37. E. 3. | Robertus Harington, *mi. fil.* 2. *ob.* 22 R. 2.

Bernardus *de* Brus, *mil. ob.* 4 E. 3. — Agneta.

Johannes Harington. — Agn. *f.* Laurenc. Fleet *de* Fleet. *in Com.* Linc.

Johannes *de* Brus, *m. ob.* 21 E. 3. — Margareta.

Nicholaus Green, *mil.* — Joanna *f. & coh.*

Johannes Harington, *de* Fleet *in* Holland, *Com.* Linc. — .... *f. & h.* Johannes *de* la Launde.

Thomas Culpeper. — Jana *f. coh.* Nich. Green.

Tho. Colepeper *de* Exton *m.* — Juliana *f.* Radulfi Crumwell, *m.*

Johannes Harington, *de* Exton, *jure vxoris.* — Katherina, *f. & h.*

Robertus Harington, *de* Exton. — .... *f.* Johannis Prescot, *mil.*

Johannes Harington, *de* Exton. — Alicia *f.* Hen. Southill *Com.* Linc.

Johan. Harington, *mil.* — Eliz. *f. & h.* Rob. Morton *de* Peckleton *Com.* Leic. | Rober. Harington, *f.* 2.

Jacobus Harington, *miles.* — Lucia *fil.* Willielmi Sidney *militis.* | Edmund. | Robert. | Johannes.

Elizabeth. *Vx.* Edw. Montigue *mil.*

Francisca *Vx.* Guil. Lee *mil.*

Marga. *Vx.* Don Benito Hispano, *de familia Ducum de* Fantasgo.

Cather. *Vx.* Edw. Dimmock *mil.*

Maria *Vx.* Edw. Wingfeild *mil.*

Mabilia *Vx.* Andr. Noel *mil.*

Sara *Vx. Dom.* Hastings.

Theodosia *Vx. Dom.* Dudley.

Johannes *Dom.* Harington, *Baro de* Exton. — Anna *fil. & h.* Roberti Kelway, *ar.*

Henricus Harington, *mil.* — .... *fil. & coh.* Franc. Agar.

Jacobus Harington, *mil. & Baronet de* Ridlington *Com.* Rot. — Francisca *fil. & h.* Roberti Sapcotes.

Kelway, *ob. infans.*

Johan. *Dom.* Harington, *ob. s. p.*

Lucia *Vx.* Edw. *Com.* Bedford.

Robertus Chichester *mil. baln.* — Francisca.

Jacob. Harington *mi. de* Elmsthorp *Com.* Leic.

Johannes Harington *mil.*

Margareta *fil. & coh.* Joh. Doyly.

Edw. Harington, *mil. & bar. f.* 1.

Thomas *Dom.* Bruce. — Anna.

Robertus *Comes de* Aylesbury.

It hath been observed by those who have strictly examin'd all the Colateral Branches of this Family, that from the above-mentioned Sir *James Harrington* and *Lucy* his Wife, have been, and are descended or neerly allyed to their descendents, no less than eight Dukes, three Marquisses, seventy Earls, nine Counts, twenty seven Vicounts, and thirty six Barons, among which number sixteen Knights of the Garter.

AND here, before I leave this noble Family of the *Harringtons*, ought to be remembred the Exemplary Charity of the pious *Ann* Lady *Harrington*, Wife to the first Lord *John* above mention'd, which Lady surviving her said Husband, did in the year 1616 (14 *Jacobi*) purchase the Grant of a Rent charge of one hundred pounds *per An.* to be issuing out of the Mannour of **Cottesmore** in this County, to the said Lady *Ann* her heirs and assignes for ever, payable at the four usual quarter days, in the South Porch of the parish Church of **Okeham**, by even and equal portions, which Grant being made in due form of Law, and dated the 20*th.* of *June* was inroll'd in Chancery 1 *Nov.* in the said 14*th.* year of King *James*. Afterwards by indenture bearing date 1 *Non.* 14. *Jac.* the said Lady limitted the said Rent charge to Sir *Edward Noel*, Sir *Edward Harrington*, Sir *William Bulstrode*, Sir *Francis Bodenham*, *Thomas Mackworth*, *John Wingfield*, and *Richard Cony* Esquires, and to their heirs and assigns for ever, in trust and confidence for the following pious uses, *viz.*

To the Vicar of **Exton** and Overseers of the poor there, to be by them distributed to the Poor of the said Parish for ever, the yearly sum of——— } *l.* 25

Also to the said Vicar and Overseers, to be imployed by them on a poor man (to be named by the Lord of the Mannor of **Exton** for the time being) for the keeping of the Tomb in **Exton** Church called Mr. *Kelways* Tomb, and other such Tombs as now are or hereafter shall be erected in the said Church, the yearly Sum of——— } *l.* 2

To the Vicar of the Parish Church of **Burly** and the Overseers of the Poor there to be by them distributed to the poor of the said Parish, the yearly Sum of } *l.* 10

To the Vicar of the Parish Church of **Okeham** and the Overseers of the poor there, to be by them distributed to the poor of the said Parish, being Tenants or under Tenants of any of the Lands, parcel of the Mannour of the said Lady *Harrington* in **Okeham**, the yearly Sum of——— } *l.* 32

To the Vicar of the Parish Church of **Hambleton** and the Overseers of the poor there, to be by them distributed to the poor, being Tenants of any of the Lands of the said Lady *Harringtons* Mannour in **Hambleton**, the yearly Sum of——— } *l.* 10

To the Parson of **Cottesmore** and **Barrow** and the Overseers of the Poor there, to be by them distributed to the poor of the said Parish the yearly Sum of——— } *l.* 16

To the Parson of the Parish Church of **Market-Oxton**, and Overseers of the poor there, to be by them distributed to the poor of the said Parish, the yearly sum of } *l.* 5

The said payments to be made quarterly to the respective persons as above appointed, by the aforesaid Trustees within ten days after the receit of the said Rent-charge of 100 *l. per An.*

Also the said Lady *Harrington*, about the same time built a convenient place for a small Library in the Parish Church of **Okeham**, and furnisht it with about two hundred Latin and Greek Folio's, consisting chiefly of Fathers, Councils, School-men, and Divines, for the use of the Vicar of that Church, and accommodation of the Neighbouring Clergy; most of which Books have been curiously bound, the Covers adorn'd with several guilded Frets (commonly call'd the *Harringtons* Knots) and

Ex Dono Dominæ Annæ Harringtonæ *Baronessæ.*

Printed and pasted in the Title Pages.

Of the Church.

Ex collec. Wingf. Bodenham m. f. 40.

IN the 11*th.* year of *E.* 1. *Bernard de Brus* Son of *Bernard de Brus* of €xton, gave and releaſed to God, and the Church of St. *Andrew* at Noꝛthampton, and the Monks there, the Church of €xton with the tithes of his Lands, and all other liberties to the ſaid Church belonging within or without the ſaid town of €xton, and all the Tithes of Hay, which in his Park of Bernazdyſhill, or elſe where they have been accuſtomed to receive : Alſo the Paſture of eight Cattle, which they had of the Almes of *Iſabel* his Grand-mother ; granting further that the ſaid Monks, and their men, in the ſaid Town of €xton, ſhall be free and quit of all ſuit of Court, or other ſecular demands and exactions whatſoever ; which Deed bears date, *Wedneſday* next before the feaſt of St. *Mark* the *Evangeliſt, Anno Domini,* 1283.

ib. f. 42.

Afterwards controverſie ariſing between the Prior of St. *Andrews* at Noꝛthampton, and the Vicar of €xton, a compoſition was made, and certified by *John D'Alderby* then Biſhop of Lincoln, the Contents of which was, that the Vicar of the Church of €xton ſhall have in the name of a perpetual Vicarage, all the Alterage of the ſaid Church, and the Tithes of Bernardyſhille, with a compitent houſe, the ſaid Vicar paying to the ſaid Monaſtery two Marks, and alſo paying the Synodals, *Monachi vero procurabunt hoſpitium Archidiaconi* , (*i. e.* The ſaid Monks were to entertain the Archdeacon in his Viſitation, with Proviſion and Lodging, which entertainment was in proceſs of time changed to a certain ſum of Mony, and call'd *Procurations*) This Deed of Certificate bears date at Lydington, 2. *Kall. Mar. Anno Domini* 1310.

Regiſt. Linc.

In the 4*th.* year of *Oliver Sutton* Biſhop of Lincoln, (which was in the 11*th.* of *E.* 1.) the abovemention'd *Bernard de Brus* did preſent *Robert de Tiſho* his Chaplain to the Free-Chappel built *in curia ſua apud* €xton.

Ib.

In the 18*th.* year of *John D'Alderby* Biſhop of Lincoln (which was 10. *E.* 2.) *Bernard de Brus,* Son of the foreſaid *Bernard,* and at that time Lord of €xton, did preſent to the Chantry of the Chappel of the Mannour of €xton.

Of which Chantry I find the following account made and certified in the 2. *E.* 6. by *Richard Cicyl,* Eſquire, and *Thomas Hays,* Commiſſioners appointed to enquire of, and ſurvey all Colledges Chauntries, Free-Chappels, Guilds *&c.* in this County, *viz.*

Certif. pro Com. Rutl. in Offic: Augm. 2 E. 6.

Memorandum, *Of late there was in* €xton *one ſtipendary or Chantry of the yearly Value of* 6 l. *going out of the poſſeſſions of the late Monaſtery of St. Andrews of* Noꝛthampton, *which Sir* John Harrington Kt. *alledgeth to have purchaſed of three years paſt, of the late famous of Memory K.* Henry *the eighth*

The Vicarage of €xton is valued in the Kings Books at, 8 *l.* 7 *s.* 8 *d.*

The preſent Patron is the Right Honorable *Edward* Earl of Gainſbozough, Lord of the Mannour.

Monuments in the Church at *Exton.*

About the Verge of an Antient Alablaſter Tomb, in the Chancel.

✠ Vous qe par ycy paſſer eȝ
    Pur l' almȝ Nichol. Grene pꝛieȝ,
Son Cozps giſt de ſouth cette pere,
Par la Moꝛt qe taunt eſt fere,
€n la cynkauntiſme an moꝛt luy pꝛiſt,
Mercy luy fate Ieſu Criſt, Amen.

On

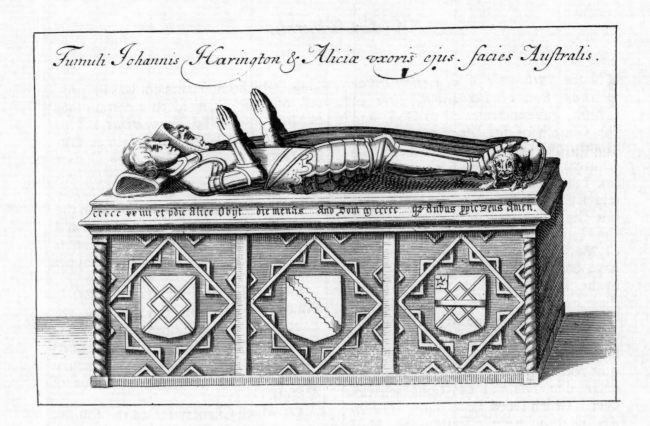

On an Antient Monument ſupporting the Cumbent Statues
of an Armed Knight and his Lady, in the body of
the Church towards the South ſide.

ORate p₂o animabus Johannis Harington ⁊ Aliciæ uxo₂is
ejus, qui quidem Johannes obiit v. die menſis Novemb.
Anno Dom. M. CCCCC. XXIIII. ⁊ p₂edicta Alicia obiit ....
die menſis .... M. CCCCC. ...... quo₂um animabus p₂opitie-
tur Deus, Amen.

In the North Wall of the Chancel, is erected a Curious
Monument with this Inſcription.

HIc ſitus eſt Jacobus Harington de **Exton** *miles, cum vxore*
Lucia, Gulielmi Sidnei *militis filia, ex qua liberos ſuſcepit* 18.
quorum matrimonium contraxerunt tres filii , filiæ octo, maximus natu
filius Johannes *miles hæredem duxit* Roberti Kelway, *Curiæ War-*
dorum, & Liberationum ſuperviſoris. ſecundus Henricus *miles uxorem*
duxit unam ex hæredibus Franciſci Agar *a Conſiliis hibernicis. Ter-*
tius Jacobus *armiger vxorem habuit unam ex hæredibus* Roberti Sapcots *armigeri. Filia natu maxima* Elizabetha *nupſit* Edwardo Montigue *militi. Secunda* Franciſca, Gulielmo Lee *militi. Tertia*
Margareta, *Don* Benito *de* Siſneros Hiſpano *de familia Ducum de*
Fantaſgo. *Quarta* Catherina Edovardo Dimmock *militi. Quinta*
Maria Edovardo Wingfelde *militi; Sexta* Mabilia Andræ Noeli
militi.

Tumulus Iacobi Harington militis & Luciæ vxoris ejus.

militi. Septima Sara *maritum habuit Dominum* Haftings. *Comitis* Huntirgdoniæ Hæredem, *Octava* Theodofia *Dominum* Dudley *de* Caftro Dudley. *Iidem* Jacobus *&* Lucia, *quinquaginta annos in matrimonio vixerunt. Illa prior diem obiit annum agens feptuageffimum fecundum. Ille jam octogenarius fato functus eft, anno affertionis humanæ* 1591. *Reginæ* Eliz. 34. *Uterque filium* Jacobum *folum Executorem conftituerunt, qui ut parentibus fuis jufta perageret, pietatifque fuæ teftimonium pofteris relinqueret, hoc monumentum in perpetuam illorum memoriam, pofuit confecravitque.*

> *Si Genus antiquum, vetere`s`que per atria ceræ,*
> *Si propriæ virtutis adorea Clavus equeftris,*
> *Si foboles numcrofa, & quinquaginta per annos*
> *Inter utramque facem cunctâ caruiffe Querelâ,*
> *Canities fi fera, & Mors matura, beatus,*
> *Denique fi cenfus, cenfuq; beatior omni*
> *Larga manus, fincera fides, reverentia Cæli,*
> *Fœlicem aut vitam, aut mortem fecêre beatam.*
> *Nobis & Vitam & Mortem fecêre beatam.*
> *Nunc cum fata jubent vixiffe, animafq; repofcunt*
> *Sidera, compoffuit cineres, juffitq; fub ifto*
> *Hæredis pietas requiefcere* Maufoleo,

In the South Ile, On a Noble Monument.

HIc jacet *Sepultus* Robertus Keylwey, *infignis (dum vixit) inter togatos armiger, Ingenio, Doctrinâ, & virtute clarus, qui femper bene latuit, vixit chriftianè, & mortuus eft in domino* 21 Februarii *anno falutis noftræ* 1580. *& ætatis fuæ* 84. *Sobolem reliquit fuperftitem* Annam, *folam Hæredem & unicam filiam fibi chariffimam, nuptam* Johanni Harington *de* **Exton**, *militi, quem pro filio & amico intimè femper dilexit: de qua quidem* Annâ *dictus* Johannes *genuit in vita prædicti* Roberti *prolem geminam,* Keylweiium *filium qui mortuus eft, fecundo die menfis* Decembris *An. Dom.* 1570. *& ætatis fuæ* 21 *hebdomodarum, & hic una cum avo tumulatur; &* Luciam *filiam ad huc fuperftitem, cui longam vitam concedat Deus. Ut ergo dicti* Johannes *&* Anna *tam charo & pio parenti jufta perfolvant, & ut gratiffim. animi fui Exemplum Pofteris relinquant, Hoc Monumentum conftruxerunt, illudq;* Keylweyo *patri, &* Keylweyo *filio, (in perpetuam eorum memoriam, fi fic Deo placuerit) dedicarunt, quod fibimet etiam Sepulchrum (Deo favente) deftinant.*

> *Qui generifq; fui fuerat, gentifq; togatæ*
>   *Gloria,* Keylweii *funera flenda vides.*
> *Contulerant in eum variè fua munera Divæ,*
>   *Jufticiæ comites,* Suada, Minerva, Fides.
> *Dum latet in Templi Vir non incautus Afylo,*
>   *Invidia caruit, crevit at ille magis.*
> *Tutius occulto creffit fic arbor in Ævo*
>   *Nititur & tandem, viribus ipfa fuis.*
> *Sed neque fic potuit, venienti obfiftere morti,*
>   *(Sed bene) dum in Chrifto molliter offa cubent.*
> *Dotibus heu nimium mors ô inimica beatis;*
>   *Horrida fic omnes, ad tua luftra trahis.*

Tumulus Roberti Kelwey armigeri, nec non Iohannis Domini Harington &c.

In the North Ile , near the Pulpit ; On a Curious Monument of black and white Marble:

ANNA

Uxor Tho. *Dom.* Bruce *Bar. de* 𝕶𝖎𝖓𝖑𝖔𝖘𝖘𝖊
Filia Roberti Chichester *Eq. Baln.*
Familia illustri in agro Devonien.
Matrem habuit
Franciscam *filiam & ex semisse hæred.*
Johan. *Dom.* Harrington *Bar. de* 𝕰𝖗𝖙𝖔𝖓.
ipsa matris Hæres ex asse.
Fæmina
Pudicitiæ, tum recti scientia, tum amore
in Conjugem intenso, munitissimæ.
Nobilissimis moribus, serenitate perpetua,
Ingeniiq; admirabili elegantia,
Placentissima.
Convixit marito An. iv *mens.* ix. *peperitq;*
ei filium Rob. Bruce *superstitem,*
Eo Partu
Cum esset absumpta omnis vis Corporis,
Sanctissimam animam, pia morte,
Paucos post dies, deo reddidit,
Die xx. *Martii Anno Ætat. suæ* xxii.
Humanæ Salut. MDCXXVII.
Dilectissimæ conjugi,
Ob egregias Virtutes & Insignia in se merita,
Monumentum hoc bremevq; titulum
faciund. cur. Moer. Mar.

On

Tumuli Annæ Dominæ Bruce, facies Borealis.

*On the other side of the same Monument
The like in English.*

ANne, Wife to *Thomas* Lord *Bruce* Baron of 𝕶𝖎𝖓𝖑𝖔𝖘𝖘𝖊, Daughter of Sir *Robert Chichester* Knight of the Bath, of an antient Family in the County of 𝕯𝖊𝖇𝖔𝖓, and of *Frances* one of the two Daughters and Coheirs of *John* Lord *Harrington* Baron of 𝕰𝖗𝖙𝖔𝖓, sole heir to her Mother; A Lady endowed with a natural disposition to Vertue, a true understanding of honour, most noble behaviour, perpetual cheerfulness, most eligant Conversation, and a more than ordinary conjugal affection. She was married *iv.* years and *ix.* months, and left one only child named *Robert Bruce.* Weakened by that birth she died in Childbirth, the *xx.* day of *March,* in the *xxii.* year of her age, *Anno Domini* M. DC. XXVII. Erected and inscribed to the memory of his most beloved, and most deserving Wife, by *Tho.* Lord *Bruce.*

On a Neat Monument, lately erected, in the North side
of the Church.

JAcobus Noel, Baptistæ *Vicecomitis de* **Campden**, *è quarta
Uxore* Elizabetâ, Montacuti *Comitis de* **Linsey** *magni Came-
rarii* **Anglie**, *filiâ, Filius quintus ; ingentis spei juvenis, formâ præcel-
lens æque ac Staturâ eminens : insigni supra annos tam animi quam
Corporis cultu, & vigore præditus, obiit* Junii 24. 1681. *Ætatis
suæ* 18.

    *Quem Puerum forsan facies dixissit & ætas,
       Fecerat hunc virtus, atque Statura Virum.
    Maturus vixit, licet immaturus obivet ;
       Ingenii vis hoc, mors dedit illud, Opus.*

Great as his birth did all his actions shew,
His very Recreations spoke him so.
Spritely his Meen, yet Grave, discreet, and Wise,
Free from the Ages grand Debaucheries.
Virtue with Stature still his years outran ;
He dyed in's Nonage, and yet lived a Man.

Eodem fato conjunctus Linseius *ejusdem* Baptistæ *&* Elizabetæ
Filius primulus, qui obiit anniculus Martii 12. *An. Domini*, 1656.

*Item eorundem parentum Filius quartus, cui ob præproperum nimis
fatum defuit Prænomen*, 1662.

Jacobus Noel
Bapt Vic Cam de

EZENDEN.

Lyes in the East Hundred. At the time of *Domesday* survey, *Walterius* held of the Bishop of **Lincoln**, in this Town, one Hide of Land; of Arable six Carucates, in demesne two Carucates, with one Servant, and five *Bordarii*, possessing four Carucates: Here was at that time a mill of 16. s. and three acres of meadow, a Wood six furlongs in length and four broad: all then worth 5 *l. Bardi tenuit cum* Saca & Soca. How this *Bardi* was related to the old *Saxon* Barons of **Easindine**, I know not. Of whom we read, that when the Danes invaded **England** about *An. Dom.* 1016. the then Baron of **Easindine** with the men of **Stamford** gave them Battail near that Town, and beat them back for a time.

In the 5th. year of H. 2. *William de Buffew* was Lord of this Mannour. Which *William* married *Rohesia*, Daughter and Coheir of *Baldwin* Son of *Gilbert de Gant* E. of **Lincoln** and Baron of **Bourn**. The said *William* dying about the 31. H. 2. it was found by office taken after his death, that *Rohesia* his Widdow was at the Kings disposal, that she was 60. years of age, that her land in **Issenden** was of the value of 10. l. that her stock was three plows and a hundred sheep, that within eight years she had received from the profits of her Wood 10. marks, and 10. s. of the profits of her Courts, and that she hath two Daughters her Heirs, one of which is married to *Hugh Wak*, the other to *John de Bully*. That which I find further memorable of this *Rohesia de Buffew* is, that she gave by her deed to the Monks of St. *Andrews* at **Northampton**, eighteen acres of Land in her demesne, with the tithes of the Asserts (or Inclosures) of **Esenden**, in perpetual almes; in like manner as they hold the Chappel with all the tithes of the said Town: quitting and discharging by the same deed the said Monks, and all their men, from all Exactions relating to any harvest works, *ad Colligendas Messes*. After the death of which Lady, the above mentioned *John de Bully* became Lord of this Mannour, in right of his wife, and dying left issue *Idonea* his Daughter and sole heir, who about 13. *Joh.* became the wife of *Robert de Veteri ponte*, or *Vipont*, Hereditary Sheriff of **Westmerland**, whose Son, another *Robert de Vipont*, had issue two Daughters his Coheirs, *Isabella* marry'd to *Robert de Clifford*, and *Idonea* first marryd to *Roger de Leiborn*, and after his death to *John* Lord *Cromwel*; to whom, and to his Wife, and her Heirs K. E. 2. in the 2. year of his reign granted liberty of Free Warren in this Lordship, among several others at that time in their possession. But this Lady *Idonea* dying about the 8th. year of E. 3. This Mannour came, upon her death, to *Edward Dispenser*, Grandson to *Hugh Dispenser jun.* who suffer'd in 20. E. 2.

Afterward in the time of *Edward* 4. the Mannour of **Ezendine** was possest by *Richard Nevil* Earl of **Warwick**, in right of *Anne* his Wife, Daughter and in fine heir to *Richard Beauchamp*, Earl of **Warwick**, and *Isabel* his Wife, Daughter and Heir of *Thomas* Lord *Dispencer*, grandson of the abovementioned *Edward Dispenser*.

How afterwards this Estate came to the Crown, *vid. infra*, in **Uppingham**.

In the 36 H. 8. this Lordship being then in the Crown as parcel of the Earl of **Warwicks** Land, was purchased by *Richard Cecil*, at that time Yeoman of the Wardrobe to the King; whose Son and Heir *William* being a person of great Learning, singular Judgment, admirable Moderation, and comely Gravity, came to be the cheifest Statesman of the Age wherein he lived: and was by Queen *Elizabeth* in the 13th. year of her Reign, advanced to the degree and dignity of a Baron of this Realm by the title of Lord **Burghley**: and in the 26th. *El.* install'd Knight of the most noble Order of the Garter; which *William* Lord **Burghley** departed this

Domesd. in Northa. n. 5.

But. Sur. of Stamford. 22.

31. H. 2. Rot. de dominabus & puellis.

M. S. Wing. Bodenham m. fo. 44.

Car. 2. E. 2ᵃ n. 49.

Bar. Eng. 1. Vol. 395.

Bar. Eng. 1. Vol. 307.

Bar. Eng. 2. Vol. 405.

this life *An.* 1598. (40. *El.*) leaving issue by *Mary* his first Wife, *Thomas* his Son and Heir, and by *Mildred* his second Wife, another Son named *Robert.* Which said *Thomas* Lord 𝕭𝖚𝖗𝖌𝖍𝖑𝖊𝖞 was in the 41. *El.* constitued Warden of 𝕽𝖔𝖈𝖐𝖎𝖓𝖌𝖍𝖆𝖒 Forest, and Constable of the Castle there, for life; and in the 3d. of King *James* created Earl of 𝕰𝖝𝖊𝖙𝖊𝖗. *Robert* the 2d. Son of the said *William* Lord 𝕭𝖚𝖗𝖌𝖍𝖑𝖊𝖞, being in the 38th. of Queen *Elizabeth* made one of the Queens Principal Secretaries of State, was in the first of King *James* created Lord *Cecil* of 𝕰𝖘𝖎𝖓𝖌𝖉𝖔𝖓 *in Com.*

𝕽𝖔𝖙𝖊𝖑. in the 2. *Jac.* Vicount 𝕮𝖗𝖆𝖓= 𝖇𝖚𝖗𝖓𝖊, in the 3. *Jac.* Earl of 𝕾𝖆𝖑𝖎𝖘𝖇𝖚𝖗𝖞, and in the 6th. of that King Lord Treasurer of 𝕰𝖓𝖌𝖑𝖆𝖓𝖉; he was also Knight of the most noble Order of the Garter, and Chancellour of the University of 𝕮𝖆𝖒𝖇𝖗𝖎𝖉𝖌𝖊; which Earl *Robert* dying, *An.* 1612. left issue *William* his Son and Heir, whose Heir apparant *Charles* dyed in his Fathers life time, but left issue *James*, who upon the death of his Grandfather *An.* 1668. became Earl of 𝕾𝖆𝖑𝖎𝖘𝖇𝖚𝖗𝖞 and Baron of 𝕰𝖘𝖎𝖓𝖌𝖉𝖔𝖓.

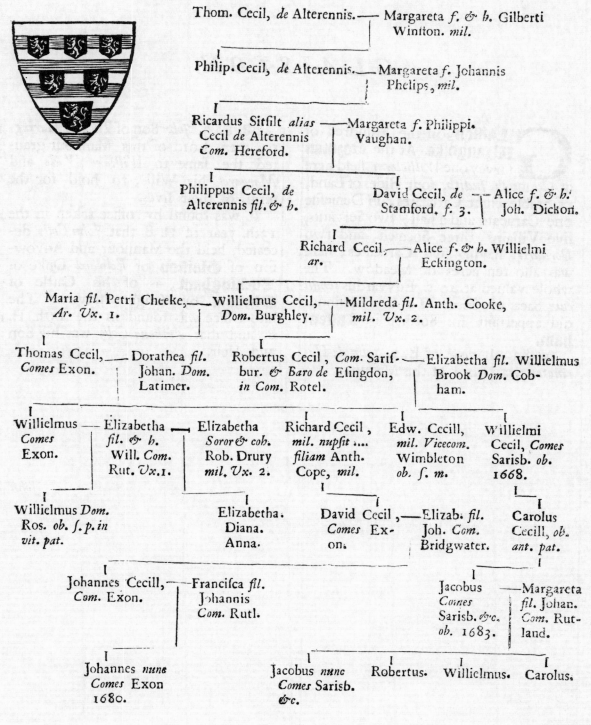

Thom. Cecil, *de Alterennis.* —— Margareta *f. & h.* Gilberti Winston. *mil.*

Philip. Cecil, *de Alterennis.* —— Margareta *f.* Johannis Phelips, *mil.*

Ricardus Sitsilt *alias* Cecil *de Alterennis Com.* Hereford. —— Margareta *f.* Philippi. Vaughan.

Philippus Cecil, *de Alterennis fil. & h.*   David Cecil, *de* —— Alice *f. & h.* Stamford. *f.* 3. | Joh. Dickon.

Richard Cecil, —— Alice *f. & h.* Willielmi *ar.* | Eckington.

Maria *fil.* Petri Cheeke, —— Willielmus Cecil, —— Mildreda *fil.* Anth. Cooke, *Ar. Ux.* 1. | *Dom.* Burghley. | *mil. Ux.* 2.

Thomas Cecil, —— Dorathea *fil.* *Comes* Exon. | Johan. *Dom.* Latimer.   Robertus Cecil, *Com.* Sarisbur. *& Baro de* Esingdon, *in Com.* Rotel. —— Elizabetha *fil.* Willielmus Brook *Dom.* Cobham.

Willielmus *Comes* Exon. —— Elizabetha *fil. & h.* Will. *Com.* Rut. *Ux.* 1.   Elizabetha *Soror & coh.* Rob. Drury *mil. Ux.* 2.   Richard Cecil, *mil. nupsit ....* *filiam* Anth. Cope, *mil.*   Edw. Cecill, *mil. Vicecom.* Wimbleton *ob. s. m.*   Willielmi Cecil, *Comes* Sarisb. *ob.* 1668.

Willielmus *Dom.* Ros. *ob. s. p. in vit. pat.*   Elizabetha. Diana. Anna.   David Cecil, *Comes* Exon. —— Elizab. *fil.* Joh. *Com.* Bridgwater.   Carolus Cecill, *ob. ant. pat.*

Johannes Cecill, —— Francisca *fil.* *Com.* Exon. | Johannis *Com.* Rutl.   Jacobus *Comes* Sarisb. *&c.* *ob.* 1683. —— Margareta *fil.* Johan. *Com.* Rutland.

Johannes *nunc Comes* Exon 1680.   Jacobus *nunc Comes* Sarisb. *&c.*   Robertus.   Willielmus.   Carolus.

Of

Of the Church.

M.S. Wingf.
Bodenham mil.

ABout the latter end of the Reign of H. 2. *Baldwin Bueloth,* who had marryed *Rohefia* the Widdow of *William de Buffey* (or *Buffew*) did with the confent of his Wife and the Heirs of the faid *William de Buffey,* give and grant in perpetual Almes, to the Monks of St. *Andrews* of 𝕹𝖔𝖗𝖙𝖍𝖆𝖒𝖕𝖙𝖔𝖓 , twelve acres of Land in his Demefnes in 𝕰𝖘𝖘𝖊𝖓𝖉𝖊𝖓. For which guift, the faid Monks undertook to find a Chaplain to refide continually in 𝕰𝖘𝖘𝖊𝖓𝖉𝖊𝖓 , and to fupply the Cure of the Chappel there.

GLAISTON.

Domefd. North.
56.

GLaifton, in the Hundred of 𝖂𝖗𝖆𝖓𝖌𝖉𝖎𝖐𝖊. At the 𝕹𝖔𝖗𝖒𝖆𝖓 furvey one *Willielmus* held here of Countefs *Judith,* four Hides of Land, of arable eight Carucates, in Demefne one Carucate and a half, two Servants, five Villains, three Socmen, and two *Bordarii,* having five Carucates, here was alfo ten acres of Meadow. The whole valued at 40 s. *Edvvardus tenuit cum* Saca *&* Soca. To this Mannour did appertain fix Socmen in 𝕷𝖚𝖋𝖋𝖊𝖓𝖍𝖆𝖒.

Nom. Vill. in
Scacc.

In the 9th year of E. 2. *John de Harington* was Lord of this Mannour.

28. E. 3. *John* Son of *Thomas Harington* then Lord of this Mannour granted the fame to *William Wade* and *Margaret* his Wife, to hold for the term of their lives.

M.S. Wing.
Bodenham m.
f. 91.

It was found by office taken in the 13th. year of H. 8. that *John Colly* deceafed, held the Mannour and Advowfon of 𝕲𝖑𝖆𝖎𝖘𝖙𝖔𝖓 of *Edward* Duke of 𝕭𝖚𝖈𝖐𝖎𝖓𝖌𝖍𝖆𝖒, as of his Caftle of 𝕺𝖐𝖊𝖍𝖆𝖒 by Knights fervice. The like Office was found in the 15th. H. 8. and that *Anthony Colly* was his Son and Heir.

Efc. 13. H. 8.

Efc. 15. H. 8.

John

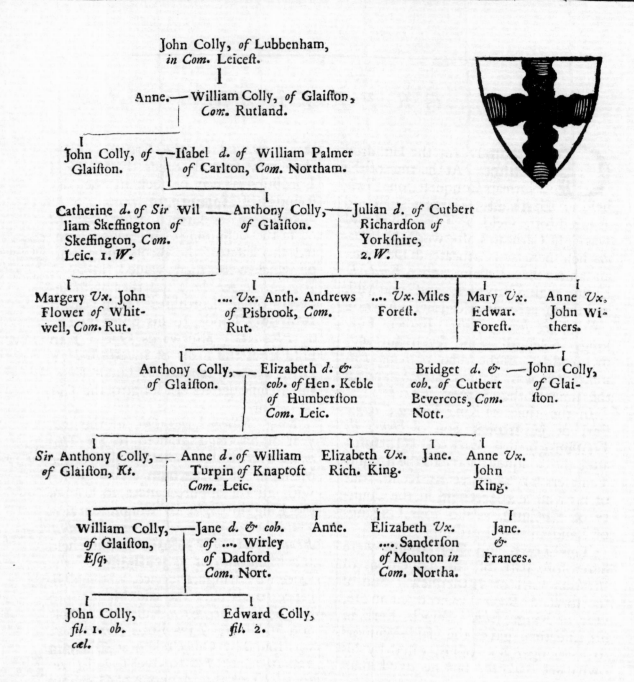

John Colly, *of* Lubbenham, *in Com.* Leiceſt.

Anne.— William Colly, *of* Glaiſton, *Com.* Rutland.

John Colly, *of* —Iſabel *d. of* William Palmer Glaiſton. *of* Carlton, *Com.* Northam.

Catherine *d. of Sir* William Skeffington *of* Skeffington, *Com.* Leic. 1. *W.* — Anthony Colly, *of* Glaiſton. — Julian *d. of* Cutbert Richardſon *of* Yorkſhire, 2. *W.*

Margery *Vx.* John Flower *of* Whitwell, *Com.* Rut. | .... *Vx.* Anth. Andrews *of* Pisbrook, *Com.* Rut. | .... *Vx.* Miles Foreſt. | Mary *Vx.* Edwar. Foreſt. | Anne *Vx,* John Withers.

Anthony Colly, *of* Glaiſton. — Elizabeth *d. & coh. of* Hen. Keble *of* Humberſton *Com.* Leic. — Bridget *d. & coh. of* Cutbert Bevercots, *Com.* Nott. —John Colly, *of* Glaiſton.

Sir Anthony Colly, *of* Glaiſton, *Kt.* — Anne *d. of* William Turpin *of* Knaptoſt *Com.* Leic. | Elizabeth *Vx.* Rich. King. | Jane. | Anne *Vx.* John King.

William Colly, *of* Glaiſton, *Eſq*; — Jane *d. & coh. of* .... Wirley *of* Dadford *Com.* Nort. | Anne. | Elizabeth *Vx.* .... Sanderſon *of* Moulton *in Com.* Northa. | Jane. *&* Frances.

John Colly, *fil.* 1. *ob. cæl.* | Edward Colly, *fil.* 2.

Of the ADVOWSON.

Reg. Linc.

Comp. Johannis Doddington, *pro com* Rutl. *in Offic. Augm.* 3. *E.* 6.

Ex Autogr. pennes Janam Andrews *Viduam.*

IN the 10. *H.* 3. The Prior of **Laund** preſented to the Church of **Glaiſton**, ſo alſo in 21. *H.* 3.

To which ſaid Priory of **Laund** the Incumbent of the Church of **Glaiſton** did pay an Annual penſion of 6 *s.* 8 *d.* at the Feaſt of St. *Michael* yearly.

In the 26. *Car.* 1 (1640.) Sir *Anthony Colly* Knight, then Lord of this Mannor, joyned with his Son and Heir apparent, *William Colly* Eſquire, in a

Conveyance of divers parcels of Land in **Glaiſton**, together with the Advowſon of the Church there, to *Edward Andrews* of **Bisbooke** in this County, Eſquire: Which Advowſon is ſince conveyed over to *Peterhouſe* in **Cambiidge**.

The Rectory of **Glaiſton** is valued in the Kings Books at 12 *l.* 16 *s.* 9 *d.*

The preſent Patron is

K

GREETHAM

GREETHAM.

Greetham lyes in the Hundred of **Alftoe**. At the time of the Norman Conqueft, one *Goda* held in **Greetham** 3. Carucates of Land as rated to the Geld or Tax. The Land was eight Carucates, afterwards K. *William* held here two Carucates in Demefne, and thirty three Villains, and 4. *Bordarii*, having eight Carucates, and one Mill, and feven acres of Meadow. A wood (*Silva per loca paftilis*) fixteen Furlongs in length, and feven furlongs in breadth. In the time of King *Edward* this was valued at 7 *l.* and at the time of the Survey at 10 *l.*

Domefday Tit. Rotel.

In the time of King *Steven*, *Roger* Earl of **Warwick** Son of *Henry de* **Newburgh**, firft Earl of **Warwick** after the Conqueft, gave to the Knights Templers 11 *s.* of yearly Rent, out of his Mill at **Greetham** in the County of **Rutland**, as alfo four Oxgangs of Land in that Lordfhip.

Bar. Eng. 1. *Vol.* 69.

This Town and **Cottefmore** were heretofore part of the poffeffions of *Walleran* Earl of **Warwick** (Son of the forefaid *Roger*) who dyed in 6*th*, year of King *John*. Which Earl in his Life time gave the faid Mannors to a younger Son of his, call'd by his own name *Waleran*, but he dyed iffuelefs.

Bar. Eng. 1. *Vol.* 71.

Which Eftate together with the Earldome of **Warwick** came not long after to *William de Mauduit*, in right of *Alice* his Mother, Daughter of the firft abovemention'd *Waleran*.

Afterwards it defcended among other large Poffeffions as well in this County as elfewhere, to the Family of the *Beauchamps* Earls alfo of **Warwick**, till forfeited by *Thomas* one of thofe Earls, it was by King *Richard* 2. granted with the reft of that Earls Eftate in this County to *Thomas Mowbray* then Earl of **Nottingham**, and afterwards advanced to the Title of Duke of **Norfolk**, from which time to the reign of *Hen.* 7. It had the fame poffeffors with **Uppingham**, and by the fame means

Bar. Eng. 1. *Vol.* 129.

was conveyed to the Crown, together with feveral other Eftates and Lordfhips, as may be feen in the defcription of **Uppingham**, *infra*.

Being in the Crown, King *Edward* 6. in the beginning of his reign, granted this Eftate (the Rents and profits of which were then valued at 26 *l.* 10 *s.* 4 *d. ob. per An.*) together with feveral other Lordfhips then called **Warwick** Lands, to his Sifter the Lady *Elizabeth* (afterwards Queen) to hold from the Feaft of St. *Michael* 38 *H.* 8. *durante beneplacito*: but it feems this demife lafted not long to the faid Lady, for

Comp. pro Com Rutland. in Offic. Augm. 3 E. 6.

King *Edward* the 6*th*. in the 3*d.* year of his reign granted to Sir *Thomas Cheyney* Knight, *inter alia*, all that the Mannour of **Greetham** (*Com. Rut.*) with all the appurtenances, to hold of the King in *Capite* by Knights Service.

Pat. 3. *E.* 6: *p.* 7.

In the 3*d.* year of Queen *Elizabeth Francis* Earl of **Bedford**, who then held the Mannour of **Greetham** of the Queen by Knights fervice, obtain'd licence to alienate the faid Mannour to Sir *James Harrington* Knight. Whofe Son and heir, *John* Lord *Harrington*, was found by Office taken at **Okeham** 22. *Mar.* 13 *Jac.* to dye feized (*inter alia*) of the Mannour of **Greetham** which he held in *Capite*, by the 40*th.* part of a Knights Fee.

3 Eliz. p. 5:

Efc. 14. *Jac. p.* 2. *n.* 116.

I find that King *James* granted his Licence, dated 1 *April* in the 21. year of his reign, to *Edward* Lord *Noel* to alienate the Mannour of **Greetham** to *George* (then) Marquifs of **Buckingham**; whofe fon and heir the right Noble *George* Duke of **Buckingham** is the prefent Lord of this Mannour.

Rot. Pat. 21 *Jac.*

Befides what relates to the Mannour of **Greetham**, it was found by Office taken in 20 *El.* that *Jane* wife of *Thomas Lynne* was the Daughter and next Heir of *Jane Troughton* deceafed, who held two Meffuages, two Clofes, of which one is called, *Temple-Barnes* the

Efc. 20. *El.*

the other *Temple fields*, lying in 𝖲𝗍𝗋𝖾𝗍=𝗍𝗈𝗇 and 𝖦𝗋𝖾𝖺𝗍𝗁𝖺𝗆, and one Wood called 𝕿𝖍𝖎𝖈𝖐𝖒𝖔𝖟𝖊 in 𝖦𝗋𝖾𝖺𝗍𝗁𝖺𝗆, by Eſtimation nine acres of Land, and one other Wood in 𝖦𝗋𝖾𝖺𝗍𝗁𝖺𝗆 call'd 𝕱𝖚𝖑𝖑𝖜𝖔𝖔𝖉, containing by Eſtimation nine acres, all which were held of the Queen in *Capite* by Knights ſervice.

Of the ADVOWSON.

Reg. Linc.

In the 22. *H.* 3. The Prior of the Holy Sepulcher at 𝖶𝖺𝗋𝗐𝗂𝖼𝗄 preſented to the Vicarage of the Church of 𝖦𝗋𝖾𝖺𝗍𝗁𝖺𝗆: *Quæ conſiſtit in toto alteragio, & manſo competenti, ſolvend. dictis Canonicis unam marcam.*

Antiq. of Warwic. p. 364.

When this Church was firſt given to the ſaid Priory is uncertain, but at the ſurvey of that Houſe 26 *H.* 8. the Rectory of this Church was found to be part of their Poſſeſſions.

In the 3 *E.* 6. the Rectory here late belonging to the Priory of *S. Sepulchers* at 𝖶𝖺𝗋𝗐𝗂𝖼𝗄 ſuppreſt, was farm'd at the yearly rent of 4 *l.* 6 *s.* 8 *d.*

Comp. pro Com Rutl. in Office Augm. 3. E. 6.

In the 11. year of King *James*, *John* Lord 𝖧𝖺𝗋𝗋𝗂𝗇𝗀𝗍𝗈𝗇 the elder dyed ſeiz'd of the Rectory of 𝖦𝗋𝖾𝖺𝗍𝗁𝖺𝗆; which Rectory he held in ſoccage of the Honour of 𝖧𝖺𝗆𝗉𝗍𝗈𝗇 Court, by Fealty onely.

Eſt. 14. Jac. p. 2. n. 116.

The Vicarage of 𝖦𝗋𝖾𝖺𝗍𝗁𝖺𝗆 is valued in the Kings Books at, 5 *l.* 3 *s.* 8 *d.*

The preſent Patron is the Duke of 𝖡𝗎𝖼𝗄𝗂𝗇𝗀𝗁𝖺𝗆.

GUNTHORPE.

𝕲Unthorp is now onely the name of certain Grounds in the Hundred of 𝖬𝖺𝗋𝗍𝗂𝗇ſ𝗅𝖾𝗒, and Pariſh of 𝖮𝗄𝖾𝗁𝖺𝗆. Yet here was formerly a Village, tho at preſent not the leaſt ſign of a Town remaining more than one poor Shepherds Cottage. And at *Domeſday* ſurvey it was included as one of the five *Berews* or Hamlets belonging to 𝖮𝖼𝗁𝖾𝗁𝖺𝗆 *Chercheſcch*, the other four being 𝖫𝖺𝗇𝗀𝗁𝖺𝗆, 𝖡𝖺𝗋=𝗅𝗒𝗍𝗁𝗈𝗋𝗉𝖾, 𝖤𝗀𝗅𝖾𝗍𝗈𝗇, and 𝖡𝗋𝗈𝗈𝗄.

Nom. Vill.

In the Reign of *E.* 2. *William de Hocot* held 𝖦𝗎𝗇𝗍𝗁𝗈𝗋𝗉𝖾 of *Margaret* Counteſſe of 𝖢𝗈𝗋𝗇𝗐𝖺𝗅𝗅, Widow of *Pierce de Gaveſton*, who at that time poſſeſt the Lordſhips of 𝖮𝗄𝖾𝗁𝖺𝗆, 𝖤𝗀𝗂𝗅𝗍𝗈𝗇, 𝖫𝖺𝗇𝗀𝗁𝖺𝗆, and divers other Revenues in this County.

Of late years this Eſtate was poſſeſt by Sir *Hugh Ducy* Knight of the Bath, 4th. Son of Sir *Robert Ducy* Knight and Baronet, Lord Mayor of 𝖫𝗈𝗇𝖽𝗈𝗇 in the year 1630. Which ſaid Sir *Hugh Ducy* dyed poſſeſt hereof, about the beginning of the year 1663. (being then high Sheriffe of this County) from whom it is derived to the preſent Owner, Mr. *John Flavell* of 𝖫𝗈𝗇=𝖽𝗈𝗇 Citizen and Merchant Taylor.

HAMBLETON·

Domesd. in Tit.
Rotel.

IN the Hundred of 𝕸𝖆𝖗𝖙𝖎𝖓𝖘𝖑𝖞. Of this Estate, thus *Domesday* book. In 𝕳𝖆𝖒𝖊𝖑𝖉𝖚𝖓𝖊 *Cherchesoch*, with the seven *Berews* or Hamlets thereunto belonging, Queen *Eddid* held four Carucates of Land, as rated to the Tax or *Geld.* The arable Land was sixteen Carucates. Here at the time of the survey the King had five Carucates in Demesne, and one hundred and forty Villains, and thirteen *Bordarii*, having forty Carucates. Here were at that time three Priests and three Churches, to which did belong one *Bovate* and eight acres of Land. Here was one Mill of 21 *s.* 4 *d.* and forty acres of Meadow. A Wood (*Silva minuta fertilis per loca*) three miles in length, and one mile in breadth. In the time of King *Edward* this estate was valued at 52 *l.* This whole Mannour with the seven Berews is computed, in that Record, to be three miles and eight

Leuca Anglicana 12. *Quarantenas continebat.*

furlongs in length, and two miles and eight furlongs in breadth.

After this 𝕳𝖆𝖒𝖇𝖑𝖊𝖙𝖔𝖓 belonged to the

M. S. *Winf.*
Bod. *mil f.* 97.

Lord *Umfrevil*, for I find that in the 11th. year of E. 3. *Gilbert* Son of *Robert de Umfrevil* Earl of *Angos*, released to *Giles de Badlesmere* all his right in this Lordship : But it seems the Father of the said *Giles* had an Estate here long before, for in the 9. E. 2.

Nom Vill.

it is recorded that *Bartholmew* Lord

Bar. Eng. 2.
Vol. 58.

Badlesmere, an eminent Baron in those days, obtain'd a Charter of Freewarren in all his Demesne Lands, in particular in this Mannour, and 𝕸𝖆𝖗𝖐𝖊𝖙 𝕺𝖗𝖙𝖔𝖓 in this County. After whose death this Estate descended to Sir *Giles de Badlesmere* his Son and Heir, who dying

Bar. Eng. 2.
Voll. 59. and 1.
Vol. 185.

without issue in 12. E. 3. 𝕳𝖆𝖒𝖇𝖑𝖊𝖙𝖔𝖓 was assigned to *William de Bohun* Earl of 𝕹𝖔𝖗𝖙𝖍𝖆𝖒𝖕𝖙𝖔𝖓, in right of *Elizabeth* his Wife one of the Sisters and Coheirs of the said *Giles.*

Bar. Eng. 1.
Vol. 559.

In the 9th. year of H. 4. *John* Lord *Lovel* died seized of the Mannour of 𝕳𝖆𝖒𝖇𝖑𝖊𝖙𝖔𝖓, which he had in right of

Maude his Wife, Daughter and Heir to *Robert de Holland*, a Baron of this Realm.

It was found by Office taken in the 7 H. 4. that *Edward* Son and Heir of *Edmund* late Duke of 𝕸𝖔𝖗𝖐 (which *Edward* was the first Earl of 𝕽𝖚𝖙𝖑𝖆𝖓𝖉) held of the King among other Lands, one Cottage, one hundred and fifty three acres of Land, eleven acres of meadow in 𝕳𝖆𝖒𝖇𝖑𝖊𝖙𝖔𝖓 *magna* in the County of 𝕽𝖚𝖙𝖑𝖆𝖓𝖉, and forty two acres of Land, and two acres of meadow in 𝕭𝖞𝖍𝖆𝖑𝖑 in the same County, called 𝕻𝖊𝖒𝖇𝖗𝖔𝖐𝖊𝖘 Lands, as members appurtaining to the Castle and Mannour of 𝕱𝖔𝖉𝖊𝖗𝖎𝖓𝖌𝖍𝖆𝖞; all which he held by the service of one Knights Fee.

H. 7. H. 4. ex
parte Rem.
Thes. in Scacc.

19 H. 7. It was found by Office that *Henry Ferrers* held the Mannour of 𝕳𝖆𝖒𝖇𝖑𝖊𝖙𝖔𝖓 with its appurtenances, of the King by Fealty onely, and that *Edward Ferrers* was his Son and Heir.

Esc. 19 H. 7.

It was found by Office taken at 𝕶𝖊𝖙𝖙𝖔𝖓 in this County, on the 7. *Nov.* 15 H. 8. Before *John Mollesworth* Escheator, that *Richard Flowr* Esquire dyed seized (*inter alia*) of the Mannour of little 𝕳𝖆𝖒𝖇𝖑𝖊𝖙𝖔𝖓, and of two hundred acres of Land, twenty acres of meadow with the appurtenances in 𝕳𝖆𝖒𝖇𝖑𝖊𝖙𝖔𝖓 aforesaid; Also of two messuages, eighty acres of Land, twenty acres of meadow in Great 𝕳𝖆𝖒𝖇𝖑𝖊𝖙𝖔𝖓 : All which he held of *Edward Ferrars* Knight, as of his Mannour of Great 𝕳𝖆𝖒𝖇𝖑𝖊𝖙𝖔𝖓, by Fealty onely; and that *Roger Flower* was his Son and next Heir.

Esc. 15. H. 8.
n. 23.

In the 43. year of Queen *Elizabeth*, *Henry Ferrers* obtain'd the Queens Licence dated 1. *Julii*, to alienate his Mannour of 𝕳𝖆𝖒𝖇𝖑𝖊𝖙𝖔𝖓 in the County of 𝕽𝖚𝖙𝖑𝖆𝖓𝖉, to Sir *John Harrington* Knight.

Rot. *Pat.* 43.
Eliz. *pars.* 19.

It was found by Office taken at 𝕺𝖐𝖊𝖍𝖆𝖒 in this County on the 22. *March*, 13. *Jacobi*, before *Edward Harrington* Knight, *William Bulstrode* Knight, *John Reading*, Gen. Feodaries, that *John* Lord *Harrington* the elder dyed seized (*inter*

Esc. 14. Jac.
P. 2. *n.* 116:

ter alia) of the Mannour of **Hambleton** *alias* **Hamblesdon** *cum pertinentiis* in **Edyweston, Manton, Normanton, Empingham, Egliston,** which he held in *Capite* by Knights Service, but by what part of a Knights Fee the Jury knew not.

The prefent Lord of this Mannour is the right Noble *George* Duke of **Buckingham.**

Of the ADVOWSON.

Reg. Linc.

In the 15 *H.* 3. the Advowſon of the Church of **Hamildon** was adjudged to belong to the Biſhop of **Lincoln,** together with the Chappel of **Brandeſton,** and a penſion of 20 *s.* from the Church of *St. Peters* in **Stamford.**

Ib.

In the 34. *H.* 3. *Robert Groſted* then Biſhop of **Lincoln,** with the conſent of the Rector of the Church of **Hamildon,** granted to *John Talbothe* of **Fincham,** Son of *Geoffry Talbothe* and to *Martina* his Wife, and to their heirs for ever, Licence to have a Chappel in their Houſe at Little **Hameldon,** *ſine fontibus & Campana, ſibi & liberæ Familiæ ſuæ, per proprium Capellanum ſuum in eadem Capella, ſumptibus propriis & oneribus.* Which Deed bears date at **Ludington** in the 15th. year of the ſaid Biſhops Conſecration.

In the 2. *E.* 1. *Robert de Bannebar* was preſented by the Chapter of **Lincoln** to the Vicarage of the Church of **Hamildon,** and inſtituted to the ſame at **Bukeden** by *Richard Graveſend* then Biſhop of **Lincoln,** 13. *Kalend. Aug.* in the 16th. year of his conſecration: Which living was found to conſiſt, at that time, not only in the Vicaral Tythes in **Hamildon,** and **Braunſton,** but alſo in certain profits ariſing from **Normanton, Lindon, Martinſthorpe, Weſton,** and **Manton.**

Reg. Linc.

The Vicarage of the Church of **Hamelden** is valued in the Kings Books at, 10 *l.* 17 *s.* 0 *d.*

The preſent Patron is

HARDWICK.

Yes in the Eaſt hundred, and was formerly a Village, though now the Name only of certain Grounds adjoyning to **Empingham:** With which Town it was no doubt ſurveyed, as a Member of the ſame, at the time of the Norman Survey, in regard I find no mention of **Hardwick** in *Domeſday* Book.

In the 9. *E.* 2. **Hardwick** had the the ſame Lord with **Empingham,** *viz. William de Baſings,* from whom both the ſaid Eſtates are derived by marriage to the *Mackworths,* who now enjoy the ſame.

Nom Vil.

HORN.

HORN, formerly a Town and Pariſh, now only the Name of certain Grounds and a *Sine-Cure,* lyes in the Eaſt hundred.

Domeſd. Northam. n. 3.

At the time of *Domeſday* Survey, the Biſhop of **Durham** held two hides of the King in **Horne,** of arable four Carucates, in Demeſne one Carucate, one Sockman, a Prieſt, twelve Villains, ſeven *Bordarii,* and one Servant, having four Carucates; here were at that time three Mills of 20 *s.* and a Wood of one furlong and twelve Perches in length, and ſeventeen Perches broad; all valued at 4 *l.* Langfer *tenuit de Rege E. cum* Saca *&* Soca.

At the ſame time *Grimbaldus* held of the Counteſs *Judith,* one Hide in **Horne,** of arable two Carucates, in Demeſne one Carucate, two Servants,

Id. ib. n. 561

& duæ ancillæ, nine Villains, and four *Bordarii*, having two Carucates; here was also in this tenure a mill of 4 *s.* 8 *d.* all formerly valued at 20 *s.* but at that time at 30 *s.*

Nom. Vill. in Scacc.

In the 9th. year of *E.* 2. *Allanus de Franckton*, and *William de Basings* were Lords of **Horne**.

Esc. 1. *Ma.*

It was found by Office taken in the first year of Queen *Mary*, that Sir *John Harington* Knight, held two parts of the Mannour of **Horne**, and divers other Lands in **Horne** of the Queen *in Capite*, by Knights service, together with several other Estates in this County, in the said Office mention'd. And that *James Harington* is his Son and Heir. In which honourable Family of the *Haringtons* this Mannor of **Horn** continued till in the Reign of King *James*, the Sisters and Coheirs of *John* the last Lord *Harington* of **Exton**, conveyed the same to Sir *Baptist Hicks*, whose Daughter and Coheir *Julian*, being

marryed to *Edward* Lord *Noel*, brought this Estate into that honourable Family, where it remains at this day.

Of the ADVOWSON.

HOrnfeild, *olim Ecclesia, modo devastata*, is valued in the Kings books at 1 *l.* 6 *s.* 8 *d.*
Reg. Linc. To which Church, in the 19 *H.* 3. Sir *John de Hamby* Knight, presented *William de Dembleby* his Clerk.

In the 33 *E.* 1. (1305.) *Richard Ibid.* Son of *Richard de Seyton* presented to the Church of **Horne** *Roger Bovile* of **Seyton**; and *Alanus de Franckton* presented *William de Hotoft* to the same Church by an other title, which it seems was not valid, for the said *Richard* recovered the Presentation, and had his Clerk admitted.

The Patron of the Sine-Cure is the Right honourable *Edward* Earl of **Gainsborough**.

INTHORPE.

IS a small Hamlet in the East Hundred, and in the Parish of **Tinwell**.

In the 9 *E.* 2. the Abbot of **Peterborough** was Lord of **Tinewell** and **Ingethorpe**. *No. Vill. in Scacc.*

KELTHORP.

IN the Hundred of **Wrangdike**, and Parish of **Ketton**.
Kelthorp did heretofore belong to the Collegiate Church of the Blessed Trinity of **Tattesbal** in the County of **Lincoln**: after the dissolution of *Rot. Pat.* 36. *H.* 8. *pars.* 6. which House King *H.* 8. by his Letters patents dated at **Westminster** 13. *Mar.*

in the 36. year of his reign, granted this Estate (*inter alia*) to *Charles Brandon* Duke of **Suffolk**.

In the 5th. of *Eliz. Francis Coleby* obtain'd Licence to alienate the Mannor of **Kelthorp** *in Com.* **Rotel.** to *John Houghton*, which License bears date 30. *Apr.* in the said 5. *Eliz.* *Pat.* 5. *El. pars.* 8.

John

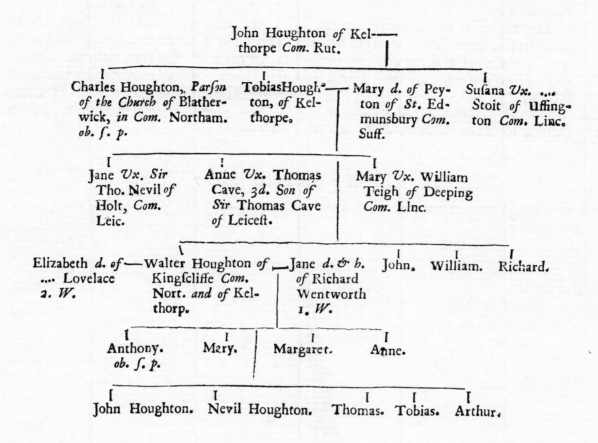

John Houghton *of* Kel——thorpe *Com.* Rut.

Charles Houghton, *Parson of the Church of* Blatherwick, *in Com.* Northam. *ob. ſ. p.*

TobiasHoughton, *of* Kelthorpe.

Mary *d. of* Peyton *of St.* Edmunsbury *Com.* Suff.

Suſana *Vx.* .... Stoit *of* Uffington *Com.* Linc.

Jane *Vx. Sir* Tho. Nevil *of* Holt, *Com.* Leic.

Anne *Vx.* Thomas Cave, 3 *d. Son of Sir* Thomas Cave *of* Leiceſt.

Mary *Vx.* William Teigh *of* Deeping *Com.* Linc.

Elizabeth *d. of* .... Lovelace 2. *W.*

Walter Houghton *of* Kingſcliffe *Com.* Nort. *and of* Kelthorp.

Jane *d. & h. of* Richard Wentworth 1. *W.*

John. William. Richard.

Anthony. *ob. ſ. p.*

Mary.

Margaret.

Anne.

John Houghton. Nevil Houghton. Thomas. Tobias. Arthur.

KETTON.

Domeſd. North.
n. 1.

THis Town lyes in the Eaſt hundred : And was at the time of the Conquerors Survey held by the King. Here were ſeven Hides, of arable Land thirteen Carucates, in Demeſne two Carucates, three Servants, twelve Sockmen, twenty four Villains, and five *Bordarii*, with a Prieſt, having eleven Carucates : Here was alſo one Mill of 6 *s.* and 8 *d.* and forty acres of Meadow, and a Wood containing ſixteen Acres. To this Mannour at that time belong'd **Tixover**, both which Towns were then valued at 10 *l.* but formerly in the time of the Confeſſor at 100 *s.* only,

Bar. Eng. 1.
Vol. 631.

In the 2 H. 2. *Richard de Humet*, being then Conſtable of **Normandy**, in conſideration of his ſervices, obtain'd from that King a grant of the Lordſhip of **Stamford** in *Com.* **Linc.** with all its appurtenances (both of the Caſtle and Borough) excepting the ſervices of the Abbot of **Peterborough**, and of *William Lanvalei* : He had alſo by that Kings Grant, at the ſame time, **Ketene** in this County, and divers other Mannours elſewhere. All which Eſtates together with the ſaid Office of Conſtable of **Normandy**, the ſaid King confirm'd to his Son *William de Humet*, after the Death of the ſaid *Richard*.

This *Richard de Humet* was Sheriff or *Cuſtos* of this County from the 10 of H. 2. to the 26 year of his reign, being the firſt that I have met with, in that Office for this County.

Nom. Vill. in
Scacc.

In the 9 E. 2. *Ralf de Greneham* was Lord of this Mannour.

Rot. pipe.

In the 18 E. 2. *Thomas* Son of the ſaid *Ralf* had Livery of a certain Mannour in **Ketton** which the ſaid *Ralf* deceaſed did hold of *John Leſtrange*, late within

within age, and in the Kings Cuſtody, by the ſervice of the 4th. part of a Knights Fee.

The Sheriff of this County is accountable in the Pipe Office, yearly, for an antient Rent of 2 *s. per An. pro Ocreis Reginæ*, ariſing out of this Town of **Ketton**.

Comp. pro Com. Rutl. in Offic. Augm. 3 *E.* 6.   King H. 8. granted the Mannour of **Ketton** to *James Gunter*, Gent. and his

Heirs reſerving for a yearly Rent, or tenth, out of the ſame the ſum of 11 *s.* 1 *d.* payable at *Michaelmas*.

In the 37 of H 8. *James Gunter* obtain'd Licence to alienate all that the Mannour of **Ketton** with the Appurtenances, and all that the Grange called **Ketilthorp** Grange *in Com.* **Rutland** to Sir *James Harington* Knight and his Heirs.   7. H. 8. *p.* 6.

Of the Church there.

Ecclesia Parochialis apud Ketton.

Visus Australis

Reg. Lin.

IN the time of *Oliver Sutton*, who, was confecrated Bifhop of **Lincoln**, 7 E. 1. it was ordain'd by the faid Bifhop, that the Vicar of the Church of **Ketton** fhould find fit and proper Minifters in the faid Church of **Ketton**, and Chapel of **Tykefbouere**, for which he fhould recover of the Prebendary of **Ketton** the fum of 20 Marks fterling, yearly.

The Prebend of **Ketton** belonging to the Church of **Lincoln**, is valued in the Kings Books at 29 *l.* 10. *s.* 2 *d.* And the Vicarage at 8 *l.*

Reg. Line.

Hugh de Wells Bifhop of **Lincoln**, by his Deed dated the 5. *Aug.* in the 23. year

of his Confecration, which was 16. H. 3. granted a Releafe of 20 days Pennance to all thofe who fhould contribute any thing to the building or reparation of the Church of the Bleffed *Mary* of **Ketton**, at that time ruinous.

This new building, here mentioned, is no doubt that which remains at this day, the neateft Parifh-Church in all thefe parts, for defign and ftructure; it is form'd in the fhape of a little Cathedral, as if intended for an Epitome of its Mother **Lincoln :** In relation to which may be apply'd the words of *Horace*, with fmall Variation,

O, Matre Pulchriori, filia Pulchra!

In the Church

On a handfome Monument erected in a Wall neer the Chancell, having the Date, 1594.

Conditur hic, natu, naturâ, Nomine, Clarus:
Quem meritis Virtus triplo veftivit honore;
Middletone tuum non eft ignobile Stemma;
Nec Whitwelle tuum; Digbeyus adæquat utrumque.
Sic Ferdinando Caldecote moriendo revixit:
Cui bis fex nati funt, cuilibet ecce Sororem.

On the fame Monument, *Caldecote* and *Digby* impail'd

In the Eaft Window of the Chancell. *Fretty az. Semy of Fowrs de Lis:* Quarter'd and impail'd diverfly, in feveral Coats.

L A N G H A M.

IN the hundred of **Okeham-Soak**; and had always, till the laft Age, the fame Owner with **Okeham**: And in the Book of *Domefday* Survey it is included in **Okeham** *Cherchefoch*, as one of the five Berews or Hamlets thereunto belonging.

In the 28, year of *E.* 1. *Edmund* Earl

Ear. Eng. 1.
Vol. 766.

of **Cornwall**, Son of *Richard* Earl of **Cornwall**, and *Senchia* his Wife (of whom more in **Okeham**) dyed fei-

ed of the Caftle in **Okeham**, with the Mannours of **Egelton**, and **Langham**, in the County of **Rutland**, and likewife of the Sheriffalty of the faid County, without iffue. After whofe Death through the mediation of the Peers in Parliament, held at **Lincoln** 29 *E.* 1. the King was pleafed to allow to *Margaret* his Widow 500 *l.* per *An.* for her fupport, and for the making good thereof, he affigned the Caftle ſtle and Mannor of **Okeham** in **Rutland**, with the hundreds of **Martinſly**, **Alneſtow** and **Eaſthundꝛed**; the Hamlet of **Egilton**, part of the Mannour of **Langham**, in the ſame County; and 14 *l*. 16 *s*. 4 *d*. yearly Rent, iſſuing out of the Court-Leets, and Sheriffs ayde in **Ketton**, **Pꝛeſton**, **Okeham**, **Hamelton**, and divers other Towns in that County: With ſeveral other Lordſhips, Lands, and Rents elſewhere. Which *Margaret* married for her ſecond Husband *Piers de Gaveſton*: And ſurviving him, *Hugo de Audely* for her third.

Ex parte Rem. Theſ. H. 7. H. 5.

In the 7. *H*. 5. it was found by Office that *William Bourchier* Chivalier, and *Anne* his Wife, Daughter and heir of *Thomas* late Duke of *Glouceſter*, held of the King *in Capite* fifty five Meſſuages, fifty five yard Land, fifty one Cottages, ſixty five acres, three Roodes and a half of Meadow, forty two acres one Rood and a half of Paſture, 7 *s*. and one pound of Pepper of free Rent in **Langham** in the County of **Roteland**, as parcels and members of the Mannour of **Okeham**, by the Service of one third part of a Knights Fee.

Bar. Eng. 2. Vol. 128.

This Sir *William Bourchier* Knight, was Nephew and Heir to *Bartholmew* Lord *Bourchier*, he was the Son of *William Bourchier* younger Brother of the ſaid Lord, and *Alianore* daughter and Heir of *John de Louvain*; he was much in the favour of King *H*. 5. from whom, in conſideration of his eminent ſervices both in this Realm and in foraign parts, he obtain'd a Grant of the whole County of **Ewe** in **Noꝛmandy**. He

married *Anne* Daughter of *Thomas* of **Woodſtock** Duke of **Glouceſter**, Widdow of *Edmund* E. of **Stafford**, and dyed in the 8th. year of H. 5. Leaving iſſue *Henry* his Son and Heir, who in 13 H. 6. had ſummons to Parliament by the title of Earl of **Ewe**, and was afterwards advanced to the Dignity of Earl of **Eſſex**; *Thomas* Biſhop of **Ely**, and in 32 H. 6. Archbiſhop of **Canterbury**; *William* Lord *Fitzwarine*; and *John* Lord *Berners*; with one Daughter, *Anne*, who marryed *John Moubray* Duke of **Noꝛfolk**.

Id. 129.

In the 5. year of King E. 6. it was found by Inquiſition taken at **Uppingham** in this County, on the 25. of *Septem*. after the Death of *Gregory* Lord *Cromwell*, that the ſaid Lord *Cromwell* dyed ſeized (*inter alia*) of the Mannour of **Langham**: which, with **Okeham** and other Lands in the Inquiſition mentioned, he held of the King *in Capite* by Knights ſervice; and that *Henry* Lord *Cromwell* was his Son and Heir. Which *Henry* had iſſue *Edward* Lord *Cromwell*, and Sir *Gregory Cromwell* Knight. In whoſe time, it ſeems, this Mannour of **Langham** was firſt ſeparated from that of **Okeham**, and ſettled in marriage upon his 2*d*. Son, Sir *Gregory Cromwell*. For I find that Queen *Elizabeth* on the 2. *Sept*. in the 42. year of her reign, granted her Licenſe to the ſaid Sir *Gregory Cromwell* and *Frances* his Wife, to alienate the Mannour of **Langham** *in Com*. **Rutland**, to Sir *Andrew Noel* Knight. From which Sir *Andrew* is deſcended the Right honourable *Edward* Earl of **Gainsboꝛough** the preſent Lord of this Mannour.

Eſc. 5. E. 6. *pars.* 2. *n.* 54.

Rot. Pat. 42. *El. pars.* 17.

In the Church.

About the Verge of an Antient Graveſtone in the North Buildiug.

✠ **Oꝛate pꝛo anima** Willielmi Byby **de** Langham **qui obiit** xi. **die** Decembris Anno Dom. M. CCC. LXXXIX.

About the Verge of an Alablaster Tombstone on the left hand going into the Chancel

✠ 𝕺F youre charyte pray for they Solls of John Clerke Jone and Anys hys wyvys the whiche John deceſſyd the iii day of February in the yere of owre Lord God M. CCCC. XXXII. of whoſe Solls Jeſu have marcy, Amen.

Armes in the Windows.

O. *a* Maunch *g. Haſtings E. of* Pembroke.
O. 3 Cheveronels. *g. Clare E. of* Clare *and* Glouceſter.
Az. 3. Ducal Crowns, *o. Kings of the Eaſt* Angles.
G. *a* Feſs *between* 6 croſſe Croſlets, *o. Beauchamp E. of* Warwick.

L E Y G H. L Y F E I L D.

Formerly a Town and Mannor, now onely a Lodge, in the Forreſt which, no doubt , was named the Forreſt of Lyfeild from this Town. Of this Town or Mannour I find no mention in *Domeſday* Book.

Nom. Vill. in Scacc. In the 9. E. 2. *Theobald de Menyle* (or rather *Nevyle*) was Lord of the Mannour of Leye.

From whom this Eſtate , together with the Office of Cheif-Forreſter of the Forreſt of Rutland , was derived to the *Chiſeldines*, as I have formerly made mention.

Bar. Eng. 1. *Vol.* 585. In the Reign of *Edward* 4. *William* Lord *Haſtings* his great Favourite, and a faithful adherer to the houſe of York, had a Grant from the ſaid King of the Mannor of Lygh or Lyfeld, a d Office of Cheif Forreſter in Rutland. He had alſo a grant of the Stewardſhip of Okeham, and Conſtablewick of the Caſtle there , for life , by *Anne* Dutcheſs of Buckingham, who held the ſame in Dower, 1. E. 4. which Lord *Haſtings* was afterward murder'd by the Command of *Richard* Duke of Gloucester in the begining of the ſhort reign of *Edward* 5. whoſe Lands being confiſcate, during the time of *R.* 3. they were by H. 7. in the firſt year

Id. 586.

of his reign, reſtored to his Son and Heir *Edward* Lord *Haſtings* , whoſe Son *George* Lord *Haſtings* was in the 21. year of *H.* 8. advanced to the title of Earl of Huntington.

In which Family this Eſtate conti- *24. El. p. 2.* nued till the reign of Queen *Elizabeth*: For I find, that in the 24*th.* year of that Queen, ſhe granted her Pardon to Sir *James Harrington* Knight for purchaſing to himſelf of *Henry* then Earl of Huntington without Licence of alienation, the Mannour of Lee in the County of Rutland , the ſame being held *in Capite.*

This Eſtate being thus in the *Harring-* *tons, John* Lord *Harrington* the Younger, by Indenture dated 18.*Feb.*11.*Jac.*ſettled *Eſt.* 14. Jac his Mannour of Lee, *alias* Leighfeld, *p.* 2. *n.* 117. among diverſe other Mannours and Lands in this County, in Truſt , to be ſold after his Death, for the payment of his , and his Fathers Debts. Which Lord ſoon after departing this life, this Eſtate was accordingly ſold to Sir *Eward Noel* Knight and Baronet , and a Fine was paſt of the ſame in the Term of S. *Michael* 12. *Jac.* wherein the ſaid Sir *Edward Noel* was demandant and *Edward* Earl of Bedford and *Lucy* his Wife, and *Anne* Lady *Harrington Rot. Fin.* M Widdow, and others, were Deforceants. 12. Jac

L 2 *Of*

Of the Forrest of RUTLAND, commonly call'd. LIFEILD.

THe firſt Original of this Forreſt is uncertain ; but ſeveral Grounds parcel of it, were afforreſted in the Reign of King *John*, as appears by the following Record.

Peramb. 29: E. 1. M. 15.

PErambulatio facta in Com. **Rote-land** coram Rogero *le* Braban-zun *& Sociis ſuis die* Lune *in* Craſti-no *Sancti* Nicholai. *Anno Regni Regis* Edwardi 28. *per Sacramentum* Johan-nis *de* Hotot, Roberti *ad* Aulam, Wil-lielmi *de* **Tolethorp**, Richardi Tayl-lard, Richardi *de* Bellaſago, Willielmi *de Sancto* Licio, Richardi *de* Middle-ton, Roberti *de* Bellaſago, Walteri *de* **Sculthorp**, Richardi *de* **Emping-ham**, Regenaldi *de* **Seyton**, Roberti *de* **Caſterton**, Henrici *le* Tanner *de* **Ok-ham**, Johannis Baſſet, Roberti *de* Ca-ſtre, Richardi *ad* Aulam, Johannis *de* **Braunſton**, *&* Roberti *de* **Sculthorp** *qui dicunt ſuper Sacramentum ſuum de cooperto Foreſte quod tam diu extitit in Foreſta quod neſciunt a quo tempore, & dicunt quod omnes ville & terre extra metas & bundas ſubſcriptas verſus le* **Stubbedeſton** *& verſus* **Stauxford**, *preter quandam placeam que vocatur* **Whichele**, *vid. de* **Braunceſton** *& alias verſus Foreſtam, & de* **Upping-ham**, *uſque in le* **Redgate** *& ſic ſequen-do le* **Redgate** *uſque in le* **Brodegate**, *& ſic uſque ad* **Lidenton** *& per medium* **Lidenton** *& de inde uſque in aquam de* **Licele** *afforeſt. fuerunt tempore Regis* Johannis. *In cujus rei teſtimonium huic ſcripto ſigilla noſtra appoſuimus. Dat apud* **Okeham** *die & Anno ſupra-dictis.*

The Bounds and Limits of **Lifeild** *and* **Beaumount** *Forreſt, ac-cording to a Survey late in the Poſſeſſion of the Right Honour-able* Baptiſt *Lord Viſcount* **Camboen**, *deceaſed,* viz.

BEginning at **Flitteriſh** Corner in the Field of **Okeham**, it goes weſtward, taking in all **Braun-ſton** high-meadow, the **Wiſp**, and **Withcot** ſail, and ſo proceeds, taking in **Bittlewell** ſail, and **Cockly** ſale, and ſo to **Steerwood**, and then taking in **Tinford** Bridge, it takes in **Belton** and **Wardly** Towns, proceeds to **Beaumont**, ſale and **Preſton Under-woods**, and ſo about to **Long bridge**, by **Caldecot**, taking in **Caldecot** and **Snelſton** Fields, and ſo up to **Lid-dington**, taking in all **Uppingham Brand**, and the Eaſt Field, and ſo tak-ing in all **Ayſton** Common feilds it, proceeds by **Ridlington** to **Brook**, and then up to **Brook** Mill, and ſo to **Flitteriſh** where the Circuit or Peram-bulation began. Containing within the ſaid limits the following Towns, viz. **Brook**, **Braunſton**, **Belton**, **Ward-ley**, the Mannour of **Leigh**, **Ridling-ton**, **Uppingham**, **Ayſton**, **Stoke**, **Lidington**, **Snelſton** and **Calde-cot.**

In the 15 E. 2. *John* Hekelut, who married *Alice* Daughter and coheir of Theobald *de* Nevill*, gave to the King 40 *s*, for the releif of the ſaid *Alice*, for the **Baliwick** of the Cuſtody of the Kings Forreſt of **Rutland**, which the late King *Edw.* 1. granted to the ſaid
Theo-

P. 15. E. 2. ex parte Rem. The-ſaur.

Theobald and his heirs, rendring yearly to the Exchequer the same Rent which *Peter de Nevil,* Father of the said *Theobald,* formerly paid for the Custody of the same.

Origines de An. 6 R. 2. King *Ric.* 2. in the 6*th.* year of his reign gave his Licence to *William de Boroughe* to grant to *Edward Calingrugg,* Chevalier, the Baliwick of the Custody of the said Forrest.

Mic. 8 H. 6. Ex parte Rem. Thesaur. In the 8*th.* year of *H.* 6. it was found that *Robert Chisulden* Esquire, and *Ann* his Wife, daughter and heir of *William de Burghe,* and *Margaret* his Wife, Defunct, held of the King, the Baliwick of the keeping the Kings Forrest of **Roteland** , by the service of paying into the Exchequer 40 *s.* yearly at the Feast of St. *Michael* in Lieu of all services.

Esc. 23 H. 6. n. 14. Of which *Ann* Daughter and heir of *William de Burghe,* and Wife of *Robert Chisulden,* it was found by inquisition taken at **Okeham** on the 23. day of *April.* 23 *H.* 6. that the said *Anne* dyed seised in her Demean as of Fee of the Mannour of **Lye,** and of the Custody of the Forrest of **Rutland,** with *Wyndfallin wode, Dere fallin wode, Cabliciis (i. e.* all decayed small wood) *Woodsylver, Heggyngsylver, Attachiaments of the Forresters,* with the issues and profits of the *Swannimots,* and *Chiminage,* as also the power of making and removing all Forresters of the said Forrest at her Will; and that the said Forrest is held of the King in *Capite,* the profits of which said Forrest was then valued at seventeen Marks, over and above all Reprises.

Of this Family of the *Chisildines,* see more in **Braunston.**

Rar. Eng. 1. Vol. 585, 586. But I find that not long after, *viz.* in the reign of King *Edward* 4*th.* that King granted to his great Favourite and faithful adherant, *William* Lord *Hastings,* the Mannour of **Lygh** or **Leyfeild,** with the office of chief Forrester in **Rutland** , which Lord being murdered, and his Estate confiscated during the reign of *R.* 3. it was by King *H.* 7. in the first year of his Reign restored to his Son and heir *Edward* Lord *Hastings.*

Esc. 14. Jac. *pars* 2. *n.* 116. It was found by Office taken at **Okeham** 22 *Martii,* 13 *Jacobi,* before *Edward Harrington* Knight , *William Bulstrode* Knight, and *John Reading* Gent. Feodaries of this County of **Rutland,** that *John* Lord *Harrington* the Elder, (who departed this life at **Wormes** beyond the Seas, on the 24 *August* 11. *Jac.*) dyed seised in this Demean as of Fee (*inter alia*) of the Mannour of **Lee** *alias* **Leighfeild** with the Office of *Custos* of the Forrest of **Rutland** and **Ridlington** Park , all which he held *in Capite.*

Rot. Finium M. 14 Jac. Not long after whose Death, this Estate, and the Office of Seneschal and Bayliff of the Forrest of **Roteland** and Keeper of **Ridlington** Park, was sold and conveyed to Sir *Edward Noel* Knight and Baronet, and a Fine was past of the same in *Michaelmas* Term 12 *Jac.* between the said *Edward Noel* Demandant, and *Edward* Earl of **Bedford** and *Lucy* his Wife, and *Anne* Lady *Harrington* Widow, and others deforceants.

LUFFENHAM, North, *and South.*

Domesd. North. n. 1. THe two **Luffenhams** lye in the hundred of **Wrangedike,** and were possibly, heretofore but one Town; for I find no distinction in *Domesday* Survey, where it is said , that the King held **Luffenham** and **Sculetorp.** There was at that time accounted here seven hides and one yard land, of arable fourteen Carucates, twelve Sockmen, and sixteen *Bordarii,* with a Priest, having twelve Carucates, there were also two Mills of fourty pence rent, and ten Acres of Meadow. All which in the time of King *Edward* was valued at 30 *s.* but at the Survey at 40 *s. Homines operant opera Regis quæ præpositus jusserit; has terras tenuit Regina* Edith, *modo tenet* Hugo de Porth *ad firmam de rege.* There was also at that time belonging to the Kings Mannour of **Berchedone,** in **Lufenham** four hides

hides, ten Carucates of arable Land, and sixteen acres of Meadow.

Maud the Empress bestowed this Mannour among several others, one *William Beauchamp* of 𝕰𝖑𝖒𝖑𝖊𝖞, who had been Steward to her Father *H.1.* and her faithful adherent in her Wars against King *Steven.* From which *Beauchamp* descended the famous Earls of 𝖂𝖆𝖗-𝖜𝖎𝖈𝖐 of that name.

Bar. Eng. 1. Vol. 225.

In the 14 *E.* 3. *Thomas Beauchamp* E. of 𝖂𝖆𝖗𝖜𝖎𝖈𝖐 held the Mannour of South 𝕷𝖚𝖋𝖋𝖊𝖓𝖍𝖆𝖒 and 𝕭𝖆𝖗𝖔𝖉𝖔𝖓 with other Lands in this County, by the service of being the Kings Chamberlain in the Exchequer.

Camb. Brit. Rutl.

Of later times the *Harringtons* had a Mannour in North-𝕷𝖚𝖋𝖋𝖊𝖓𝖍𝖆𝖒. For I find that *John* Lord *Harrington* the younger by Indenture dated 18. *Feb.* 11. *Jac.* Settled his Mannour of North-𝕷𝖚𝖋𝖋𝖊𝖓𝖍𝖆𝖒, among other Mannours and Lands in this County, in Trust, to be sold after his Death for the payment of his and his Fathers Debts. Soon after which, the said Lord dying, this Estate was accordingly sold: and became the Seat of that truly Noble and Loyal Gentleman, *Henry Noel* Esq; second Son of *Edward* Lord *Noel*, Vicount *Campden*. Which Mr. *Noel* in the times of the late Rebellion, residing here, and refusing to deliver up his house, Armes, and person to the Lord *Grey* of 𝕲𝖗𝖔𝖔𝖇𝖞, who demanded them for the Parliament, was forced by Fire and Batteries, to Capttulate; and tho the Articles were, 1. That the Rebells should see the Fire quencht; 2. That all in the house should have Liberty to depart whether they would; 3. That none should enter the House but Commanders. Yet not regarding any obligation, Promise or Agreement, they enter the house, as well Common Souldiers as Officers, Rob, plunder, wast, burn, and destroy, his Goods accounts, writings, and Evidences, ravilh his maid Servants, enter the adjoyning Church, and there deface a goodly Monument erected to his deceased Lady : And having thus ranfakt all from the living to the dead, they carryed the said Mr. *Noel* Prisoner to 𝕷𝖔𝖓𝖉𝖔𝖓, where he remained a long time in *Peter-house*, a constant sufferer for the Royal Interest.

Esc. 14 Jac. p. 2. n. 117.

Mercur. Rusti-cus. p. 66.

This Estate is at present the Seat of the honourable *Baptist Noel* Esq; second Son, now living, of the right honourable *Baptist Vicount Campden*, late deceased.

THe Town of South 𝕷𝖚𝖋𝖋𝖊𝖓𝖍𝖆𝖒 may be famous for having a Case in Law arising from hence whereby the Kings Ecclesiastical Jurisdiction was asserted. The Historial part of which Case is thus. *Robert Caudrey* Parson of the Rectory of South 𝕷𝖚𝖋𝖋𝖊𝖓𝖍𝖆𝖒 in the County of 𝕽𝖚𝖙𝖑𝖆𝖓𝖉 was in 31. year of *Qu. El.* deprived of his said Benefice before the high Commissioners, as well for that he had preached against the Book of Common prayer, as also for that he refused to celebrate divine service according to the said Book : After which, the Validity of the said deprivation coming to be examined before the Judges of the common Law in an action of Trespasse brought by the said *Caudrey*, *Term. Hill*. 33. *El.* against one *Atton* for breaking his Close in North 𝕷𝖚𝖋𝖋𝖊𝖓-𝖍𝖆𝖒. It was urged by the Council of the Plantiff that the said Deprivation was void, as not being Warranted by the *Stat*. 1.*El. ch*.1. whereby the Queen is enabled by Letters patents under her great Seal to authorise Commissioners to exercise under her Highness all manner of Jurisdiction Ecclesiastical within this Realm and *Ireland*, &c. But the Objections being over-ruled, it was resolved by the whole Court that the said act concerning Ecclesiastical Jurisdiction was not a Statute introductory of a new Law, but declaratory of the Old, and in case that act had never been made, yet the King or Queen of *England* for the time being, may authorise ecclesiastical Commissioners by the antient Prerogative and Law of *England* : And for that, Sir *Edward Coke* in the Report of that Case produces divers antient Presidents.

Co. Rep. li. 5. f. 1.

Id. f. 8.

A younger Branch of the Family of the *Digby's* of 𝖂𝖊𝖑𝖙𝖔𝖓 have been many years seated at North 𝕷𝖚𝖋𝖋𝖊𝖓-𝖍𝖆𝖒 and Lords of a moitey of that Mannour.

Robert

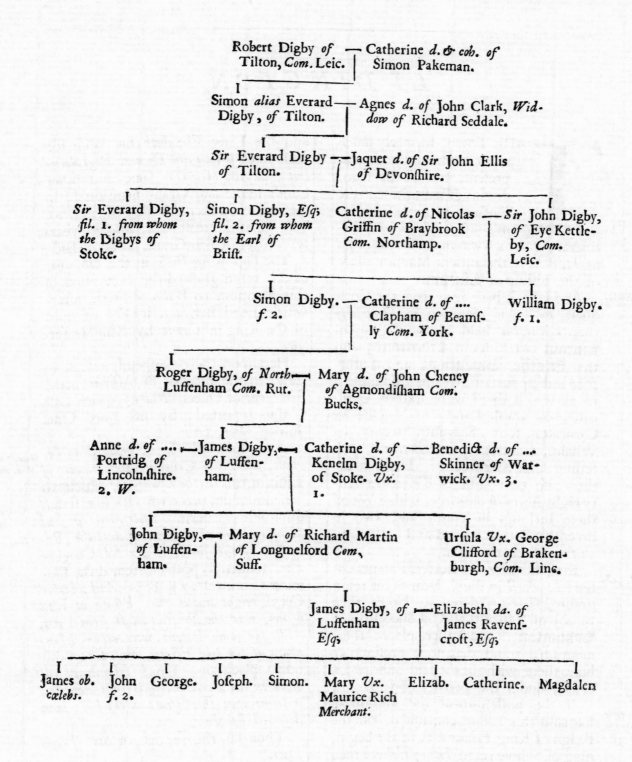

Robert Digby *of* — Catherine *d. & coh. of*
Tilton, *Com.* Leic. | Simon Pakeman.

Simon *alias* Everard — Agnes *d. of* John Clark, *Wid-*
Digby, *of* Tilton. | *dow of* Richard Seddale.

Sir Everard Digby — Jaquet *d. of Sir* John Ellis
of Tilton. | *of* Devonshire.

Sir Everard Digby, | Simon Digby, *Esq;* | Catherine *d. of* Nicolas — *Sir* John Digby,
fil. 1. *from whom* | *fil.* 2. *from whom* | Griffin *of* Braybrook | *of* Eye Kettle-
the Digbys *of* | *the* Earl *of* | *Com.* Northamp. | by, *Com.*
Stoke. | Brist. | | Leic.

Simon Digby. — Catherine *d. of* .... | William Digby.
f. 2. | Clapham *of* Beamf- | *f.* 1.
| ly *Com.* York.

Roger Digby, *of* North- — Mary *d. of* John Cheney
Luffenham *Com.* Rut. | *of* Agmondifham *Com.*
| Bucks.

Anne *d. of* .... — James Digby, — Catherine *d. of* — Benedict *d. of* ...
Portridg *of* | *of* Luffen- | Kenelm Digby, | Skinner *of* War-
Lincoln.fhire. | ham. | *of* Stoke. *Ux.* | wick. *Ux.* 3.
2. *W.* | | 1.

John Digby, — Mary *d. of* Richard Martin | Urfula *Ux.* George
of Luffen- | *of* Longmelford *Com,* | Clifford *of* Braken-
ham. | Suff. | burgh, *Com.* Linc.

James Digby, *of* — Elizabeth *da. of*
Luffenham | James Ravenf-
Efq; | croft, *Efq;*

James *ob.* | John | George. | Jofeph. | Simon. | Mary *Ux.* | Elizab. | Catherine. | Magdalen
cœlebs. | *f.* 2. | | | | Maurice Rich
| | | | | *Merchant.*

Of the ADVOWSON.

Reg. Linc:

Ib.

IN the Reign of *E.* 1. *Edmund* Earl of Cornwall was Patron of the Church of North Luffenham, and prefented to the fame *John de Molef-worth,* in the twelve year of that King. In the 46 *H.* 3. *William de Bello-campo* Earl of Warwick prefented to the Church of South Luffenham.

The two Rectories of South and North Luffenham are valued in the Kings Books, each at 17 *l.* 0 *s.* 5 *d.*

The Prefent Patrons are

LYDING-

LYDINGTON.

Lel. Itin. 1. Vol.

Domesd. North. n. 5.

Rot. Pat. 3. E. 3. n. 46.

Comp. in Offic. Augm. pro Com. Rutland. 3 E.6.

Comp. ub. sup.

THis Town, formerly much more confiderable than at prefent, lyes in the Hundred of **Wrangdike**, in the South parts of this County. **Luddington**, fays *Leyland* in his Itinerary (which was made in the reign of *H.* 8.) is the antient Mannor place of the Bifhop of **Lincoln**.

And fuch it had been from the Conqueft, for it is recorded in *Domefday* that *Walterius* held of the Bifhop of **Lincoln** two hides in **Lidentone**; and that **Stoche, Smeliftone** and **Caldecote** did appurtain to this Mannour, in all which there were fixteen Carucates, of arable Land; in demefne fix Carucates, four Servants, twenty fix Villains, and twenty four *Bordarii*, poffeffing nine Carucates. There were then alfo two Mills of 8 *s.* and twenty eight Acres of meadow, with a Wood three furlongs in length and two in breadth, all then valued at 8 *l. Bardi tenuit cum* Saca *&* Soca.

King *E.* 3. by his Letters Patents dated 12 *April* in the 3. year of his reign granted Free Warren to *Henry* then Bifhop of **Lincoln** and his Succeffors in **Lydington** (and other places there mention'd) and that none prefume to hunt there without the faid Bifhops Licenfe, under the penalty of 10 *l.*

In the poffeffion of the Bifhop of **Lincoln** this Eftate continued, till the Reign of King *Edward* 6. in the beginning of whofe reign *Henry Holbeth* then Bifhop of that Sea, did give and grant to the faid King (but upon what confideration I find not) the Dominion or Mannour of **Liddington** with all and fingular its rights and Appurtenances in the County of **Rutland**, then valued at the yearly Rent of 63 *l.* 14 *s.* 9 *d.*

All which the faid King *Edward* 6. foon after granted by Letters Patents under the feal of the Court of Augmentations, dated 24 *May* in the 2 year of his reign, to *Gregory* Lord *Cromwell*,

and the Lady *Elizabeth* his Wife for their lives, *fi tam diu Domino Regi placuerit*, paying for the fame and other Lands in the faid Grant mention'd, in the name of a Rent the fum of 14 *l.* 3 *s.* 5 *d. ob.* at the feaft of St. *Michael*, yearly. After which Grant, as abovefaid,

The faid King *E.* 6. in the 5*th.* year of his reign granted the Reverfion of this Mannour to *William Cecyl*, afterwards Lord *Burghley*, in Fee to hold of the King in *Capite* by Knights fervice.

5. E. 6. p. 7.

Hereupon there happend a Cafe in Law, in the term of St. *Michael* in the firft year of Queen *Mary*; which Cafe is thus reported, by the Lord Chief Juftice *Dyer, viz.*

King Edward *the* 6. *granted to his Aunt, the Lady* Crumwel *the manner of* **Liddington** *in the County of* **Rutland** *habendum fibi pro term. vitæ fuæ, fi tam diu nobis placuerit. Afterwards the faid King reciting that grant, grants the Reverfion of the fame, to Sir. W. Cecyl in Fee, reddendo poft mortem dictæ Dominæ* Crumwel *27 l. &c. And whether* Cecyl *might avoid this Eftate at Will or not, was the Queftion. It feem'd not.*

Dyer. fo. 94. M. 1. Mar. n: 29.

In the fame Patent were other Mannours of the like Eftate, fcil. fi tam diu nobis placuerit, Which Mannours remain in the Queens hands that now is; it feems that this Eftate might have been defeated by the Queen.

Thus far the report of Sir *James Dyer.*

Which abovemention'd Sir *William Cecyl*, Lord *Burghly* left iffue by *Mary* his firft Wife, *Thomas* Lord *Burghley*, who in the 3. year of King *James* was created Earl of *Exeter*, in which honourable Family this Lordfhip remains at this day.

The aforefaid *Thomas* Lord *Burley* in or about the year 1602. converted part of the old Pallace here, formerly belonging to the Bifhops of **Lincoln**, into an Hofpital for a Warden, twelve poor Men, and two Women,

and

and call'd it **Jesus** Hospital. In the Hall of which Hospital, being a fair Chamber, and (as reported) part of the Bishops own Lodgings heretofore, is still to be seen in the Windows in great Capital Letters *Dominus exaltatio mea:* And almost in every Quarry, *Delectare in Domino.*

There are also remaining in the same Windows the following Coats of Arms, belonging to two of the ancient Bishops.

John Russel Bish. of *Linc.*

John Longland Bish. of *Linc.*

Fitz. N. B. 184. a.

Lydington had formerly a Market belonging to the Bishop of **Lincoln**, and in *Fitzherberts Natura Brevium* the form of a Writ of Nusance directed to the Sheriff of **Rutland** upon that occasion, is to be seen in these words, *Rex Vic.* &c. *Prec.* P. *quod juste,* &c. *permittat Episcopum* **Lincoln.** *prosternere quoddam Mercatum in* **Uppingham**, *quod* P.

de M. pater præd. P. *cujus hæres ipse est, injuste,* &c. *levavit ad nocumentum liberi mercati.* C. *nuper Episcop.* **Linc.** *prædecess. præd. Episcopi in* **Luddington** *ut dicit, & nisi fecer. & præd. Episcopus sec. te secur.* &c. *tunc sum. præd.* P. *quod sit,* &c. *ostens. quare,* &c.

This Writ we may presume to be granted in the Reign of *H.* 3. when *Peter de Monfort* was Lord of the Mannour of **Uppingham**.

Of the ADVOWSON.

In the 32 *H.* 3. *Nicholas de Evesham* Cannon of **Lincoln**, presented to the Vicarage of the Prebendary Church of **Lidington**, *Quæ consistit in Alteragio, & in omnibus minutis Decimis de* **Lidington**, *exceptis minutis Decimis de Curia Domini Episcopi, in Decimis etiam molendinorum omnium in Parochia de* **Lidington** *integre, & in duobus marcis, singulis annis, de Ecclesf. de* **Caldecote** & **Snelleston**.

Reg. Lin.

The Prebend of **Lidington**, belonging to the Church of **Lincoln**, is valued in the Kings Books at, 20 *l.* 00 *s.* 00 *d.* And the Vicarage at 8 *l.* 2 *s.*

The present Patron of the Vicarage is

Monuments remaining in the Church.

Before the Steps going up to the Communion Table are Two fair Marble Gravestones adorned with brass Figures, Arms, and Epitaphs: On one are these Words;

Here lyeth Helyn Hardy **the wyf of** Robert Hardy **Gentilman which deceffid on** Wisson-day, **the yere of oure Lord God,** An. M.CCCC. lxxxvi. **On whose Soule God have mercy,** Amen.

Under the other lies one of the Ancestors of the now Lord **Rocking-ham**, as seems by the Arms (on a *Chevron* between 3 *Martlets,* as many *Cressents*) which Coat graved on four several Plates of Brass, is fixt towards the four Corners of the Gravestone; and about the Verge

✠**Of your charite pray for the Soule of Master** Edwarde Watson **Esquier Justice of Peace, and** .... **to three reverend Fathers in God, that is to say to my Lord** William Smith, **to my Lord** Wil-

M

liam

liam Attwater, **to my Lo2d** John Longland **late fucceſ=**
ſibely beping Biſhops of Lincoln, **which** Edward **De=**
ceſſyd the x. **Day of** October, **the pere of our Lo2d**
M. Vᶜ xxx. **on whoſe Soule and on the Soule of**
Miſtreſ Emme **his wpfe** Jeſu **habe mercp.**

Armiger hic ſitus eſt Edwardus Watſon *honorus,*
   Juſticiæ cultor , arteq; Cauſidicus.
Hunc Lincolniæ *habuit præſul digniſſimus olim.*
   Scribam,& cauſarum hunc legit ad officium.
Ferre inopi auxilium, longas componere lites,
   Conſilio promptus quoſq; juvare fuit.
Quid memorem Dotes animi ? quid munera ſortis ?
   In Patriam clarum quid pietatis opus ?
Parce Virum *conjunx, proles terquina parentem*
   Parce precor lacrimis ſolicitare tuum.
Ingenium, Mores, Virtus & fama, Fideſq;
   Nunc illi ad ſuperos concomitantur Iter.

LYNDEN.

IN the Hundred of **Martinſly.** Of this Town I find no mention in *Domeſday* Book, it being no doubt Surveyed under the Title of **Hamel-Dune** *Chercheſoch.*

Nom. Vill.   In the 9 *E.* 2. the King was Lord of this Mannour.

Pip. Vet. Eſch.   In the 18 E. 2. *Matthew Bron* did account in the Exchequer the ſum of 14 *s.* 4 *d.* for the iſſues of one yard land in **Lyndon** in *Com.* **Roteland** then in the Kings hands on the death of *Simon de Lindon.*

Rot. Pat. 22 E. 3. n. 12.   King *Edward* 3. by his Letters Patents, dated 23. *June* in the 22 year of his Reign granted to *Robert de Corby,* and to *Joan* his Wife, and the Heirs of the ſaid *Robert* for ever, the Mannor of **Lyndon** *cum pertinen.* and the Advowſon of the Church there, formerly granted to *Hugh de Montegomeri* for life : And this was in conſideration of the ſervice, which he perform'd to his dear Mother *Iſabel* the Queen, and alſo in exchange for certain Lands, which the ſaid *Robert* held in **Eltham** and **Mandebill.**

Ex parte Rem. Theſ. H. 10. H. 4.   It was found by Office taken 10 *H.* 4. That *John Daneys* Son and Heir of *John Danneys* held of the King *in Capite* the Mannor of **Lindon** in the County of **Rutland,** by the Service of one Knights Fee. Afterwards in the 13 *H* 6. it was found, That *Robert Daneys,* Son and Heir of *John Daneys,* Kt. held the ſaid Mannor by the Service of one third part of a Knights Fee. *Ib.* *P.* 13 *H.* 6. *R.* 1.

King *Edw.* 6. in the Sixth year of his Reign, granted his Licenſe to *Francis Peyton* to alienate the Mannor and Advowſon of **Lindon** with the appurtenances, in the County of **Rutland** to *John Hunt* and his Heirs. *Pat.* 6 *E.6. p.* 2.

This *John Hunt* (as appears by the following Pedigree) was the Father of *Remigius Hunt,* who in the 39. year of *Elizabeth* borrowing 110 *l.* of *Tobias Loveday* of **Stamfo2d** in the County of **Lincoln,** Gent. did joyn in a Leaſe, with *Elizabeth* his Wife, *Thomas* and *Francis* his Sons, whereby they demiſed certain Farms in this Town to the ſaid *Loveday* for 21 years, by way of Mortgage, for the ſecurity of the ſaid ſum ; the Rent of which Farms being received by *Loveday,* and amounting to 30 *l.* per *An.* clear, one *Will. Cook* of **No2manton** in this County exhibited an Information againſt the ſaid *Loveday* in the Exchequer, upon the Statute of Uſury, but became Nonſuit. The perticulars of which Caſe, being too prolix to be here inſerted may be ſeen at large in *Co. Entrys, Tit. Inform. fo.* 393. *b.*

                               Turgitus

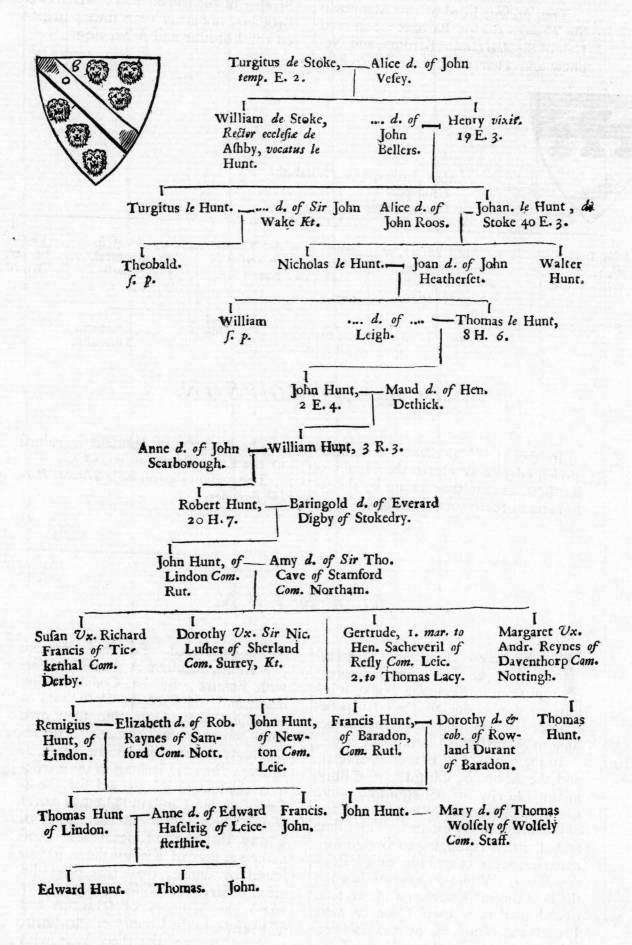

Turgitus *de* Stoke, —— Alice *d. of* John
temp. E. 2. | Vesey.

William *de* Stoke, ... *d. of* —— Henry *vixit.*
Rector ecclesiæ de John 19 E. 3.
Aſhby, *vocatus le* Bellers.
Hunt.

Turgitus *le* Hunt. —— ..... *d. of Sir* John Alice *d. of* —— Johan. *le* Hunt, *di*
Wake *Kt.* John Roos. Stoke 40 E. 3.

Theobald. Nicholas *le* Hunt. —— Joan *d. of* John Walter
ſ. p. Heatherſet. Hunt.

William ..... *d. of* ..... —— Thomas *le* Hunt,
ſ. p. Leigh. 8 H. 6.

John Hunt, —— Maud *d. of* Hen.
2 E. 4. Dethick.

Anne *d. of* John —— William Hunt, 3 R. 3.
Scarborough.

Robert Hunt, —— Baringold *d. of* Everard
20 H. 7. Digby *of* Stokedry.

John Hunt, *of* —— Amy *d. of Sir* Tho.
Lindon *Com.* Cave *of* Stamford
Rut. *Com.* Northam.

Suſan *Ux.* Richard Dorothy *Ux. Sir* Nic. Gertrude, 1. *mar. to* Margaret *Ux.*
Francis *of* Tic- Luſher *of* Sherland Hen. Sacheveril *of* Andr. Reynes *of*
kenhal *Com.* *Com.* Surrey, *Kt.* Resly *Com.* Leic. Daventhorp *Com.*
Derby. 2. *to* Thomas Lacy. Nottingh.

Remigius —— Elizabeth *d. of* Rob. John Hunt, Francis Hunt, —— Dorothy *d. &* Thomas
Hunt, *of* Raynes *of* Sam- *of* New- *of* Baradon, *coh. of* Row- Hunt.
Lindon. ford *Com.* Nott. ton *Com.* *Com.* Rutl. land Durant
Leic. *of* Baradon.

Thomas Hunt —— Anne *d. of* Edward Francis. John Hunt. —— Mary *d. of* Thomas
of Lindon. Haſelrig *of* Leice- John. Wolſely *of* Wolſely
ſterſhire. *Com.* Staff.

Edward Hunt. Thomas. John.

The preſent Lord of this Mannor is Sir *Thomas Barker*, Baronet, Son and Heir of Sir *Abel Barker*, Baronet, and Nephew and Heir of *Thomas Barker*, Eſq; Brother of the ſaid Sir *Abel*; which two Brothers, not many years ſince purchaſed this Lordſhip and Advowſon.

Abell Barker, of ——— Elizabeth.
Hambleton *in*
Com. Rutland.

John Barker, | Sir Abell Barker, *of* ——— Anne *da. of* Sir Thomas | Mary *da. of* A- | Thomas
fil. 1. *ob.*   Hambleton, *created*   Burton *of* Stockerſon *in*   lexander Noel,   Barker,
cælebs 1648.   *a Baronet* 9 Sept.   *Com.* Leic. Baronet *Ux.*   *of* Whitwell   *ob. cælebs*
                   1665. *ob.* 1679.   I.   Eſq; *Ux.* 2.   1680.

Sir Thomas Barker,   Mary.   Eliſabeth.
of Linden Baronet.   Thomaſin.

Of the ADVOWSON.

Reg. Lin. In the 19 *H.* 3. *Alanus de* **Lindon** preſented *John de Tyes* to the Church of **Lindon**, at that time vacant by the reſignation of *Steven de* **Sandwic**.

The Rectory of **Lindon** is valued in the Kings Books at, 6 *l.* 17 *s.*
The preſent Patron is Sir *Thomas Barker*, Baronet.

MANTON.

LYes in the Hundred of **Martinſly**. Of this Town is no mention in *Domeſday* Book, it being, no doubt, one of thoſe ſeven Berews or Hamlets there mentioned to belong to **Hameldune** *Cherckeſoch*.

Nom. Vill. in Scacc. In the 9 *E* 2. The Earl of **Warwick**, and the Abbot of **Clugny** or **Cluny**, in the Dutchy of **Burgundy**, were Lords of **Manton** : Which Abbot was of the Order of Ciſtertians. This Eſtate and all others belonging to foreign Monaſteries, were commonly called Priories *Aliens*. *Co.* 2. *Inſt.* *P.* 583. Whoſe Superiours beyond the Seas did in former times uſe to ſend over hither their own Country men, French and Normans, by means whereof daily Alms was decay'd, the Treaſure of this Realm tranſported to their Superiour Houſes, and the ſecrets of this Realm diſcovered. For theſe Reaſons our Kings, as often as they had Wars with **France**, by the Common Law might and did ſeize the Poſſeſſions of *Co. ubi ſup.* of theſe Priors *Aliens* into their own hands, without any Office, *&c.* And accordingly I find, that in the 18 *E.* 2. *Matthew Bron* did account in the Exchequer the ſum of 8 *l.* 4 *s.* 4 *d.* for the iſſues of certain Lands in **Manton** parcel of the Temporalities of the Abbot of **Cluny**, then in the Kings hands. And in the 22. year of *Richard* the 2. it was found by Office, that that King did grant to Sir *Gilbert Talbot*, Knight (*inter alia*) the Mannors of **Manton** and **Tykeſore** in the County of **Rutland**, to hold during the then War with *Eſc.* 22 *R.* 2: *n.* 47: **France** : With Licenſe to the ſaid *Gilbert*, to obtain a Grant of the ſame from the

the Abbot and Covent of **Cluny**, for the term of his Life, and one year longer, which said Sir *Gilbert* died the 6. of *Feb.* in the abovemention'd 22 *R.* 2.

But for the Reasons above specified, and other considerations, these Priories *aliens*, having been often complained of in Parliament, were at last totally suppreſt, and their Poſſeſſions given to the King and his Heirs for ever, in the Parliament holden at **Leicester** in the Second year of King *Henry* 5. to the number of an hundred and ten Religious Houses, says *Speed*. Moſt of their Lands and Revenues were afterwards by King *Henry* 6. given to other Monaſteries and Houſes of Learning, especially to the two famous Colledges of that Kings erection. Kings Colledge in **Cambridge**, and **Eaton**.

Rot. Parl. 2. H. 5. n. 9.

Speeds Chron. pag. 786. Stows Annals pag. 345.

But it seems this Mannor became part of the Poſſeſſions of the Collegiate Church of the bleſſed Trinity of **Tatteshall** in the County of **Lincoln**: And such it continued till the suppreſſion of that Houſe; It being then valued at 7 *l.* 2 *s.* 7 *d. per annum.*

In Offic. Augm. Bundel poſſ. Duc. Suff.

After which this Eſtate being in the Crown, King *H.* 8. by Letters Patents dated at **Westminster** 13 *Mar.* in the 36 year of his Reign, granted among divers other Lands belonging to the said Colledge of **Tatershal**, all thoſe his Mannors of **Tekeſore**, **Manton**, and **Kilthorp** *in Com.* **Rutland** to *Charles Brandon* Duke of **Suffolk**, his Heirs and Aſſigns, to be held of the King *in Capite* by the twentieth part of a Knights Fee.

Patent 36 H. 8. p. 6.

Which Eſtate after the death of the said Duke (37 *H.* 8.) and the deceaſe of his two Sons *Henry* and *Charles* without Iſſue (5 *E* 6.) deſcended to ſeveral Heirs general, *Sidney, Lovel,* and others.

Bar. Eng. 2. Vol. p. 300.

Concerning whom, it was found by Office in the 1 *Mar.* That *Thomas Lovel*

Eſc. 1 Mar.

held the fifth part of the Mannours of **Tixover**, **Manton**, and **Kilthorp**, with their appurtenances, being part of the Poſſeſſions of the late diſſolved Colledge of **Tatersal** *in Com.* **Lincoln** of the Queen *in Capite* by Knights Service, and that *Margaret* the Wife of *John Kerſey* was his Siſter and Heir.

But it seems not long after, the whole intereſt (by partition, compoſition, or otherwise) became united in the Heir of *Sidney*: For in 21 *Eliz.* that Queen granted her Licenſe to Sir *Henry Sidney*, Kt. Lord Preſident of the Marches of **Wales**, to alienate this Mannour together with that of **Teekſore** in this County to *Michæl Lewis* and his Heirs, which said *Michael Lewis* dying without iſſue 4. *June* 26 *Eliz.* the said eſtate deſcended to *Clement Lewis* his brother and Heir. Who in 33 *Eliz.* obtained Licenſe to alienate the said Eſtate to *William Kirkam jun.* Eſq; and accordingly the said *Clement Lewis* did convey the said Eſtate to the said *Will. Kirkam*, who in the 37 *Eliz.* obtained the Queens Licenſe to alienate the Mannour of **Maunton** *alias* **Manton** to *Roger Dale* then of **Collyweſton** in the County of **Northampton**, Eſq; his Heirs and Aſſigns for ever, which accordingly he did by his Deed of Feoffment dated 1 *Apr.* 37 *Eliz.* and by a Fine levied *Octab. Mic.* 2 *Jac.* In whoſe name and Family it continued, till of late years *Charles Dale* Eſq; Grandſon and Heir of the aforeſaid *Roger Dale*, leaving at his death four Daughters his Coheirs, ſome of which being within Age, certain Truſtees were inabled by a ſpecial Act in the Parliament, held at **Westminster** 31 *Car.* 2. to sell and convey this Eſtate, which accordingly they did, by due and effectual Conveyance in the Law, *An. Do.* 1682. to *Abraham Wright*, Clerk, his Heirs and Aſſigns for ever.

21 El. p. 7.

Ex Autag. pen. A. W.

Of the Church there.

Reg. Linc.

IN the 10 *E.* 1. *Edmund* Earl of **Cornwal** preſented to the Church of **Manton**, as Patron of the ſame.

The Rectory of **Manton** is valued in the Kings Book, at 8 *l.* 19 *s.* 7 *d.*

HEre was formerly within our Lady Chappel in this Church one Chantry or Colledge, founded in the Reign of King *Edward* 3. by *William Wade*, and *John Wade* Capellanus, which *William Wade* appears to be a man of Eminent eſteem in this County in thoſe dayes, for

Eſc. 31 E. 3. n. 57.

I

I find his name in the List of Knights of the Shire serving in Parliament for the County of **Rutland** from the 15 E. 3. to the 25. year of that King, without any intermission.

The particulars of which Foundation were in the 2 E. 6. Surveyed and thus certified by *Richard Cecil*, Esq; and *Thomas Hays* Commissioners for that purpose, *viz.*

Certif. pro Com. Rutl. in Offic. Augm. 2 E. 6.

The said Chauntry or Colledge was founded for the maintenance of one Master or Governour, and two Stipendaries Brethren, to celebrate Divine Service there for ever; and had then at the time of the Suppression, Possessions Spiritual and Temporal thereunto belonging in the Counties of **Rutland** *and* **Leicester***, to the value of* 26 l. 18 s. 8 d. *Whereof in Rents resolute* 36 s. *Procurations and Synodols* 10 s. 5 d. *Pensions* 3 s. 4 d. *Alms to the Poor* 30 s. 5 d. *Remains clear, per An.* 22 l. 18 s. 6 d.

The Pension of the then Master named Sir John Gorle *of the age of* 78. *years, of honest Conversation and Repute, but unable by reason of his age to serve a Cure* 13 l. 10 s. 6 d. *Out of which per annum to the King for a tenth* 2 l. 4 s. 10 d.

The said Master was also Vicar of **Aynsford** *in Com.* **Oxford***.*

The Pension of Sir Will. Smith *Brother of the said Chantry* 9 l. 3 s. *He served the Cure of the Parish there, for which he was certified to receive per An.* 3 l. 6 s. 8 d. *With his Diet, which rated at* 2 s. 4 d. *the Week, amounts in the whole to* 6 l. 1 s. 4 d.

Plate belonging to the said Chauntry seven Ounces. Delivered to the Jewel House.

Ornaments and Houshold stuff with other Goods and Chattels prised at 27 l. 3 s. 4 d.

Debts owing by the Master since and not

before the 8. *of December last, whereof he prayeth to be consider'd* 4 l. 13 s. 4 d.

Then follows in the said **Certificate**, this Memorandum or Advice from the abovementioned **Commissioners**, *Viz.*

A Vicar of necessity is to be endowed for the serving of the Cure there, which heretofore was served by one of the Brethren of the said Chauntry, for that the Rectory there is appropriated to the same Chantry, and the number of Howsling people (i. e. Communicants*) within the same Cure are an hundred.*

At the time of the suppression of this Chantry or Colledge, which was in the 2 E. 6. that King was pleased to grant to *Gregory* Lord *Cromwel*, and the Lady *Elizabeth* his Wife, the Scite of the said Colledge or Chantry with all Buildings, Gardens, and Orchards thereunto appertaining, and all Lands and Tenements to the said Chantry belonging in **Manton**, then valued at 20 l. 8 d. *per annum.* As also the profits of the Rectory of **Manton**, then valued at 10 l. *per an.* to have and to hold the premises during their two lives, and the life of the Survivour of them, *si tam diu Regi placuerit.* And this was by Letters Patents under the Seal of the Court of Augmentations, dated 15 May 2 E. 6.

Comp. pro Com. Rutl; 3 E. 6. in Offic. Augm.

There was also at that time certain Lands in **Pykewell** in *Com.* **Leicester** belonging to this Colledge or Chantry to the yearly value of 6 l. 18 s.

Comp. ut supra

Which said Estate and Tythes, formerly belonging to the Chantry was afterwards granted by Queen *Elizabeth* (among other Lands) to *Robert* Lord *Dudley*, which Grant bears date 9. *June* in the 5. year of her Reign.

Rot. Pat. 5. El. pars. 4.

Monuments in the Church.

Cut on a Plate of Brass fixt in the Wall of the North Building.

ORate pro animabus Magistrorum Willielmi Villers in Legib⁹ Baccallarii quondam Magistri hujus Cantarie, Thome Vellers fratris ejusdem Ciuis & Pannarii Civitatis London, ac Roberti Neuton in Decretis Baccallarii quondam Apprehenticii dicti Thome posteaque Magistri hujus Cantarie, qui multa bona eidem Cantarie contulit ad Edificia reparavit, Parentum & Benefactorum suorum, Quorum animabus propicetur Deus, Amen.

On

On a small Plate of Brass, fixt on a Grave Stone, in
the same North Building.

Hic jacet VVillielmus VVade Fundatoz hujus Cantarie,
cujus anime ppicietur Deus.

MARKET OVERTON.

*Camb. Brit.
lat. Edit.* 1590.
p. 419.

THis Town lies in the Hundred of Alstoe, and is so called I presume, in regard it was formerly a Market Town: Yet Mr. *Cambden* in his *Britannia* printed in *Octavo*, gives it the name of Margedoverton; and from the resemblance of that name, thinks it to be the old Margidunum mentioned in the Roman Itinerary of *Antoninus.* Which Observation I find omitted as erroneous, in the following Edition, in *Folio.*

*Antiq. of War-
wikſh. p.* 8.

It was called Overton from its situation, as standing upon a hilly ground, and all Towns of that name are observed to stand high; *Over*, importing as much as *supra*.

*Domeſday Tit:
Rotel.*

At the time of the Norman Conquest, Earl *Wallef* held in Overtune and Stratone (then esteemed as a Berew belonging to this Town) three Carucates of Land and a half, as rated to the Geld or Tax. The Arable Land was twelve Carucates. Here at the time of *Domeſday* Survey Countess *Judith* held three Carucates, thirty nine Villains, and eight *Bordarii*, having nine Carucates, and forty Acres of Meadow. A Wood (*paſtilis per loca*) being one mile in length, and half a mile in breadth. In the time of King *Edward* it was valued at 12 *l.* at the Survey at 20 *l.*

Bar. Eng. 2.
Vol. 58.

In the Reign of *Edward* 2. *Bartholomew* Lord *Badleſmere* was seized of this Mannour, and in the ninth year of that King obtained a Charter for divers Markets and Fairs in sundry of his Lordships: In perticular for one Market every week upon the *Tueſday* at Market Overton in *Com.* Rutland, and two Fairs, on the Eve, day, and morrow of *John* Port-Latine (*May* 6.) and the other on the Eve, day, and morrow of St. *Luke* the Evangelist (*Octob.* 18.) As also for

free Warren in all his demesn Lands, in particular in his Lordships of Overton, and Hameldon in this County. Which Lord adhereing to the rebellious Barons of that Age, he was taken at Burrow-Bzig, and executed at Canterbury, leaving issue *Giles* his Son and Heir. Which *Giles* found such favour with the King, that notwithstanding his Nonage, yet doing his Homage he had Livery of his Fathers Lands, 7 *E.* 3. and died seized of the said Estate 12 *E.* 3. without Issue.

In 33 year of *Edward* 3. *John Vere* Earl of Oxfozd dyed seized of this Mannour, which he had by *Maud* his VVife one of the Sisters and Coheirs of the said *Giles* Lord *Badleſmere*, and VVidow of *Robert* Son of *Robert Fitz Pain. John* Lord *Tibetot* (who married *Margaret* another of the Sisters and Coheirs of the said *Giles*) held also certain Tenements here.

Bar. Eng. 1.
Vol. 193.

Bar. Eng. 2.
Vol. 39.

In the 2 *E.* 4. *Richard* Duke of Gloucester (afterwards King by the name of *Richard* the third) obtain'd a Grant of the fee of this Lordship, and many others which were part of the estate of *John* Earl of Oxfozd attainted, which *John* was the third of that Name and Family, a zealous Lancastrian, and flying over into France to *Henry* Earl of Richmond return'd with him into England, and stood high in his favour ever after.

Bar. Eng. 2
Vol. 165.

Afterwards this Town became part of the Possessions of *Henry Courtney* Marquess of Exeter, but upon his attainder of High Treason, *anno* 1538. and the attainder of *Gertrude* his Widow, *an.* 1539. it came to the Crown. And accordingly I find that *Richard Darington* the Kings Receiver in these parts 3 *E.* 6. did then account in the Court of Augmentations

*Comp. in Offic:
Augm. pro Com.
Rutland.* 3 *E.* 6.

tions, fot the Rents and profits of this Mannour, then in the Kings hands by reason of the abovesaid attainder, the Sum of 19 *l*. 14 *s*. 6 *d*. *ob*.

Esc. 14 Jac.*p.*2. *n.* 116.
It was found by Office taken at 𝕺𝕶𝖊𝖍𝖆𝖒 22 *March* 13 *Jac.* after the death of *John* Lord *Harrington* the Elder, that the said Lord died seized, among other Lands and Possessions in this County, of the Mannour of 𝕸𝖆𝖗𝖐𝖊𝖙 𝕺𝖛𝖊𝖗𝖙𝖔𝖓, which he held *in Capite* by the 40. part of a Knights Fee.

Bar. Eng. 2.*Vol. p.* 146.
John Lord *Molines* held one Messuage, fifty one Acres of Land, and one Acre of Meadow in this Lordship, by grant of *E.* 3. in the 20. year of his Reign.

P. 1 H. 6. *ex parte Rem.Thes.*
In the first of *H.* 6. It was found by Office that *Robert Sousex* Son and Heir of *Robert Scusex* held of the King *in Capite* one Messuage, 51 Acres of land, and one Acre of Meadow in 𝕸𝖆𝖗𝖐𝖊𝖙 𝕺𝖛𝖊𝖗𝖙𝖔𝖓 in the County of 𝕽𝖚𝖙𝖑𝖆𝖓𝖉, by the Service of the fiftieth part of a Knights Fee : And afterwards in the 24. of the

Ib. H. 24. H. 6.
same King, *Thomas Sussex* Brother and Heir of *Robert Sussex, jun.* was found to hold the said Estate by the same Services.

VVhich Estate of the *Sussex*'s did formerly belong to *Simon de Beresford* Enemy and Rebel of King *Edward* 3. and being by that means forfeited, and in the said Kings hands, it was by him first granted to *Robert Sussex* for life only at the yearly farm of 16 *s*. 4 *d*.

Ex Collect.Win. Bodenham, mil. fo. 36.

Of the *ADVOWSON*.

IN the 38 *E.* 1. Sir *Batholomew de Badlesmere* Kt, presented to the Church of 𝕺𝖛𝖊𝖗𝖙𝖔𝖓 𝕸𝖊𝖗𝖈𝖆𝖙.

Reg. Linc.

It was found by Office in the 14. of King *James*, that *John* Lord *Harrington* Sen. dyed seiz'd of the Advowson of this Church.

Esc. 14 Jac.*p.*2. *n.* 116.

The Rectory of 𝕸𝖆𝖗𝖐𝖊𝖙 𝕺𝖛𝖊𝖗𝖙𝖔𝖓 is valued in the Kings Books at 14 *l*. 11 *s*. 1 *d*.

The present Patron is

MARTINSTHORP.

M𝖆𝖗𝖙𝖎𝖓𝖘𝖙𝖍𝖔𝖗𝖕 is situate in the Hundred of 𝕸𝖆𝖗𝖙𝖎𝖓𝖘𝖑𝖞, and hath perhaps given name to that Hundred. Of this Place (formerly a Town) is no mention in *Domesday* Book, it being one of those seven Berews mentioned and surveyed under the Title of 𝕳𝖆𝖒𝖊𝖑𝖉𝖚𝖓𝖊 *Cherchesoch*.

Nom. Vill.

This Mannour formerly belonged to the Family of St. *Liz*, otherwise called *de Seyton* (a Branch of the most noble Family of St. *Liz*, sometimes Earls of 𝕹𝖔𝖗𝖙𝖍𝖆𝖒𝖕𝖙𝖔𝖓 and 𝕳𝖚𝖓𝖙𝖎𝖓𝖌𝖙𝖔𝖓) till about the Reign of *H.* 6. Sir *William Feilding*, Kt. marrying *Agnes* the Daughter and Heir of *John de St. Liz*, alias *Seyton*, this Estate first came by that match, into the Noble Family, who at this day enjoy it. From which *William* descended Sir *William Feilding*, Kt. advanced in the 18. year of King *James* to the de-

Bar. Eng. 2 *Vol.* 441.

gree of a Baron of this Realm, by the Title of Lord *Feilding* of 𝕹𝖊𝖜𝖍𝖆𝖒-𝕻𝖆𝖉𝖔𝖝, as also to that of Viscount *Feilding*, and in the 20. of the said King he was created Earl of 𝕯𝖊𝖓𝖇𝖎𝖌𝖍. This Noble Lord died in the service of his late Majesty King *Charles* the First of blessed memory, 8 *April* 1643. leaving issue by *Mary* Daughter of Sir *George Villers*, and Sister to the late Duke of 𝕭𝖚𝖈𝖐𝖎𝖓𝖌𝖍𝖆𝖒, two Sons, *Basil*, who succeeded him in his Honours, and *George* created Lord *Feilding* of the 𝕮𝖆𝖌𝖍𝖊 in 𝕴𝖗𝖊𝖑𝖆𝖓𝖉, Vicount 𝕮𝖆𝖑𝖑𝖊𝖓, and Earl of 𝕯𝖊𝖘𝖒𝖔𝖓𝖉; which said *Basil* Earl of 𝕯𝖊𝖓𝖇𝖎𝖌𝖍 deceasing without issue, *Anno*, 1675. *William* his said Brothers Son and Heir succeeded to the Honours and Estate, and is the present Earl of 𝕯𝖊𝖓𝖇𝖎𝖌𝖍 and 𝕯𝖊𝖘𝖒𝖔𝖓𝖉.

Galfridus

Galfridus *Comes de* Hapsburg *&*
Dominus de Lauffenburgh *&*
Rinfelden *in* Germania. *Temp.* H. 3.

Galfridus Felden.— Matilda *de* Colevile.

Galfridus Felden.— Agnes *f.* Johannis *de* Napton.

Willielmus Feilding.— Johanna *f.* Willielmi Prudhome.

Johannes Feilding,— Margareta *f.* .....
miles.   Purefoy.

Willielmus Feilding,— Agnes *f. & h.* Johannis
miles.   *de St.* Liz.

Everardus Feilding,— Jellis *f.* .... Ruffel.
mil. Balnei.

Willielmus Feilding,— Elizabetha *f.* Thomæ Pultney
mil. ob. 2 E. 6.   *de* Mifterton *mil.*

Bafilius Feilding,— Goditha *f. & coh.* Willielmi Willington,
arm.   *de* Burchefton *in Com.* Warw. *ar.*

Willielmus Feilding — Dorathea *f.* Radulphi Lune,
mil.   *mil.*

Bafilius Feilding, *ar.*— Elizabetha *f.* Walteri Afton *de*
                          Tixal *in Com.* Staff. *mil.*

Willielmus Feilding, *mil.*— Maria *f.* Georgii Villers,
Dominus Feilding, *& Comes*   *de* Brookesby *in Com.*
de Denbigh.   Leic. *mil.*

Bafilius *Comes de*   Georgius *Dominus* Feilding— Brigetta *f.* Milonis
Denbigh *ob. f. p.*   *Comes de* Defmond *in*   Stanhop *militis.*
                              Hiber.

Maria *Soror nuper Domini*— Willielmus *Comes de* — Maria *f.* Henrici Cary
de Kingfton *in* Hi-   Denbigh *&* Defmond.   *Comitis de* Monmouth.
bernia.

Bafilius *Dominus*   Willielmus.   Maria.
Feilding.

Martinsthorp House, on the South Side.

Of the ADVOWSON.

Reg. Linc:

MArtinsthorp was formerly a Rectory presentative, and in the Reign of *E.* 1. (*Benedict de Gravesend* being then Bishop of **Lincoln**) the Lady *Alice de Monteforte* presented to the Church of **Martinsthorp**. Which *A-*

lice was Daughter of *Henry de Aldithley,* and Widow of *Peter de Montfort,* who died 50 *H.* 3.

The Rectory of **Martenthorp** (at present a Sine-Cure) is valued in the Kings Books at, 6 *l.* 0 *s.* 4 *d.*

The Patron of the Sine-Cure is the Earl of **Denbigh**.

MORCOT.

Domesd. North. n. 5.

MOrcote lies in **Wrangdike** Hundred: In this Town there was formerly belonging to the Kings Mannour of **Barowdon** four Hides of Land, eight Carucates of Arable, and Six Acres of Meadow.

Rot. de Dominabus, &c. 31 H. 2.

In the 31 *H.* 2. It was found that *Alice de Bidune* sister of *William Mauduit* was at the Kings disposal, that she was

then fifty years of Age, that her Land in **Morcote** *cum pertinent.* was of the yearly value of 10 *l.* with one Plow: and that she had four Daughters, one married to *Hugh* (or rather *Henry*) *de Clinton,* a second to *Milo de Bellocampo,* a third to *Richard de Bellocampo,* and the fourth to *Gaufridus* Son of *Gaufridus.*

In

Pipe 11 *Joh.*
Rot. 5.

In the 11 *John* the said *Hugh* (or *Henry*) *de Clinton* and *Amicia* his Wife, *Milo de Bellocampo* and *Amabilis* his Wife, *Gaufridus* the Son of *Gaufridus* and *Matilda* his Wife, and *Hugh de Bellocampo*, and *Adulphus de Gattefden* and *Armegard* his VVife, claimed againſt *Iſabel Malduit* the Town of 𝔐o𝔯cote *cum pertinent.* as their right, who came and called to VVarranty *Robert Mauduit* the Lord thereof, in regard ſhe claims nothing but in Dower.

Nom. Vill.

In the Reign of *E.* 2. *Thomas de Beauchamp* was Lord of 𝔐o𝔯cote.

Mic. 11 *E* 4.
Ex parte Rem. Thef.

It was found by Office taken in 11. year of *Edw.* 4. That *Edward Dodingsels* held at the time of his Death, among other Lands, the Mannour of 𝔐o𝔯cote (*Com.* 𝕽utl.) of the King *in Capite*, by the ſervice of the third part of a Knights Fee.

Eſch. 3 *El.*

It was found by Office in the third year of Queen *Eliz.* that *Simon Digby* (*inter alia*) held certain Lands of the yearly value of 4*l.* in 𝔐o𝔯cote, of the Queen *in Capite* by Knights Service, and that *Roger Digby* was his Son and Heir. VVhich Lands by another Inquiſition taken in the ſaid Queens time, appeared to be ſix Meſſuages, one Cottage, an hundred thirty and four Acres of land, eight acres of Meadow, and thirty four Acres of Paſture.

The Lord Paramount here, is (at the writing hereof) the Right Honourable the Earl of 𝔈xeter, and *Joſeph Herendine*, Eſq; mean Lord of this Mannour.

HEre is erected in this Town a ſmall Hoſpital for ſix poor People, men or VVomen unmarried : Their Proviſion 6 *l. per annum* a peice. It was founded in the tenth year of King *James* by one Mr. *George Jilſon*, a Roman Catholick (and as ſome ſay, a Prieſt) for the maintenance of which he ſettled certain lands at 𝔖cre𝔡ington or 𝔖creekington, in *Com.* 𝕷incoln, (let at that time for the ſum of 40 *l.* 13 *s.* 4 *d.* yearly, over and above all repriſes) on certain Truſtees and their Heirs, for the ſole uſe and behoof of the ſaid poor people , twenty ſhillings onely being yearly deducted for the Church VVardens of the Pariſh, in conſideration of their trouble in collecting the ſaid Rents, and quarterly diſtributing the ſame.

Ex relatione Johannis Savage, Cler.

The ſame Mr. *Jilſon* built alſo about the ſame time, another Hoſpital, more conſiderable than this, (as I have heard) at 𝔄ſhby-𝔉allows in 𝔏eiceſterſhire.

Of the ADVOWSON.

IN the Reign of King *John*, *Ernaldus* ſon of *Richard*, claim'd the Advowſon of the Church of 𝔐o𝔯cot, againſt *Iſabel Malduit*, who came and call'd to VVarranty *Robert Malduit* her Son in regard ſhe held in Dower only.

Ex Collect. Win. Bodenham, mil. fo. 19.

The perpetual Advowſon of this Church was of late years purchaſed by *William Halls*, Clerk, Rector of 𝔊laiſton in this County ; who dying deviſed the ſaid Advowſon to his Son *William Halls* of 𝔏ondon, Citizen and Merchant Taylor, who very lately conveyed the ſame to the preſent Incumbent, *John Savage*, Clerk, his Heirs and Aſſigns for ever.

The Rectory of 𝔐o𝔯cot is valued in the Kings Books at 10 *l.* 19 *s.* 5 *d.*

The Preſent Patron is the abovementioned Mr. *Savage.*

In the Church.

Cut about the Verge of an Ancient Tomb ſtanding on the South ſide of the Church, and let into the VVall by a kind of Niche, or Arch.

✠ VVillielm. 𝔡e Overton giſt icy
𝔇ieu 𝔡e 𝔖alme eyt mercy, Amen.

In the middle of the Chancell, cut about the Verge of a plain Graveſtone.

Heare lyeth the Body of Eliſabeth Beeſton *buried the* 9. *day of* March *in the year of our Lord,* 1622.

NOR-

NORMONTON.

IN the Hundred of 𝕸𝖆𝖗𝖙𝖎𝖓𝖘𝖑𝖞. Of 𝕹𝖔𝖗𝖒𝖆𝖓𝖙𝖔𝖓 there is not any mention in *Domesday* Book, it being, no doubt, one of those seven Berews or Hamlets, mentioned and Surveyed under the title of 𝕳𝖆𝖒𝖊𝖑𝖉𝖚𝖓𝖊 *Cherchesoch.*

Soon after the Conquest the *Normanvilles* were Lords of this Town; a Family of great account in those elder times, who were also seated at 𝕶𝖊𝖓𝖆𝖗𝖙𝖔𝖓 in the hundred of 𝕭𝖑𝖆𝖈𝖐𝖇𝖔𝖗𝖓 in 𝕶𝖊𝖓𝖙, till their male issue failing, both that Estate, and this in 𝕽𝖚𝖙𝖑𝖆𝖓𝖉 went by Match to the *Basings.*

Nom. Vill. In the Reign of *E.* 2. *William de Basings* was Lord of 𝕹𝖔𝖗𝖒𝖔𝖓𝖙𝖔𝖓. It is not improbable that this *William de Basings* might be related to *Adam de Bassing* who was Lord Mayor of 𝕷𝖔𝖓𝖉𝖔𝖓, in 36 *H.* 3. (1251) whose habitation was where *Blackwell-hall* now *Stow. Sur.* stands in 𝕷𝖔𝖓𝖉𝖔𝖓, and from whom the *London 298.* Street and Ward thereunto adjoyning took the denomination of *Bassings-hall Street*, and *Bassinges-hall Ward.* The Armes of which Family, *viz. Gerundee of* 12 *peices O. and az.* were till the last age, to be seen in the stone work, and painted in abundance of places about the said hall. But in what degree of Consanguinity they were allyed, I know *Vil. Cant.* not. Mr. *Philpot* in his *Villare Cantia-* *p. 201.* *num* makes them to be of the same blood and family: And I have seen some notes of discent that makes this *William de Basings* to be Grandson to the above-mentioned *Adam de Bassing*, *viz.* Son of *Robert de Basing* Sheriff of 𝕷𝖔𝖓𝖉𝖔𝖓 in 7 *E.* 1. and he Son of the said *Adam.* But whether it be so or not, I cannot affirm: in regard the Arms of this *William de Basings* and his issue are so very different from the former, namely, *az. a Crosse moline voided, Or*, which Coat is to be seen at this day in the Church Windows here at 𝕹𝖔𝖗𝖒𝖆𝖓𝖙𝖔𝖓,

and also at 𝕰𝖒𝖕𝖎𝖓𝖌𝖍𝖆𝖒 in this County. However, I am apt to believe that this *William de Basings* is the same person with *William Basing*, who was one of the Sheriffs of 𝕷𝖔𝖓𝖉𝖔𝖓 in 2 *E.* 2. and a great Benefactor to the Priory *Stows Sur.* of Black Nuns called St. *Hellens* with- *Lon. p. 178.* in *Bishopsgate* in 𝕷𝖔𝖓𝖉𝖔𝖓: Which Priory *Weavers Fun.* was first founded by *William Basing*, *Mon. p. 421.* Dean of *Pauls*, about the year 1212. in the Reign of King *John.*

Certain it is, that the said *William de Basings*, enjoyed this Estate by reason that he marryed *Margaret* Daughter and heir of *Thomas de Normanville*, Lord of this Town, by which *Margaret* he had issue *Thomas de Basings*, whose Grandson Sir *John de Basings* Knight, depar- *Ex Stem.* ted this life in the 24 *H.* 6. without issue: After whose death this Estate came by discent into the name and family of the *Mackworths, Thomas Mackworth* of *Mackworth* in *Com.* 𝕯𝖊𝖗𝖇𝖞, having marryed *Alice*, the Sister and heir, of the said Sir *John de Basings.* Brother to which *Thomas Mackworth*, was *John Mackworth*, Dean of 𝕷𝖎𝖓𝖈𝖔𝖑𝖓 in the Reign of King *H.* 6. * To whom * *Stow. Sur.* did formerly belong the Messuage in *Lond. p. 430.* *Holborn* now known by the name of *Dug. Orig.* *Bernards Inn*, but antiently called *Jurid.* *Mackworths Inn.*

From which said *Thomas* descended *George Mackworth* Esq; who in the space of forty years, was five times high Sheriff of this County, and dyed 28 *H.*8. whose great Grandson *Thomas Mackworth* of 𝕹𝖔𝖗𝖒𝖆𝖓𝖙𝖔𝖓 Esq; was by Patent dated 4 *Jun.* in the 17 *Jac.* (1619) advanced to the Degree of a Baronet of this Kingdom, being the 106th. in the List of that Honour: from whom descends Sir *Thomas Mackworth* Baronet, the present Lord of this Mannour and 𝕰𝖒𝖕𝖎𝖓𝖌𝖍𝖆𝖒: the 14th. in degree from *Thomas de Normanville* who departed this life in 3 *H.* 3.

Thomas

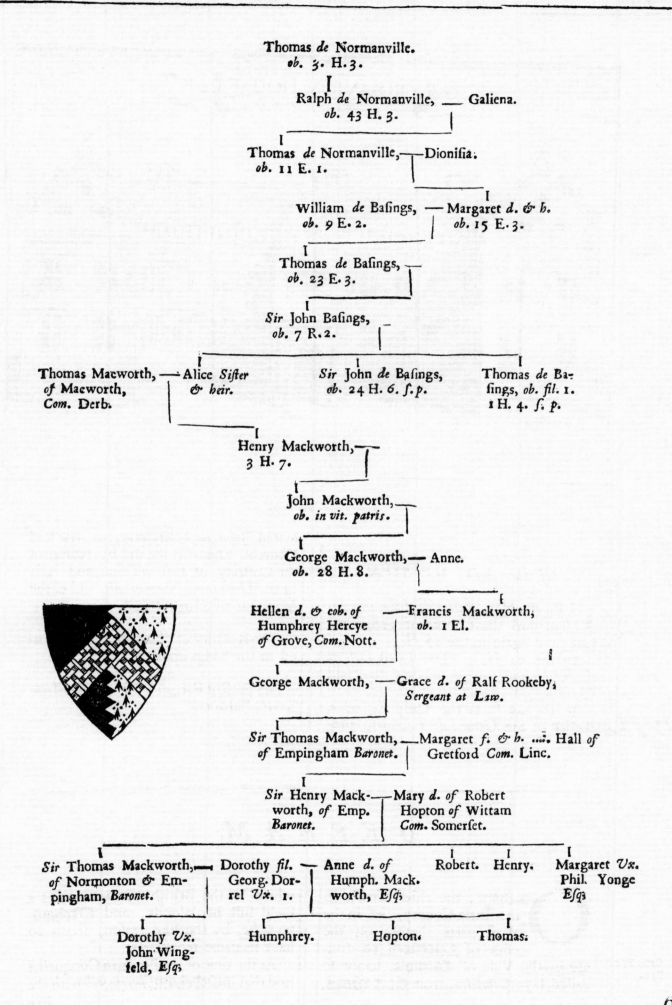

Thomas *de* Normanville.
ob. 3. H. 3.

Ralph *de* Normanville, ___ Galiena.
ob. 43 H. 3.

Thomas *de* Normanville, ——Dionifia.
ob. 11 E. 1.

William *de* Bafings, — Margaret *d. & h.*
ob. 9 E. 2.   *ob.* 15 E. 3.

Thomas *de* Bafings, —
ob. 23 E. 3.

Sir John Bafings,
ob. 7 R. 2.

Thomas Macworth, ——Alice *Sifter*   *Sir* John *de* Bafings,   Thomas *de* Ba-
of Macworth,   *& heir.*   *ob.* 24 H. 6. *f. p.*   fings, *ob. fil.* 1.
Com. Derb.   1 H. 4. *f. p.*

Henry Mackworth, ——
3 H. 7.

John Mackworth, __
ob. in vit. patris.

George Mackworth, — Anne.
ob. 28 H. 8.

Hellen *d. & coh. of* ——Francis Mackworth,
Humphrey Hercye   *ob.* 1 El.
of Grove, *Com.* Nott.

George Mackworth, ——Grace *d. of* Ralf Rookeby,
                     Sergeant at Law.

Sir Thomas Mackworth, __Margaret *f. & h.* .... Hall *of*
of Empingham *Baronet.*   Gretford *Com.* Linc.

Sir Henry Mack-——Mary *d. of* Robert
worth, *of* Emp.   Hopton *of* Wittam
Baronet.   *Com.* Somerfet.

Sir Thomas Mackworth,——Dorothy *fil.* — Anne *d. of*   Robert. Henry. Margaret *Vx.*
of Normonton *& Em-*   Georg. Dor- Humph. Mack.   Phil. Yonge
pingham, *Baronet.*   rel *Vx.* 1. worth, *Efq;*   *Efq;*

Dorothy *Vx.*   Humphrey.   Hopton.   Thomas.
John Wing-
feld, *Efq;*

O

NORMANTON HOUSE
on the East side.

Of the ADVOWSON.

Reg. Linc.

IN the 12 *H.* 3. *Robert de Albiniaco* presented to the Church of 𝕹𝖔𝖟𝖒𝖆𝖓𝖙𝖔𝖓; and again in the 17 *H.* 3.

Ibid.

In the 21 *H.* 3. The Lord *Gilbert de Umfreville* presented. to the said Church.

Ex Collect. Wingf. Bod. mil.

In the 25 *E.* 1. the Lady *Euftachia*, Relict of Sir *Gerard de Fauecart*, presented *John de Schireborne*, to the said Church, and this she did by reason of the Custody of *Edmond* Son and Heir of Sir *Thomas de Normanville*, and of the Mannour of 𝕹𝖔𝖟𝖒𝖆𝖓𝖙𝖔𝖓.

The Rectory of 𝕹𝖔𝖟𝖒𝖆𝖓𝖙𝖔𝖓 is valued in the Kings Books at 5 *l.* 4 *s.* 7 *d.*

The present Patron is Sir *Thomas Mackworth*, Baronet.

O K E H A M.

Cam. Brit. Rutl.

O𝖐𝖊𝖍𝖆𝖒, the chief Town in this little County, lies in the West parts thereof on the edge of 𝕷𝖊𝖎𝖈𝖊𝖘𝖙𝖊𝖗𝖘𝖍𝖎𝖗𝖊, situate in the Vale of 𝕮𝖆𝖙𝖒𝖔𝖘𝖊, haply so called, sayes *Cambden*, from 𝕮𝖔𝖊𝖙 𝕸𝖆𝖊𝖟, which in the British tongue signifies a Field full of Woods, and 𝕺𝖐𝖊𝖍𝖆𝖒, sayes he, by the like reason, seems to have its name from *Oakes*.

At the time of the Norman Conquest, I find that in 𝕺𝖈𝖍𝖊𝖍𝖆𝖒 *Cherchesoch* with the five

five Berews, or Hamlets, thereunto belonging, Queen *Eddid* held four Carucates of Land, as rated to the Tax or Geld. Of arable Land there were fixteen carucates. Afterwards the King had here two Carucates *ad aulam*, and befides which about four Carucates more. Here were a hundred and thirty eight Villains, and nineteen *Bordarii* having amongft them thirty feven Carucates, and a quarter, and twenty Acres of Meadow. There was here at that time one Prieft and a Church, to which did belong four Bovates of this Land. Here was alfo a Wood (*filva paftilis*) being one mile in length, and half a mile in breadth. All which was, in the time of King *Edward*, valued at 40 *l.*

Here alfo one *Levenot* did before the Conqueft hold one Carucate of Land as it was rated to the Tax or Geld. Which at the time of the Survey, *Fulcherus Mala opera* enjoyed, being five Bovates, and fix Acres of Meadow, valued then at 20 *s.*

The whole Mannour of Ocheham with the faid Hamlets or Berews, is faid in the Record of *Domefday* to contain three miles in length, and one mile and eight quarantenes, or furlongs in breadth.

Albertus Clericus (or *Aubrey* the Clerk) held at the time of *Domefday* Survey the Churches of Ocheham, and Hameldun, and St. *Peters* in Stanford, which belongs to Hameldun, together with the Lands adjoyning to the faid Churches, *viz.* feven Bovates; all which the faid *Albertus* had by the Kings Grant and favour. And he held in Demefne four Carucates, and eighteen Villains, and fix *Bordarii* having five Carucates. Which laft mentioned eftate was valued in the time of King *Edward* at 8 *l.* but at the Conquerours Survey at 10 *l.*

At the time of the aforementioned Survey there was in Noffitone (now called Knofton in *Com. Leiceft.*) three Carucates of Land appurtaining to the Soke of Ocheham, there were feventeen Socmen, and fix *Bordarii*, having fix Carucates; there was alfo a Wood of one furlong in length and half a furlong in Breadth, all then valued at 20 *s.* and held by the King in Demefne.

Afterwards this Mannour of Oke-

ham became part of the Poffeffions of the *Newburgs*, a Noble family of the Normans, who came into England with Duke *William*, and by him made Earls of Warwick: for I find that the younger Son of the faid *William* the Conquerour, *viz.* King *Hen.* 1. granted the Lordfhip of Sutton in *Com.* Warwick, in a very ample manner, together with a free Chace, and other Liberties, to *Roger de Newburg*, the fecond Earl of Warwick of the Norman Race; in Exchange for the Mannours of Hocham and Langham in *Com.* Roteland, then held by the faid Earl.

But it feems that this Mannour of Okeham continued not long in the Crown, but was regranted to another eminent Subject, of the Noble Family *de Ferrariis*.

The firft Baron of Okeham was *Walkeline de Ferrers* a younger Son to *William de Ferrers* Earl of Darby, which *Walkeline* held Okeham by the fervice of one Knights fee, and a half, in the 12 *H.* 2. and in the 22 *H.* 2. paid a hundred marks for trefpaffing in the Kings Forrefts in thofe parts. In 33 *H.* 2, he anfwered 30 *s.* for one Knights fee and a half, upon Collection of the Scutage of Galweye. And in the 1 *R.* 1. was acquitted for the affarting of eighty acres of Land in the Forreft of Roteland; *viz.* in the fields of Okeham fifty five acres, in the fields of Braunfton twenty acres, and in the fields of Broc five acres. But that which is moft memorable of him, is that he was at the famous Seige of Acon in the Holy Land, with King *Ric.* 1. in the third year of his Reign. *Hugh* the Son of this *Walkeline* dying without iffue about the begining of King *John*, *Ifabel* his Sifter, Wife to *Roger* Lord *Mortimer*, became his heir. Who in the ninth year of the faid King *John*, gave feven hundred marks, and feven Palfreys for Livery of the faid Mannor of Okeham.

In the 36 *H.* 3. *Richard* Earl of Cornwall a younger Son of King *John*, obtained a Grant of the Mannor of Okeham in Rutland (fometime belonging to *Ifabel de Mortimer*) in part of payment of 500 *l.* due to him from the King, on the marriage of *Senchia* his Wife, Daughter of the Earl of Province

vince to hold to himself, and the Heirs of his Body by her. This *Richard* Earl of 𝕮𝖔𝖗𝖓𝖜𝖆𝖑 was crowned King of the Romans at 𝕬𝖎𝖗 in 𝕲𝖊𝖗𝖒𝖆𝖓𝖞, *anno* 1257. whose Son, *Edmund* Earl of 𝕮𝖔𝖗𝖓𝖜𝖆𝖑, died without Iſſue, 28 *E.* 1. After whoſe death, *Margaret* his Widow held this Eſtate for her life, *Vide* 𝕷𝖆𝖓𝖌𝖍𝖆𝖒 *ſupr.*

Bar. Eng. 2 Vol. 92. In the 15 *E* 2. The Caſtle of 𝕺𝖐𝖊𝖍𝖆𝖒, and Shrevalty of the County of 𝕽𝖚𝖙𝖑𝖆𝖓𝖉 was granted to *Edmund* Earl of 𝕶𝖊𝖓𝖙, the ſaid Kings ſecond Brother: which *Edmund* was attaint of Treaſon in Parliament, and executed 4 *E.* 3.

Bar. Eng. 1. Vol. p. 185. In the 11 *E.* 3. *William de Bohun*, Earl of 𝕹𝖔𝖗𝖙𝖍𝖆𝖒𝖕𝖙𝖔𝖓, had a grant from the Crown, of the Caſtle and Mannour of 𝕺𝖐𝖊𝖍𝖆𝖒, and of the Shrevalty of the County of 𝕽𝖚𝖙𝖑𝖆𝖓𝖉, to hold to himſelf, and the Heirs Males of his Body, under certain conditions in the ſaid Grant expreſſed. Whoſe Son *Humphrey de Bohun* Earl of 𝕹𝖔𝖗𝖙𝖍𝖆𝖒𝖕𝖙𝖔𝖓, by deſcent from his Father, and Earl of 𝕳𝖊𝖗𝖊𝖋𝖔𝖗𝖉 and 𝕰𝖘𝖘𝖊𝖝, as heir to his Unkle, died ſeized of this Mannour, 46 *E.* 3. leaving only two Daughters; *Eleanor*, who became the Wife of *Thomas of* 𝖂𝖔𝖔𝖉𝖘𝖙𝖔𝖈𝖐, (ſixth Son to King *Henry* the third) and *Mary* married to *Henry* Earl of 𝕯𝖊𝖗𝖇𝖞, afterwards King of 𝕰𝖓𝖌𝖑𝖆𝖓𝖉; by the name of *Henry* 4. It reverting thus again to the Crown in default of iſſue male, *Rich.* 2. in the ninth year of his Reign, *Bar. Eng. 1 Vol. 194.* having retain'd *Robert Vere* Earl of 𝕺𝖝𝖋𝖔𝖗𝖉 (and afterward Marqueſs of 𝕯𝖚𝖇𝖑𝖎𝖓, and Duke of 𝕴𝖗𝖊𝖑𝖆𝖓𝖉) into his imployment; did in conſideration of the great coſts and expences he was at in his ſervice, give him the Caſtle and Lordſhip of 𝕺𝖐𝖊𝖍𝖆𝖒, with all the Forreſt of 𝕽𝖚𝖙𝖑𝖆𝖓𝖉, to hold for the term of his Life, the Remainder to the heirs Males of his Body : Yet this was but an earneſt of what follow'd; for in the ſame year, he granted him the Land and Dominion of 𝕴𝖗𝖊𝖑𝖆𝖓𝖉 with all profits, *&c.* as amply as the King himſelf ought to have the ſame, excepting to the King the Homage, Reſort, and Superiority of that Country. But this great and invidious Favourite, being (not without cauſe) highly diſguſted by the Nobility, more eſpecially the aboveſaid *Henry* Earl of 𝕯𝖊𝖗𝖇𝖞, he was forced to flie the Kingdom, baniſht in Parliament, outlaw'd, and his Eſtate ſeized; and being beyond Sea, he was wounded by a wild Boar in

hunting, of which he died at 𝕷𝖔𝖇𝖆𝖎𝖓𝖊 16 *R.* 2. (1392.) without iſſue.

But his Eſtate in 𝕺𝖐𝖊𝖍𝖆𝖒, was it ſeems revoked long before his death, for during his troubles, the abovemention'd *Thomas of* 𝖂𝖔𝖔𝖉𝖘𝖙𝖔𝖈𝖐 Duke of 𝕲𝖑𝖔𝖚𝖈𝖊𝖘𝖙𝖊𝖗, one of his Arch enemies, *Bar. Eng. 2. Vol. 170.* obtain'd of the ſaid King about the 12. year of his Reign, a Grant of the Caſtle, Town, and Mannour of 𝕺𝖐𝖊𝖍𝖆𝖒 with the Shrevalty of the County, late part of the Poſſeſſions of *William de Bohun* Earl of 𝕹𝖔𝖗𝖙𝖍𝖆𝖒𝖕𝖙𝖔𝖓 Which *Thomas* left iſſue *Anne* his Daughter and ſole Heir, who was firſt married to *Edmund* Earl of 𝕾𝖙𝖆𝖋𝖋𝖔𝖗𝖉, and after his death to Sir *William Bourchier*, Kt. Earl of 𝕰𝖜𝖊.

But in 13 *R.* 2. *Edward.* eldeſt ſon of *Edmund of Langley* Duke of 𝕻𝖔𝖗𝖐 fifth ſon of King *Edward* the Third, being created Earl of 𝕽𝖚𝖙𝖑𝖆𝖓𝖉 for his Fathers *Bar. Eng. 2. Vol. 156.* life; had therewithal a Grant of the ſaid Caſtle, Town, and Lordſhip of 𝕺𝖐𝖊𝖍𝖆𝖒, with the Shrevalty of the ſaid County, in part of ſatisfaction of eight hundred Marks *per Annum* intended to him: Which *Edward* was in the 21. of the ſaid Kings Reign made Conſtable of 𝕰𝖓𝖌𝖑𝖆𝖓𝖉, and Duke of 𝕬𝖑𝖇𝖊𝖒𝖆𝖗𝖑𝖊; but after upon the depoſal of King *Richard*, the title of Duke was taken from him: and tho at firſt he oppoſed King *Henry* the Fourth, yet afterwards he became much in his favour; and in the Parliament 7 *H.* 4. was reſtored to his Hereditary Dignity of Duke of 𝕻𝖔𝖗𝖐; and loſt his Life in the Battle of 𝕬𝖌𝖎𝖓𝖈𝖔𝖚𝖗𝖙. 3 *H.* 5.

In the Reign of *Henry* 6. *Humphrey Stafford* Duke of 𝕭𝖚𝖈𝖐𝖎𝖓𝖌𝖍𝖆𝖒, deſcen- *Bar. Eng. 1 Vol. 166.* ded from the aboveſaid *Thomas of* 𝖂𝖔𝖔𝖉𝖘𝖙𝖔𝖈𝖐 (*viz.* Son of *Edmund* Earl of 𝕾𝖙𝖆𝖋𝖋𝖔𝖗𝖉, and *Anne* Daughter and ſole Heir of the ſaid *Thomas*) was joyntly with *Anne* his Wife ſeized of the Caſtle, Mannour, and Lordſhip of 𝕺𝖐𝖊𝖍𝖆𝖒, with two * Parks there, the one *Eſc. 38, 39 H. 6. n. 37.* called 𝕱𝖑𝖊𝖙𝖊𝖗𝖎𝖘, the other 𝕾𝖙𝖔𝖓𝖊-𝕻𝖆𝖗𝖐, and ſo ſeized died the 38 *H.* 6. which Eſtate the ſaid *Anne* held after his death: and in the 1 *E* 4. made *William* Lord *Haſtings* her Steward of the ſaid Mannour, and Conſtable of the ſaid Caſtle. *Bar. Eng. 1 Vol. 584.* The ſaid *Anne* Dutcheſs of 𝕭𝖚𝖈𝖐𝖎𝖓𝖌𝖍𝖆𝖒, was Daughter to *Ralph Nevil* the firſt Earl of 𝖂𝖊𝖘𝖙𝖒𝖔𝖗𝖊𝖑𝖆𝖓𝖉, and married for her ſecond Husband Sir *Walter Blount*, Kt. Lord *Mountjoy*, and departed ed this life in the twentieth year of *E.* 4. After whose deceafe, *Henry* Duke of **Buckingham**, Son and Heir of the faid *Humphry* and *Anne*, fucceeded his Father in his Honours, and poffeft alfo (no doubt) this Eftate; till endeavouring to depofe *Richard* 3. whom he (cheifly) had lately advanced to the Throne; he was by that Kings command beheaded at *Salisbury*, without any legal Tryal, *An.* 1484. (1 *R.* 3.)

Bar. Eng. 1 *Vol.* 712.

After whofe Death *Henry* Lord *Grey* of **Codnoure** in *Com.* **Derby** obtain'd a grant, in the faid firft year of *R.* 3. of the Mannors of **Okeham**, **Langham**, and **Egefton**, from that King to hold to the faid Lord *Henry*, and the heirs Males of his body lawfully begotten. But this gift ended with his life, (if not fooner) for in the 11th. of *H.* 7. he dyed without any lawful iffue. After which *Edward Stafford* the laft *Duke* of **Buckingham** of that family, enjoyed this Eftate, till his Attainder, 13. *H.* 8.

Bar. Eng. 2. *Vol.* 371.

At which time it reverting to the Crown, and King *Hen.* 8. having created his great Mignion, *Thomas Cromwell*, a Baron of this Realm by the name of Lord *Cromwell* of **Okeham**, among other his many Bounties, in the 30th. year of his reign, granted him the Caftle and Lordfhip of **Okeham**, which faid Lord, not long after falling into the Kings disfavour, and accufed of feveral high Crimes was on the 24th. of *July* 32 *H.* 8. beheaded on the Tower hill: Leaving iffue *Gregory Cromwell* his Son and heir. Which *Gregory* was by a new patent bearing date the 18th. of *December* 32 *H.* 8. created a Baron of this Realm, by the Title of Lord *Cromwell*, but not diftinguifht by any Place.

Id. 375.

The faid Lord held the Caftle and Mannour of **Okeham**, the Mannour of **Langham**, two Windmills, three other Mills, fixty Meffuages, twenty Cottages with their appurtenances in **Okeham**, **Langham**, and * **Flittereys**,

Efc. 5 *E.*6. *pars* 2. *n.* 45.

of the King *in Capite*, by Knights fervice in Fee : Alfo the Mannour of **Lyddington**, and Lands belonging to the late Chantry at **Manton**, with their appurtenances in **Lyddington**, **Belton**, **Wardly**, **Stokedry**, and **Snelfton**, with the Advowfon of **Ward-**

* *Formerly a Park belonging to the Lords of Okeham; firft inclofed in the* 36 *H.* 3. *by Richard Earl of Cornwall. Vid. Efch.* 36 *H.* 3. *n.* 44.

ly, of the King, by the Rent of 14 *l.* 3 *s.* 5 *d. ob. per an.* for all fervices as appear'd by Letters Patents granted by King *Edward* the 6th. to the faid *Gregory* Lord *Cromwell*. And this laft mention'd eftate was for the lives of himfelf and *Elizabeth* his Wife. All this was found by office taken at **Uppingham** 25 *Sept.* 5 *E.* 6. Upon the Death of the faid *Gregory*, and that *Henry* Lord *Cromwell*, was his Son and heir. Whofe Son and heir *Edward* Lord *Cromwell*, obtain'd licenfe, dated 12 *Feb.* 38. *Eliz.* to alienate the Caftle and Mannour of **O-keham** with the appurtenances, to Sir *John Harrington* Knight (created Lord *Harrington* 1 *Jac.*) And accordingly it was found by office taken on the 22 *March*, 14 *Jac.* That *John* Lord *Harrington* the Elder, dyed feized (*inter alia*) of the Mannor, Caftle, and Lordfhip of **Okeham** with the appurtenances, in **Okeham**, **Braunfton**, **Wardly**, and **Belton**, all which he held *in Capite* by Knights Service. And this Eftate was after the faid Lords Death enjoy'd by *Anne* Lady *Harrington*, his Widdow, as part of her joynture. But was, not long after, conveyed to the late Duke of **Buckingham**, whofe Son and heir, the right Noble *George*, now Duke of **Buckingham**, is the prefent Owner of the Caftle, Mannour, and Lordfhip of **Okeham**.

Rot. Pat. 38 *El. pars* 6.

Efch. 14. *Jac. pars* 2. *n.* 116.

The Family of *Flore*, alias *Flowr* (an antient and Worfhipful name, of which fee more in **Whitwell**, *infra*) was formerly Seated in this Town, on a fair Eftate of Freehold, viz. ten Meffuages, an hundred Acres of Land, ten Acres of Meadow *cum pertinent.* held of the Lord of this Mannour by Fealty only, which Eftate, or the greateft part of it was afterwards, in the Reign of Queen *Eliz.* purchafed of one *William Flowr*, a younger Branch of that family, by *Hugh Booth* Rector of **Cuffington** in *Com. Leic.*

Efch. 15 *H.* 8. *n.* 23.

H Ere is alfo another Mannor, containing part of this Town, and all **Barlythorp** a Hamlet in this Parifh, belonging to the Dean and Chapter of **Westminster** Of which fee more in **Barlythorp**, *Supra.*

O

Of

Of the Church there.

Reg. Linc.

IN the 12 *H.* 3. the Abbot of Weſt=minſter preſented to the Church of Pocham, *Gilbert Mareſcallus. Salvo* Willielmo *ejuſdem eccleſiæ vicario, &* Rogero *de* Sancto Johanne *Vicario Capellæ de* Bzanteſton *jure ſuo quod habent in iſtis Vicariis, &* Salvo Galfrido *qui Capellam de* Gnoſſington *tenuit jure ſuo in eadem, proviſum eſt etiam per dictum Epiſcopum quod dictus* Gilbertus *nullum habuit jus in eccleſia de* Hameldon *per hanc inſtitutionem.*

Ibid.

In the 29 *E.* 1. the ſaid Abbot and Convent of *Weſtminſter,* preſented *John de Langford* to the Benefice of the Church of Ockam, which Benefice did then appear by inquiſition, to be in *Rectoria & non in vicaria: & conſiſtere in portionibus infra ſcriptis, viz. in toto alteragio Eccl. de* Ockam, *& capellarum de* Langham, Egleton, Bzock, Gun=thozp, *& de* Thozp, *cum omnibus minutis Decimis ad alteragium qualitercunq; ſpectantibus, & cum medietate ſeni om-*

nium parochanorum tam Eccl. de Ockam *quam capellarum prædict. & in una Carucata Terræ cum pertinentiis, & uno manſo ex parte auſtrali Eccleſiæ de* Ockam *ſcituato, & in decimis Garbarum in parochia de* Ockam *ad eſtimationem trium marcarum, & in una Marca quæ Capella de* Knoſſington *Eccleſiæ de* Ockam *ſoluerit annuatim.*

After the Deſolution of *Weſtminſter* Abby, King *E.* 6. in the 4*th.* year of his reign, granted among other things the Advowſon of the Vicarage of the Church of Ockeham, to *Nicholas Ridley* Biſhop of London and to his Succeſſors for ever ; and this was by his Charter dated 12 day of *April* in the ſaid 4*th.* year of his reign.   *4 E.6. pars 4.*

The Vicarage of Ockeham *cum Capellis*, is valued in the Kings Books at, 28 *l.* 3 *s.*

The preſent Patron is the Biſhop of London.

Monuments remaining in the Church of Okeham.

In a Chappel on the South ſide of the Chancel, on a Plate of Braſs fixt in a Marble Graveſtone.

Sub hoc marmoze requieſcit tumulatus Franciſc. Waryn de Okeham Mercatoz Staple Uille Callec. filius Williel. Waryn hic cozam iſto altare beate Mariæ Sepulti qui quidem Franciſcus Duzit in uzozem Elizabetham Aſheby quondam filiam Willielmi Aſheby De Lowesby in Com. Leiceſt. Armigeri qui quidem Franciſc. diem ſuum clauſit extremum xx. Die Auguſti An. Dom. M. Vᶜ x. Et An. R.R. Henrici viii. ii. cujus anime ppittetur Deus.

In the Body of the Church, about the Verge of a Graveſtone.

✠ Hic jacent Willielmus Flore & Elena Uxoz ejus qui quidem Willielmus obiit pzimo .... Septuogeſimo nono quoz animabus pzopicietur Deus, Amen.

Facies Ecclesiæ parochialis de Okeham ab Austro.

Near the North building, on a Graveſtone adorn'd with
Braſs Plates and Sculpture.

HIc jacet Thomas Flore **quondam de** Okeham **Armiger qui quidem** Thomas **obiit die** Lunæ **prima poſt feſtum. S.** Nicholai **Epiſcopi An. Dom.** Mil. CCCC. Lxxxiii. **cujus anime ppicietur De⁹.** Amen.

On the North ſide of the Middle Chancel is erected a plain **Tomb** of
Freeſtone, about which the following words
were lately remaining.

ORate p𝔯o animabus .... Wyght **iſtius Uille qui obiit** xi. **die menſis** Octobris **An. Dom.** M. Vᶜ .... **& con-ſo𝔯tis ſui, Quo𝔯um animabus ppicietur Deus.**

In the Body of the Church near the North Door, on a plain Graveſtone.

..........**filia** Rogeri Flore **quondam u𝔯o𝔯** Henrici Pleſſington..........

In the Chancel on a plain Graveſtone.

Subtus jacet Venerab. Vir Guil. Peachie *S. T. B. quondam Coll. D.* Joh. *Cant. Soc. nuper hujus Eccleſiæ Vic. Morum innocentia ſatis laudatus, in arte concionandi Verſatiſſ.*

Quatuor }   *Inſignum Theologor.*   { *Pater.*
Trium }   { *Soror.*
          Qui Octob. 6.

Non tam morbo confectus, quam vivendi tædio laſſatus, placide expiravit.

      { *Dom.* 1643.
A⁰. { *Ætat.* 78.
      { *Reſidentiæ,* 47.

Noli vexare : Quieſcit.

South of the Chancell on a ſmall neat Monument, in the Wall.

Ann *the Daughter of* Andrew Burton *of* **Okeham,** *Eſq;* *Fellow of* **G𝔯ayes Inn,** *departed this Life,* June 19. A. D. 1642. *Æt.* 15.

> *Reader ſtand back; dull not this marble Shrine*
> *With irreligious breath : the Stone's divine,*
> *And does incloſe a Wonder; Beauty, Wit,*
> *Devotion, and Virginity with it.*
> *Which like a Lilly fainting in its prime,*
> *Wither'd and left the World; deceitful Time*
> *Cropt it too ſoon : and Earth the ſelf ſame Womb*
> *From whence is ſprung, is now become its Tomb.*
> *Whoſe ſweeter ſoul, a Flower of matchleſs price;*
> *Tranſplanted is from hence to Paradice.*

Andreas *&* Anna Mæſtiſſ. *Parentes, P P.*

On a plain Monument or Memorial, lately erected
This Inscription.

IN memory *of* John Booth *of this Parish, Gent. who departed
this Life,* Apr. 1. An. Dom. 1649. *and of* Mabella *his Wife,
only sister to* Andrew Burton, *Esq; who also departed this Life,
on the 6. day of* March, An. Dom. 1656.
Death is to us a New Life.

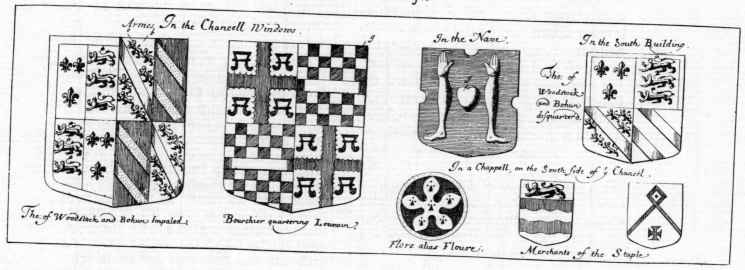

Armes In the Chancell Windows.

In the Nave.

In the South Building.

Tho: of Woodstock and Bohun disquartered.

Tho: of Woodstock and Bohun Impaled.

Bourchier quartering Lowain.

In a Chappell, on the South side of ye Chancel.

Flore alias Floure.

Merchants of the Staple.

Of the Market, and Fairs, here.

Rot. Pat. 36
H. 3. m. 10.

KIng *Henry* the 3*d.* by his Charter dated at *Westminster,* the 5*th.* day of *June* in the 36 year of his reign, granted to his beloved Brother *Richard* Earl of **Cornwall,** and to his heirs by his Wife *Sanchia* Daughter of the Earl of **Province,** that they should have, at their Mannour of **Okeham** in the County of **Rutland,** two Merkates weekly, *viz.* one on the *Monday,* and the other on the *Saturday:* And two Fairs there yearly, *viz.* one on the Vigil-day, and Morrow, of the Decollation of St. *John Baptist* (*Aug.*29.) the other on the Vigil, Day, and Morrow, of the invention of the Holy Cross (*May* 3.) *Nisi mercata illa, & feriæ illæ sint ad nocumentum,* &c.

Esc. 38,39 H.6.
m. 37.

But it seems in process of time, the *Monday* Mercate, and one of the Fairs were discontinued or grown out of use. For in the Inquisition taken after the death of *Humphrey* Duke of **Bucks,** in the 39 *H.*6. There is mention made only of one Merkate here weekly on the *Saturday,* and one Fair on the Feast of the decollation of St. *John Baptist* yearly; the profits whereof were then valued at 14 *s. per annum.*

Of the Old Hospital in **Okeham.**

Mon. Ang. 2.
Vol. 473.

OF the Hospital of St. *John* and St. *Anne* in this Town, I find that King *Richard* 2*d.* in the 22*th.* year of his Reign gave License to *William Dalby* of **Extone** to found and establish a certain Hospital at **Okeham,** to consist of two Chaplains, whereof one to be *Custos* and perpetual, the other removeable, and of twelve poor men, to pray for the good estate of the said King and *Isabel* his Queen, and after their Decease for their Souls, and for the Soul of *Anne* his late Queen deceased, and for the late King, and Queens souls, for the good Estate of the said *William Dalby* and *Agnes* his Wife, and after their decease for their souls, and the souls of all the Faithful deceased; with License to the said *William Dalby* to give and assign to the said Hospital, one Messuage and two acres of Land; with License also to give and assign the Advowson, Patronage, and Collation, of the said Hospital to the Prior and Covent of St. *Anne* of the order of Carthusians neer **Coventry,** being of the said Kings Foundation, with License also to the said Prior and Covent to give and assign out of their possessions a yearly Rent of 40 *l.* to the *Custos* of
the

Ex Autogr. penes Vic. de Okeham.

the said Hospital for the maintenance of the said *Custos*, and twelve poor men, and their successors for ever.

After this, in the year 1421 (1 H. 5.) *Roger Flore* of 𝕺𝖐𝖊𝖍𝖆𝖒 Esquire (who had married *Catherine* Daughter and heir of the said *William Dalby*) reciting the foundation of the said Hospital according to the above specified License in a certain place, called 𝕮𝖍𝖆𝖒𝖇𝖊𝖗=𝖑𝖊𝖞𝖓𝖊𝖘 𝕮𝖗𝖔𝖋𝖙 within the parish of 𝕺=𝖐𝖊𝖍𝖆𝖒, reciting also that the said *Wiliam Dalby* had reserved power to himself and the said *Roger* (now by the Death of the said *William* Patron of the Hospital) to declare, correct, reform, or add to the Statutes of the said Hospital, he therefore the said *Roger*, with the License of the said King *H.* 5. *Richard* then Bishop of 𝕷𝖎𝖓𝖈𝖔𝖑𝖓, and all others then concern'd, made several alterations and additions to the former Statutes of *Dalbys* Constitution, *inter alia*, that in case his heirs or Successors should at any time be negligent and remiss in bestowing the respective places of the *Custos*, Chaplain, or twelve poor men (any of the said places being void by death, removal, or otherwise) that then the power, *illa vice*, of conferring the said places shall devolve to the Vicar of the parish Church of 𝕺𝖐𝖊𝖍𝖆𝖒, so also in case the heir of the said *Roger* the Patron, shall at that time happen by reason of his Nonage to be in Ward; in case the said Vicar of 𝕺𝖐𝖊𝖍𝖆𝖒 be negligent, or in parts beyond the Seas, then the said power to remain, *illa vice*, to the Abbot and Covent of *Westminster*, Proprietaries of the said Church of 𝕺𝖐𝖊𝖍𝖆𝖒, and in case at that time the Abby of *Westminster* be void of an Ab-

bot, the said power to remain to the Abbot of 𝕺𝖘𝖊𝖑𝖜𝖊𝖘𝖙𝖔𝖓 *in Com.* 𝕷𝖊𝖎𝖈. The aforesaid Rent of 40 *l. per an.* to be thus distributed, to the *Custos* 6 *l.* 13 *s.* 4 *d. per an.* to the Chaplain 5 *l. per an.* to each poor man 10 *d. ob. per* week, To the Vicar of 𝕺𝖐𝖊𝖍𝖆𝖒 3 *s.* 4 *d. per an.* for a composition late made and confirmed by the Bishop: The residue being 16 *s.* 8 *d.* to be disposed of for Repairs: The *Custos*, Chaplain, and poor men at their several admissions to be sworn in the presence of the Patron or his Deputy, and the Vicar of 𝕺𝖐𝖊𝖍𝖆𝖒. The form of which Oath to be as follows, J. A. B. 𝕿𝖍𝖊 𝖜𝖍𝖎𝖈𝖍 𝖆𝖒 𝖓𝖆𝖒𝖊𝖉 𝖎𝖓𝖙𝖔 𝖆 𝖕𝖔𝖔𝖗 𝖒𝖆𝖓 𝖙𝖔 𝖇𝖊 𝖗𝖊𝖈𝖊𝖕𝖛𝖊𝖉 𝖎𝖓𝖙𝖔 𝖙𝖍𝖎𝖘 𝕳𝖔𝖘𝖕𝖎𝖙𝖆𝖑 𝖆𝖋𝖙𝖊𝖗 𝖙𝖍𝖊 𝖋𝖔𝖗𝖒𝖊 𝖔𝖋 𝖙𝖍𝖊 𝕾𝖙𝖆𝖙𝖚𝖙𝖊𝖟 𝖆𝖓𝖉 𝖔𝖗𝖉𝖆𝖓𝖆𝖈𝖎𝖔𝖓𝖘 𝖔𝖗𝖉𝖊𝖞𝖓𝖊𝖉 𝖎𝖓 𝖙𝖍𝖊 𝖘𝖆𝖒𝖊 𝕳𝖔𝖘𝖕𝖎𝖙𝖆𝖑 𝖘𝖍𝖆𝖑𝖑 𝖙𝖗𝖊𝖜𝖑𝖞 𝖋𝖚𝖑𝖋𝖎𝖑𝖑𝖊 𝖆𝖓𝖉 𝖔𝖇𝖘𝖊𝖗𝖛𝖊 𝖆𝖑𝖑 𝖙𝖍𝖊 𝕾𝖙𝖆𝖙𝖚𝖙𝖊𝖘 𝖆𝖓𝖉 𝖔𝖗𝖉𝖊𝖓𝖆𝖓𝖈𝖊𝖘 𝖔𝖋 𝖙𝖍𝖊 𝖘𝖆𝖎𝖉𝖊 𝕳𝖔𝖘𝖕𝖎𝖙𝖆𝖑 𝖎𝖓 𝖆𝖘 𝖒𝖔𝖈𝖍𝖊 𝖆𝖘 𝖞𝖊𝖞 𝖑𝖔𝖓𝖌𝖊𝖓 𝖔𝖗 𝖙𝖔𝖚𝖈𝖍𝖊𝖓 𝖒𝖊 𝖙𝖔 𝖒𝖞 𝖕𝖔𝖚𝖗 𝖋𝖗𝖔 𝖍𝖊𝖓𝖘𝖇𝖔𝖗𝖙𝖍-𝖜𝖆𝖗𝖉𝖞𝖘 𝖉𝖚𝖗𝖎𝖓𝖌 𝖒𝖞 𝖙𝖎𝖒𝖊 𝖎𝖓 𝖙𝖍𝖊 𝖘𝖆𝖎𝖉𝖊 𝕳𝖔𝖘𝖕𝖎𝖙𝖆𝖑 𝖜𝖎𝖙𝖍𝖔𝖚𝖙 𝖔𝖓𝖞 𝖋𝖗𝖆𝖚𝖉𝖊 𝖘𝖔𝖊 𝖍𝖊𝖑𝖕𝖊 𝖒𝖊 𝕲𝖔𝖉 𝖆𝖓𝖉 𝖒𝖞 𝕳𝖔𝖑𝖞𝖉𝖔𝖒 𝖆𝖓𝖉 𝖇𝖞 𝖙𝖍𝖊𝖘𝖊 𝖍𝖔-𝖑𝖞 𝕰𝖛𝖆𝖓𝖌𝖊𝖑𝖎𝖊𝖘 𝖙𝖍𝖊 𝖜𝖍𝖎𝖈𝖍𝖊 𝖞 𝖙𝖔𝖚𝖈𝖍𝖊 𝖆𝖓𝖉 𝖑𝖊𝖞 𝖒𝖞 𝖍𝖔𝖓𝖉𝖊 𝖚𝖕𝖔𝖓.

In the 26 *H.* 8. this Hospital was valued at 12 *l.* 12 *s.* 11 *d.* But in *Speeds* Catalogue it is not valued. *Mon: Ang.* 1. *Vol.* 1043.

This Hospital is still in being, but the present Governors pretend it to be of a new foundation and Patronage.

In the Chappel Windows, North side.

𝕺𝖗𝖆𝖙𝖊 𝖕𝖗𝖔 𝖇𝖔𝖓𝖔 𝖘𝖙𝖆𝖙𝖚 Williel. Grafford & Ellene 𝖈𝖔𝖓𝖘𝖔𝖗𝖙𝖎𝖘 𝖘𝖚𝖊.

𝕺𝖗𝖆𝖙𝖊 𝖕𝖗𝖔 𝖇𝖔𝖓𝖔 𝖘𝖙𝖆𝖙𝖚 Henerici Bell 𝕰𝖙 Isabelle 𝖈𝖔𝖓𝖘𝖔𝖗𝖙𝖎𝖘 𝖘𝖚𝖊.

In the Hall Windows at the Old Hospitall.

Of the New Hospital, and School in Okeham.

Cam. Brit. Rutl.

ABout the year 1584. *Robert John-son* Parson of North-**Luffenham** in this County, and Archdeacon of **Leicester**, by his charitable Collections (or as *Cambden* calls it, *è Stipe Collaticia*) and more especially, out of certain conceal'd Lands, which he begg'd of Queen *Elizabeth* for this purpose, built and endowed a second Hospital in this Town by the name of *Christs Hospital*, and a free School; concerning which (long after the foundation) he made certain Statutes and Ordinances containing,

1. That there be twenty four Governours; of which the Bishops of **London**, and **Peterborough**, the Deans of *Westminster*, and **Peterborough**, the Archdeacon of **Northampton**, the Masters of Trinity and St. *Johns* Colledges in **Cambridge**, to be perpetual, and without election, the rest to be elected by the Major part of the then Governours, out of the Neighbouring Gentry or beneficed Clergy.

2. That the School-master be a Master of Arts at the time of his Election, his stipend 24 *l. per An.* that the same person be Warden of the Hospital, for which he is to receive 6 *l. per An.* more.

3. That there be an Usher, his salary 12 *l. per An.* that the said Usher be Sub-Warden in the Hospital, and read prayers twice a Week in the Chappel, for which 3 *l. per An.* more.

4. That there be fifteen poor men and a Woman, of which number eight to be Townsmen, their stipend, each 3 *l. per An.*

5. Seven Schollers to be chosen to receive each an exhibition of 40 *s per An.* at the University for seven years, if they so long continue there.

6. That there be a Receiver of the Revenues *&c.* his stipend 5 *l. per An.* and that there be two Audits *per An.* and that each Governour then present ceive 4 *s.* 4 *d.* for his Dinner, and Gloves.

Which Statutes and Ordinances are dated, *June* 17. 1. *Car.* 1.

The same *Johnson* founded also at **Uppingham**, another Hospital and Free School; both which foundations, as well that there as this here, have the same Patron, the same Governours, the same indowments, and the same Statutes, *mutatis mutandis.* See more in **Uppingham.**

Of the CASTLE.

Camb. Brit. Rutl.

THe Castle at **Okeham**, saith *Cambden*, was built by *Walkeline de Ferraiis*, of whom before.

In this Castle was formerly a Free Chappel, the Patronage of which belonged to the Lords of the Castle, as appears by Inquisition taken on the death of *Humphrey Stafford* Duke of **Buckingham**, *An.* 39. *H.* 6. And accordingly in the 32 *H.* 3 the Lady *Isabella* widow of *Roger de Mortuomari* presented to *Robert Grosted* then Bishop of **Lincoln**, *Richard* the son of *Hugh de Cliva* to be her Chaplain in the said Chappel, and this was by Deed, to which were Witness *John de Watton* then Prior of **Brook**, *William de Bellocampo*, *James de Bellocampo*, *Henry de Mortuomari*, *Gilbert de Meinell*, *Henry de Bevill*, *Henry de Murdac*, and others. *(Esc. 38, 39 H. 6. n. 37. / Reg. Linc.)*

In the 46 *H.* 3. the King of the Almains or Romans presented to the same. *(Ibid.)*

In the 17 *E.* 1. *Edward* E. of **Cornwall** presented to this Chappel, then void by the death of *William Dixi.* *(Ibid.)* The profits or revenue of which, was at that time thus valued, and did consist in 50 *s.* which the Chaplain received out of the Chamber of the said Earl, also in two Marks and a half, which he received from the Market of **Okeham**, and in the Tithes of the Earls Pasture grounds, which one year with an other, amounted to one Mark, also in the Obventions accruing to the said Chappel in the absence of the Earl and his Countess, also in the Tithes of the wool, Lamb, and Milk of six Cottagers, and lastly in (*uno honesto Domicilio*) one convenient house in the Town of **Okeham.**

In the 47 *E.* 3. This Castle being then in the Crown, upon the death of *Humphrey de Bohun*, that King granted his Precept to *Simon Ward* then Keeper of this Castle, to pay to *Nicholas de Stoke* parson of the Chappel here, the yearly Rent of eight Marks, 7 *s.* 1 *d. ob.* and four Loads of Wood, accustomably paid to the said Parson and his predecessors time out of mind. *(Rot. Pat. 47 E. 3. m. 28.)*

The

Aula Comitatus apud Castrum de Okeham.

The **Lord** of the Caſtle and Mannour of 𝕺𝕜𝖊𝖍𝖆𝖒 for the time being, claims by preſcription a Franchiſe or Royalty very rare, and of ſingular note ; *viz.* That the firſt time that any Peer of this Kingdom ſhall happen to paſs through the Precincts of this Lordſhip, he ſhall forfeit, as a Homage , a Shoe from the Horſe, whereon he rideth, unleſs he redeem it with mony.   The true Original of which cuſtome I have not been able on my utmoſt endeavour, to diſcover. But that ſuch is, and time out of mind hath been, the Uſage, appears by ſeveral Monumental Horſeſhoes, (ſome gilded and of curious Workmanſhip) nail'd upon the Caſtle Hall Door.

Some of which Horſeſhoes are ſtampt with the names of thoſe Lords who gave 'em, with the times when given, as follows ;

Henry Lord *Mordant,* 1602.
Edward Lord *Dudley.*
William Earl of 𝕻𝖊𝖒𝖇𝖟𝖔𝖐𝖊.
Phillip Earl of ·𝕸𝖔𝖓𝖙𝖌𝖔𝖒𝖊𝖗𝖞.
Henry Lord *Montegle,* 1607.
Henry Lord *Clifford,* 1607.
Lancelot Andrews Lord B. of 𝕰𝖑𝖞, 1614.
Lord *Noel,* 1617.

Henry Earl of 𝕳𝖚𝖓𝖙𝖎𝖓𝖌𝖙𝖔𝖓, 1620.
Ferdinando Lord *Haſtings,* 1621.
John Lord *Vaughan,* 1621.
Spencer Lord *Compton,* 1621.
Thomas L. *Cromwell* Vic. 𝕷𝖊 𝕮𝖆𝖑𝖊, 1631.
Nicholas Earl of 𝕭𝖆𝖓𝖇𝖚𝖗𝖞, 1655.
John L. *Bellaſis* Bar. of 𝖂𝖔𝖟𝖑𝖊𝖇𝖞, 1667.

With many others ; ſome of later date, and ſome more antient, whoſe inſcriptions are now hardly legible.

To the Lords Court, held within the Caſtle of 𝕺𝖐𝖊𝖍𝖆𝖒, ſeveral Towns, as well in this County as in 𝕷𝖊𝖎𝖈𝖊𝖘𝖙𝖊𝖗𝖘𝖍𝖎𝖗𝖊, owe ſuit ; namely 𝕭𝖟𝖆𝖚𝖓𝖘𝖙𝖔𝖓, 𝕭𝖊𝖑𝖙𝖔𝖓, and 𝖂𝖆𝖗𝖉𝖑𝖞 in 𝕽𝖚𝖙𝖑𝖆𝖓𝖉, and 𝕿𝖜𝖎𝖋𝖔𝖟𝖉 and 𝕿𝖍𝖔𝖟𝖕𝖊-𝕾𝖆𝖈𝖍𝖛𝖎𝖑𝖊 in 𝕷𝖊𝖎𝖈𝖊𝖘𝖙𝖊𝖗𝖘𝖍𝖎𝖗𝖊.

I read in *Stows* Survey of 𝕷𝖔𝖓𝖉𝖔𝖓, of a Lord Mayor of that City, born here : *Viz.* Sir *John Brown,* otherwiſe called *John de Werks,* Mercer, Son of *John Brown* of 𝕺𝖐𝖊𝖍𝖆𝖒 in 𝕽𝖚𝖙𝖑𝖆𝖓𝖉𝖘𝖍𝖎𝖗𝖊, and Lord Mayor of 𝕷𝖔𝖓𝖉𝖔𝖓, in the year 1481. (21 E. 4.) The Armes aſcribed to him are, *az. a Cheveron between three Eſcollop Shells Or, within a Bordure in-graled*

Stows Surv: Lond. f. 570.

graled Gules. I find in the same Author that he dyed *Anno.* 1497. and was buried in the Church of St. *Mary Magdalen* in *Milk-ſtreet.* Whoſe Son, Sir *William Brown* Knight, was twice Lord Mayor of the ſaid City 23 *H.* 7. and 5 *H.* 8. and had iſſue by *Margaret* daughter of Sir *Edmund Shaa* Knight, his firſt Wife, *William Brown* his Son and heir, and by his ſecond VVife *Allice* Daughter of Sir *Henry Keeble* Knight, *John Brown* whoſe poſterity remain'd for many years ſeated at **Ho?ton-Kirby** in the County of **Kent.**

Let me alſo remember another man of remark, who was born here in this laſt Age, and the rather becauſe Dr. *Fuller,* in his book called the VVorthies of *England,* hath already placed him in the Liſt of memorable Perſons, tho he knew but little of his Story. It is *Jeoffrey Hudſon* the Dwarf, memorable on ſeveral Accounts. He was the Son of one *John Hudſon,* a perſon of very mean Condition, but of a luſty Stature and and ſo were all his Children, except this *Jeoffrey,* born in the year 1619. Being above ſeven years old, and ſcarce eighteen inches in highth, he was taken into the Family of the late Duke of **Buckingham** at **Burly** on the Hill, in this County, as a Rarity of Nature: And the Court being about that time in Progreſs there, he was ſerved up to the Table in a cold Pye. After the Marriage of King *Charles* the firſt with the excellent Princeſs *Henrietta Maria* of *France,* he was preſented to that Queen, and became her Dwarf; and being ſent over into *France* to fetch the Queens Midwife, in this Journey he was taken at Sea by a Flemiſh Pirate, and carryed Priſoner into **Dunkirk:** Of which captivity there is in Print a very pleaſant Poem conſiſting of three Canto's, writ

by Sir *William Davenant,* and call'd *Jeoffreido's.* Afterwards, when the Rebellion broke out he became a Captain of Horſe in the Kings ſervice, till he went over with his Royal Miſtreſs into *France:* during his abode there it was his unhappineſs to kill Mr. *Crofts* (Brother to the Lord *Crofts*) in a Combat on horſeback; for which he was expell'd the Court. After this he was a ſecond time taken Priſoner at Sea, but that was a much more fatal Captivity than the firſt. It was a Turkiſh Pirate that took and carried him to *Barbary,* where he was ſold, and remain'd a ſlave for many years. Being at laſt redeem'd, he came into *England,* and lived in theſe parts on certain Penſions allowed him by the Duke of **Buckingham,** and other Perſons of Honor, for ſeveral years. But occaſions cauſing him to remove and abide at **London,** he was there in the late troubleſome times, which began in the year 1678; and being known to be a Roman Catholick, he was taken and clapt up in the Gate-Houſe, where he lay a conſiderable time; from whence being at laſt enlarged, he lived not long after, and died about two years ago. But that which in my opinion ſeems the moſt obſervable is what I have heard himſelf ſeveral times affirm, that between the 7*th.* year of his Age and the 30*th* he never grew any thing conſiderable, but after thirty he ſhot up in a little time to that highth of ſtature which he remain'd at in his old age, *viz.* about three foot and nine Inches. The cauſe of this he aſcribed (how truly I know not) to the hardſhip, much labour, and beating, which he endured when a Slave to the Turks. This ſeems a Paradox, how that which hath been obſerved to ſtop the growth of other perſons, ſhould be the cauſe of his. But let the Naturaliſts reconcile it.

PICKWORTH.

PICKWORTH (formerly a Town, and Parish, of which nothing remains at this day but a Steeple, now known by the Name of *Mockbegger*) stands in the East hundred. Of this place I find no mention in *Domesday* Book, it belonging possibly, at that time (as a member) to some other Neighbouring Town, but to which I cannot say.

Nom. Vill.
in Scacc.

Clauf. 29 E. 1.
m. 13. dorso.

In the 9th. year of King *E. 2. Roger de Geneye* was Lord of **Pickworth**: The same *Roger de Gyneto* (no doubt) who in the 29 *E.* 1. received the Kings writ of Summons to attend him at **Berwick** on the Feast of the Nativity of St *John Baptist*, well fitted with Horse and Armes, from thence to march against the Scots. In which name this Estate continued till the Reign of *Hen.* 6. at which time, *John Geney*, Kt. then Lord of this Mannour, by his Testement dated on the Feast of St. *Hillary* the Confessor *An. Domini* 1422. did bequeath his body to be buryed among the Friers Augustines in **Norwich**, neer to the Sepulcher of *Roger* his Son, and by the same will devised his Mannour of **Pickworth** in the County of **Rutland**, to be sold by his Executors, presently after his death, to *Henry Inglose* Knight for 1000 Marks of Silver. Which Will was proved, 5 *Nov.* 1433.

M. S. Wingf.
Bodenham,
mil. f. 83.

Id. ib.

The said Sir *Henry Inglose* being accordingly possest of this Lordship, made his Testament on the 20th. of *Jan.* 1451. and by the same order'd his body to be buried in the Presbitery of the Priory of St. *Faiths* at **Horsham**, neer *Amicia* his Wife, to the Prior and Canons of **Ingham** he bequeathed 20 *s.* to *Henry* his Son all his sheep at **Askeby** (*Com. Suff.*) To his Son *Robert* one Bason and Ewre of Silver, &c. and devised his Mannour of **Pikeworth** (*Com. Rotel.*) to be sold: Which Will was proved, 14 *July*, 1451. (29 H. 6.)

Afterwards this Lordship came into the possession of Sir *John Hussy* the first and last Baron of that name created by King *H.* 8. who builded himself a fair Seat at **Sleford** in the County of **Lincoln**. Which said Baron was executed at **Lincoln** in the year 1537. for high Treason, he having been ingaged in the Commotion of the Commons rais'd in **Lincolnshire**, the preceding year, on the account of Religion. Whereupon this Estate Escheated to the Crown: and accordingly I find in the 3 *E.* 6. *Thomas Astewood* the Kings Bayly accounted in the Augmentation Office for the Rents of **Pikeworth**-*Infield* and **Pikeworthe** *Outfield*, then in the Kings hands, by reason of the attainder of Sir *John Hussey* Lord *Hussey* of high Treason, the sum of 38 *l.* 7 *s.* 4 *d.*

Camb. Brit.
Linc. p. 535.

Comp. in Offic.
Augm. pro Com.
Rutland. 3 E. 6.

Certain Lands in this Lordship did formerly belong to the Monastery of **Olveston** in *Com.* **Leicest.** for I find in the account of *Jeoffrey Radcliffe* the Kings Receiver in that County 28 *H.* 8. that the said Accountant did, among other parcels belonging to the said Monastery, account for the sum of 13 *s.* 4 *d.* for the farm of one Pasture called *Abbots* **Stocking** in the fields of **Pykeworth** in the County of **Rutland** *cum suis pertinent.* also certain Lands called **Withawe Pitts** with fifteen acres of Land and Pasture late demised to *Sir John Hussey* Knight for fifty years, by Indenture under the Seal of that Covent, dated 11 *Jan.* 15 *H.* 8.

Comp. in Offic.
Augm. pro Com.
Leic. 28 H. 8.

It was found by Inquisition taken at **Okeham** 22 *Mar.* 13 *Jac.* after the Death of *John* Lord *Harrington* the Elder, that the said Lord dyed seized (*inter alia*) of **Pickworth**, *alias* **Pickworth Stocking.**

Esch. 14 Jac.
pars 2. n. 116.

The present Lord of this Estate is the right honourable *John* Earl of **Exeter.**

ADVOW-

Of the ADVOWSON.

Reg. Linc.

IN the 11*th.* year of *H.* 3. *William de Gisneto* prefented to the Church of 𝔓𝔦𝔩𝔨𝔢𝔴𝔬𝔯𝔱𝔥. So alfo in the 19*th.* year of that King.

Ibid.

In the 12*th.* year of *E.* 1. *William* Son of *Thomas de Deggeville*, Clerk,

was prefented to the Church of 𝔓𝔦𝔩𝔨𝔢= 𝔴𝔬𝔯𝔱𝔥, by *Thomas* then Lord of that Mannour.

In the 19 *E.* 1. *Roger de Gynney* prefented to the Church of 𝔓𝔦𝔨𝔢𝔴𝔬𝔯𝔱𝔥.

Ibid.

The Rectory of 𝔓𝔦𝔨𝔢𝔴𝔬𝔯𝔱𝔥 is valued in the Kings Books at, 4*l.* 0 *s.* 0 *d.*

The Patron of the Sine-Cure is the Earl of 𝔈𝔵𝔢𝔱𝔢𝔯.

PILTON.

LYes in the hundred of 𝔚𝔯𝔞𝔫𝔤= 𝔇𝔦𝔨𝔢. Of this Town is no mention in *Domefday* Survey, it being, no doubt, at that time furveyed as a member to fome other Neighbouring Town, but to which I cannot learn.

Nom. Vil. in Scacc.

In the Reign of *E.* 2. *Thomas Beauchamp* Earl of 𝔚𝔞𝔯𝔴𝔦𝔠𝔨 was Lord of 𝔓𝔦𝔩𝔱𝔬𝔫𝔢.

The Prefent Lord of this Mannour is *John Digby* of North-𝔏𝔲𝔣𝔣𝔢𝔫𝔥𝔞𝔪, Efq;

Of the ADVOWSON.

IN the 36 *E.* 1. *William de Offington* prefented to the Church of 𝔓𝔦𝔩𝔱𝔬𝔫.

Reg. Linc.

The Rectory of 𝔓𝔦𝔩𝔱𝔬𝔫 is valued in the Kings Books at, 4*l.* 17 *s.* 2 *d.*

The prefent Patron is *John Digby* Efq; Lord of the Mannour.

PRESTON.

𝔓Refton lyes in the Hundred of 𝔐𝔞𝔯𝔱𝔦𝔫𝔣𝔩𝔶, a full mile North of 𝔘𝔭𝔭𝔦𝔫𝔤𝔥𝔞𝔪; and tho it be a Parifh of it felf, yet it is part of the fame Mannor with 𝔘𝔭𝔭𝔦𝔫𝔤𝔥𝔞𝔪, to which Town (fo far as I can difcover) it hath always been joyned in the poffeffion of the fame Lords. *See* 𝔘𝔭𝔭𝔦𝔫𝔤= 𝔥𝔞𝔪.

Of this Town I can find no mention in *Domefday* Book, no more than of 𝔘𝔭𝔭𝔦𝔫𝔤𝔥𝔞𝔪, they both being no doubt, two of thofe feven Berews, or Hamlets, which in thofe days belong'd to 𝔅𝔢𝔡= 𝔩𝔦𝔫𝔠𝔱𝔲𝔫𝔢 *Cerchefoch.*

Of the ADVOWSON.

IN the 23 *H.* 3. Sir *Peter de Montfort* Knight prefented to the Church of 𝔓𝔯𝔢𝔣𝔱𝔬𝔫.

Reg. Linc.

In the 4 *E.* 1. the Lady *Alice*, Widdow of Sir *Peter de Montfort* prefented to the faid Church.

Ibidem.

The Rectory of 𝔓𝔯𝔢𝔣𝔱𝔬𝔫 is valued in the Kings Books at, 9*l.* 17 *s.* 4 *d.*

The Prefent Patron is *Edward Fawkener*, Efq;

RIDLINGTON.

Domesday Tit.
Rote.]

Yes in the Hundred of 𝕸𝖆𝖗𝖙𝖎𝖓-𝖘𝖑𝖞. In 𝕽𝖊𝖉𝖑𝖎𝖓𝖈𝖙𝖚𝖓𝖊 *Cherche-foch* with feven Berews or Hamlets thereunto belonging, Queen *Eddid* at the Conqueſt, held four Carucates of Land as it was rated to the Tax or Geld. The Land was fixteen Carucates. Here at the time of *Domefday* furvey the King held four Carucates in Demefne, and a hundred and feven Villains, and twenty fix *Bordarii*, having thirty Carucates, and two Sockmen having two Carucates: Here were then two Prieſts and three Churches, and two feats or places for Mills, and fourty Acres of Meadow, a Wood (*per loca paſtilis*) three Miles in length and eight furlongs in breadth. All which in the time of King *Edward* was valued at 40 *l.* This whole Mannour with the faid Berews, was then accounted three Miles and feven furlongs long, and two miles and two furlongs broad.

Nom. Vill.

In the 9 *E* 2. *Robert de Hoyland*, and *John de Wynill* were Lords of 𝕽𝖎𝖉𝖑𝖎𝖓𝖌-𝖙𝖔𝖓.

Rot. Pat. 1, 2.
P. M. pars 12.

In the 1. and 2. *P.* and *M. Chriſtopher Smith* obtain'd Licenfe dated 17*th. May* to alienate his Mannour of 𝕽𝖎𝖉𝖑𝖎𝖓𝖌𝖙𝖔𝖓 in *Com.* 𝕽𝖚𝖙𝖑𝖆𝖓𝖉 with the appurtenances late parcell of the Poffeffions of the Duke of 𝕽𝖎𝖈𝖍𝖒𝖔𝖓𝖉, to Sir *John Harrington* Knight. And accordingly it was found by inquifition taken at 𝕺𝖐𝖊𝖍𝖆𝖒 22 *Mar.* 13 *Jac.* that *John* Lord *Harrington* the elder dyed 24 *Auguſt* 11 *Jac.* feized (*inter alia*) of the Mannour of 𝕽𝖎𝖉𝖑𝖎𝖓𝖌𝖙𝖔𝖓, and that he held the fame of the King in Soccage by Fealty, and the Rent of 12 *s.* and one pound of Pepper yearly. In which Family this Mannour continued till it was conveyed by the Siſters and Coheirs of *John* laſt Lord *Harington*, to Sir *Edward Noel* then refiding at 𝕭𝖗𝖔𝖔𝖐 in this County, which Sir *Edward Noel* being made a Baronet (the 34*th.* in number) upon the firſt erection of that honour, was a perfon of fo great eſteem and merits, that on the 23*th.* of *March*, 14 *Jacobi*, he was advanced to the de-

Efch. 14. Jac.
pars 2. n. 116.

Rot. Fin. M.
12 Jac.

gree and dignity of a Baron of this Kingdome, by the title of Lord *Noel* of 𝕽𝖎𝖉𝖑𝖎𝖓𝖌𝖙𝖔𝖓 in *Com.* 𝕽𝖚𝖙𝖑𝖆𝖓𝖉 (* which honour he received from the King at 𝕭𝖚𝖗𝖑𝖞 in this County) and having marryed *Julian* eldeſt of the Daughters and Coheirs of Sir *Baptiſt Hicks* Knight and Baronet, upon the advancement of the faid Sir *Baptiſt* to the titles of Lord *Hicks* of 𝕴𝖑𝖒𝖎𝖓𝖌𝖙𝖔𝖓 in *Com.* 𝖂𝖆𝖗-𝖜𝖎𝖈𝖐, and Vicount 𝕮𝖆𝖒𝖕𝖉𝖊𝖓 of 𝕮𝖆𝖒𝖕-𝖉𝖊𝖓 in *Com.* 𝕲𝖑𝖔𝖚𝖈. 5 *May,* 4 *Car.* 1. obtain'd a grant of the faid honours to himfelf and the heirs Males of his Body in Reverfion, in cafe the faid Sir *Baptiſt* fhould dye without iffue male; which titles afterwards he did accordingly enjoy. This worthy Lord approving himfelf alway moſt loyal to his Majeſty King *Charles* the firſt in the times of the late Rebellion, departed this life in the Kings Garrifon at 𝕺𝖝𝖋𝖔𝖗𝖉, 10 *Mar.* 1643. and is buryed at 𝕮𝖆𝖒𝖕𝖉𝖊𝖓 abovemention'd, leaving *Baptiſt* his Son and Heir, Lord Vicount *Campden*, Baron of 𝕽𝖎𝖉𝖑𝖎𝖓𝖌-𝖙𝖔𝖓 and 𝕴𝖑𝖒𝖎𝖓𝖌𝖙𝖔𝖓 (and fince his Majeſties Reſtauration) Lord Leiutenant of this County of 𝕽𝖚𝖙𝖑𝖆𝖓𝖉) who in like manner with his Father, proving faithful to his late Majeſty in the grand defection of thofe times, raifed and maintained at his own Coſts, a Troop of Horfe and a Company of foot in the Kings fervice, at his then Garrifon of 𝕭𝖊𝖆𝖛𝖊𝖗; and departed this life at 𝕰𝖝-𝖙𝖔𝖓 in this County, *Oct.* 29. 1682. To whofe hereditary honours fucceeded his Son and Heir *Edward* at that time Lord Leiutenant of the County of 𝕾𝖔𝖚𝖙𝖍-𝖆𝖒𝖕𝖙𝖔𝖓, Warden of 𝕹𝖊𝖜𝖋𝖔𝖗𝖗𝖊ſ𝖙, and Governour of 𝕻𝖔𝖗𝖙ſ𝖒𝖔𝖚𝖙𝖍, who, by his Majeſties fpecial favour, was fummon'd to the Houfe of Lords in Parliament during his Fathers life, by the name of *Edward* Lord *Noel* of 𝕿𝖎𝖙𝖈𝖍-𝖋𝖊𝖎𝖑𝖉; and foon after his Fathers death created Earl of 𝕲𝖆𝖎𝖓ſ𝖇𝖔𝖗𝖔𝖚𝖌𝖍, in *Com.* 𝕷𝖎𝖓𝖈𝖔𝖑𝖓. and Lord Leiutenant of this County, and *Cuſtos Rotulorum*, of the fame.

Bar. Eng. 2.
Vol. 435.

* *Hows continuation of Stows Chron.* f. 102ƺ.

Noel

Noellus *Dominus de* Elenhall *in Com.* Staff.

Robertus *qui fundavit* —— Alicia.
Cœnobium de Raunton
in Com. Staff. *temp.* H. 2.

Thomas Noel, *Dominus*   Philippus Noel, *de*
de Elenhall & Raunton   Hilcot *Com.* Staff.
fil. & *b.*   *f.* 2.

Robertus Noel. —— Johanna *f.* Johannis
Acton, *mil.*

Philippus Noel, *de* Ceftford
vixit 52 H. 3.

Philippus Noel, *de* Ceftford & Newbold.

Philippus Noel, *ob.* —— Cecilia ..... *vixit*
ante patrem.   12 E. 2.

Thomas Noel. —— Alicia *f.* & *h.* Henrici
de Wyverfton.

Willielmus Noel, *de* Newbold.

Richardus Noel, *de* Newbold.

Thomas Noel, —— Jana *f.* Rogeri Draycot *de* Panefley
de Newbold.   *in Com.* Staff. *Ux.* 2.

Robertus Noel, *de* —— Matilda *f.* .....
Hilcot, 6 E. 4.   Brereton.

Jacobus Noel, —— ... *f.* .... Pool *de* Lang-
de Hilcot.   ley *in Com.* Derb.

Robertus Noel   Arthurus Noel,   Andreas Noel, *de* —— Eliza. *f.* & *h.* Willielmi Hopton
de Hilcot *in*   *f.* 2.   Dalby *in Com.*   *de* Hopton *in Com.* Salop, *viduâ*
Com. Staff. *f.* 1.   Leiceft.   Johannis Perient *militis. Ux.* 2.

Andreas Noel, *de* Dalby —— Mabella *f.* Jacobi Harington *de*   Henricus Noel,
miles, ob. 1607.   Exton *in Com.* Rutl. *mil.*   *ob.* 1596.

Edwardus Noel, *mil.* & *Bar.* —— Juliana *f.* & *coh.* Baptiftæ Hicks   Carolus   Arthurus   Alexander —— Maria *Sor.* Galfred
Dominus Noel *de* Ridling-   *mil.* Vicecomitis Campden *ob.*   Noel, *mi.*   Noel.   Noel, *ar.*   Palmer *mi. Attor-*
ton. *Vicecomes* Campden.   25 Nov. 1680.   *ob.* 1619.   *nati Generalis.*

Eliz. *f.* & *coh.* Tho. —— Baptifta *Vicecomes* —— Elizabetha *f.* Monticuti   Henricus Noel,   Andreas Noel, *de* Whit-
Dom. Wotton.   Campden *ob.* 1682.   *Comitis de* Lindfey.   *ob. f. p.*   well *in Com.* Rutl. *miles.*

Edwardus *Vice-* —— Elizab. *f.* &   Henricus   Maria.   Lindfey   Baptifta Noel,   Johannes   Jacobus   Catherina.
comes Campden   *coh.* Thomæ   Noel,   Juliana.   *ob. in-*   *de* Luffenham   Noel, *ar.*   *ob.*   Bridgetta.
& *Comes de*   *Com. de* South-   *arm.*   Elizab.   *fans.*   *in Com.* Rut.   *ob. f̃ m.*   1681.   Penelope.
Gainsborow.   ampton.   Hefter.   *drm.*

Wriothfley-Baptift *Dominus* Campden.

Esc. 23 H. 8. It was found by Office taken in the 23 *H.8.* that *John Calcot* held two Messuages and three Cottages with their appurtenances in **Ridlington** of the King, as of his Mannour of **Preston**, but by what services they knew not.

Of the ADVOWSON.

Reg. Linc. In the 5 *H. 3. William de Cantilupo* presented to the Church of **Ridlington**.

In 42 *H. 3.* the Lady *Alice de Mont-* *Reg. Linc.* *fort* presented to the Church of **Ridlington**.

The Rectory of **Ridlington** is valued in the King Books at, 10 *l.* 12 *s.* 0 *d.*

The present Patron is the Right honourable *Edward* Earl of **Gainesborough**.

In the Church.

On a neat Monument erected in the North Wall of the Chancel.

Here lyeth intombed James Harrington, *Kt. and Baronet, youngest Son of Sir* James Harrington *of* Exton, *Kt. and* Fraunces *his first Wife one of the Daughters and Heirs of* Robert Sapcots *of* **Elton** *in the County of* **Huntingdon**, *Esquire, by whom he had yssue sixteen Children, viz. nine Sons and seven Daughters; which said* Fraunces *deceased in* September 1599, *and the said* James Harington *deceßed the* 2 Febr. 1613.

RYHALL.

Bar. Eng. **L**Yes in the East hundred.
1. Vol. p. 5. Before the Conquest *Godive*, a Widow, who became the second Wife of *Siward* Earl of **Northumberland**, gave for the health of her Soul (by the consent of King *Edward* the Confessour) **Righale**, and **Boelmesthorpe**, to the Abbey of **Peterborough**; but after her Death the said *Siward* obtain'd the Lordship of **Righale**, by agreement with the said Monks, to hold for his life, and after to return to the Abby.

Domesd. Nort. At the Conquerours survey, *Judith* *n. 56.* Countess of **Huntington** (who married *Waltheof* Son of the abovemention'd *Siward* Earl of **Northumberland**) held of the King one Hide and a half in **Riehale**, of arable Land eight Carucates *cum-appendicis,* in Demesne one Carucate, four Servants, ten Villains, and four Sockmen possessing four Carucates. Here were also at that time two Mills of 26 *s.* and a Wood of four furlongs in length,

and two in breadth. To this Mannour did then appurtain **Belmesthorpe**, both being at that time valued at 6 *l.*

This estate did once belong to *Regi-* *Car.* 11 H. 3. *nald* Earl of **Bollen**, who dying, King *m. 4.* *H. 3.* by his Charter dated at **Abbindon**, *Aug.* 22. in the 11*th.* year of his reign (*donec illud hæredi ipsius Reginaldi* *Bar. Eng.* 1. *reddiderimus*) gave the Mannor of **Ry-** *Vol. 389.* **hall** to *Hugh Despenser* an eminent Baron in those days, whose Grandson, a second *Hugh,* held the said Lordship of that King in Fee farm, and in the 40*th.* year of the said King *H. 3.* was made Governour of **Hareston**-Castle (*Com.* **Derby**) This last mention'd *Hugh* was Father to *Hugh Despenser* Senior, who with his Son *Hugh Despenser* Junior, were the two great favourites of that unfortunate Prince, King *Edw.* 2*d.* but for ill using their power with him, were both banisht in Parliament, 15 *E.* 2. Notwithstanding this, the younger *Spencer* obtain'd the next year a formal revocation of that
sentence

sentence under the Kings great Seal, as also a special Protection from any disturbance whatsoever by reason thereof, and became more in favour than ever, with the Grants of many new honours and Estates, among which a new grant of this Mannour of **Ryhall**, tho not long after they both suffered the Ignominious Death of Traytors.

Id. 392.

In the first of *Edw.* 3. *Edmund* Earl of **Kent** surnamed of **Woodstock** second Son to King *Edward* 1. obtain'd a grant of this Mannour, of which Lordship he dyed seized, being executed for treason in the 4th. year of *Edw.* 3. leaving issue *Edmund* and *John* his Sons, both which departing this life without issue, *Joan* their Sister, then wife of Sir *Thomas Holland* Knight, was found to be the next Heir, which Sir *Thomas* dyed seized of this Mannour in right of his Wife in 35 *E.* 3. But the said *Joan* surviving, became soon after the Wife of *Edward* the *Black* Prince. The foremention'd Sir *Thomas Holland* having in his life time assumed the Title of Earl of **Kent** in his Wives right, left issue *Thomas* Earl of **Kent** his son and Heir, who after his Mothers death in the 9th. year of *R.* 2. obtain'd a special livery of all the *Lands* of his mothers Inheritance, among which **Ryhall**; and **Wyssendene** in this County of **Rutland**; and of the same died seised in 20 *R.* 2. leaving issue *Thomas Holland* his son and heir. Which *Thomas* was afterwards in the 21 of *Ric.* 2. created Duke of **Surrey**, tho from that great title again deposed in the 1 *H.* 4. and soon after, *viz* on *Wednesday* after the Feast of the Epiphany in the same year endeavouring a Rebellion against that King, he lost his life. After whom *Edmund* his brother succeeded in the honour and most part of the Estate, by reason of an antient entail; which *Edmund* was killed

Bar. Eng. 2 *Vol.* 92.

Id. 94.

Id. 75.

Id. 76.

at the siege of **Briack** in **Normandy** 9 *H.* 4. being at that time seized of this Mannour. His Estate was afterwards divided among several heirs general, he leaving no issue of his own.

Id. 77.

The present Lord of this Mannour is the right honourable *John* Earl of **Exeter.**

Mr. *Cambden* tells us that in former Ages one *Tibba*, whom he calls *Minorum gentium Sancta*, was here at **Ryhal**, like a second *Diana* worshipped by *Faulkners*, as the Patroness of Hawking. But upon what authority he delivers this he expresses not. Certain it is that this *St. Tibba* was a Virgin-Anchoresse at **Godmanchester**, a Kinswoman of *Penda* King of **Mercia**, and lived in or about the year of Christ 696. Of so great Reputation for piety, that our Historical Poet *Michael Drayton*, enumerating all the Holy women amongst our Ancestors the English Saxons, writ thus,

Camb. Brit. Rut.

Cressy Ch Hist. li. 20. *c.* 11. *p.* 503.

— *And to these, Saint* Tibba *let us call,*
In solitude to Christ, that past her whole delight,
In **Godmanchester** *made a constant Anchorite.*
Amongst which of that house for Saints that reckon'd be
Yet never any one more graced the same than She.

Poly-Olbion, 2. *Part, Song* 24. *p.* 110.

How this Character agrees with a second *Diana*, or how Saint *Tibba* came from **Godmanchester** to be Worshipt in **Rutland**, I know not.

The Family of the *Bodenhams* have for serveral discents enjoy'd a Fair Estate of Freehold in this Town.

The Pedigree of which Worshipful Family is thus derived.

Hugo

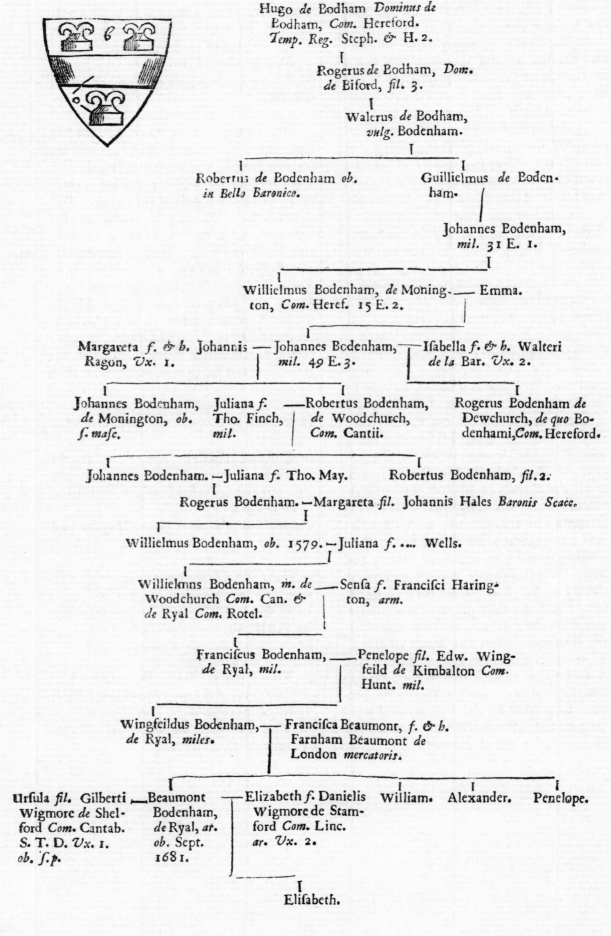

Hugo *de* Bodham *Dominus de*
Bodham, *Com.* Hereford.
Temp. Reg. Steph. *&* H. 2.

Rogerus *de* Bodham, *Dom.*
de Biford, *fil.* 3.

Walerus *de* Bodham,
vulg. Bodenham.

Robertus *de* Bodenham *ob.*
in Bello Baronico.

Guillielmus *de* Boden‑
ham.

Johannes Bodenham,
mil. 31 E. 1.

Willielmus Bodenham, *de* Moning‑——— Emma.
ton, *Com.* Heref. 15 E. 2.

Margareta *f. & h.* Johannis ——— Johannes Bodenham, ——— Isabella *f. & h.* Walteri
Ragon, *Vx.* 1.   *mil.* 49 E. 3.   *de la* Bar. *Vx.* 2.

Johannes Bodenham,   Juliana *f.* ——— Robertus Bodenham,   Rogerus Bodenham *de*
de Monington, *ob.*   Tho. Finch,   *de* Woodchurch,   Dewchurch, *de quo* Bo‑
f. masc.   *mil.*   *Com.* Cantii.   denhami,*Com.* Hereford.

Johannes Bodenham.—Juliana *f.* Tho. May.   Robertus Bodenham, *fil.* 2.

Rogerus Bodenham.—Margareta *fil.* Johannis Hales *Baronis Scacc.*

Willielmus Bodenham, *ob.* 1579.—Juliana *f.* .... Wells.

Willielmns Bodenham, *m. de*——Sensa *f.* Francisci Haring‑
Woodchurch *Com.* Can. *&*   ton, *arm.*
de Ryal *Com.* Rotel.

Franciscus Bodenham, ——Penelope *fil.* Edw. Wing‑
de Ryal, *mil.*   feild *de* Kimbalton *Com.*
   Hunt. *mil.*

Wingfeildus Bodenham,——Francisca Beaumont, *f. & h.*
de Ryal, *miles.*   Farnham Beaumont *de*
   London *mercatoris.*

Ursula *fil.* Gilberti —Beaumont —Elizabeth *f.* Danielis   William.   Alexander.   Penelope.
Wigmore *de* Shel‑   Bodenham,   Wigmore *de* Stam‑
ford *Com.* Cantab.   *de* Ryal, *ar.*   ford *Com.* Linc.
S. T. D. *Vx.* 1.   *ob.* Sept.   *ar. Vx.* 2.
ob. s. p.   1681.

Elisabeth.

Of the *ADVOWSON.*

Ex Collect.
Wingf. Bod.
m.f. 45.

IN the 5 *E.*3. *John* Bishop of **Lincoln** did certifie the Vicarage of the Church of **Ryal**, (which Church was at that time appropriated to the Priory of St. *Andrews* of **Northampton**) to consist in the Tithes of Wool, Milk, Lambs, Poultry, Swine, Geese, Calves, Sheep, *&c.* two yard Land, Tithes of Hay and Mills, and in a Pension of two Marks.

The Vicarage of **Ryal** is valued in the Kings Books at, 13 *l.* 17 *s.* 00 *d.*

The Present Patron is

In the Church of **R**yall.

On two hansome Monuments erected in the East end of the Chancel, are ingraved the following Inscriptions.

ULtimum *Christi adventum hic expectat* Gulielmus Bodenham *Eques auratus. Duas habuit Uxores,* Sence *filiam* Francisci Harington *de South* **Witham** *in Com.* **Lincol.** *Armigeri unam ex Hæredibus Matris suæ* Barbaræ Sutton *de* **Aram** *in Com.* **Nott.** *&* Isabellam *filiam* Jacobi Quarlis *de* **Ufford** *in Com.* **Northam.** *armigeri. Ultimam hujus lucis usuram amisit,* An. Dom. 1613.

ULtimum *Christi adventum hic expectant* Franciscus Bodenham *alias* Bodenden *Eques auratus & duæ ejus Uxores, quarum prima fuit* Penelope *filia* Edwardi Wingfeild *de* **Kimbalton** *Castle equitis aurati, secunda* Theodocia *filia Prænobilis* Francisci *Domini* Hastings *de* **Ashby** *de la* Zouch. *Ultimam hujus lucis usuram amiserunt Annis.* 1625. 1645. 1671.

S E T T O N.

Domesd. Nort.
n. 1.

Setton lyes in the Hundred of **Wrangkdike.** At the general Survey in the Conquerors time, I find that this Town was a Member or parcel of the Mannour of **Berchedone** (or **Barowdon**) then held by the King, who had in this Town, belonging to the said Mannour, one Hide of *Land* and a half, and one Bovate of Land; six Carucates of arable, and two Acres of Meadow. Also one Mill of 36 *d.* A Wood, and *Spinetum,* or ground over-run with Thorns.

Ibid.

At the same time *Robertus de Todeni* held in this Town (then called **Segetone**) one Hide and one Bovate of Land : Arable four Carucates, of which two in Demesne, two Servants, four Villains, and two Cottagers, with a Priest. All which possest one Carucate and a half, there was also three Acres of Meadow, and a Wood of forty perches in longitude and as many in latitude. But the said *Robert* held only a third part of the Wood, and arable Land. To this estate of the said *Robert* did appurtain at that time one yard Land in **Berchedone**, and four Villains, with half a Carucate, which had been worth 40 *s.* but at that time

Q   was

Ear. Eng. 1.
Vol. 111.

was worth no more than 20 s.

This *Robert de Todenei* was a Noble Norman who came into 𝕰𝖓𝖌𝖑𝖆𝖓𝖉 in the Conquerours Army, and having a large Estate given him by the Victorious *William*, for his Military service, he built 𝕭𝖊𝖑𝖛𝖔𝖎𝖗 Castle, and seated himself there: From whom the now Earl of 𝕽𝖚𝖙𝖑𝖆𝖓𝖉 does lineally descend.

The same *Robert* also founded a Priory for Monks near his said Castle of 𝕭𝖊𝖑𝖛𝖔𝖎𝖗, and annexed it as a Cell to *St.* 𝕬𝖑𝖇𝖆𝖓𝖘.

Rot. de Domi-
nabus, & Puel-
lis. 31 H. 2.

M. S. Wingf.
Bodenham. m.

In the 31. *H.* 2. *Alice de Beaufow* widow of *Thoms de Beaufow* was found to be at the Kings disposal; that she was the Daughter of *Walterus Oiry*, and Neece of *Alexander* the Son of *Nigellus*; that she was at that time 20 years of age, and that she had a Daughter her sole heir two years of Age. Her Land in 𝕾𝖊𝖆𝖙𝖔𝖓 was valued at eight Marks *per an.* with the following Stock, *viz.* two Plows, a hundred Sheep, two Beasts, five Sows, one Boar, and four Cows. For the Farm of her Land she received the first year 36 s. 10 d. and two pound of Pepper.

Nom. Vill.

In the 9 *E.* 2. *John de Bellafage,* (or *Beaufoe,*) *John* Son and heir of *Nicholas de Seyton*, at that time within Age,

and *William de Sancto Licio,* were Lords of 𝕾𝖊𝖞𝖙𝖔𝖓 and 𝕿𝖍𝖔𝖗𝖕𝖊.

Of the CHURCH.

IN the 23 *H.* 3. *Robert de Cycester,* and *Ralf de Bellasago* presented to the Church of 𝕾𝖊𝖞𝖙𝖔𝖓.   *Reg. Lina.*

In the 26. *E.* 1. *John de Bellasago* presented *William de Bellasago* to the Church of 𝕾𝖊𝖞𝖙𝖔𝖓, then vacant on the removal of *Thomas de Bellasago*, by reason that he was infected with the Leprosie.   *Idem.*

In the Church of 𝕾𝖊𝖆𝖙𝖔𝖓 is an antient Monument, erected in an Arch in the south Wall of the Body of the Church but without any Epitath to be seen at this Day: Yet there are two Coats of Armes cut in the stone, uncoullered; The first of which is quarterly, in the first two Lioncells passant, the second Bendy of ten pieces, the third two Bars surmounted of a Bend, the fourth as the first; the other Coat is a Lyon passant Crowned.

The Rectory of 𝕾𝖊𝖞𝖙𝖔𝖓 is valued in the Kings Books at, 20 *l.* 7 *s.* 5 *d.*

The present Patron is *James Tryan,* Esq; Lord of this Mannour.

STOKE-DRY:

Nom. Vill.

Camb. Brit.
Rut.

LYes in the hundred of 𝖂𝖗𝖆𝖓𝖌- 𝕯𝖎𝖐𝖊, and was formerly parcel of the Bishop of 𝕷𝖎𝖓𝖈𝖔𝖑𝖓𝖘 Mannour of 𝕷𝖎𝖉𝖉𝖎𝖓𝖌𝖙𝖔𝖓. For which *vide supra.*

𝕾𝖙𝖔𝖐𝖊 in Old English signifies a Village, and it had the addition of 𝕯𝖗𝖞, by reason of its scituation on the side of a Hill.

In the reign of *E.* 2. *Roger de More-wode* was Lord of 𝕾𝖙𝖔𝖐𝖊-𝕯𝖗𝖞.

Of latter time this Town hath been the habitation of a right antient Race of the *Digbys*; which *Digbys* of 𝕯𝖗𝖞- 𝕾𝖙𝖔𝖐𝖊 tho formerly blemisht by Sir *Everard Digby*, drawn in (sayes *Cambden*) to the powder Treason, yet *I* may add it hath since been rendred famous through the Christian World, by the singular-

ly Learned Sir *Kenelm Digby* of the same family, and eldest Son of the said Sir *Everard*.

This Lordship, notwithstanding the Attainder of the said Sir *Everard* for that Treason, remains in his Posterity, by reason that the said Sir *Everard* had, long before any Treason by him committed, conveyed this and other Mannours, to the use of himself for life, and after to the use of his son and heir apparent in Tayl, with divers Remainders over to his other Children : So that when afterwards he was attainted and executed for the said Powder Treason, he being only Tenant for life, his estate remain'd to the abovemention'd *Kenelm Digby* his eldest Son, who at that time being within age, this point   *Co. Rep. lib.*
8. f. 165. b.

in

in Law arofe; whether the King fhould have the Wardfhip of the Body and Lands of the faid *Kenelm*, or any part of the fame? they being held of the King in *Capite*? And it was refolved by the two chief Juftices, and chief Baron, and the whole Court of Wards, that the King could not have the faid Wardfhip but only where there was an heir, general or fpecial, which in this cafe there was not: The blood being corrupted, and the faid *Kenelm* having no inheritable blood in him from his Father; neither was he a fpecial heir in Tayl, by force of the Stat. of *Weft.* 2. but came to the Eftate as a meer Purchafer: And for the fame reafon, had he been of Age, the King could not have had the *Primer Seifin*.

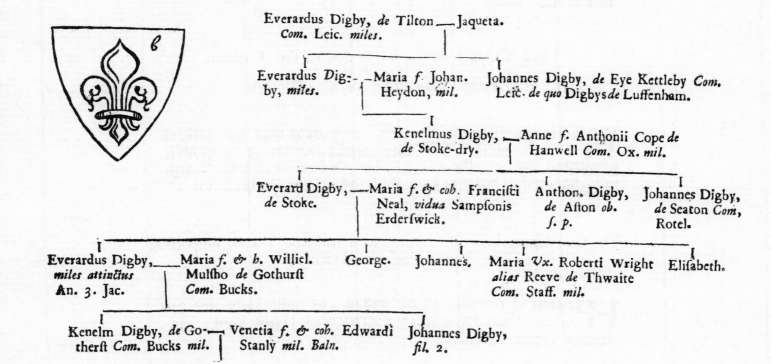

Everardus Digby, *de* Tilton — Jaqueta.
Com. Leic. *miles*.

Everardus Dig- — Maria *f.* Johan.   Johannes Digby, *de* Eye Kettleby *Com.*
by, *miles*.   Heydon, *mil.*   Leic. *de quo* Digbys *de* Luffenham.

Kenelmus Digby, — Anne *f.* Anthonii Cope *de*
de Stoke-dry.   Hanwell *Com.* Ox. *mil.*

Everard Digby, — Maria *f. & coh.* Francifci   Anthon. Digby,   Johannes Digby,
de Stoke.   Neal, *vidua* Sampfonis   *de* Afton *ob.*   *de* Seaton *Com,*
   Erderfwick.   *f. p.*   Rotel.

Everardus Digby, — Maria *f. & h.* Williel.   George.   Johannes.   Maria *Vx.* Roberti Wright   Elifabeth.
miles attinctus   Mulfho *de* Gothurft   *alias* Reeve *de* Thwaite
An. 3. Jac.   Com. Bucks.   Com. Staff. *mil.*

Kenelm Digby, *de* Go- — Venetia *f. & coh.* Edwardi   Johannes Digby,
therft Com. Bucks *mil.*   Stanly *mil.* Baln.   *fil.* 2.

Johannes Digby,
Ar.

Of the ADVOWSON.

Reg. Linc.

IN the 4 *H.* 3. the then Prior of the Hofpital of St. *John* of *Jerufalem* in *England* prefented to the Church of **Drieftoke**: And again in the 21*th.* year of that King.

38 H. 8. p. 7. In the 38 *H.* 8. *Richard Andrews* obtain'd Licenfe of the King to alienate (among other things) all thofe Lands commonly called *Dyngly Lees* containing by eftimation four acres of Land, in **Stoke-Dzy**, in *Com.* **Rot.** *nuper Preceptorio de* Dingly *Spectant.* with the Advowfon of **Stoke-Dzy**, to *Kenelm Digby* and his heirs.

Thefe Preceptories were Cells, or Religious houfes in the Country, belonging to the Knights Templers, or Knights of St. *John,* fubordinate to their chief manfion at **London.** Such were **Balfhall** in **Warwickfhire, Dalby** in **Leiceftserfhire, Temple-Bzewer** in **Lincolnfhire,** and this of **Dingly** in **Nozthamptonfhire,** with abundance of others throughout **England.**

Antiq. Warwickfh. p. 704.

The Rectory of **Dzy-Stoke** is valued in the Kings Books at, 11 *l.* 2 *s.* 1 *d.*

The Prefent Patron is

Monuments in the Church.

In the Nave, about the Verge of an Alabaster Tomb,
adjoyning to the South Wall.

Hic jacet Jaqueta Digbi **quondam Uxor** Everardi Digbi **Armigeri que quidem obiit vicessimo nono Die mensis** Junii Anno Domino M°· CCCC. Lxxxxvi. **cujus anime propicietur Deus,** Amen.

In a Chappel on the South side of the Chancel.

About the Verge of an Alabaster Gravestone.

Hic jacent Ricardus Digbi **& Agnes uxor ejus qui quidem** Ricardus **obiit** XVII°· **Die mensis** Octobris **& Agnes obiit penultimo die mensis** Octobris A°· Domini M......... CCC. **septuagessimo nono, quozum animabus propicietur Deus,** Amen.

In the same Chappel about the Verge of a hansome Tomb, supporting
the figure of an armed Kinght.

Hic jacet Everardus Digbi **Miles qui obiit undecimo die** Aprilis Anno Domini M. CCCCCXL°· **cujus anime propicietur Deus,** Amen.

In the Chancel, adjoyning to the partition Wall of the aforesaid Chappel
about the Verge of a hansome Tomb supporting
the Images of a Man and Woman:

Here lyeth the Bodyes of Kenelme Digby *Esquire which* Kenelme *deceased the* 21. *of* April, 1590. *and of* Anne *his Wife which* Anne *deceased the* ...:.................

On the West end of the same Tomb are cut in the
Stone, the Arms of *Digby* and *Cope* Impaled, with this Word,

Nul que ung,   *None but one.*

STRETTON.

Domesday Tit. Rotel. IN the Hundred of **Alſtoe. Stra-tone** was at the Conqueſt a *Berew* or Hamlet belonging to **Overtune**, and had the ſame owner, *viz. Judith* Counteſs of **Huntington**, the Conque-rors Neice. Yet did one *Alured* Chal-lenge or claim, at that time, the 4*th.* part of **Stratune.** Before the Conqueſt it was poſſeſt by Earl *Wallef.*

Nom. Vil. in Scacc. In the 9*th.* year of E. 2. the King was the immediate Lord of this Mannour.

Rot. Pipe 15 E. 2. In the 15*th.* year of *E.* 2. *John de Ro deney* the Kings Eſcheator ſouth of **Trent** did account for certain Tenements in **Stratton** in the County of **Rotel.** formerly belonging to *Nicholas de Se-grave,* and which he held of *John de Segrave, per ſervicium unius Clavis* Gari-ofolii, by the ſervice of one Clove. The Daughter and heir of which *Nicholas de Segrave, Maud,* was married to *Edmund de* **Bohun.**

Rot. Pat. 17. H. 6. pars 2. m. 15. In the reign of King *Henry* 6*th.* The Town and Lordſhip of **Stretton** did belong to *Humphrey* Duke of **Glou-ceſter** that Kings Uncle, at whoſe In-ſtance and requeſt the ſaid King by his Letters Patents dated at **Wyndeſore** 24 *July* in the 17*th* year of his Reign, granted to the Tenants of his ſaid Un

cle in **Stretton** in *Com.* **Roteland,** their heirs and ſucceſſors, to be for e-ver freed and exonerated from all tenths, and *quota's* of tenths, of goods and Chat-tells, which may or ſhall hereafter be granted in Parliament from the Laity. And that they ſhall be taxt to the *Fif-teenth* after the ſame manner with the Burroughs and antient Vills, demeans of the Crown. At the ſame time par-doning to the ſaid *Men* of **Stretton** all Debts, actions, and Demands, then due to the ſaid King.

Eſc. 14. Jac. pars 2. n. 116. It was found by Office taken at **Oke-ham** in this County on the 22 *Mar. An.* 13 *Jac.* after the death of *John* Lord *Har-rington* the elder, that the ſaid Lord dy-ed ſeiſed (*inter alia*) of the Mannour of **Stretton** ; which he held in Soc-cage of the Mannour of Eaſt **Green-wich**, and by the rent of 10 *s. per Annum.*

Of the CHURCH.

THE Rectory of **Stretton** is valu-ed in the Kings Books at, 7 *l.* 17 *s.* 0 *d.*

The preſent Patron is

Stretton Stocking.

Ithin the Pariſhes of **Stretton,** tho neer a mile diſtant from the Town, and on the very edge of **Lin-colnſhire** lyes a fair Seat called **Stock-in hall,** the habitation of *Samuel Brown* Eſq; who ſerved for this County, a

Member of the Houſe of Commons, in the Parliament which ſate at *Weſtminſter* in the 12*th.* year of his now Majeſty (1660.) And hath been ſince High She-riffe of **Rutland** in the year 1677. (29 *Car.* 2.)

Nicholaus

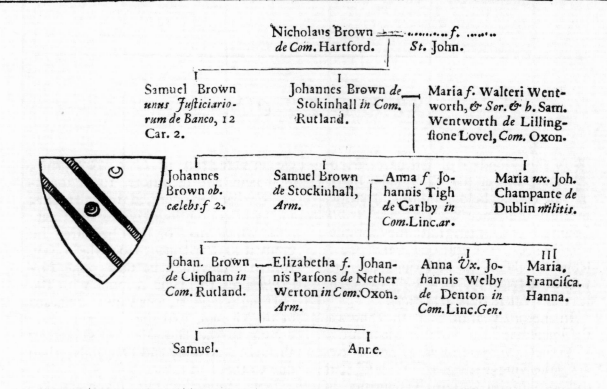

Nicholaus Brown ————— f. ——
de *Com*. Hartford. | *St.* John.

Samuel Brown
*unus Jufticiario-
rum de Banco*, 12
Car. 2.

Johannes Brown *de*
Stokinhall *in Com.*
Rutland.

Maria *f.* Walteri Went-
worth, & *Sor.* & *h.* Sam.
Wentworth de Lilling-
ftone Lovel, *Com.* Oxon.

Johannes
Brown *ob.
cælebs.f* 2.

Samuel Brown
de Stockinhall,
Arm.

Anna *f* Jo-
hannis Tigh
de Carlby *in
Com.* Linc.*ar.*

Maria *ux.* Joh.
Champante de
Dublin *militis.*

Johan. Brown
de Clipfham *in
Com.* Rutland.

Elizabetha *f.* Johan-
nis Parfons *de* Nether
Werton *in Com.*Oxon.
Arm.

Anna *Vx.* Jo-
hannis Welby
de Denton *in
Com.*Linc.*Gen.*

III
Maria,
Francifca.
Hanna.

Samuel.

Anr.e.

THISSLETON.

IN the Hundred of **Alſtoe**. At the Conqueſt One *Erich* (a *Saxon*) had here half a Carucate of Land as rated to the Geld or Tax : But afterwards when the Survey of *Domefday Book* was made, one *Hugo* the Fermour of Counteſs *Judith* held in this Town, then call'd **Tiſtertune**, one Carucate, and ſix Villains having one Carucate, which eſtate in the time of King *Edward* was valued at 20 *s.* but at the ſaid Survey at 40 *s.*

Domefday Tit.
Rotel.

Here was alſo another Mannour poſſeſt at the Conqueſt by one *Siuuard*, containing half a Carucate of Land as taxt to the Geld. At the Survey *Aluredus de* **Lincole** (the ſame of whom I made mention in **Stretton**) held here one Carucate and three Villains, and two *Bordarii*, having half, a Carucate, this was alſo valued at 20 *s.* in the time of King *Edward*, but at the Survey at 60 *s.*

Ib.

In the 29 *E.* 1. *Hugo de Buſſey* Knight then Lord of this Mannour receiv'd the Kings Writ of Summons to attend him well fitted with Horſe and arms at **Berwick** upon **Tweed**, from thence to march againſt the Scots.

Clauf. 29 *E.* 1.
m. 13.

In the 35 *E.* 1. *John Buſſey* Knight then Lord of **Thiſtleton** divided the ſaid Mannour into two parts, giving one to *Nicholas* his Son, and the other, with the *Advowſon* of the Church to his Son *John.*

M. S. W. Bod.
mil.f. 101. *b.*

In the 9th. of *E.* 2. *John de Buſſey* was Lord of this Mannour.

Nom. Vill.
in Scacc.

In this name and Family the Lordſhip of **Thiſleton** continued till the 28 *H.* 8. In which year *John Buſſey* dying without iſſue Male, left only one Daughter *Agnes* his ſole heir, who became the Wife of Sir *Edmund Brudnell* of **Deen** (*Com.* **North.**) Knight ; but the ſaid *Agnes* dying without iſſue, her eſtate deſcended to *Anthony Meers* her next Kinſman and heir at Law, who in the 24th. *Eliz.* ſold and conveyed this Mannour , together with other Lands elſewhere, which he had by Inheritance from the ſaid *Agnes*, to the ſaid Sir *Edmund Brudnell* and his heirs for ever.

M. S. Wing.
Bodenham, m:
f. 102.

It was found by Inquiſition taken at **Okeham**, on the 22 *March* 13 *Jac.* that *John* Lord *Harrington* the elder dyed ſeized (*inter alia*) of two Meſſuages and fifty acres of Land in **Thiſtleton** in the County of **Rutland**, which he held *in Capite*, by the hundreth part of a Knights Fee.

Efc. 14 Jac.
p. 2. *n.* 116.

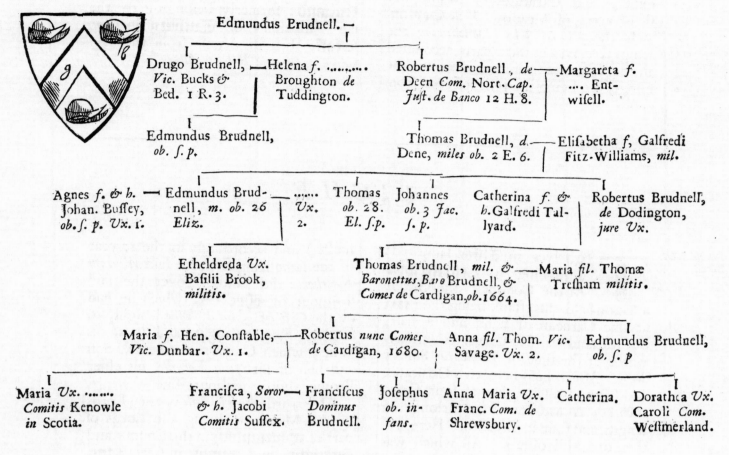

Edmundus Brudnell. ─

Drugo Brudnell, ─ Helena *f.* ....   Robertus Brudnell, *de* ─ Margareta *f.*
Vic. Bucks *&*   Broughton *de*   Deen *Com.* Nort. *Cap.*   .... Ent-
Bed. 1 R. 3.   Tuddington.   *Just. de Banco* 12 H. 8.   wifell.

Edmundus Brudnell,   Thomas Brudnell, *d.* ─ Elifabetha *f,* Galfredi
ob. f. p.   Dene, *miles ob.* 2 E. 6.   Fitz-Williams, *mil.*

Agnes *f. & h.* ─ Edmundus Brud-   .... Thomas   Johannes   Catherina *f. &*   Robertus Brudnell,
Johan. Buffey,   nell, *m. ob.* 26   *Ux.*   *ob.* 28.   *ob.* 3 *Jac.*   *h.* Galfredi Tal-   *de* Dodington,
ob. f. p. Ux. 1.   Eliz.   2.   El. *f.p.*   *f. p.*   lyard.   *jure Ux.*

Etheldreda *Ux.*   Thomas Erudnell, *mil. &* ─ Maria *fil.* Thomæ
Bafilii Brook,   *Baronettus, Baro* Brudnell, *&*   Trefham *militis.*
militis.   *Comes de* Cardigan, *ob.* 1664.

Maria *f.* Hen. Conftable, ─ Robertus *nunc Comes* ─ Anna *fil.* Thom. *Vic.*   Edmundus Brudnell,
Vic. Dunbar. *Ux.* 1.   *de* Cardigan, 1680.   Savage. *Ux.* 2.   *ob. f. p*

Maria *Ux.* ....   Francifca, *Soror* ─ Francifcus   Jofephus   Anna Maria *Ux.*   Catherina.   Dorathea *Ux.*
Comitis Kenowle   *& h.* Jacobi   *Dominus*   *ob. in-*   Franc. *Com. de*   Caroli *Com.*
in Scotia.   *Comitis* Suffex.   Brudnell.   fans.   Shrewsbury.   Weftmerland.

Of the Church there,

IN the 13 H. 3. *Lambert de Buffey* pre-
fented to the Church of **Thiſleton**
In the 33 H. 3. Sir *Hugh de Buffey*
Knight prefented to the Church of
Thiſleton.

In 7 E. 2. Sir *John de Buffey* Knight,
Son and heir of Sir *Hugh de Buffey* Knight,
prefented *Thomas de Botham* his Chaplain to the Church of **Thiſleton**, and
this was by deed dated at **Okeham**,
die Natalis Domini, An. 1313.

I find that *John Doddington* the Kings
Receiver in thefe parts 3 E. 6. accounted in the Court of Augmentations for
the fum of 20 *s.* going out of the Rectory of **Thiſtleton** to the late Preceptory of **Temple Brewer** in *Com.* **Lincoln**: And alfo for the fum of 12 *d.*
going out of the faid Rectory of **Thiſtleton** to the late Preceptory of **Ding-
ley** in *Com.* **Northampton.**

The Rectory of **Thiſleton** is valued in the Kings Books at, 3 *l.* 11 *s.* 0 *d.*

The Prefent Patron is

Reg. Linc.

Ex Collect.
Wingf. Bod.
m. f. 90. 91.

Comp. pro Com.
Rutland *in*
Offic. Augm.
An. 3. E. 6.

T H O R P E.

Thorpe, a fmall Village, lyes in
the Hundred of **Wrangdyke**,
and in the parifh of **Seaton.**
In the time of the Conquerour it was
Parcel of the Mannour **Berchedone**
(or **Barowden**) then held by the
King, who had here belonging to the
faid Mannour one Hide and one yard
Land

Domefd. No
n. 56.

Land, four Carucates of Arable and three acres of Meadow. *Vide* Seyton

Comp. pro Com. Rutland in Offic. Augm. An. 3. E. 6.
In the 3 E. 6. *John Doddington* the Kings Receiver in these parts accounted in the Court of Augmentations for the sum, of 8 *s.* being the rent reserved from

a Parcel of Tithes in Thorpe in *Com.* Rutland, formerly belonging to the late Monastery of Tutbury in *Com.* Staff. then in demise from the said Covent to one *Robert Annes.*

TIGHE.

Domesday Tit. Rotei.
Tigh lyes in Alstoe Hundred, adjoyning to Leicestershire At the Conquest one *Goduin* a Saxon held this estate, being then taxt at one Carucate of Land and a half, but the land was five Carucates. Afterwards at the time of *Domesday* Survey *Robert Mellet* held here two Carucates, and fifteen Villains, having four Carurucates; A Meadow four furlongs in length, and four in Breadth. Here was then one Mill of 2 *s.* All which was valued at that time at 4 *l.*

Clauf. 29 E. 1. m. 13.
In the 29*th.* year of E. 1. *John de Folville* then Lord of this Mannour received the Kings Writ, commanding him to attend him well fitted with horse and armes on the day of the Nativity of St. *John Baptist*, at Berwick upon Tweed, from thence to march against the *Scots.* The same *John* was one of the Knights. of the shire for this County of Rutland in several Parliaments, during the Reign of that King.

M. S. Wingf. Bodenham. m.
In the 16 E. 3. *John Folville* Lord of Ashby-Folvile, granted to *William Kay thorpe* Parson of the Church of Ashby, The Mannor of Tye in the County of Rutland, and all other Lands and Tenements, which *Alice de Forville* his Mother held in Dower, after the death of *Eustachius de Folville* his Father. Which Grant was no doubt, in trust (Clergy men appearing in those days the most proper Trustees in divers re-

spects) and accordingly in the 37 year of the same King E. 3. the said *William Kaythorpe* did convey over the said mannour of Tye *&c.* which he had of the Gift of *John Folville* Knight, to *Geoffrey Folville* Knight, and *Isabel* his Wife; which *Geoffrey* was the 2*d.* Son and heir of Sir *John Folville*, his elder Brother dying without issue.

Afterwards the *Helwells* became Lords of this Mannour, being also Lords of part of Whitsundine in this County, and Stansby, and Gunby in *Com.* Linc. all which Lordships came by match into the Family of the *Sherards*, *Thomas Sherard* of Stapleford Esq; having a-bout the Reign of H. 7. marryed *Margaret* sole heir of *John de Helwell* Esq; Which said *Thomas* was great Grand-Father to Sir *William Sherrard* Knight, whom his late Majesty King *Charles* 1*st.* of blessed memory, by his Letters Patents dated 10 *Julii* in the third year of his reign, created Lord *Sherard*, and Baron of Le Trym in the Kingdom of Ireland, whose Son and heir, the right honourable *Bennet* Lord *Sherard* now living, is the present Lord of this Mannour. Whose antient discent from *Schirard*, who lived in England in the time of the Conqueror, and held great possessions in the Counties of Chester and Lancaster, I have here briefly Exemplify'd.

Ex Stemmate.

Pat. 3. Car. 1. pars 6. n. 15.

Schirard

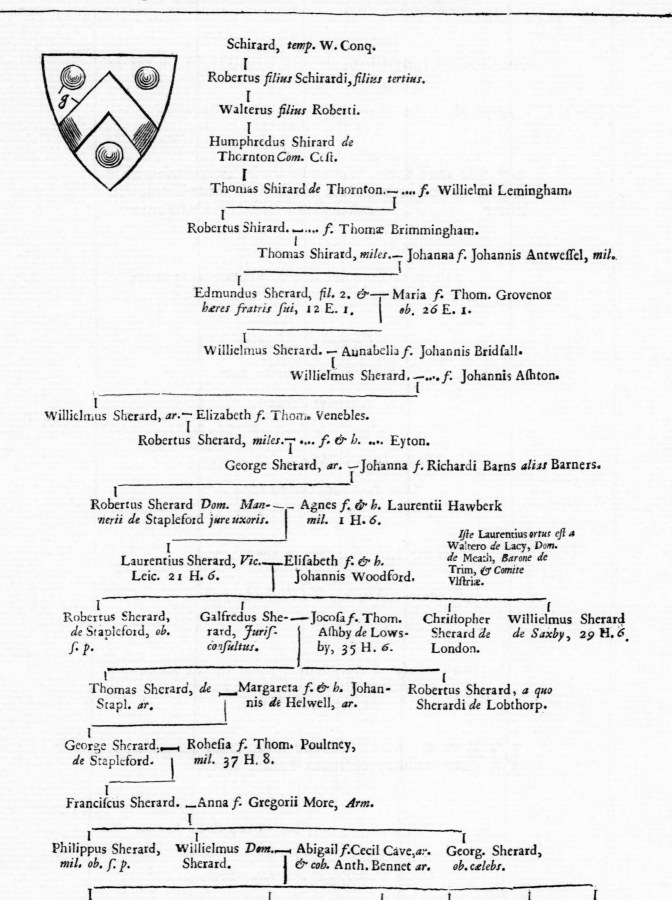

Schirard, *temp.* W. Conq.

Robertus *filius* Schirardi, *filius tertius.*

Walterus *filius* Roberti.

Humphredus Shirard *de* Thornton *Com.* Cest.

Thomas Shirard *de* Thornton. —.... *f.* Willielmi Lemingham.

Robertus Shirard. —.... *f.* Thomæ Brimmingham.

Thomas Shirard, *miles.* — Johanna *f.* Johannis Antweffel, *mil.*

Edmundus Sherard, *fil.* 2. *&* — Maria *f.* Thom. Grovenor *hæres fratris fui,* 12 E. 1. | *ob.* 26 E. 1.

Willielmus Sherard. — Aunabella *f.* Johannis Bridfall.

Willielmus Sherard. —.... *f.* Johannis Afhton.

Willielmus Sherard, *ar.* — Elizabeth *f.* Thom. Venebles.

Robertus Sherard, *miles.* — .... *f. & h.* .... Eyton.

George Sherard, *ar.* — Johanna *f.* Richardi Barns *alias* Barners.

Robertus Sherard *Dom.* Man- — Agnes *f. & h.* Laurentii Hawberk nerii *de* Stapleford *jure uxoris.* | *mil.* 1 H. 6.

Laurentius Sherard, *Vic.* — Elifabeth *f. & h.* Leic. 21 H. 6. | Johannis Woodford.

Ifte Laurentius ortus eft a Waltero de Lacy, Dom. de Meath, Barone de Trim, & Comite Viftriæ.

Robertus Sherard, *de* Stapleford, *ob. f. p.*

Galfredus Sherard, *Jurif-confultus.* — Jocofa *f.* Thom. Afhby de Lows-by, 35 H. 6.

Chriftopher Sherard *de* London.

Willielmus Sherard *de* Saxby, 29 H. 6.

Thomas Sherard, *de* Stapl. *ar.* — Margareta *f. & h.* Johannis *de* Helwell, *ar.*

Robertus Sherard, *a quo* Sherardi *de* Lobthorp.

George Sherard, *de* Stapleford. — Rohefia *f.* Thom. Poultney, *mil.* 37 H. 8.

Francifcus Sherard. — Anna *f.* Gregorii More, *Arm.*

Philippus Sherard, *mil. ob. f. p.*

Willielmus *Dom.* — Abigail *f.* Cecil Cave, *ar.* Sherard. | *& coh.* Anth. Bennet *ar.*

Georg. Sherard, *ob. cælebs.*

Bennet *Dom.* Sherard. — Elizab. *f. & h.* Roberti Chri-ftopher, *mil.*

Philippus Sherard, *de* Witfundine, *Ar.*

Georgius.

Francif-cus.

Henricus.

Anna *Uxor* Nicho. *Com.* Banbury.

Chriftopher, *ob. cælebs.* 1681.

Bennet.

Elizabeth.

R

Monuments

Monuments remaining in the Church of *T I G H.*

About the Verge of an Ancient Tomb on the North fide
of the Chancel.

✠ **Hic jacet Dom.** Willielmus Shoile **Baccalarius in lege qui obiit quarto die** Januarii **Anno Dom. Mil-
lissimo** .... xi. **cujus anime ppicietur Deus,** Amen.

On a Plate of Brafs fixt in a Graveftone lying in the
middle of the Chancel.

Jacobus Adamfon

Natu Scotus, Anglus vitâ

Moribus Antiquis,

Cum fuo Rege in profperis & adverfis,

Rector hujus Ecclefiæ per 31 annos.

Obiit die Martii *Octavo* 1661.

In the Eaft Window of the Chancel.

Azure, 3 *Mafcles, Or. Creft a Lyonefs.*

In the Body of the Church, about the Verge of
an ancient Graveftone joyning clofe
to the South VVall.

Hic jacet Johannes Blonfyld **Anno Dom.** .... Vᵒ·
cujus anime pzopicietur Deus, Amen.

In the VVindow juft over the fame, thefe Armes.

Or, 3 *Pallets, gu. a Canton, Ermine.*

Of the ADVOWSON.

Reg. Linc.

IN the 33 H. 3. *William de Folvile* Knight, prefented to the Church of **Tye**, as Patron of the fame.

Ibidem.

In the 10 E. 1. which was in the 3d. year of *Oliver de Sutton* Bifhop of **Lincoln**, the Lord *Edmund* the Kings brother, (who bore the Title of King of **Sicily**) prefented to the Church of **Tye**. Which prefentation, though at firft oppofed by the Lady *Joan de Folville* by reafon of the Cuftody of *Alice* her Daughter, heir of *William de Folville* deceafed, yet the faid Lady foon after withdrew her Pretentions.

The Rectory of **Tighe** is valued in the Kings Books at 14 *l.* 2 *s.* 10 *d:*

The prefent Patron is the right honourable *Bennet* Lord *Sherard.*

TIKENCOTE.

Domefd. North. No. 56.

LYes in the *Eaft* hundred. At the Conquerors Survey, *Grimbaldus* held of the Countefs *Judith* three Hides bating one Bovate in **Tichecote**, the Arable Land was fix Carucates, in demefne one ; eight Sockmen, twelve Villains, and one Cottager, all poffeffing five Carucates. Here was alfo one Mill of 24 *s.* and twelve acres of Meadow, formerly valued at 30 *s.* and then at 50 *s.*

Nom. Vil.

In the reign of E. 2. *Britius Danyes* was Lord of this Mannour. Which *Britius Daneys* was one of thofe eminent perfons in this County, who in the 29

Clauf. 29 E. 1. *m.* 13.

E. 1. received the Kings writ of fummons to attend him at **Berwick** upon **Tweed** well fitted with horfe and armes, from thence to march againft the Scots.

M. S. Wingf. Bodenham, m.

In the 18 E. 3. *Roger Daneys* did releafe to *Roland Daneys* his Brother, and to his heirs all his right in the Mannour of **Tikencote**, and in all fuch Lands and Tenements which did at any time belong to *Bricius Daneys* in **Empingham**.

In the 10 H. 4. It was found that *John Danneys*, fon and heir of *John Danneys*, held of the King the Mannour of **Tikencote** in the County of **Rotel**, by the fervice of one Knights fee ; and two Carucates of Land with the appurtenances in **Horum** (*i. e.* **Horn**) in the faid County, by the fervice of the fixth part of a Knights Fee.

Ex parte Rem. Thef. H. 10 H. 4.

In the 5 E. 6. *John Campynet* and his Wife obtain'd Licenfe to alienate the Mannour of **Tikencote** in the County of **Rutland** to *John Bevercots,* and *John Fixton,* and their heirs, to the ufe of the faid *John Campynet &c.* which Mannor was held of the King in *Capite* by Knights fervice.

Lic. Ali. 5 E. 6. *p. 2.*

But of later time a younger Branch of the *Wingfeilds* of **Upton** *in Com.* **Northampton**, became Lords of this Mannour.

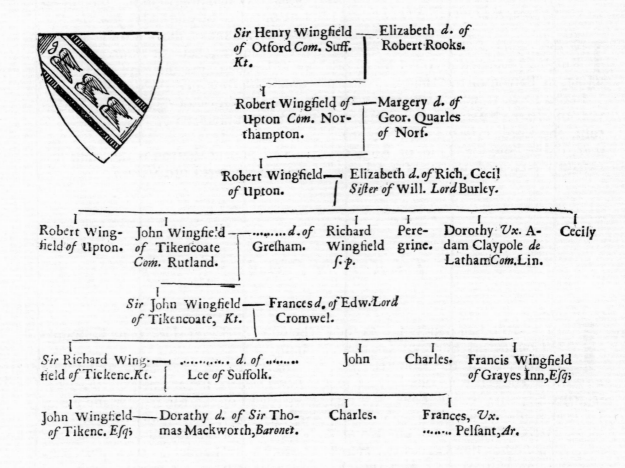

Sir Henry Wingfield ——— Elizabeth *d. of*
of Otford *Com.* Suff.　　Robert Rooks.
Kt.

Robert Wingfield *of* ——— Margery *d. of*
Upton *Com.* Nor-　　　　Geor. Quarles
thampton.　　　　　　　*of* Norf.

Robert Wingfield ——— Elizabeth *d. of* Rich. Cecil
of Upton.　　　　　　*Siſter of* Will. *Lord* Burley.

Robert Wing-　John Wingfield ——— ....*d. of*　Richard　Pere-　Dorothy *Vx.* A-　Cecily
field *of* Upton.　*of* Tikencoate　　Greſham.　Wingfield　grine.　dam Claypole *de*
　　　　　　Com. Rutland.　　　　　　*ſ. p.*　　　　　Latham*Com.*Lin.

Sir John Wingfield ——— Frances *d. of* Edw. *Lord*
of Tikencoate, *Kt.*　　Cromwel.

Sir Richard Wing-　——— .... *d. of* ....　John　Charles.　Francis Wingfield
field *of* Tickenc. *Kt.*　　Lee *of* Suffolk.　　　　　　　　*of* Grayes Inn, *Eſq;*

John Wingfield ——— Dorathy *d. of Sir* Tho-　Charles.　Frances, *Vx.*
of Tikenc. *Eſq;*　mas Mackworth, *Baronet.*　　　　.......... Pelſant, *Ar.*

Of the ADVOWSON.

Reg. Linc.

IN the 28 E. 1. the Abbot of 𝕺𝕤𝕠𝕝𝖜𝖊-
𝖘𝖙𝖔𝖓 (now call'd 𝕯𝖚𝖘𝖙𝖔𝖓) did preſent to the Church of 𝕿𝖎𝖐𝖊𝖓𝖈𝖔𝖙𝖊, on
one part, and Sir *Bricius Daneys* then
Lord of the Mannor preſented *William*
his Son, on the other; but Sir *Bricius
Daneys* revoked his preſentation.

The Rectory of 𝕿𝖎𝖐𝖊𝖓𝖈𝖔𝖙𝖊 is valued
in the Kings Books at 6 *l.* 5 *s.* 8 *d.*

The preſent Patron is

TINWELL.

Domeſd. North.
N. 6.

𝕿Inwell lyes in the *Eaſt* hundred
and did formerly belong to
the Church of St. *Peters de*
𝕭𝖚𝖗𝖌, or 𝕻𝖊𝖙𝖊𝖗𝖇𝖔𝖗𝖔𝖚𝖌𝖍, for at the
Conquerors Survey, it was found that
that Church held 𝕿𝖊𝖉𝖎𝖓𝖜𝖊𝖑𝖑𝖊, where
were five hides and one yard Land, of
arable eight Carucates, in Demeſne
two; twenty four Villains, and eleven
Bordarii poſſeſſing ſeven Carucates.
Here were alſo two Mills of 24 *s.* and
twenty acres of Meadow, formerly valued at 10 *s.* but at the time of that Survey, at 7 *l.*

And in the poſſeſſion of that Abby
did this Town continue till the diſſolution. After which,

King *Edward* 6. in the 7*th.* year of 7. E. 6. p. 8.
his reign granted his Letters Patents of
Confirmation of the Mannour of 𝕿𝖎𝖓-
𝖜𝖊𝖑𝖑 in this County, and 𝕾𝖔𝖗𝖙𝖍𝖔𝖗𝖕
in *Com.* 𝕹𝖔𝖗𝖙𝖍𝖆𝖒𝖕. (formerly granted
to *Richard Cecyl* and his heirs) to *William Cecyl* Knight, afterwards Lord
Burley, to hold of the King in *Capite*
by Knights ſervice, reſerving the yearly
Rent of 65 *s.* 7 *d.* for a tenth payable
at *Mic.* From whom is lineally deſcended
the right honourable *John* Earl of 𝕰𝖝𝖊𝖙𝖊𝖗 the preſent Lord of this Mannour,
and of 𝕴𝖓𝖙𝖍𝖆𝖗𝖕 a ſmall Village within
this Pariſh.

Monuments

Monuments in the Church.

On a Plate of Brafs fixt upon a plain Grave-ftone, near the Weft end of the Chancell.

EN (*Hofpes*) *Sepulchrum* Gulielmi Robinfon *Armigeri, Viri docti, prudentis, pii : Sapientiam & gravitatem multa Lectio conciliavit : Virorum nobilium amicitiis cognitus, quos fine adulatione coluit : duas filias reliquit quas pie educaverat : interim Mors oppreffit anno ætatis* 48. & *Redemptoris,* 1640.

On two plain Grave-ftones placed in the South Eaft Angle of the Chancel.

HEre *lyeth the body of* Elifabeth Cecil *daughter of* David *Earl of* Exeter *by* Elifabeth *his Countefs, Daughter of* John *Earl of* Bridgewater. *Buried* November 13. Anno Domini 1638.

HEre *lyeth* Thomas Cecil *fixth Son of* David *Earl of* Exeter *by* Elifabeth *his Countefs, Daughter of* John *Earl of* Bridgewater: *buried* May 28. Anno Domini 1641.

In the South Wall of the Chancel is erected a hanfome Monument (but without date) to the memory of *Elifabeth,* Daughter of *Richard Cecil,* Efq; and Sifter of *William* Lord *Burley,* who was firft married to *Richard Wingfield* Efq; and after his death to .... on which Monument are the following infcriptions,

Deo æterno opt. Max. & memoriæ Sacrum.

Fide   *Charitate*
certaque Spe   *Refurgendi.*

Ut viret occato denatum femen in Agro,
Mortua fic vivent Corpora noftra Deo.

On this Monument are thefe three Efcutchions reprefenting a Feme and her two Husbands, *Viz.*

In the middle *Cecil* with the diftinction of the younger Houfe, and over the Coat, *ELIZABETH.*

On the Dexter, *arg. on a Bend. gu. Cottifed fab,* 3 *pair of Wings conjoyn'd, of the firft,* and over the Coat. *R. W.*

On the Sinifter, *S. a Bend engraled between* 6 *Billets ar.* Over the Coat *H. A.*

Of the ADVOWSON.

Reg. Linc.

IN the 4 *H.* 3. the Abbot of 𝕻eter-bourough prefented *Roger de Welles* to the Church of 𝕮inewell.

The Rectory of 𝕮inwell is valued in the Kings Books at 12 *l.* 10 *s.* 5 *d.*

The Prefent Patron is the right honourable the Earl of 𝕰xeter.

TIXOVER.

Domefd. North. Nº. 1.

TIxover (in *Domefday* writ 𝕮ichefouze) lyes in the hundred of 𝖂zangdike. At the time of the Norman Survey this Town was appurtenant to the Kings Mannor of 𝕮hetene, and here were then reckoned two Hides, of arable eight Carucates, fixteen Sockmen, and four *Bordarii,* or Cottagers, having fix Carucates; here was alfo one Mill of 5 *s.* Rent, eight acres of Meadow, and three acres of Thornes.

Nom. Vil.

In the 9 *E.* 2. the Abbot of 𝕮lugny or 𝕮luny in 𝕭urgundy, was Lord of 𝕮ykefoze. Which being a Priory Alien, this Eftate was often (in time of Wars with France efpecially) feiz'd by the King.

Pipe.Vet.Efc.

In the 18 *E.* 2. *Matthew Bron* did account in the Exchequer the fum of 12 *l.* 9 *s.* 5 *d. ob.* for Rents and other iffues out of the Mannour of 𝕮ykefovere *Com.* 𝕽ot. parcel of the Temporalities

of the Abbot of the *Cluniacs ,* which were at that time in the Kings hands.

After the total fuppreffion of all Priories Alien, which was 2 *H.* 5. this Mannour became part of the poffeffions of the Collegiate Church at 𝕮atteſbal, in *Com.* 𝕷incoln , and fo continued till the fuppreffion of that Houfe.

After the fuppreffion of which Houfe, this Eftate being in the Crown,

In the 36 *H.* 8. that King granted *36 H. 8. p, 6.* to *Charles Brandon* Duke of 𝕾uffolk all thofe his Mannours of 𝕮ikefoze , 𝕸anton, and 𝕶ylthozp, to be held of the King *in Capite* by Knights fervice. Which *Charles* left iffue male only two *Bar. Eng.* Sons, *Henry* and *Charles,* both which *2 Vol.* 300. dying iffuelefs in the 5 *E.* 6. their Eftate became divided among feveral collateral heirs , *Sidney, Lovel, Cavendiſh &c.* Whofe relation I have expreft in the Scheme here annext.

	Sir William Brandon ___ *Kt.* 12 H. 7.	Elizabeth *d. of Sir* Robert Wingfield, *Kt.*	

Margaret.	*Sir* Gregory Lovel, *Kt.*	*Sir* Will. Brandon, *Kt.* Standard Bearer to King H. 7.	Eliz. *da. &* coh. of *Sir* Hen. Bruin, *Kt.*	*Sir* Thomas Brandon *Kt. of the Garter,* ob. f. p.	Anne ___ John Sidney of Penhurft, *Com.* Kent.	Eleanor *Vx.* Joh. Glenham.	Katherine *Vx.* Henrici Gurney.	Elizabeth *Vx.* Joh: Cavendiſh.
	Sir Thomas Lovel, *Kt.*	*Sir* Charles Brandon, *Kt. Duke of* Suffolk.		*Sir* William Sidney. *Kt.* ___ Anne *da* of Edmund Pakenham. Banneret, *ob.* 7 *E.* 6.				
	Thomas Lovel, ob. f. p.	Margaret *Wife of* John Kerfey, *Efq;*		*Sir* Henry Sidney, *Kt.* ___ Mary *da.* of John *of the Garter,* Lord Deputy *of* Ireland. Dudley *Duke of* Northumberland.				
				Sir Philip Sidney, *Kt,* Governour *of* Fluſhing.		*Sir* Robert Sidney *created Earl of* Leicefter, 16 Jac.		

In

Efc. 1 Mar.

In the firſt year of Queen *Mary*, it was found by office, that *Thomas Lovel* dyed ſeized of the fifth part of the Mannours of **Tixover**, **Manton**, and **Kylthorp**, with their appurtenances, being parcel of the poſſeſſions of the late diſſolved Colledge of **Tatterſal**, all which he held of the Queen *in Capite* by Knights ſervice : And that *Margaret* the Wife of *John Kerſey* was his Siſter and heir.

21 El. *p.* 7.

But it ſeems not long after the whole Eſtate became united in the heir of *Sidney* by partition, for in the 21 *El.* that Queen granted Licence to *Henry Sidney* Knight to alienate the Mannours of **Teekſore** and **Manton** (*Com.* **Rotel.**)

to *Michael Lewis* and his heirs.

In the 33 *Eliz.* the ſaid Eſtate was conveyed to *William Kirkham*, who not long after conveyed the ſame to *Roger Dale* of **Colly Weſton** Eſq; in whoſe name and family it continued till of late years *Charles Dale* Eſq; Grandſon of the ſaid *Roger*, leaving at his Death four Daughters his Coheirs, two of which being within age, certain Truſtees were enabled by a ſpecial act in the Parliament held at *Weſtminſter* 31 *Car.* 2. to ſell this Lordſhip, which accordingly they did by due and effectual conveyance in the Law to *Henry Stafford* of **Blatherwick** in the County of **North.** Eſq; the preſent Owner hereof.

Ralph *de* Stafford *deſcended from the ancient Barons of* Stafford, 49 E. 3. —— Matilda *da. & coh.* of *Sir* John Haſtang *of* Lemmington, *in Com.* Warwick, *Kt.*

Sir Humphrey Stafford *of* Grafton, *in Com.* Worceſt. 21 R. 2.

Sir Humphrey Stafford, *Kt.* ob. 7 H. 5. —— Elizabeth *da. and h.* of *Sir* John Burdet, *Kt.*

John Stafford, *f. & h.* ob. *ſ. p.*

Sir Humphrey Stafford, *Kt.* 9 H. 6. —— Alianore *da.* of *Sir* Thomas Aylesbury, *and heir of* John *her Brother ; by whom came the Mannour of* Blatherwick, *in Com.* Northamp.

Sir Humphrey Stafford, *Kt. attainted,* 1 H. 7.

Sir Humphrey Stafford, *Kt. reſtored* 37 H. 8.

Sir Humphrey Stafford, *Kt. ob.* 2 E. 6. —— Margaret *ſiſter and coh.* of *Sir* Edmund Tame, *Kt.*

Sir Humphrey Stafford, *Kt. ob.* 17 Eliz.

John Stafford, *Eſq;*

Humphrey Stafford, *Eſq;*

William Stafford, *of* Blatherwick, *Eſq;* —— Margaret *da.* of *Sir* John Corbet, *Kt.*

Henry Stafford, *Eſq;*

William

TOLE.

TOLETHORP.

Tolethorp lyes in the *East* Hundred, and was formerly a Town and had a Chappel.

Domesd. North. *N°.* 35.

I find at the time of the Conquerors Survey, *William* the Son of *Ansculfus*, held half a hide in Tolethorp, of Arable four Carucates, *Rex inde habet Soca.* In Demesn one Carucate, twelve Villains, and fifteen *Berdarii*, having three Carucates, here were four Mills of 40 *s.* and twenty Acres of Meadow, held by eight Sockmen, all formerly valued at 40 *s.* but at the time of the Survey at 5 *l.*

Nom. Vil.

In 9 *E.* 2. *Nicholas de Burton* was Lord Tolethorp,

Disc. of Leic. *by* W. B. 108.

Afterwards in the time of *Edw.* 3. It was the chief seat of Sir *William de Burton* Knight, one of the Justices of the Kings Bench from 17. *E.* 3. to the 36 year of that Kings reign; who dyed '49 *E.* 3. leaving issue by *Elleonor* his Wife, Sir *Thomas de Burton* Knight, who deceased 8 *R.* 2. from whom descend the *Burtons* of Stockerson, Okeham, and Braunston, as seems by their Armes, *S a Cheveron Argent between three Owles membred and Crowned, Or.*

Which said Sir *Thomas Burton*, did by his deed dated at Tolethorp on the *Saturday* next after the Feast of St. *Martin* the Bishop, 50 *E.* 3. convey unto *John Brown* of Stamford Esq; this Mannour of Tolethorp, together with all its appurtenances, and the perpetual *Advowson* of the Chappel of the same; also all his Lands, Tenements, Rents, and services in the Village of *Little* Casterton with the Reversion of the Patronage of the Church of the same.

Ex Stem. penes Chr. Brown, *ar.*

TOLETHORPE *From the South*

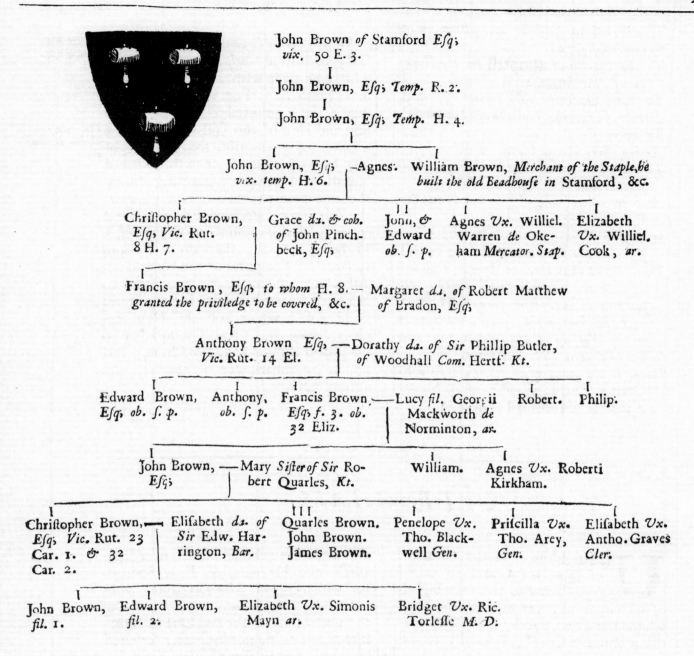

John Brown *of* Stamford *Esq;*
vix. 50 E. 3.

John Brown, *Esq; Temp.* R. 2.

John Brown, *Esq; Temp.* H. 4.

John Brown, *Esq;* —Agnes. William Brown, *Merchant of the Staple, he*
vix. temp. H. 6. *built the old Beadhouse in* Stamford, &c.

Christopher Brown, | Grace *dz. & coh.* | Jonn, & | Agnes *Ux.* Williel. | Elizabeth
Esq, Vic. Rut. | of John Pinch- | Edward | Warren *de* Oke- | *Ux.* Williel.
8 H. 7. | beck, *Esq;* | *ob. f. p.* | ham *Mercator. Stap.* | Cook, *ar.*

Francis Brown, *Esq; to whom* H. 8. — Margaret *da.* of Robert Matthew
granted the priviledge to be covered, &c. | of Bradon, *Esq;*

Anthony Brown *Esq,* —Dorathy *da. of Sir* Phillip Butler,
Vic. Rut. 14 El. | of Woodhall *Com.* Hertf. *Kt.*

Edward Brown, | Anthony, | Francis Brown——Lucy *fil.* Georgii | Robert. | Philip.
Esq, ob. f. p. | *ob. f. p.* | *Esq, f.* 3. *ob.* Mackworth *de*
| | 32 Eliz. Norminton, *ar.*

John Brown, —Mary *Sister of Sir* Ro- | William. | Agnes *Ux.* Roberti
Esq; | bert Quarles, *Kt.* | | Kirkham.

Christopher Brown,—Elisabeth *da. of* | Quarles Brown. | Penelope *Ux.* | Priscilla *Ux.* | Elisabeth *Ux.*
Esq, Vic. Rut. 23 | Sir Edw. Har- | John Brown. | Tho. Black- | Tho. Arey, | Antho. Graves
Car. 1. & 32 | rington, *Bar.* | James Brown. | well *Gen.* | *Gen.* | *Cler.*
Car. 2.

John Brown, | Edward Brown, | Elizabeth *Ux.* Simonis | Bridget *Ux.* Ric.
fil. 1. | *fil.* 2. | Mayn *ar.* | Torlesse *M. D.*

Butchers *Sur-*
vey of Stamf.
p. 32, *and* 37.

Of this Family was *William Brown* Merchant of the Staple, who in the year 1493. (8 *H.* 7.) Built the Old *Beadhouse* in 𝕾𝖙𝖆𝖒𝖋𝖔𝖗𝖉, for a Warden Confrater, twelve poor old men, and a Nurse; and endow'd the same with the Mannour of 𝕾𝖜𝖆𝖕𝖋𝖊𝖎𝖑𝖉 (*Com.* 𝕷𝖎𝖓𝖈.) and with divers Lands and Tenements elsewhere. He also built at his own proper charges the beautiful Steeple, with a great part of the Church, of *Alhallows* in 𝕾𝖙𝖆𝖒𝖋𝖔𝖗𝖉, in which Church he lyeth buried after he had been twice Alderman of the said Town, *viz.* in the years 1466. and 1470.

Which *William* was younger Brother of *John Brown* Esq; who lived in the Reign of *H.* 6. Whose Widdow, *Agnes Brown,* was also a charitable Bene-

factress, according to the Practice of that age; as appears by her Will, dated on the day of St. *John Baptist An. Domini* 1470. (10 *E.* 4.) Whereby she devised, her body to be buryed in *Alhallows* Church at 𝕾𝖙𝖆𝖒𝖋𝖔𝖗𝖉, beside her Husband, and among other matters, the Charities following.

Penes Christ.
Brown *de* Tole-
thorp, *Armig.*

To our moder *Church of* 𝕷𝖎𝖓𝖈𝖔𝖑𝖓 6 s. 8 d.
To the Church of Alhallows *of* 𝕾𝖙𝖆𝖒𝖋𝖔𝖗𝖉,
a Vestment *of a suite the which shall cost*
me by the oversight of my Friends that
shall occupy for me, 100. *Marks.*
To the Gray Fryers. 20 s.
To the Black Fryers. 20 s.
To the Augustine Fryers. 20 s.
To the White Fryers. 13 s. 4 d.
To the Nuns. 13 s. 4 d.

*To a Priest to sing for me fifteen years
continually, 75 l.
To the Church of* Amptell *in the Coun-
ty of* Bedford, *40 s.
To every Godchild that I have 3 s. 4 d.
To every Curate that comes to my Dirige 6 d.
To every Priest, 4 d.
And to every Parish Clark. 2 d.
To every Prior and Warden of the four hou-
ses that comes (*ut sup.*) o s. 6 d
And to every other Fryer that comes (*ut
sup.) 4 d.
Item for a Vestment and Chalis to the Chap-
pel that my Husband and I lig in, 8 l.
Item I will that there be bought a Cloath
of Silk and Gold with a Valence ef the
same to be born with four Petyt Staves
over the Sacrament, on Palme Sunday
in the Worship of the Sacrament, and
I will that it cost 4. Marks.
Item, to the painting of the Tabernacle in
Corpus Christi Chapple in St. Marys
Kyrke in* Stamford. *40 s.*

Which *John Brown* and *Agnes* afore- *Fullers Worthies of Eng:
Rut.*
said, had issue *Christopher Brown* Esq;
who came over with *H.* 7. and assisted
him against *R.* 3. For which good ser-
vice *K. H.* 8. granted to *Francis Brown* *Chart. penes
Christ. Brown,
ar.*
Son and Heir of the said *Christopher*, a
Charter of exemption from serving of
any Jury whatsoever, or in the Office of
Sheriff or Escheator , granting also by
the same deed to the said *Francis Brown*,
the Liberty and Priviledge to be cover'd
in the presence of him the said *K. H.* 8.
his heirs, and all other great Persons
spiritual or Temporal of this Kingdome;
All which immunities were granted to
the said *Francis Brown* for the term
of his Life ; whose Son and Heir *Anthony Brown* was great Grandfather to
Christopher Brown Esq, now living and
possest by inheritance of this fair and
antient Estate.

UPPINGHAM.

Camb. Brit.

UPpingham is in the Hundred
of Martinfly, and so called
says *Cambden*, from the highth
of its scituation : yet in truth the place
where the Town stands, tho it be something above a Level , is hardly to be
called a hill.

Of Uppingham I can find no mention in *Domesday* Book, it being at that
time (no doubt) one of those seven
nameless Berewics or Hamlets included
in Redlinctune *Cherchesoch*, of which
see more under the Title of Ridling
ton.

*Bar. Eng.
1 Vol. 409.*

In the time of the Barons Wars Up
pingham belong'd to the *Montforts*:
For I find that *Peter de Montfort* an e-
minent Baron in those times, gave the
Mannour of Uppingham to *William* his
2d. Son, about 50 H. 3. Preston also
had the same Lords. But *Guy de Montfort* a descendant from the abovesaid
Peter, having married a Daughter of
Thomas Beauchamp Earl of Warwick,
Id. 410. the *Montforts* estate in this County was
settled in Tayl on the said *Guy*, the

Remainder to the said Earl of Warwick, and his heirs, 22 E. 3. Soon after which *Guy de Montfort* dying without issue , this Estate became part of
the possessions of the said Earl of Warwick, but being not long after ferfeited
by him , and in the Crown, King *Ri-* *Bar. Eng. 1.
Vol. 129.*
chard the 2d. granted the same together
with the Mannours of Gretham, and
Barodon in this County , to *Thomas
Mowbray* Earl of Nottingham, and
Duke of Norfolk, a great favourite of
that King. With whom , as it seems,
this Estate continued not very long ;
for in the time of the Civil Wars, all
the foresaid Towns and Essington in
this County were part of the large possessions of *Richard Nevil* commonly cal- *Bar. Eng. 1.
Vol. 307.*
led the stout Earl of Warwick, he having married *Anne* Daughter of *Richard Beauchamp*, and Sister to *Henry*
Duke of Warwick, after whose death
she became heir to the said Earldome.
But her Husband being kill'd in Barnet
field, on *Easter-Day* 11 E. 4. fighting
on the part of the house of Lancaster ;
his

his Countefs after his Death underwent no little diftrefs, all her vaft inheritance being by Authority of Parliament taken from her, and fettled on her two Daughters, *Ifabel* married to *George* Duke of **Clarence**, and *Anne* to *Richard* Duke of **Gloucefter**, and was accordingly withheld from her till 3 *H.* 7. when the King (having himfelf a mind thereto, and her Daughters being then both dead) by a new act of Parliament repealed the former, and reftored her in to the poffeffion of the premifes, with power to alien the fame or any part thereof: Purfuant to which power, fhe by her deed bearing date the 13 of *Decemb.* 3 *H.* 7. and a fine thereupon, conveyed the abovefaid Towns in this County, with many others elfewhere, to the faid King, entailing them upon the iffue male of his Body, with remainder to her felf and her Heirs.

Ubi fup.

Which faid King *H.* 7. in the firft year of his reign (being then it feems, *de facto,* poffeft of this eftate) granted the Stewardfhip of the Lordfhips of **Uppingham, Prefton, Baroughden, Efenden,** and **Gretham,** and of all the Lands formerly belonging to *George* Duke of **Clarence,** to *Simon Digby* a 2d. Son of Sir *Everard Digby* of **Pilton** (*Com.* **Leic.**) Whofe Son and heir

Bar. Eng. 2. *Vol.* 436.

Reginald Digby was great Grandfather to *John Digby,* who in the 16 year of King *James* (1618.) was advanc'd to the Title of Lord *Digby* of **Shirburne** in the County of **Dorfet,** and in the 20. of that King created Earl of **Briftol.**

It appears by the account of *Richard Darrington* the Kings Receiver for thefe parts in the 3 *E* 6. that the faid King *Edward* the fixth granted the Mannor of **Prefton** and **Uppingham** (the Rents and Profits of which did at that time amount to the Sum of 80 *l.* 3 *s.* 6. *d.* *ob. q;* *per an.*) to his Sifter the Lady *Elizabeth,* (afterwards Queen) to hold from the Feaft of *St. Michael* in 38 *H.* 8. *durante bene placito ipfius Domini Regis.*

Compt. pro Com. Rutland in Offic. Augm. 3. E. 6.

Afterwards in the Reign of Queen *Elizabeth,* the Mannour of **Prefton** and **Uppingham** was granted out of the Crown to the then Earl of **Exeter,** from which Family it went in marriage with *Anne,* one of the Daughters and Coheirs of *William* Earl of **Exeter,** to the Earl of **Stamford,** from which Family it was conveyed to the prefent Owner.

Ex relatione Edwardi Fawkener, Arm.

The prefent Lord of **Uppingham** and **Prefton,** is *Edward Fawkener,* Efq; which Eftate he enjoyes by inheritance from his great Uncle *Everard Fawkener,* a wealthy Citizen and Mercer of *London.*

Anthonius *Fawkener* de Stokedry, *in Com.* Rutland.

Kenelmus *Fawkener* de Stokedry. .... *f.* .... Wilcox *de* Knaufton *in Com.* Leic.

Everardus *Fawkener de* London, & *de* Uppingham, *Vic.* Rutland, 1628. *ob. f. p.* 1653.

Edwardus *Fawkener* de Dryftoke. Maria *f.* .... Cowper *de* Wefton *in Com.* Northamp.

Kenelmus *Fawkener* de Braunfton *in Com.* Rutl. *ob.* 1667. Catherina *f.* Thomæ Ireland *de* Prefton *in Com.* Rutl.

Edwardus *Fawkener* de Uppingham, *ar.* Dorcas *f. & coh:* Willielmi Nevil.

Edwardus *Fawkener Med.* Temp. *Jurifconfultus.*

Here

Here is alſo in this Town another ſmall Mannour, belonging to the Parſon of the Church of **Uppingham** for the time being, in right of his Perſonage.

Of the Hoſpital, and School.

ABout the year 1584. *Robert Johnſon* Archdeacon of **Leiceſter**, and Parſon of North-**Luffenham** in this County, built (out of Collections for that purpoſe) a free School in this Town, and an Hoſpital for the maintenance of thirteen poor men and one Woman, of which number ſix to be Townſmen: Their Stipend, three pounds a piece *per ann.* At the ſame time he erected the like at **Okeham**; both which Foundations he afterwards indow'd with certain Conceal'd Lands, and impropriations, which he had beg'd of Queen *Elizabeth* for that purpoſe, and for both conſtituted the ſame Orders of Government. Which ſee in **Okeham**, *ſupra.*

Of the MERCATE, &c.]

Rot. Cart. 9 E. 1. n. 46.

KIng *Edward* 1. in the 9*th* year of his Reign did grant and confirm to *Peter de Monteforti* then Lord of this Mannour, that he and his heirs for ever ſhall have one Mercate at their Mannor of **Uppingham** in *Com.* **Rotel.** weekly on the *Wedneſday*, and alſo one Fair yearly, for three days, *viz.* the Eve, day, and morrow of the bleſſed *Margaret* the Virgin, (*i e.* 20 *Julii.*) *Niſi mercatum illud & feria illa ſint ad nocumentum vicinorum mercatorum & vicinarum feriarum.*

By the Stat. 11 *H.* 7. *ch.* 4. the Standard of Weights, and meaſures for this County of **Rutland**, is appointed to be kept at **Uppingham :** It not being allways appointed to be kept at the County Town; for by that *Stat.* the Standard for the County of **Warwick** is to remain at **Coventry.**

Of the ADVOWSON.

Reg. Linc.

IN the 42 *H,* 3. *Benedict de Gravend* being then Biſhop of **Lincoln**, the then Abbot of *Weſtminſter* preſented to the Church of **Uppingham.**

4 E. 6. pars 4.

But after the diſſolution of *Weſtminſter* Abby, the Temporalties of that houſe being in the Crown, King *Edward* 6. in the fourth year of his Reign, granted, among other things, the *Advowſon* of this Church to *Nicholas Ridley* then Biſhop of **London** and to his Succeſſours for ever; and this was by his Letters Patents dated the 12*th.* day of *April* in the ſaid 4*th.* year of his reign.

The Rectory of **Uppingham** is valued in the Kings Books at, 20*l.* 0*s.*9*d.*

The preſent Patron is the Biſhop of **London.**

In the Church of Uppingham.

Memoriæ Sacrum

VIro honoratiſſimo *Everardo* Fawkener *Armigero in hoc Comitatu olim* Vicecomiti, *qui obiit* 2. *die* Maii *An. Dom.* 1653. *Annoque Ætat. ſui* 75.

> *Clarus ab ingenuis jacet hic* Fawkenerus *Avitis*
> *Quem magè virtutum nobilitavit Amor.*
> *Geſtantem ſummos* Rutlandia *vidit honores*
> *Quos ambit juris militiæque Decus.*
> *Spectat ab Aurora quaq;* Uppinghamia *Templum*
> *Sumptibus illius compita ſtrata nitent :*
> *Promptior ut Cælum qua nos gradiamur ad altum*
> *Et conſtipato ſit via* Munda *foro.*

Pauperibus

Pauperibus Solamen erat : Juvenumque solebat
Angustam larga spem relevare manu.
Lector, ne luges ; nec vos lugetis Amici,
Post hæc en superest nescia fama mori.

In grati animi Testimonium Edvardus Fawkener Armiger in hæredem sibi as-
citus hoc mærens posuit Monumentum.

WARDLY.

Lyes in the Hundred of **Okeham Soak.** Of **Wardly** there is no mention in *Domesday* Book, it being at that time surveyed as a member to some other Neighbouring Town, but to which I cannot say.

This Town, together with **Ayston** in this County, did belong to the *Murdocs* of **Stokerson** (*Com.* **Leic.**) by whose heir general it came to the *Boyvilles*, *Alice de Boyville* Sister and Heir of *Hugh Murdac* being Lady of this Mannor in the 9th. year of *E.* 2. which *Alice* was the Wife of *Thomas de Boyville*, in whose name and posterity this Estate continued till 8 *E.* 4. in which year *John Boyville* the last Lord of this Mannour of that name dying without issue male, his E-

Nom. Vil. in Scacc.

state became divided among his three Daughters and Coheirs, in which division this Town and **Ayston** in this County were assigned to the Purparty of *Thomas Restwold* and *Margaret* his Wife, one of the said three Daughters.

E Collect. Wingf. Bod. m. f. 101,102.

Of the ADVOWSON.

Walterus de Baskerville & Isolea uxor ejus petunt versus Priorem de **Launda** de Advocatione ecclesiæ de **Wardly.** An. 4 *Johannis.*

Fragmenta Johan. An. 4. Rot. 13.

The Rectory of **Wardly** *Cum* **Belton,** is valued in the Kings Books at, 10*l.* 15*s.* 11*d.*

The present Patron is

WHISSUNDINE.

IN the Hundred of **Alstoe.** At the time of the *Norman* Conquest. Earl *Wallef*, a Saxon, held **Wichinge-Dene** then rated at four Carucates to the Tax or Geld. The Land was twelve Carucates. Afterwards at the time of *Domesday* Survey, *Hugo de Hotot* Farmer of *Judith* Countess of **Huntington**, held here five Carucates, and twenty seven Villains, and six *Bordarii* (or Cottagers) having eight Carucates. In the time of King *Edward* the Confessor this Mannour was valued at 8 *l.* but at the abovemention'd Survey at 13 *l.*

In the 9 *E.* 2. *Thomas Wakes* and *Robert de Helewelle* were Lords of one moi-

Domesday Tit. Rotel.

Nom. Vill. in Scacc.

ety of **Whissindon**, and *Richard de Harington* and *John de Wyttelebirye* were Lords of the other moiety. Of all which in order. First,

Concerning the *Wakes* Estate in this Town, I find that *Thomas* Lord *Wake* dyed seised of the Mannour of **Wyssingden** (*Com.* **Rotel.**) in the 23 year of *Edw.* 3. leaving *Margaret* Countess of **Kent** (Widow of *Edmund* of **Woodstock** second Son to King *E.* 1. and Earl of **Kent**) his Sister and Heir , whose Sons *Edmund*, and *John*, successive Earls of **Kent** dying seized of this Lordship without issue, *Joan* their Sister then Wife of Sir *Thomas Holland* Knight, became

Bar. Eng. 1 Vol. 541.

became their heir. Which *Joan* was afterwards marryed to *Edward* the Black Prince. But she dying seised of this Mannour, 9 *R.* 2. *Thomas Holland* Lord *Wake* & Earl of **Kent**, her Son and Heir, had the same year a special Livery of this and the rest of her Estate; which *Thomas* departing this Life in the 20. year *R.* 2. left issue *Thomas* his Son and Heir, and *Edmund*, both which dying without issue, his five Sisters, *Alianore*, *Joan*, *Margaret*, another *Alianore*, and *Elisabeth*, became their Coheirs.

margin: Bar. Eng. 2. Vol. 75.

margin: Ed. 76. 77.

This Mannour it seems fell at that time to the purparty of *Alianore* the Eldest Sister, (who being the Widow of *Roger Mortimer* Earl of **March**, marryed for her second Husband *Edward Cherlton* Lord *Powis*:) For in the 25th. year of *H.* 6. it was found by Office that *Henry Gray* Son and Heir of *Joan* third Daughter and Coheir of *Alianor* first sister and Coheir of *Edmund* late Earl of **Kent**, held the Mannour of **Whissundine** *cum pertinent.* in the County of **Rut.** of the King in *Capite*, by the service of the hundredth part of a Knights Fee. Which *Henry* left issue *Richard* his Son and Heir, who departing this Life, 6 *E.* 4. being then seized of this Mannour of **Wissenden**, left issue by *Margaret* his Wife, Daughter of *James* Lord *Audley*, *John Gray* Lord *Powis*, who in the 10th year of *H.* 7. was found to dye seized of this Estate, and that he held the same of the King in *Capite* by Knights service.

margin: Ex parte Rem. The. Trin. 25. H 6.

margin: Bar. Eng. 1. Vol. 284.

margin: Esc. 10. H. 7.

The *Helewells* Estate in this Town remain'd in that name, till about the reign of *H.* 7. it came by an heir Female to the *Sherards*, and is at present possest by the right honourable *Bennet* Lord *Skerard*, Heir of that family now living. Of which see more in **Tigh.**

In the 18 *E.* 2. *Matthew Bron*, the Kings Escheator in this County, accounted for the Mannour of **Wissenden**, late the Estate of *Richard de Harrington* deceased, and which he held of the Earl of **Richmond** by the service of 4 *l. per an*, and not of the King. This was called the Mannour of **Morehall.**

margin: Rot. Pipe 18 E. 2.

margin: Esc. 18. E. 2. n. 75.
Esc. 51. E. 3. n. 18.

Concerning the *Wittleburys* Estate, which hath been of great antiquity in this Town: I find that in the 12 *E.* 3. *Albericus de Wytelbury*, who was son of *John de Wytelbury*, paid to the King 12 *s.* 6 *d.* as a relief for one Messuage, twenty two yard Land and a half, and twenty acres of Meadow in **Wyssenden** with the appurtenances in the County of **Roteland**, held of the King in *Capite* by the service of the 8th. part of a Knights fee.

margin: Ex parte Rem. Thes. H. 12. E. 3. r. 1.

In the 25 *E.* 3. *Thomas* Son and heir of the said *Albericus de Witelbury* paid the King a relief of the said sum, for the same Estate as abovespecifyed.

margin: Ib. P. 25. E. 3.

In the 3 *H.* 4. it was found by Office that *Albredus* Son and Heir of *John Wittlebury* held the Estate above specifyed of the King in *Capite* as of his Mannour of **Huntington**, by the service of the 8th. part of a Knights Fee.

margin: Ib. P. 3. H. 4.

Which Family of the *Wittelburys* were heretofore Lords of the Mannour of **Brinklow** in *Com.* **Warwick**, which they held by the service of a Sore Sparhawk, yearly at *Lammas*, or 2 *s.* in Mony.

margin: Dugd. Warw. p. 143.

This Estate with two other Mannonrs in this Town, are all three united by the Name of the Mannour of *Moorhall*, *Whittlebury*, and *Powis*, and are now possest by the honourable *Phillip Skerard* Esq; second Son of *William* late Lord *Sherard*. Of which Family *vid.* **Tigh.**

To which antient discent, as there exprest, may be added the alliance of this younger branch, *viz.*

Philippus Sherard, *Ar.* fil. 2. Willielmi *Dom.* Sherard, *mar.* 3.	Margareta fil. Thomæ Denton, *mil.* Vidua Johannis Poultney, Arm.	Willielmus Eure Arm. fil. 2 Will. *Dom.* Eure, *occisus in servicio* Car. 1. *Regis*, Anno 1645. *mar.* 2.

Bennet Sherard, ar. — Dorathea fil. Dom. Fairfax Vidua ..... Stapleton, ar.	Philip. Sherard de Car-Colson in Com. Nottingham fil. 2. — Anna fil. & coh. Johan. Thoroughton, M. D.	Denton Sherard fil. 3.	Abigail Ux. Johan. Pckering, arm.	Margareta consanguinea & coh. Will. Dom. Eure, ux. Tho. Danby, ar.	Maria consang. & coh. Will. Dom. Eure, ux. W. Palmes ar.

Philippus.	Elizabetha.	Margareta.	Philippus.	Robertus	Willielmus.	Anna.	Maria.	Elizabetha.

Of the Church there:

IN the 17 *E.* 1. Sir *John de Swine-borne* Knight, and Frier *John de Luxdors* Sacrist of the Monastery of *Lundors* (*Lindores*) in Ꝼꝼe, in Ꞩcꞷtland, as Procurators of the Abbot and Covent of the said Monastery, did present to the Church of Ꝃlꝓꞩꞷendeu.

Reg. Linc.

In the 14 *E.* 2. *John* Priest of Ꞩtyꞏclington was presented to the Vicarage of the Church of Ꝃhiꞩꞩonden by the Prior and Covent of Ꞩempzingham, and admitted to the same at Ꞑeꝃark

Reg. Linc.

by *Henry Burghersh* then Bishop of Lincoln, 4. *Kall. Junii* 1321.

At the time of the dissolution of the said Priory of Ꞩempzingham the Rectory of Ꝃhiꞩundine was in Lease to *Michael Rayne* at the yearly Rent of 22 *l.* and this was by indenture of Demise from that Covent, *Dat.* 20 *Junii* 26 *H.* 8.

Comp. pro Com. Rutl. in Offic. Augm. an, 3 E. 6,

The Vicarage of Ꝃhiꞩꞩendine is valued in the Kings Books at, 7 *l.* 1 *s.*

The Present Patron is the Righ honourable *Bennet* Lord *Sherard.*

In the Church of Whitsundine.

About the Verge of an Alabaster Tomb in the Chancel.

Hꝺc jacent Bartholomeus Villars, ꞩecundus ꝼilius Willielmi Villars de Brokesby, ᵹ Margareta UꝜoz ejus una Fꝺliarum ᵹ heredum .... de Whytstondyn, quꝺ obꝺꝺt xx ꝺꝺe Martii .... quozum anꝺmarum pzopꝺcꝺetur Deus, Amen.

W H I T W E L L.

IN the hundred of Alꞩtoe. At the time of the Norman Conquest one *Besy* a Saxon was Lord of Ꝃꝺtewelle which was then taxt to the Geld at one Carucate. The Land was three Carucates. Afterwards at the time of the Survey call'd *Domesday* Book one *Herbertus* held here in farm of Countess *Judith* one Carucate of Land, and six Villains, and four *Bordarii* having two Carucates. Here was at that time a Church and a Priest, and twenty acres of Meadow, and one Mill of the value of 12 *d.* A pasture Wood (*Silva per loca pastilis*) of six furlongs, and six perchers in length, and three furlongs, and thirteen Perches in Breadth. All which was then valued but at 40 *s.*

Domesd. Tit. Rotei.

In the 9 *E.* 2. The Prior of the Hospital of St. *John* of Ꝺeruꞩalem was Lord of Ꝃhꝺtwell. These were the Knights Hospitallers or Knights of St. *John,* who

Nom. Vil. in Scacc.

are now called Knights of Malta.

But after the dissolution of that Order in Englꝛnd, which was by Statute made in the 32 year of *H.* 8. *ch.* 24) it seems that this Estate was granted to the *Harringtons* of Ꝺrton; and accordingly it was found by Office taken in the first year of Queen *Mary,* that Sir *John Harrington* Knight, among other Lordships in this County, dyed seized of the Mannour of Ꝃhꝺtwell, which he held of the Queen in *Capite* by Knights service. In like manner it was found by inquisition taken at Ꝺkeham 22 *March,* 13 *Jac.* before *Edward Harrington* Knight, *William Bulstrode* Knight, and *John Reading* Gent. Feodarys, that *John* Lord *Harrington* the elder, dyed seized (*inter alia*) of the Mannour of Ꝃhꝺtwell, but by what tenure is not there exprest.

Esch. 1. Mar.

Esc. 14. Jac. pars 2. n. 116.

In which Family it continued till

In

Lucy Counteſs of 𝕭𝖊𝖉𝖋𝖔𝖗𝖉 one of the heirs general of *John* laſt Lord *Harington*, conveyed the ſame to Sir *Baptiſt Hicks* Knight and Baronet, from whom by *Julian* one of his Daughters and Coheirs, it was derived to the right honourable *Baptiſt* Vicount *Campden* late deceaſed.

The preſent Lord of this Mannour is the honourable *Baptiſt Noel* Eſq; ſecond Son, now living of the ſaid Vicount *Campden*.

The Family of *Flore, alias Flower*, (a name of great note, in former times, in this Country) had in this Town an antient Seat and Eſtate of Freehold

thereunto belonging : *viz.* Two Meſſuages, forty acres of Land, twenty acres of Meadow, and one Water Mill, which they held of the Prior of St. *John* of 𝕵𝖊𝖗𝖚𝖘𝖆𝖑𝖊𝖒 in 𝕰𝖓𝖌𝖑𝖆𝖓𝖉, as of his Mannour of 𝖂𝖍𝖎𝖙𝖜𝖊𝖑𝖑, by the Rent of 7 *s.* yearly, and ſuit of Court there. As appears by Inquiſition taken at 𝕶𝖊𝖙𝖙𝖔𝖓 in this County 7 *Nov.* 15 *H.* 8. before *John Molleſworth* Eſcheator ; after the death of *Richard Flower* Eſq; which *Richard* deceaſed, 16 *Sept.* before, and left *Roger Flower* his Son and next heir, aged at that time thirty years and above.

Eſc. 15 H. 8. *n.* 23.

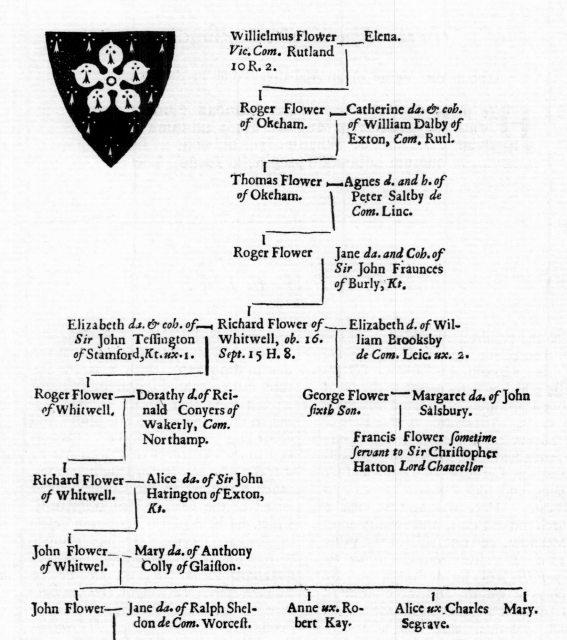

Willielmus Flower ⎯⎯ Elena.
Vic. Com. Rutland
10 R. 2.

Roger Flower ⎯ Catherine *da. & coh.*
of Okeham.   *of* William Dalby *of*
Exton, *Com.* Rutl.

Thomas Flower ⎯ Agnes *d. and h. of*
of Okeham.   Peter Saltby *de*
Com. Linc.

Roger Flower   Jane *da. and Coh. of*
Sir John Fraunces
of Burly, *Kt.*

Elizabeth *da. & coh. of* ⎯ Richard Flower *of* ⎯ Elizabeth *d. of* William Brooksby
Sir John Teſſington   Whitwell, *ob.* 16.   *de Com.* Leic. *ux.* 2.
of Stamford, *Kt. ux.* 1.   *Sept.* 15 H. 8.

Roger Flower ⎯ Dorathy *d. of* Rei-   George Flower ⎯ Margaret *da. of* John
of Whitwell.   nald Conyers *of*   *ſixth Son.*   Salsbury.
Wakerly, *Com.*
Northamp.

    Francis Flower *ſometime*
    ſervant to Sir Chriſtopher
    Hatton *Lord Chancellor*

Richard Flower ⎯ Alice *da. of* Sir John
of Whitwell.   Harington *of* Exton,
Kt.

John Flower ⎯ Mary *da. of* Anthony
of Whitwel.   Colly *of* Glaiſton.

John Flower ⎯ Jane *da. of* Ralph Shel-   Anne *ux.* Ro-   Alice *ux.* Charles   Mary.
    don *de Com.* Worceſt.   bert Kay.   Segrave.

John Flower.

The said *Richard* dyed feized alfo of the Mannour of Little **Hambleton**, with other *Lands* in great **Hambleton**, and a fair Eftate in **Okeham**, of which I have already made mention in the proper places. He was alfo feized in Fee of the mediety of one Meffuage, fifteen acres of Land, and five Acres of Meadow *cum pertinent.* in **Langham**, which he held of the Lord of the Caftle and Mannour of **Okeham**, by Fealty only. Alfo of an hundred acres of Wood in **Burly** *cum pertinent.* which he held of the King in *Capite*, but by what fervices is not expreft. Alfo of one Meffuage, ten acres of Land, and ten acres of Meadow, with the appurtenances in **Exton**, which he held of *John Harrington* Efq; as of his Mannour of **Exton**, but by what fervices is not expreft : All which appears by the abovefaid Inquifition.

Efc. ub. fup.

It appears by the Account of *John Doddington* in the Court of Augmentations 3 *E.* 6. that there were certain Lands (the particular of which I have not feen) in **Belton**, **Whitwell**, and **Ashwell**, formely belonging to the Hofpital of *Burton St. Lazarus*, in *Com.* **Leicest.** All which Lands were by King *H.* 8. on the 4. *Maii* in the 36 year of his reign, granted to *John Dudly* then Vicount *Lifle*, and afterwards Earl of **Warwick**, referving the Rent of 49 *s. per an.*

Comp. pro Com. Rutl. in Offic. Augm. an. 3 *E.* 6.

Of the Church there.

Reg. Linc.

IN the 32 *E.* 1. *Frier William de* **Tolehale** Prior of the Houfe of St. *John* of **Jerufalem**, prefented to the Church of **Whitwell**.

Certif. pro Com. Rutl. in Offic. Augm. 2. *E.* 6.

Here was formerly in our Lady Chapple in this Church One Chauntry, founded by *Richard Wyghtwell* Prieft, one of the Canons of the Cathedral Church of **Lincoln**. The particulars of which foundation were in the 2 *E.* 6. Surveyed and thus certifyed by *Richard Cicyl* Efq; and *Thomas Hays* Commiffioners

for that purpofe, *viz.*

Founded for the maintenance of one Prieft to fing there for ever, and hath of Lands and Tenements lying in divers places in the Counties of **Rutland** *and* **Lincoln** *to the yearly value of* 107 s. 1 d. *whereof in Kent Refolute* 3 s. 4 d. *Remaineth cleer to the Chauntry Prieft there named Sir* Robert Suckling, *aged* 46 *years, of honeft Converfation, and hath always heretofore been exercifed in the Education of Youth in learning, yet unable to ferve a Cure by reafon he is purblind* 103 s. 9 d. *inde pro decima Regi* 9 s. 11 d.

At the fuppreffion in the faid 2 E. 6. *here was one Challice weighing* 20 *Ounces, delivered to the Jewel-houfe,*

Certif. ut fup.

Ornaments Goods and Chattels prized at 13 s. 11 d.

Belonging to which Chantry I find mention of one Tenement fcituated at the eaft end of the Town of **Normanton** towards **Empingham**, with one little Croft or pightel at the North end of the fame, and divers Lands in the fields of **Normanton**, then in the Tenure of *John Shorwood* at the Rent of 11 s. *per an.* Alfo one Tenement in great **Hambleton**, fcituated over againft the Church-yard, called the Chantry houfe, with a fmall parcel of Land on the North fide of the fame, and a Clofe in nether **Hambleton**, with certain lands thereunto belonging, demifed to *William Fowler* at the Rent of 22 s. 8 d. All which Lands and Tenements King *Edward* 6. by his Letters Patents bearing date 16 *Feb.* in the 3 d. year of his Reign, granted to *Edward Warner* and *John Gofnolde*, who by their Deed dated 20 *Feb.* 3 *E.* 6. convey'd over the fame to *Robert Harbottle* his heirs and affigns for ever.

Comp. pro Com. Rutl. an. 3. *E.* 6. *in Offic. Augm.*

The Rectory of **Whitwell** is valued in the Kings Books at 5 *l.*

The Patron is the honourable *Baptift Noel* Efq; Lord of the Mannour:

WINGE.

This Town lyes in the hundred of Martinſley. Of Winge I find no mention in *Domeſday* Book : It being at the time of that Survey included, no doubt, as a member to ſome other neighbouring Town ; but to which does not appear.

Wing, in the times of the firſt Norman Kings, belong'd to the *Montforts*, whoſe Anceſtor, *Hugh de Montfort* came into England with the Conquerour, and was of great note in his Army and Affairs, but loſt his life in a Duel with *Walkeline de Ferrers*. After this *Robert de Montfort* having given a moiety of Wing to the Monks of Thorney, *Thurſtan* his brother and Heir would have avoided the Guiſt till compell'd by King *Steven* to make it good. Whereupon by his ſpecial Charter, for the health of his Soul, as alſo for the Souls of his Wife and Sons, and eſpecially for the Soul of his Brother *Robert*, and the Souls of all his Anceſtors and Succeſſors, he granted to the ſaid Monks the one half of the ſaid Town of Wenge, with the moiety of the Church and Mill, excepting the Fee of *Thurſtan* his Eſq; and the fee of *Ralf Fitz-Nigel*, for which grant thoſe Monks gave to *Robert* his Son a *Marc* of Gold.

The ſaid Monks had alſo by the gift of the aboveſaid *Ralph Fitz-Nigel* three Bovates of Land in the ſaid Town of Wenge, alſo of the gift of *Hugh de Grantemainil* one yard Land in the ſaid Town. Alſo *John de Stutavill* gave and confirmed to God and the Church of Thorney (in like manner as *Robert de Montfort* had given) half the Town of Wenge, with all appurtenances lawfully belonging to the ſame, with the whole Church there, to hold in free Almes for the health of his Soul, the Souls of his Wife, Brethren, Anceſtors and Succeſſors, and of all the faithful of God departed, and for the fraternity of the place. This Grant and Con-

firmation was alſo made in the time of *Giſlebert*, who was Abbot of Thorney in the 16*th.* year of King *Steven*, 1151. Which ſaid mediety of the Town of Wenge, and the half of the Mill of the ſaid Town, as alſo one Villain, by name *Normannus*, with his Land, *viz.* one yard Land in the ſaid Town, with all other Lands elſewhere at that time belonging to the ſaid Abbot and Church of Thorney, or which hereafter by lawfull means might be acquired by them, were confirm'd to the ſaid Church by the Bul of Pope *Alexander*, 3. *An. Dom.* 1162.

In the 9*th.* year of E. 2. there were three Lords of Wenge, *viz.* The Abbot of Thorney, the Prior of St. *Neots*, and *Peter de Montfort.*

At the time of the ſuppreſſion of the Monaſtery of Thorney this Mannour of Winge *cum pertinent.* was in Leaſe to *Henry Lacy*, and *Robert Lacy* his Son, by Indenture under the Covent Seal of the ſaid Monaſtery dated the laſt day of *Septemb. An.* 28 H. 8. for the term of fourſcore and twelve years at the Rent of 10 *l.* payable yearly at the Feaſts of the purification of the Bleſſed Virgin, and of St. *Martin.*

The ſaid Farmers were to keep, or cauſe to be kept, the yearly Courts there, and to receive for their Fee 20 *s.* out of the Rents of the ſaid Mannour. The Rents of the Cuſtomary Tenants of the ſaid Mannour were at that time 4 *l.* 5 *s.* 3 *d.* payable at *Mic.* and Lady day.

The Preſent Lord of the Mannour of Winge is

Of the ADVOWSON.

IN the 11*th.* year of the reign of King *John*, a fine was paſt at *Weſtminſter* between *William* Prior of St. *Neots* plaintiff, and *Robert* Abbot of Thorne, and *Thurſtan de Montfort* deforcients, of

---

Margin notes (left column):

Bar. Eng.
1.*Vol.* 407.

Mon. Ang. 1.
Vol. 249.

Mon. Ang. 1
Vol. 247.
a. 50.

Mon. Ang. 1.
Vol. 249.
a. 50.

Margin notes (right column):

Id. 350.

*Nom. Vil.
in Scacc.*

Comp. pro Com.
Rutland *in
Offic. Augm.*
3. E. 6.

Ubi ſup.

Ex Collect.
Wingf. Bo
denham, *m.*
f. 93.

of the *Advowson* of the Church of 𝔚**enge**, whereby the right was acknowledged to be in the Prior of St. *Neots* to hold of the Lord *Thurſtan* and his heirs; and for this the said Prior granted to the Abbot of 𝕿**hoꝛne**, and his Succeſſors, the Moiety of the Mill at 𝔚**enge.**

Frag. Jo. *an.* 7. This was really the final Concord of
Rot. 5. 10. a ſuit, touching the right of the Ad-

vowſon of this Church, begun four years before in the 7. *Jo.* but at that time adjourn'd, *ſine die*, in regard the ſaid *Thurſtan* was then in the Kings ſervice, beyond the Seas.

The Rectory of 𝔚**ing** is valued in the Kings Books at, 7 *l.* 5 *s.* 5 *d.*

The preſent Patron is the King.

In the Church of Winge.

Painted on the Wall.

Templum Sancti Petri.

Dominus Henricus *de* Clipſtoe *in Foreſtia*

de Shirwood *in*

Comitatu Nottinghamiæ *me fecit.*

On a Plate of Braſs, fixt in a Marble Graveſtone, in the Chancel.

𝕻**ꝛay foꝛ the ſoulle of** 𝔐**aſtyꝛ** Robert Gilbert **late parſon of this Pariſhe Chyrch of** Wynge, **and foꝛ all Chriſten Soules. wych deceſſed the** xi **day of** December **in the yere of of our Loꝛd a** M. Vᶜ. **and** iii.

Poly-Olbion, 2. Having now finiſht my Obſervations and Hiſtorical Collections relating to the
Part, Song 24. ſeveral Towns, Villages, and places of Remark in 𝕽**utland**, I will conclude all
p. 103. with the Encomium given to this County by *Michael Drayton*, in his *Poly-Olbion.* Where we may find the Muſe thus ſpeaking to this Little Shire.

Love *not thy ſelf the leſs, although the leaſt thou art,*

What thou in greatneſs want'ſt, wiſe Nature doth impart

In goodneſs of thy Soyl; and more delicious Mould,

Surveying all this Ile, the Sun did ne're behold.

Bring forth that Brittiſh Vale, and be it ne're ſo rare,

But Catmus *with that Vale for richneſs may compare.*

What Foreſt Nymph is found, how brave ſo ere ſhe be,

But Lyfeild *ſhews her ſelf as brave a Nymph as ſhe?*

What

What River ever rose from Bank, or swelling Hill,
Then Rutlands *wandring* Wash, *a delicater Rill?*
Small Shire that canst produce to thy proportion good,
One Vale of special Name, one Forest, and one Floud.
O Catmus, *thou fair Vale, come on in Grass and Corn,*
That Beaver *ne're be said thy sisterhood to scorn,*
And let thy Ocham *boast to have no little Grace,*
That her the pleased Fates did in thy Bosom place:
And Lifeild, *as thou art a Forest, live so free,*
That every Forest-Nymph may praise the sports in thee:
And down to Wellends *course, O* Wash, *run ever cleer,*
To honour, and to be much honour'd by this Shire.

FINIS.

Viro honorabili & præclaro Johanni Noel Armigero
Tabula meritò dicata.

ADDITIONS
TO THE
History and Antiquities
OF
RUTLANDSHIRE

SInce the printing and publishing of the foresaid Book, the Honourable *John Noel* Esq; Third Son (now living) of the Right Honourable *Baptist* late Viscount *Campden*, hath bestowed the Sum of One thousand Pounds in erecting a most Noble and Exquisite Monument in the North-side of 𝕰𝖗𝖙𝖔𝖓 Church in this County, to the Memory of the said Lord his Father. It is in Height 22 Foot, and 14 Foot in Breadth, and contains, at a convenient distance from the Floor, two admirable Statues, of the said Viscount *Campden*, and *Elizabeth* his last Lady, standing upright, somthing bigger than the Life. Between these two Statues is a Pedestal supporting an Urne. On the outward sides of the Statues are placed two great Pyramids, each supporting a Vase of black Marble twisted about with Festoons of white. And in several parts of the Monument, are represented in Baf-releif, the several Matches of the said Lord, and all the Issue, as well living as dead, by those Matches. The whole is the Workmanship of that justly admired Artist Mr. *Grinlin Gibbon*, whose Carvings at *Windsor*, *Whitehall*, and elsewhere, not only in this Nation, but in Foreign parts, have caused him to be esteem'd the best of *English* Statuaries, and perhaps inferior to none beyond the Seas.

On two Tables of black Marble, below the two Pyramids, are the following Inscriptions in Letters of Gold, *viz.* on that on the Left Hand, these words:

Here resteth Baptist Noel *Lord Viscount* Campden, *Baron of* 𝕽𝖎𝖉𝖑𝖎𝖓𝖌𝖙𝖔𝖓 *and* 𝕴𝖑𝖒𝖎𝖓𝖌𝖙𝖔𝖓, *Lord Lieutenant of the County of* 𝕽𝖚𝖙𝖑𝖆𝖓𝖉. *His eminent Loyalty to his two Sovereigns, King Charles I. and II. his Conjugal Affection to Four Wives; his Paternal Indulgence to Nineteen Children; his Hospitality and Liberality to all that desired or deserved it (notwithstanding inestimable Losses in his Estate, frequent Imprisonments of his Person, Spoil and Havock of several of his Houses, besides the Burning of that Noble Pile of* 𝕮𝖆𝖒𝖕𝖉𝖊𝖓 *) have justly rendred him the Admiration of his Contemporaries, and the Imitation of Posterity. He left this Life for the Exchange and Fruition of a better, the* 29th *day of* Octo-ber, *in the* LXXI *year of his Age.* A. D. MDCLXXXIII.

And on that on the other Hand, these Words:

He took to his First Wife Ann Fielding, *2d Daughter to* William *Earl of* 𝕯𝖊𝖓𝖇𝖎𝖌𝖍, *by whom he had Three Children, who Dyed in their Infancy. By his Second Wife,* Ann *Countess of* 𝕭𝖆𝖙𝖍, *he had One Son Still-Born. By his Third Wife,* Hester, *One of the Four Daughters and Coheirs of* Thomas *Lord* Wootton, *he had Two Sons and Four Daughters;* 1. Edward, *present Earl of* 𝕲𝖆𝖎𝖓𝖊𝖘𝖇𝖚𝖗𝖌𝖍, *Governor of* 𝕻𝖔𝖗𝖙𝖘𝖒𝖔𝖚𝖙𝖍, *Lord-Lieutenant of* 𝕳𝖆𝖒𝖕𝖘𝖍𝖎𝖗𝖊 *and* 𝕽𝖚𝖙𝖑𝖆𝖓𝖉; *2d.* Henry Noel, *late of* 𝕹𝖔𝖗𝖙𝖍-𝕷𝖚𝖋𝖋𝖊𝖓𝖍𝖆𝖒 Esq; *who Died in the* 35 *year of his Age; 3d.* Mary *present Countess of* 𝕹𝖔𝖗𝖙𝖍𝖆𝖒𝖕𝖙𝖔𝖓; *4th.* Juliana, *Wife of* William *Lord* Allington; *5th.* Hester, *who Died an Infant; 6th.* Elizabeth, *Wife of* Charles *Lord* Duresly, *Son and Heir apparent of* George *Earl of* Barkley. *By his 4th Wife (who standeth by his Side)* Elizabeth Bertie, *eldest Daughter of* Mountagu *Earl of* Lindsey, *Lord Great Chamberlain of* 𝕰𝖓𝖌𝖑𝖆𝖓𝖉, *he had Nine Children,* 1st. Lindsey Noel, *who Died in his Infancy; 2d.* Catherine *now Wife of* John *Earl of* 𝕽𝖚𝖙𝖑𝖆𝖓𝖉; *3d.* Baptist Noel Esq; *now living; 4th.* John Noel Esq; *likewise living; 5th.* Bridget Noel *also living; 6th. A Son, whose early Birth prevented his Baptisme; 7th.* James Noel Esq; *who died in the* 18th *year of his Age; 8th.* Martha Penelope *now living; 9th. A Son Still-Born.*

In the middle of the Pedestal which stands between the two Great Figures.

To the Pious Memory of Her said Husband, his Wives, their, and her own Children, Elizabeth *his last Wife in her Life time gave Monies, and left Orders for the Building this Monument, which by her Third Son and Executor, the Honourable* John Noel *was punctually perform'd,* 1686.

HEre follow certain Ancient Epitaphs, and Monumental Inscriptions, not now in being, but totally decay'd, or in the times of Rebellion erazed and obliterated, mentioned in a Manuscript Collection of Church-Notes, long since read and observed in the several Churches under-named, by that skilful Herald Mr. *Augustin Vincent*; when in the year 1618, he Visited in **Rutland**, as Deputy to the famous *Cambden Clarencieux*: Which with many other Manuscripts of the said Mr. *Vincent's*, formerly in the possession of *Ralph Shelden* of **Bealy**, in the County of **Worcester** Esq; were, since his death, lately given to the Heralds-Office, where they now remain.

In the Church at **Glasson.**

Hic jacet Walterus Collie Dominus & Patronus hujus Villæ, & Agnes Uxor ejus, qui obiit, Ann. Dom. 1407.

On another Monument.

In Lindon Natus, Johannes sic vocitatus,
Linguæ limatus, apud Oxoniam graduatus,
Doctor formatus, Aulæ Merton sociatus,
Oxoniæ gratus, Commissarius reputatus,
Glastonæ Prælatus, jacet sub marmore stratus
Moribus ornatus, sit tecum, Christe, beatus.
Annos millenos, quadringenos lege plenos
Trinos & senos, nunc Cælos scandit amænos.

On Another.

Here lieth Sir *John Bramspath*, which was made Knight; He died in the year of our Lord, 1443.

On Another.

Orate pro animabus Johannis Basset, & Agnetis Uxoris ejus.

In the Chancel at **Ketton.**

Orate pro anima Roberti Whytbie quondam Præbendarii de Ketton.

In the Church of **North-Luffenham.**

Upon a Monument, on the South-side of the Church.

Simon Digby Esq; Pensioner to King *Henry* the 8th. Second Son to Sir *John Digby* Knight-Marshal, which *Simon* Married *Katherine* Daughter of *Christopher Clapham* of **Beamelly**, in the County of **York** Esq; and *Roger Digby* their Son and Heir, Married *Mary* Daughter of *John Cheiney* of **Shordelous** in **Buckinghamshire**, Ann. Dom. 1582.

In the Church of **Okeham.**

Upon a Grave-stone; in Brass,

Hic jacet Willielmus Waren quondam hujus Villæ Burgensis & Mercator Stapulæ Villæ Calisiæ, ac etiam Domina Agnes Uxor ejus & relicta, qui quidem Willielmus obijt Ann. 1499. Decimo die Septemb.

On Another.

Hic jacet Willielmus Dalby & Agnes Uxor ejus, qui quidem Willielmus obiit in vigilia Annuntiationis beatæ Mariæ Virginis. Ann. 1404. & prædicta Agnes——

Painted on the Wall in the said Church.

Mr. *John Pooly* of **Martinsthorp** Which lyeth Buried here, Hath given the Poor in **Okeham** Ten pounds by the year. } Ann. 1557.

Other Supplemental Additions.

Pa. 27.

OF the Priory of Canons here at **Brook**, I have this further to add, out of certain old Deeds and Grants now in my Possession. Their Estate lay at **Brook**, **Braunston**, **Knauston**, **Okeham** and **Langham**, all Towns near adjoyning. As to what they held in **Braunston**, I find that *Reginald*, Son of *Robert de Brantefton*, gave to God, and the Sacrifty of the Church of the Blessed *Mary* of **Broc**, the yearly Rent of 12 *d.* which the Canons there did use to pay yearly to the said *Reginald*, as Capital Lord of **Braunston** for one Bovate of Land holden of him; which said Rent he did appoint for the maintaining of the 4th and 5th Lamp at our Ladys Vespers and Matins; And in like manner for the maintenance of the 4th and 5th Candle at the High Mass, and at our Ladies Morning Mass. A little before the Suppression, *Robert Orwell* Prior, and the Covent of this House, did by their Lease, Dated 12th of *May* 23. H. 8. Demise to *Robert Reve*, *John* his Son, and *Joan* his Wife, Dwelling in **Knofton** in the County of **Leicefter**, a Mese place, and four Yard Lands, with all Houses, Meafages, Pastures, Commons and Liberties, late in the Tenure of the said *Robert Reve*, lying in the Town and Fields of **Knowfington** and **Braunston** for their several Lives, at the yearly Rent of 43 *s.* 4 *d.* And besides usual Covenants, the Lessees obliged themselves to Set and Plant 100 Ashes upon the Lands and Ground so Demised, within the space of five years next ensuing from the Date of the Lease. This Lease was confirmed by *Anthony Coope* Esq; to whom the Lands belonging to this Priory were Granted after the Suppression. The rest of the Lands, belonging to this House, with the Reversion upon this Lease, were Sold and Conveyed 20 *Jan.* 36, H. 8. By *Anthony Coope* of **Hardwicke** in the County of **Oxford** Esq; to *John Burton* of **Braunston**: Yet some of the Lands being held *in Capite*, were not alienated till 30 *Octob.* 13 *Eliz.* At which time that Queen Granted her Licence of Alienation to *Anthony Cope* Esq;, and *John Peck*, to Convey the same to *William Burton*, Son and Heir of the foresaid *John Burton*. This parcel was exprest by the Name of **Fleetmeadow**, with the Appurtenances in **Braunston**, containing by estimation 15 Acres, late in the tenure of *Joan Ryve* Widow. Their Estate in **Okeham** and **Langham** was of a very antient Grant, but of no great value; and as I believe, they lost the Possession of part of it long before the Suppression. *Walkelinus de Ferrariis* (who was Lord of **Okeham**, **Langham**, and **Brook**, in the time of King *Hen.* 2d. and seems to be the First Founder of this House) Gave to God, and to the Church of *St. Mary* of **Broch**, and the Canons there, in pure and perpetual Alms, the Homage and Service of *Jordanus de Saxonis*, and whatsoever Right he had in him and his Tenement; and also the Tithes of the Profits arising from the Fair at **Okeham**, held at the Feast of the Decollation of *St. John Baptist*; and of the Mills of the said Town of **Okeham**, and of **Langham**. Witnesses to which Deed were *Simone Presbitero de* **Okeham**, *Gilberto Fratre ejus*, *Hugone de Ferrariis*, *Willielmo de Freues*, *Galfrido de Carento*, *Magiftro Johanne Medico*, &c. This Deed was afterwards confirmed by *Henry de Ferrariis*, Son of *Walkeline*, and after that by *Isabel de Mortuomari*, Widow of *Roger de Mortuomari*, Sister and Heir of the said *Henry de Ferrariis*. Long after this, *viz.* At the Great Court of *Edward* Duke of **York** (who was also Earl of **Rutland**,) held at **Okeham** on the Wednesday next after the Feast of *St. Michael*, in the 6th. H. 4. the then Prior of **Brook** exhibited his Claim to the Tithes of the Mills of **Oeham** and **Langham**, valued at 24 *s. per Ann.* which his Predeceffors had formerly enjoy'd, except for fix years laft paft: But whether he ever enjoy'd them afterwards, does not appear. The before-mentioned *Ifabel de Mortuomari* Granted to the Prior and Canons of **Broke** a Tenement in **Langham**, which *Gilbert Carecarius* held of her, and directed her Precept under her Seal to *William de Hampton*, her then Bayliffe at **Okeham**, to deliver to the said Prior, full Seifin of the same. Of their Estate at **Brook**, I have already Treated, to which I shall only add, That in the place where the Priory of **Brook** formerly stood, *viz.* about a Flight-shot West of the Town, hath been since the Diffolution of the said Priory, erected a very fair House, which has been for many years past the Residence of the Noble Family of the *Noels*; and was, of late years, a noted Seat of Hospitality, during the Life of *Julian* late Viscountess *Campden*, Relict of *Edward* Viscount *Campden*: which Lady was the eldest of the two Daughters and Co-Heirs of Sir *Baptift Hicks* Knight and Baronet, Lord *Hicks* of **Ilmington**, and Viscount *Campden*; who at his own proper Charges built the Seffions-house in *St.* **John-ftreet** at **London**, well known by the name of *Hicks's Hall*. He also did divers other publick Works of Charity; Among the reft he Founded an Hospital for fix poor Men, and Women, at **Campden** in **Gloucefterfhire**; wherein he appointed to each of them two Rooms, a little Garden, and two shillings a week for their maintenance; which Endowment his said Daughter *Julian* Viscountess *Campden* did much enlarge, and departed this Life at **Brooke** her conftant Residence, on the 25th of *November*, in the year 1680. being then about One hundred years of Age. She had Iffue by her said Husband, *Edward* Viscount *Campden*, two Sons and two Daughters, *viz. Baptift* Viscount *Campden*, *Henry Noel* of **Luffenham** Esq; *Elizabeth* Married to Sir *Erafmus de la Fountaine* Kt. and *Penelope* to *John* Viscount *Chaworth*.

Brook House on the South side

TOUT RIEN
BIEN OU

Illustrissimo Dn̄ø
Dn̄ø EDOARDO Comiti
de Gaineſborough Vicecomiti
Campden, Dn̄ø NOEL & Hick-
Baroni de Ridlington & Ilming-
ton in Comitatibus Hantoniæ
& Rotelandiæ Locumtenenti, No-
væ Foreſtæ Gardiano, & Gu-
bernatori de Portſmouth,
Hanc Tabulam,
H.D. I.W.

Pa. 50.

WHich moſt Noble Lord, *Robert* Earl of *Aylesbury*, Our now Gracious Soveraign King *JAMES* II. as a further remuneration of Honor, did conſtitute Lord Chamberlain of His Majeſties Houſhold in *July* 1685. but he ſurvived not long to en-joy the Office, departing this Life at his Seat at *Ampthill* in *Bedfordſhire*, on the 20th of *October* the ſame year, to the great grief of all that knew him. He being a Perſon of ſingular Merit for his conſtant Loyalty, un-feigned Religion, Virtue and Honour; of great Learning Himſelf, and a Noble *Mecænas* to all the Learned; a lover of Hoſpi-tality, and a conſtant Benefactor to the Poor. He Married the Lady *Diana*, Daughter of *Henry* Earl of *Stamford*, and by her left Iſſue ſurviving of both Sexes. Whoſe eldeſt Son and Heir, the Right Honourable *Thomas* now Earl of *Aylesbury* and *Elgin*, is the true Inheritor of both his Father's Honours, and Virtues, and is one of the Gentlemen of

His now Majeſties Bed-Chamber, as he was alſo to His late Majeſty King *CHARLES* II. of ever Glorious Memory.

Pa. 78.

OF late years *Luffenham-Houſe* (which was in the War-time ſo Nobly held out againſt the Rebels by *Henry Noel* Eſq;) became the Seat and Reſidence of another Noble Gentleman of the ſame name, the Ho-nourable *Henry Noel* Eſq; Second Son of the Right Honourable *Baptiſt* Viſcount *Campden*. Which laſt *Henry* Married *Elizabeth*, Daugh-ter and Co-heir of Sir *William Wale* Kt. but died without Iſſue-Male, in *Septemb.* 1677. leaving only one Daughter his ſole Heir. Since when, this Houſe is become the Seat of the Honourable *Baptiſt Noel* Eſq; another Son of the ſaid Viſcount *Campden*, who hath aug-mented, and much beautified the Building.

Luffenham House   *On the East side*

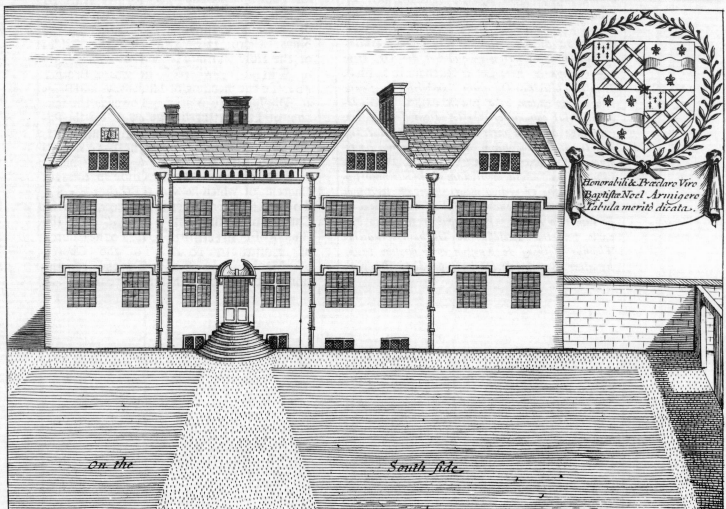

On the   *South side*

Honorabili & Præclaro Viro Baptistæ Noel Armigero Tabula meritò dicata.

Pa. 98.

THE Church at Okeham is Dedicated to *All-Saints*, as appears by an antient Will, Dated in the 15th year of King *Henry* VII. and Proved before the Official of the Arch-Deacon of Northampton, 10 *May* 1501. Which Will containing several obfervable *Matters* relating to this Church, and the old *Cuftoms* of thofe times, I have here tranfcribed at large, as follows:

In Dei nomine Amen. Anno Domini M. quincentefimo, die vero menfis Maij primo. Ego Robertus Blakburn *de* Okeham *condo Teftamentum meum in hunc modum, primo lego animam meam Deo patri omnipotenti, beatæ Mariæ ac omnibus Sanctiis ejus; Corpufq; ad fepeliendum in Ecclefia Omnium Sanctorum de* Okeham *prædicta; Item lego pro Mortuario meo meum optimum animal quod juftum eft; Item lego fummo altari pro decemis oblitis* xij d. *Item lego trefdecem denarios ut dentur in Elimofina pro falute animæ meæ; Item lego pro obfequiis meis in primo die* ij s. *fex presbiteris, in fecundo die hoc eft ad feptimum diem fex presbiteris iftius villæ* ij s. *& ad diem trigefimum taliter fex presbiteris* ij s. *& ad Clericos in quolibet die* j d. *Item lego Campanis Ecclefiæ de* Okcham iij s. iiij d. *Item lego Guyldiis Omnium Sanctorum & Beatæ Mariæ de eadem villa prædicta* xij d. *Item lego ad vias communes* xij d. *Item lego* Aliciæ *filiæ meæ de bonis meis propriis decem Marcas: Refiduum vero omnium bonorum meorum do & lego* Aliciæ *uxori meæ &* Willielmo Blakburn *filio meo quos quidem* Aliciam *&* Willielmum *facio, conftituo & ordino meos veros & legitimos Executores ut difponant pro falute animæ meæ, & fit laus Deo Amen. Hiis teftibus Magiftro Vicario perpetuo Ecclefiæ de* Okeham *prædicta,* Thomas Wilkoks *de* Knofton, *&* Willielmo Manby *alias* Smyth *de* Okeham *prædicta die prædicto.*

IN this Town of Okeham did formerly refide divers wealthy Merchants of the Staple at Calais, who dealt in feveral Staple Commodities of this Kingdom, chiefly Wooll; a Trade of very great account, while that Town was poffeft by the Englifh. Of what Quality and Condition thefe Merchants were, may be gueft by the Charities expreft in their Wills, Regiftred in the *Prerogative-Office.* One of which I will here mention, as it may be feen in the faid Office, *Lib. Horn.* 36.

William Waryn of Okeham Merchant of the Staple at Calais (who lyeth Buried in our *Ladies Ifle*, or *Chappel*, being on the South-fide of the *Chancel* in the Parifh Church at Okeham,) by his Will, Dated 1499. (14. *H.* 7.) among other things, gave to the High Altar of the faid Parifh-Church for Tithes and Duties forgotten, 5 *l.* To every Prieft that helpeth at his Obfequies the Firft, Seventh, and Thirtieth days 4 *d.* each day; to every poor Man, Woman and Child prefent at the faid Obfequies thofe three days, 1 *d.* To find two Priefts to fing and fay Maffes and Service for the Souls of Him, his Father and Mother, and all Chriftian Souls in the Parifh Church of Okeham for 20 years next enfuing, 200 *l.* To the reparation of the faid Church 10 Marks. For a fuit of Veftments for the faid Church 100 Marks. To provide Freefe Cloth, and Linen Cloth for Garments, Shirts and Sheets for poor People the fpace of five years 10 Marks. To every Houfe of the four Orders of Fryers in Stanford 13 s. 4 d. To the Nuns there 13 s. 4 d. To the Gildes of the Holy Trinity, and of our Lady in Okeham, whereof he was a Brother 40 s. To the mending of High-ways and Brigs at Okeham 10 Marks. Towards the making of Rochefter-Bridge 40 s. To the Parifh-Church of Lydington in Rutland 20 s. To the Church of Uppingham 10 s. To the Church of Afton 6 s. 8 d. To the Church of Prefton 10 s. To the Gilde in the faid Church, of which he was a Brother 6 s. 8 d. To the Church of Pysbroke 10 s. To the Church of Somerby 13 s. 4 d. To the Church of Cottefmore 10 s. To the Church of Langham 10 s. To the Church of Broke 6 s. 8 d. To the reparation of the Priory Church there 13 s. 4 d.

To

To the Abby of **Dfolwefton** in the County of **Leiceſter**, for the making of their Fraytour 40 l. And 40 l. more to find a Prieſt of their Houſe, to ſing for Him and his Wife for ever. As for his Lands and Tenements which he held in **Okeham**, he Deviſed them all to *Agnes* his Wife for her Life; the Remainder to his Son *Francis Waryn* in Tayl; The Remainder to his Son *James Waryn* in Tayl; The Remainder to his Daughter *Elizabeth Waryn* in Tayl; the Remainder to be ſetled on Feoffees (if it conveniently might be) to the following Uſes, *viz.* The Houſe wherein he dwelt, with the Appurtenances, to the Uſe of the Vicar and Wardens of the Pariſh Church of **Okeham**; conditionally, That the ſaid Vicar and his Succeſſors in the ſaid Church, ſhould for ever Commemorate his Soul, and the Souls of his Father and Mother at Maſs, every Sunday in the year; otherwiſe, that the ſaid Manſion be ſold, and the Monies to be diſtributed in Works of Mercy, and Deeds of Charity, for the Wele of his Soul. Three other Tenements in the ſaid Town, to the Uſe of the Abbot and Covent of **Dfolwefton**, conditionally, that they maintain in their Covent, a yearly *Obit*, or Anniverſary for his Soul, his Fathers and Mothers, Wife, Children, and Benefactors, and all Chriſtian Souls; And at the ſame *Obit* diſtribute to the Abbot there 20 d. to every Chanon of that Houſe, being a Prieſt, 1 s. and to every Novice 8 d. &c.

IN former times, before the Reformation there was a Pilgrimage of Devotion, in Honour of the Bleſſed Virgin, performed to a Spring in this Pariſh, about a Quarter of a Mile North of **Okeham**, which is ſtill known by the name of **Dur Ladies Well**; near which, one may yet perceive ſeveral places where have been the Foundations of a houſe or two; And this appears more plain from a Record. in the Firſt-fruits Office, *Inter communia de Term. Trin.* 8 *Eliz. rot.* 5. containing among other things———— *Quod plurima Commoda & Emolumenta Vicariæ de Okeham prædictæ pertinentia & ſpectantia conſtabant in diverſis Oblationibus & Perigrationibus utpote nuper Imagini Beatæ Mariæ ad fontem, & etiam Sancti Michaelis Archangili, & aliis compluribus ritubus & Oblationibus————————— Quæ jam una cum Com-*

modis & Emolumentis inde Vicario prædicto renovantibus prorſus evannerunt.

Pa. 103.

BEſides theſe two Hoſpitals, there are other conſiderable Charities belonging to the Town of **Okeham**, *viz.*

Anne Lady *Harington* gave in the year 1616. the ſum of 32 l. *per Ann.* for ever, to the Poor of the Lords-Hold in this Town, as I have already mentioned, *Pa.* 52.

Alſo Mrs. *Parthenia Lowman* of **London**, Widow, gave to the Town of **Okeham**, the ſum of 100 l. for a perpetual Stock; The Profits or Intereſt of which Money was on the 6th of *March* 1662. thus ſetled, *viz.* Ten Shillings part of the ſame, for a Sermon in the Church of **Okeham** yearly, on *Aſhwedneſday*, the reſidue to be yearly diſpoſed to ſuch Poor People as are paſt their Work and Labour, or Sick, and not able to maintain themſelves otherwiſe; Three Quarters of the Sum to be diſtributed to the Lords-Hold, and a Fourth Part to the Deans-Hold in the ſaid Town of *Okeham.*

HEre alſo ought to be remembred the Remarkable Charity of Mr. *Endymion Canyng*, an old Cavalier, and a Captain of Horſe in the Service of King *Charles* I. of ever Bleſſed Memory. After the Civil Wars, he lived for many years at **Brook** in this Country, in the Family of the Right Honourable *Julian*, late Viſcounteſs *Campden*, to which Lady he was Steward, and her Principal Servant. He Died a Batchelor at **Brook** in the year 1683. And by his Will, Dated on the 24th day of *May*, in the year 1681, gave to Pious Uſes as follows, *viz.*

To

To the Poor of **Chipping-Campden** and **Berrington**, in the County of **Gloucester**. ———— 200 *l.*

To the Poor of the Parish of **Monysend** in **Essex**, where he was Born and Baptized. ———— 50 *l.*

To the Poor of **Terback** in the County of **Worcester**, where he was sometime an Inhabitant. ———— 50 *l.*

To the Poor of **Okeham** in the County of **Rutland**. ———— 50 *l.*

To the Poor of **Uppingham** in the said County. ———— 50 *l.*

To the Poor of **Brook** in the said County. ———— 20 *l.*

To the Poor of **Ilmington** in the County of **Warwick**. ———— 20 *l.*

To the Poor of **Aston-Subedge** in the County of **Gloucester**. ———— 20 *l.*

To the Poor of **Bradfarton** in the County of **Worcester**. ———— 20 *l.*

And by a Codicel annext, Dated *April* 2. 1683. a little before his death he gave further.

To the Town of **Castle-Bytham** in the County of **Lincoln**, to buy a Clock for the use of the Town. ———— 6 *l.*

To the Poor of the said Town. ———— 10 *l.*

To the Poor of **Etton** in the County of **Rutland**. ———— 5 *l.*

To the Poor of **Whitwel** in the said County. ———— 5 *l.*

To the Poor of **North-Luffenham** in the said County. ———— 5 *l.*

To the Poor of **Ridlington** in the said County. ———— 5 *l.*

To the Poor of **Belton** in the said County. ———— 5 *l.*

To the Poor of **Braunston** in the said County. ———— 5 *l.*

To the Poor of **Langham** in the said County. ———— 5 *l.*

To the Poor of **Halsted** in the County of **Leicester**. ———— 5 *l.*

Besides other Legacies to his Relations, and Chief Friends, and to some Poor People particularly nam'd, of which I make no mention here, but only of the Sums given as above exprest to Pious and Publick Uses, which in all amount to the Sum of 536 *l.*

P. 108.

WHich most Noble Lord *Edward*, Earl of **Gainesborough**, hath been twice Married, First, to the Lady *Elizabeth Wriothsley*, Eldest Daughter and Co-Heir of *Thomas* late Earl of **Southampton**, Lord High Treasurer of **England**, by whom he hath Issue, One Son, *Wriothsley-Baptist* Lord **Campden**, who is joyn'd in Commission with his Father for the Lieutenancies of **Hampshire** and **Rutland**; and Four Daughters; 1st. The Lady *Frances Noel*, late Wife of *Simon* Lord *Digby*, Baron of **Geashil** in **Ireland**, which Lady died in Child-Bed of her First Child, a Daughter; not long after whose death, her Husband also departed this Life at his House at **Colshil** in **Warwickshire**, on the 19th of *Jan.* 1685; whose Loss was much regretted by all that knew him, He being a Person of very great Honour and Virtue, and of Signal Charity; 2d. The Lady *Jane Noel*, Married to the Right Honourable *William*, now Lord *Digby* of **Geashil**, Brother and Heir-male of the foresaid *Simon* Lord *Digby*; 3d. The Lady *Elizabeth Noel*; and 4th The Lady *Julian Noel*. The said Earl's Second Wife, the present Countess of **Gainesborough**, is *Mary* Daughter of the Honourable *James Herbert* Esq; Son of *Philip* Earl of **Pembroke** and **Montgomery**, Widow of Sir *Robert Wortesley* Knight and Baronet.

Pa. 128.

SIR *William Burton* here mentioned (who as I have already observed out of the description of **Leicestershire**, Pa. 108. is by that Author affirmed to be one of the Justices of the *Kings-Bench*, in the Reign of King *Edward* III.) was Lord of **Forton**, and other Lands in the County of **Leicester**; But **Colethorp** in **Rutland** was his chief Seat. I have seen a Pedigree setting forth his Issue, and their several Matches, as follows;

Sir *William Burton*══**Elleonor**.
Knight. Ob. 49. E. 3.

Sir *Thomas Burton*══**Margaret** Daughter
Kt. Ob. 8. R. 2. of *Thomas Grenham*.

Sir *Thomas Burton*══...... Dau. of
Kt. *Simon Louthe*.

.... Dau. of══*Thomas Burton*══......Dau. of
Sir *Robert Brabeson* Esq; Sir *Hugh Bushey* Kt. Ux. 2.
Kt. Ux. 1.

Robert Burton
Ob. S. M.

William Burton══.....Dau. of *John Foluille*
of **Ashby Foluille**, Com. **Leic.**

John Burton of══......Dau. of *Thomas*
Uppingham. *Baffing.*
Com. **Rutland.**

Thomas Burton══.......Dau. of *Ralph Lowe*
of **Denbigh**, Com. **Derb.**

John Burton of **Braunston.**══...... Da. of ......
Com. **Rut.** Ob. 1 Mariæ. *Blackwell.*

William Burton of ══ *Alice* Daugh. of
Braunston. *Richard Peck.*

1
John Burton══*Ann* Dau. and Heir
of *Thomas Digby* Esq;

2
Bartin Burton of══*Abigail* Dau. of
Okeham, Com. *John Cholmley* Esq;
Rut.

3
Simon Burton
of **Braunston.**

Sir *Tho. Burton*══*Philip*══*Anne* Da.
of **Stockerton** Dau. of of *Robert*
Co. **Leic.** *Henry* *Reinolds* of
Baronet. creat. *Cobham* **London,**
22. *Jul.* 20. *Jac.* *al. Brook* Gent. Ux. 2.
1. vx. 1.

Andrew Burton.══*Ann* Daught. of
of **Okeham** *William Fairmedow*
Esq; of **London**, Merch.

Mabell Wife
of *John Booth*
of **Okeham** Gent.

Anne *Eliza-* *Fran-*
Wi. of *beth* *ces*
Sr *Abell*
Barker
Baronet.

Sir *Thomas*══*Elizabeth*
Burton, Bar. Da. of Sir *John*
Prittyman Bar.

Sir *Thomas*══*Anne* eldest Dau.
Burton Bar. of Sir *Thomas*
Clutterbuck Kt.

Cornelius Bur-
ton of **Okeham** Esq;

Andrew Bur-
ton of **Exton** Gent.

Anne
Abigail
Mabel
Elizabeth
Mary
Sara.

Pa. 136.

ROger *Flower* of Okeham, here named, who Married *Catherine*, Daughter and Coheir of *William Dalby*, was a Person of so great Note in this County, that I ought not to omit here what I find memorable of him, out of his Will, Regiſtred in the *Prerogative-Office, Lib. Luffnam, f.* 69.

By his ſaid Will, Dated 15 *April* 1424, he appointed his Body to be Buried in the Church of *All-Saints* at Okeham. His beſt Animal he gave for a Mortuary. To the Vicar of Okeham for Tithes forgot, 10 *s.* To the Guilds of the Holy Trinity, the Bleſſed Virgin, and *St. Michael* at Okeham, 40 *s.* To the Chaplain of the ſaid Pariſh, 2 *s;* and to every other Chaplain of the ſaid Town, 1 *s.* To every Order of Friers at Stanford, the Carthuſians at Coventry, the Abby of *Weſtminſter,* and the Priory of Laund, 6 Marks, to pray for the Souls of *Katherine* his late Wife, *William* his Father, *Ellen* his Mother, *William* his Brother, *William Dalby* and *Agnes* his Wife, *William* and *John* his Sons, *Agnes Pleſſington* his Daughter, and *Edward* late Duke of *York.* To certain Chaplains by his Executors to be appointed to celebrate for his Soul, the Soul of King *Henry* 5*th,* and the other Souls aforeſaid, 40 *l.* To be diſtributed to the Poor, and for the performing of his Exequies; 50 Marks. To the Almshouſe of Okeham, towards the Repairs of the Chappel, and Ornaments of the Altar there, 50 *s.* To every poor Man of the ſaid Houſe, 4 *d.* To the mending of the Highways, Bridges, and Cauſeways at Okeham, 50 *s.* To every Monk of *Weſtminſter* being a Prieſt 1 *s.* not a Prieſt, 8 *d.* To the great Guild at Coventry, 40 *s.* To the Prior and Canons of Brooke, 13 *s.* 4 *d.* To the Nuns of Langly and Huntington, and Prior, and Canons of Newſted near Stamford, each Houſe 13 *s.* 4 *d.* To 20 poor People of Okeham, each a Gown of *Coventry* Freeſe, and a new Shirt. To the Maſter of the Chantry at Manton (whom he made one of his Executors,) he gave his pair of Beads which he uſed himſelf, with the Ten *Aves* of Silver, and a *Pater noſter* over-Gilt, praying him to be mindful of him ſomtimes when he ſaith our Ladies Sawter on them. It appears by the ſaid Will, that he was the Principal (if not only,) Benefactor to the Building of the Voute (*i.e.* the Spire) of the Steeple at Okeham: And that he was the Farmer or Leſſee of the Parſonage Tithes at Okeham, under the Abbot and Covent of Weſtminſter. Beſides his Lands and Revenues in Okeham, Whitwell, and Little-Hambleton, in this Coun-

ty, he had divers Lands in Lincolnſhire; and in Leiceſterſhire, Leeſthorp, and the Mannours of Steneby and Braceby, which two laſt he deviſed to his Second Wife *Cecily,* during Widowhood, or (as the words of the Will are,) *In caſe ſhe take upon her the Mantle and Ring, and avow Chaſtity.* He left Iſſue at his death five Sons, *Thomas* his Son and Heir, *Robert* deſigned to be a Prieſt, *James, Roger,* and *John,* and *Agnes* a Daughter.

Pa. 38. Col. 2. l. 12. add, Which *Ezekiel Johnſon* hath ſince, by Deed of Bargain and Sale, bearing Date 2. *July* 1686. and Inrolled in *Chancery* the 5th of the ſame Month, Sold, Granted, and Conveyed, the Mannor of Clipſham, with all the Lands, Tenements, Paſtures, and Wood-Grounds to him belonging in Clipſham, Pickworth, Stretton, and Thiſtleton in the County of Rutland, And the perpetual Advowſon of the Church of Clipſham, to *Richard Snow,* Gentleman, (one of the Clerks in *Chancery*) his Heirs and Aſſigns for ever. Which *Richard* is the youngeſt Son of *John Snow,* heretofore of Gunnerby in the County of Lincoln, Gent. and hath Married *Grace* the eldeſt Daughter of *Edmund Bolſworth,* Citizen of London, by whom he hath had iſſue of both Sexes.

P. 30. col. 2. l. 31. add, *in Auguſt* 1621.

P. 43. col. 2. l. 17. add, *Theſe Antient Guilds in England were of the ſame nature with theſe Fraternities of Houſholders, and others of both Sexes, which are now called* Sodalities, *beyond Seas.*

Corrigenda.

IN the Pedigree p. 63. for, Elizabetha fil. & h. Will. Com. Rut. Ux. 1. *read* Elizabetha fil. & h. Edw. Com. Rut. Ux. 1. *In the Ped.* p. 79. *for, Maurice Rich read Maurice Roche.* p. 96. col. 1. l. 29. *for Henry read Edward. In the Pedigree,* p. 109. *for Eliz. f. & coh. Tho. Dom. Wotton. read Heſter f. & coh. Tho. Dom. Wotton. In the ſame Pedigree theſe Letters* [*ob. ſ. m.*] *which by miſtake are miſplaced under the Name* [Johannes Noel *Arm.*] *ſhould be removed, and ſtand under the Name* [Henricus Noel *Arm.*] *who died without Iſſue Male.*

Licenſed Jan. 4. 1686.
Roger L'Eſtrange.

LONDON, Printed for the Author by *Edw Jones,* 1687.

THE
TABLE.

FINIS.

ERRATA.

PAg.2. col.1 l.15.r.this County. p.18.col.1.l.ult.r.who. p.19.col.1.l.28.r.Thirlby. p.27.col.1. l.37.r.perfit. col.2. l.36.r. with the other. p.26.col.1.l.ult.del. and. p.28.col.1.l.15.r.per. p.77. col.2.l.23.r.his. p.78. col.2.l.10.r.Historical p. 86.l penul.r.ac Edificia. p.89.l.17.r.Radulphi Lane. p.100.l.20.f.Soror,r.Socer. p.103. col.1. l.50. r.receive. p.117. col.1. l,33 r.Parish. p.128.col.1.l.15 r. of Tolethorp. p.134.col.1.l.11. f. his,r. their.

Literal Mistakes and false Pointings, the Reader is desired to excuse, as com-mon Errours of the Press.

Farther ADDITIONS
TO THE
History and Antiquities
OF THE
COUNTY of *RUTLAND.*

By the same Author.

B U R L E Y.

P. 32. add,

THIS great Lordſhip, and ſeveral others adjoining, *viz.* Oakham, Egleton, Hambleton, and Gretham, with the Foreſt of Lyfield, formerly belonging to the laſt Duke of Buckingham of the Name and Family of *Villars* (who died without Iſſue *Apr.* 16. 1687,) have been, ſince his Death, purchaſed by the Right Honourable *Daniel Finch* Earl of Nottingham; who in the Place of the Old Houſe (burnt down by the Rebels, as before is ſaid) hath erected here a moſt beautiful and noble Edifice, with all thoſe other requiſite Imbelliſhments about it, that are ſuitable to ſo magnificent a Building.

Which, with the Advantage of its eminent Situation, in a wall'd Park of five or ſix Miles Compaſs, and therein the no leſs pleaſant than large and ſpacious Woods, rich Paſtures, and Store of Game, has render'd this Seat of ſo extraordinary and ſingular Regard, that, I believe, there are not many in England that can equal, and few or none ſurpaſs Burley *on the Hill*; the very great Grace of this little County.

I may truly ſay, this exquiſite Structure, being the third Degree of Improvement, is the ſuperlative of its Kind. For *John* Lord *Harington* in his time built a new Houſe here, much better than he found; which the Great Duke of *Buckingham* in the Reign of King *James* I. either wholly built anew, or ſo very much improved that the Alteration was then more than double in Value : But this laſt is as much beyond the ſecond, as that excell'd the firſt.

And here let it not be thought improper to inſert in a Collection of Antiquities, a Poem writ on this Subject : There want not Examples of the like Nature ; but perhaps there never was a more inviting Occaſion for the Muſe's pleaſing Labours than upon the many Beauties and Advantages of this Place.

HAIL

HAIL happy Fabrick, whoſe auſpicious View
   Firſt ſees the Sun, and bids him laſt adieu !
Seated in Majeſty, your Eye commands
A Royal Proſpect of the Richeſt Lands :
Whoſe better Part, by your own Lord poſſeſt,
May well be nam'd the Crown of all the reſt.
The under-lying Vale ſhews with Delight
A thouſand Beauties at one charming Sight :
No Penſil's Art can ſuch a Landskip feign ;
And Nature rarely yields the like again.
Few Situations may with this compare,
None can excel, for View, for Soil, for Air.

   Tryumphant Structure ! while you thus aſpire.
From the dead Ruins of a Rebel Fire ;
Methinks I ſee the Genius of the Place
Advance his Head, and with a ſmiling Face,
Say, Kings have on this Spot made their Abodes ;
'Tis fitted now to entertain the Gods !

   Okeham, that ſtands below, in diſtance near,
(The Capital both of the Vale and Shire)
Though ſmall and humble in her lowly Seat,
Thinks of her Neighbourhood, grows proud and great.
She looks but up, and o'er the Wood appears
An Object never known to former Years ;
Which riſing as a new Diſcover'd Star,
Darts from that Eminence, her Rays ſo far
That all the neighbouring Shires with Joy partake
The Ornament which this alone does make.
Diffuſive Beauty, ſuch as opens here,
Can not be bounded in a ſingle Shire.

   So ſhines the outward Form : The Inward Dreſs
Sutes with the reſt ; and what can more expreſs ?
The Rooms ſo exquiſite for Uſe and Grace,
And all things ſo imbelliſh'd on the Place
One knows not which excels, the Jewels, or the Caſe.

   A beauteous Frame adorn'd with utmoſt Art
Unites the Lower to the Higher Part.
Whither does this Majeſtick Stair-caſe lead ?
Can there be leſs than Heaven at the Head ?
Far hence be all Profane, or Thoughts or Words !
'Tis ſuch a View of it as Earth affords ;
Where all the Powers of Artful Beauty ſhine :
'Tis an Imperial Room, tho' not Divine.
Yet is the Doctrine of the Penſil, there,
Such as the Pulpits frequently declare ;

               A 2   The

The Inftability of humane State :
In *Cæfar*'s Tryumphs, and in *Cæfar*'s Fate.
Where fhall I firft applaud, what moft admire ?
Since all we fee does all we can require.
Shall I the penfil'd Beauties firft difclofe ;
Or Tapiftry, whofe Luftre equals thofe ?
Raphael's Cartoons did doubtlefs ne'er appear
With more Advantage to themfelves, than here.
Shall I the fplendid Furniture relate ;
The various Utenfils of Maffy Plate,
(Where the rich Mettle is the meaner Part ;
The richer Value's Workmanfhip and Art)
Or fhall thofe Cabinets my Subject be,
The Choice of *Indian Marts*, and *Italy* ?
In which the greateft Rarities that are
Become more precious, being treafur'd there.
Ceafe, daring Mufe, ceafe to attempt a Task
Would the luxuriant Wit of *Ovid* ask :
And *Ovid*'s felf might fail in this, tho' he
So well defcrib'd the Starry *Galaxy*.

Nor be the Beauties of this Seat lefs fair,
Lefs to be fam'd, without, than thofe within it are.
The curious Gardens full of Charms appear ;
And the whole Park feems but one Garden, here.
So ravifhing the Walks, Woods, Ponds, and all
Within the Compafs of its Six-Mile-Wall !
As *Rutland* has been *England*'s Garden writ,
So this muft be allow'd th' Epitome of it.

Behold yon' fpacious Grove of kingly Oakes,
Whofe reverend Gloom to folemn Joy provokes :
Such were the Trees, beneath whofe awful Shade
The antient *Druids* once their Altars made :
From fuch *Dodona*'s Oracle was fpoke,
When *Jove* himfelf did animate an Oak :
Lodg'd on fuch Boughs, our *Charles* by Heaven was fav'd,
When hellifh Force had all his Realms enflav'd.
Bleft Prefervation ! which has honour'd more
That Tree, than ever *Jove* had done before.
In happy, blifsful, Shades, and like to thefe,
The Infant World converft with Deities.

Farther into the thick whoe'er advance
Are loft, not in the Wood, but pleafing Trance.
Nature does here the Powers of Art defy,   )
Exerting all her Faculties, to try   }
Who beft can lull the Ear, moft charm the Eye.   )

What

What Pen, what Words, can to the Life depaint
The Lark's tryumphing Joy, the Philomel's Complaint?
The fable Mearl's loud, clear, and early Note,
The fweet *Sonatas* of the Scarlet-throat?
The Finch (whofe very Name has Mufick in't)
With others more, whofe Numbers know no Stint:
All different Parts, and all in Confort fet
To the grave Turtle's Flute, and Linnet's Flagiolet,
While Silvan Songs enchant us all around
Trees eccho Trees, and feather'd Choirs refound:
Diana's Herd forget to feed, or fear,
Lofe all their other Senfe, and only learn to hear.

Nor the wild Beauties of the Cops delight
In lefs Degree the captivated Sight:
So various are the Objects which furprize
And pleafe, that we cou'd wifh our felves all Eyes.
Each feveral Riding to the Eye and Ear,
The Seat of Joy and Pleafure does appear?
And reprefents the feign'd *Elizium,* here.
Deluded Poets, heed no longer Fame:
No longer boaft *Theffalian Tempe's* Name:
This is the finifh'd *Tempe!* *Greece,* of old,
Shew'd but the rough Defign of what we now behold.

They who love Exercife and healthy Game,
For Chafe, or Flight, or of what other Name,
Meet here thofe manly Sports in fuch Excefs,
Envy herfelf muft certainly confefs,
This fingle Park may with fome Forefts vie,
As well for Store, as for Variety.
What Admiration to the Place is due,
That's a vaft Garden for its pleafing View,
And for its Game a little Foreft too.

But fince even Pleafure tires, and what we guefs
To be Delight, much ufed, proves nothing lefs;
The truly noble Peer who here abides,
To recreate Man's better Part provides:
A Room of State, where Joys of unconfin'd
And univerfal Relifh, feaft the Mind;
A lofty Stand, from whence one takes a View
Quite through the World, and fees beyond it too;
An airy Scale by which Thoughts backward clime
Up to the firft Original of Time;
Such is the *Library:* fair to be feen
Without, more fair the Furniture within.

Doubtlefs

Doubtlefs the Pleafures of the Mind are beft,
And moft refemble a Celeftial Feaft :
Books are Eternal Food, and always ready dreft.
This mental Treat does well become the Care
Of fuch a Prince in Science to prepare :
As Learn'd as Great ; Renoun'd for deepeft Senfe,
Paternal Loyalty, and Eloquence !
Head of a Family, whofe Sons all fhew
Such wondrous Parts, 'tis difficult to know
Whether to Birth or Study moft they owe.

    Thrice happy he ! and truly bleft the Man,
Who thus, retir'd from Noife and Bufinefs, can
On his own Ground, in Nature's Freedom, find
All the foft Joys of Primitive Mankind !
At eafe from foreign Arms, and inward Fear,
In Mind ferene, in Fame and Honour clear ;
He cultivates, and bleffes where he lives,
Builds and improves what bounteous Fortune gives.
This is the Life for which wife *Horace* fhews
Such high Efteem, and which in Fact he chofe :
Tybur to *Rome* preferring, did confefs,
He found a better Greatnefs in Recefs.
And yet in fuch Recefs, the generous Mind
Will make a Palace where it cannot find.
Be witnefs *Burley Houfe* ! a Dwelling fit,
And worthy Him, who built and fafhion'd it.

    Thus mighty Kings, when Martial Labours ceafe,
Employ the quiet Hours of fought-for Peace :
Through all their Lands new Wonders they erect ;
And beautify by Arts, what Arms protect :
Higher than this can no Ambition climb ;
They fight to conquer Men, they build to conquer Time.
Where's now the *Roman* Grandeur ? What's become
Of thofe unbounded Conquefts of old *Rome* ?
While all her Glories vanifh into Air,
That Nation too, as if it never were,
Two Giant-Columns ftill fupport her Name ;
And ftand the Vouchers of Eternal Fame.
I will not any Parity fuppofe
Between the Youth of this fair Pile, and Age of thofe ;
Beauties of different kind : But fure I may
With Modefty enough, yet boldly, fay,
Not *Antonine*'s, nor *Trajan*'s Pillar's Sight
Can ftrike the diftant Eye with more Delight :
Nor are from nobler Situation fhewn,
Though they boaft Seven Hills, this only One.

To

    To raife a Work like this, muſt be agreed,
Though by a Subject done, 'tis yet a Kingly Deed;
Short is that Word! 'tis fomething ſtill more great:
For thus to *build*, half ſignifies *create*.
Fair Form from Rubbiſh, ſeems a like Effect
(Let it be ſaid with all profound Reſpect)
As Earth on Chaos built, by the firſt Architect.

    A *Roman* Poet hertofore did dare
The Heavens and *Cæfar*'s Palace to compare.
'Twas a bold Thought! But when I view this Place,
Where Height of Art joins with the native Grace;
Where all thoſe Decorations that we ſee
Excel, and ſmile in a juſt Harmony:
When I confider thoſe who here abide,
The Seats chief Glory, and the Country's Pride,
Thoſe equal Partners of a noble Bed;
He, Good as Great, as Loved as Honoured!
She, (the bleſt Counterpart of ſuch a Pair)
Joy of the Earth, and Heaven's peculiar Care;
Preſerved by Miracle, and hither ſent
To be our *Rutland*'s ſignal Ornament:
When I obferve what happy Cyons ſhoot,
What Olive Branches ſpring from ſuch a Root
To bleſs their Parents, and this Age to grace
With all the Beauties of the Mind and Face;
Struck with Amazement, I may well prefume
The Heaven-like Palace This, not that at *Rome*.

    Juſtly has Fame extoll'd one *Burley* long,
And will, while Man can hear, and ſhe can find a Tongue.
For many years the Monarch Building ſtood
And reign'd in Beauty o'er the Neighbourhood;
Till this her Rival, emulous of Fame,
Starts up and makes a ſtrenuous Counter-Claim.
See a new *Phœnix* 'ere the other dies;
So nearly plac'd, ſo match'd, as Sifter Eyes:
As Sifter Eyes, they eminently grace
The middle of fair *England*'s lovely Face.
Survey the Globe, ſearch every Province round;
In no Place elſe, not *Italy*, is found
Two Seats like theſe, diſtant, and yet the ſame,
If not in all Perfections, yet in Name.
What can this younger Wonder more require?
It is a *Burley*! View it, and admire;
Farther Encomium needs not; in that Word
Is center'd all that Language can afford.

                       O K E-

O K E H A M.

P. 98. add,

THIS Advowson has been of late Years changed, and transferred by Dr. *Henry Compton*, Bishop of 𝕷𝖔𝖓𝖉𝖔𝖓, to *Daniel* Earl of 𝕹𝖔𝖙𝖙𝖎𝖓𝖌𝖍𝖆𝖒, Lord of the Castle and Mannor of 𝕺𝖐𝖊𝖍𝖆𝖒, for two other Advowsons, 𝕻𝖗𝖎𝖙𝖙𝖑𝖊𝖘𝖜𝖊𝖑𝖑 and 𝕷𝖊𝖎𝖌𝖍, lying in the County of 𝕰𝖘𝖘𝖊𝖝 and Diocess of 𝕷𝖔𝖓𝖉𝖔𝖓: To enable which Exchange a special Act of Parliament was past in *March* 1696 (8, 9. *W.* III.) N. 18. entituled, *An Act for the Exchonge of certain Advowsons between the Bishop of* 𝕷𝖔𝖓𝖉𝖔𝖓, *and the Earl of* 𝕹𝖔𝖙𝖙𝖎𝖓𝖌𝖍𝖆𝖒.

P. 101. add,

IN the North Building, or cross Arm of this Church, are the following Inscriptions.

On several Gravestones.

Jacet in hoc Tumulo Maria Booth *Vidua Reverendissimi* Hugonis Booth *de Cussington in Comitatu Lecestriæ Pastor.* Obiit *An.* Dom. 1640. *Ætatis* 93.

Jacent in hoc Tumulo Josiah Peachie *Venerabilis Verbi Dei Minister,* Obiit *An.* Dom. 1639. *Ætatis* 37. *Una cum Uxore* Maria Peachie. *Obiit An.* Dom. 1634. *Ætatis* 26. *Cum Filia* Hephzibah. *Obiit An.* Dom. 1640. *Ætatis* 10.

Jacet in hoc Tumulo Johannes Pierypont *Filius Magistri* Johannis *&* Elizabethæ *hujus Scholæ quondam Alumnus nuper Academiensis.* Obiit *An.* Dom. 1637. *Ætatis* 27.

On a plain Table of White Marble, in the North Wall.

P. M. S.
Propè jacet Corpus
Venerabilis ABRAHAMI WRIGHT, A. M.
quondam hujus Ecclesiæ
Vicarii,
Natu Londinensis, eruditione Oxoniensis,
& olim Collegii D. Johan. Baptistæ
in celeberrima ista Academiâ
Socii.
Qui nono die Maii,
⎧ Salutis Christianæ 1690.
Anno ⎨ Ætatis suæ 79.
⎩ Vicariatûs 30.
Piè & tranquillè expiravit.
*Beati Mortui qui in Domino moriuntur.
amodo jam dicit Spiritus, ut
Requiescant a laboribus suis.*

LONDON: Printed for the Author, 1714.

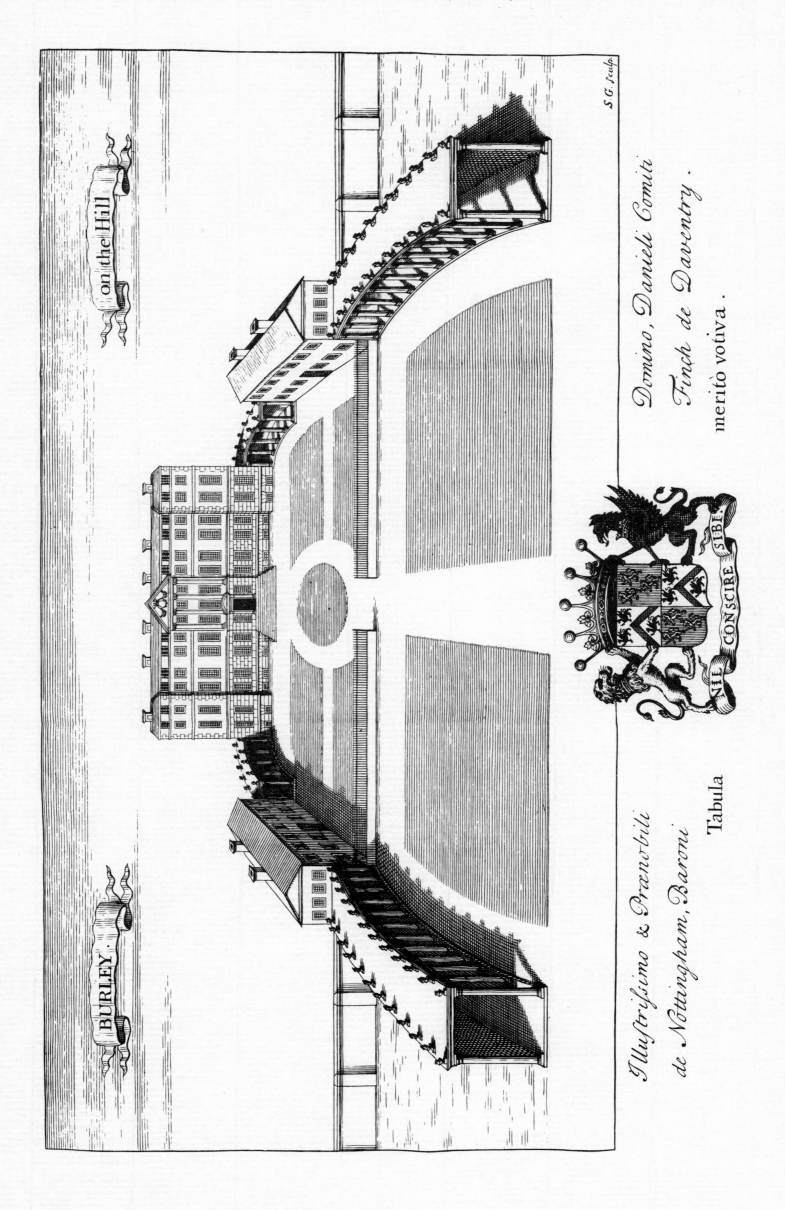

BURLEY . on the Hill .

Illuſtriſſimo & Prænobili
de Nottingham, Baroni .

Tabula

Domino, Danieli Comiti
Finch de Daventry .
meritò votiva .

NIL CONSCIRE SIBI.

S. G. Sculp.

This day is publifhed, Price One Shilling, containing a compleat Lift of the Sheriffs from the earlieft Accounts to the prefent time, and ornamented with an Engraving of Burley Hall, executed by PAGE,

No. I of

WRIGHT's

ANTIQUITIES

OF

RUTLAND,

With Additions ;

Bringing it down to the prefent Time,

By W. HARROD.

☞ The Publifher did not intend to have printed this Work by Subfcription, having obferved that Applications to the Public on this bufinefs are too often treated with indifference and inattention --- the Advice of his Friends, however, added to the unfolicited number of refpeƈtable Names, have fet afide this objeƈtion, and he now humbly folicits the Patronage of the Public, hoping that the Lift of Subfcribers on the cover of each fucceeding Number will be ornamented with the addition of kind Encouragers, the perufal of which cannot fail of infpiring him with GRATITUDE.

Stamford: Printed by W. HARROD, 1788.

DESCRIPTION *of BURLEY HOUSE.*

THIS Noble Manfion is built of fine freeftone which was fetched with great labour and expence from Clipfham and Ketton. The north and fouth fronts are exactly fimilar, being 196 feet in length ; the eaft and weft fronts are alfo fimilar, and in length 96 feet. The grand terrace to the fouth commands a fine profpect of rich country, fine vales and hanging woods, and this grand terrace, it is thought, exceeds every thing of the kind in the kingdom, being nearly 300 yards long and 30 wide, from whence you defcend by feveral flights of fteps into an extenfive vale of fine hanging woods, &c.

To the north is the grand entrance to this elegant houfe, which is fingular and grand, furpaffing every thing of the kind in this kingdom, and perhaps in Europe. You enter a noble court, by two handfome lodges, which is fpacious and ftriking, being 800 feet from thefe lodges in a ftraight line to the hall door : to the left is a handfome line of ftables, and to the right are other offices anfwerable --- from thefe offices you enter a beautiful circular colonade of great length fupported by Doric columns, which carries you to the houfe.

This Noble Palace has lain in a neglected ftate many years during the prefent Earl's minority, who has already done confiderable repairs, having fitted up a new dining room, drawing room, &c. with great tafte, and new fafhed the lower part of the houfe which gives great life to the building.

There is a fine painted room on the firft floor called the Salloon, which is more admired for it's magnificent and fine proportion than for the value of it's paintings which reprefent the Hiftory and Wars of Julius Cæfar : the length of this fine room, which extends the whole depth of the houfe from north to fouth, is 65 feet long, 36 wide, 28 high, and was painted by Lanfcroon, pupil of Verrio, who painted many excellent rooms and compofitions the work of many years at Burghley near Stamford.

The Library is of great length, and contains, befides a valuable collection of Books, fome curious fubjects in Anatomy and Natural Hiftory, and many valuable Portraits of this ancient family.

....

* *The above Account is the beft that can be procured at prefent — it is intended to fpeak more largely on the fubject in it's proper place. The publifher will be very thankful for further information.*

ERRATUM. In page IV. line 26, dele the words, *this has nearly if not quite loft it's name, perhaps the Catmofe.*

B. Christian del.

Page sculp.

The South East Prospect of BURLEY HALL, the Seat of the Rt. Hon.ble the Earl of Winchelsea.

Publish'd Sept.r 16th 1788, by W. Harrod, of Stamford.

WRIGHT'S
PREFACE to the READER.

I Suppose there needs no appology for a work of this argument, or that I should set forth the usefulness of this sort of learning in any long discourse, it being already sufficiently known to all gentlemen and scholars. Let me however borrow a few lines extremely pertinent to to this subject, out of an epistle formerly writ by *Thomas Wotton Esquire*, Father of the first Lord *Wotton*, and printed before *the Perambulation of Kent*, composed by the learned *John Lambert, Esquire*, formerly a bencher of *Lincoln's Inn: Mr. Wotton's* words are these, *I must needs say that (the sacred Word of Almighty God always excepted) there is nothing either for our Instruction more profitable, or to our minds more delectable, or within the compass of common understanding more easy or facile, than the study of Histories, nor that study for none estate more meet than for the estate of gentlemen; nor for the gentlemen of* England, *no History so meet as the History of* England. *For the dexterity that men have either in providing for themselves, or in comforting their friends (two very good things) or in serving their King and Country (of all outward things the best thing) doth rest chiefly upon their own and other folks experience.*

Since *Mr. Lambert* writ his abovementioned *Perambulation of Kent*, it hath been much desired by several worthy Persons, that all the counties of *England* might be accordingly described by others; which perhaps may be in time: some are done already, as *Kent, Cornwall, Leicestershire, Cheshire, Nottinghamshire*, but above all *Warwickshire*; several cities and towns also, as *London, Canterbury, Oxford, Cambridge, Windsor, Exeter, Stamford, Feversham*, all which have been treated of in several distinct volumes, writ by several Authors. Other Counties I hear are now in hand as *Yorkshire, Staffordshire*, and *Hartfordshire*.

As to this undertaking of mine, I must acquaint the reader, that having been above twenty years past, for the most part, resident in the County of *Rutland*, (tho' no native of the same) I collected many years ago something of this nature for my own private satisfaction. Which notes, tho' few and those imperfect, I have since been encouraged by several persons of honour and Quality to compleat into a just volume as it is now published. In the performing of which I have had some help from certain papers collected by Sir *Wingfield Bodenham, Knight*; formerly, while he lived, of *Ryhall*, in this county, who in the late times of Anarchy being a prisoner in the Tower for his faith and loyalty to his King, had there sufficient leisure to make several collections of antiquity, which he did chiefly from the labours of that Industrious and famous antiquary *Mr. Roger Dodsworth*; among which miscellaneous papers of his, I found divers notes relating to this county, as will appear by my citations. Also through the favour of the right worthy Sir *John Cotton Baronet*, I have had the perusal of his famous and incomparable Library of Manuscripts at *Westminster*, tho' in truth my affairs would not permit me to spend so much time there, as I might have done, had I no other Avocations. Nor ought I to forget to acknowledge the assistance which I have found; as well from the learned works as personal friendship and encouragement of the highly deserving Sir *William Dugdale, Knight* Garter King at arms, Sir *Henry St. George, Knight, Clarencieux*; with other gentlemen belonging to the office of arms, to whose civilities I am obliged. Yet all this I thought not sufficient till I made an actual search among the records themselves remaining in the Tower, at the chapel of the rolls, and in the Exchequer at *Westminster*, especially the Augmentation Office.

The Pedigrees, which I have inserted in this treatise, are some transcribed from the authentic rolls of descent remaining in the possession of the respective families; but the most of them are copied out of the Visitation books made for this county, and remaining in the Office of Arms. Several of which pedigrees may possibly be reduced much higher, if the parties concern'd will give themselves the trouble and charge to search further; for my part I have set down only such things as have arrived to my knowledge without importuning any for intelligence; some gentlemen being unwilling (for reasons best known to themselves) to have the evidences of their families or estates viewed by any stranger. For this reason chiefly, I have been cautious and sparing in treating of the modern proprietors and present possessors of the estates mention'd in this book, for whereas the antient titles are to be found in public records, or to be gathered from printed authors, or other authentic writings; on the contrary he that treats exactly of the present must be of necessity beholden to report and personal information, which will betray him that relies thereon to error, in regard of those many dormant conveyances upon condition, and settlements in trust, &c. which abound now a days more than ever. But if notwithstanding all my endeavours to the contrary, I have been guilty of any mistakes, I am very willing and ready, upon better evidence to annex the *Errata* in a Supplement or appendix.

As to the method in my description of this county, I have in several particulars followed that which hath been heretofore used by the industrious *William Burton, Esquire*, formerly a member of the *Inner Temple*, in his *Description of Leicestershire*, which precedent being drawn by the hand of an antient and learned barrister, seems most proper for me to observe; not only placing the towns alphabetically, and such other slighter matters, but chiefly in the concise, yet satisfactory account of the subject. The said *Mr. Burton*, as a lawyer, tells us in his preface to his reader, *That those cases of law which of latter times have happen'd within his shire, he hath briefly remember'd, in some shewing the arguments and reasons of the judgments.* And so have I in like manner here in *Rutland*. And that such antiquities as these are not inconsistent with a lawyer's observation, he tells us further in the same preface, *that for his own part, he of his knowledge can affirm, that the antiquity of a church window, for the proof of a match and issue had, hath been delivered in evidence to a jury at the assizes, and been accepted. And therefore he hath set down the arms in church windows, and the inscriptions of tombs; for that perhaps they may rectify armories and genealogies, and may give testimony, proof, and end to many differences.* These are his words, which I think I may not improperly apply also to my own undertaking.

A
This

This was, I confess, a subject much more facile and delightsome to be writ of by those who lived before the late civil wars, that is before the rebels had tore up so many brass inscriptions in churches, and broke the windows of God's house, where they saw any memorial of antiquity; as if they had a mind thereby to exterminate the memory of their forefathers, and do what in them lay, that posterity should not know that there ever was a better generation of people than themselves.

The violation of funeral rites was formerly esteem'd a thing abhorrent not only to christian religion, but also to the bare humanity of the antient Romans and all the civilized parts of the world, tho' heathen. And tho' the old common laws of *England* have given an action to the widows, and to the heirs of those whose monuments are defaced, as may be seen in *Sir Edward Coke's* 3d. Institutes. p. 202. and in other books there cited; yet in the reign of *E.* 6. some covetous and ill principled people began to be mighty busy at this work, and so also in the beginning of the reign of *Queen Elizabeth,* till that wise Queen put a stop to their career, by her proclamation dated 19. *Sept.* in the 2d. year of her reign, and by another in the 14th. year of her reign, forbidding under severe penalties, that any should *break or deface any monument of antiquity or inscription set up in churches, or other public places, for the memory of the deceased to their posterity, only, and not for any religious honour.* The said proclamation of *Sept.* 19. (too long to be here transcribed) may be seen at large in *Weaver's Funeral Monuments,* fol. 50. But the causes that procured the prohibition of such actions are extreamly worthy note : And they are thus exprest in the words of that proclamation.— *By which means not only churches remain at this day spoiled, broken, and ruinated, to the offence of all noble and gentle hearts, and the extinguishing of the honorable and good memory of sundry virtuous and noble persons deceased, but also the true understanding of divers families of this realm (who have descended of the blood of the same persons deceased) is thereby so darken'd, as the true course of their inheritance may be hereafter interrupted contrary to justice, besides many other offences that do hereof ensue.*

Thus much I thought not improper to insert in this place, to shew not only the impiety but also the illegality of such actions, which tend only to the disornament of churches, and to blind the truth of history.

I begun my account of every town with the state and condition that it was in at the *Norman Conquest,* above 600 years ago. This I have out of the old record in the Exchequer call'd *Domesday-Book :* which is the oldest public record in *England;* begun to be made in the year 1081 (14. *W.* 1.) by the command of that king; to serve for a punctual and certain information of all the lands in *England,* who were at that time the present owners thereof, and who had been, before the Conquest; how much the several lordships were worth yearly, and of what contents the same were. At the time of the composing it was a meer *Liber censualis* or tax-book; but of later time it is become the most sacred and unquestionable evidence that is in matters of tenure.

And in regard the rights of advowson and presentation to churches hath been always esteemed a material part of a lordship, I have inserted the antient patrons of the several churches in this county, with the endowments of several vicarages, as they remain of record in the registry of *Lincoln;* and these notes I have had, I must confess, from an abstract of that register, formerly transcribed by the abovementioned *Mr. Roger Dodsworth.*

In reading what I cite, out of *Domesday-Book* especially, you will meet with several obsolete and uncommon words, as *Berwica, Bordarii, Sockmen, Villain, Saca and Soca, &c.* Of all which I will here in the beginning of this work give an exposition, chiefly, out of our law-books, as the most proper interpreters, they being all old words relating to tenures and estates.

Berwica, in English a *Berew* or *Berwit,* in *Domesday-Book* signifieth, a hamlet or village appurtenant to some other town or manor. And *Sir Henry Spelman* in his *Glossary,* describes it to be *Manerium minus, ad majus pertinens, non in gremio Manerii sed vel in confinio, vel disjunctius interdum situm est :* And according to this signification is *Sir Edward Coke's* citation out of *Domesday* in *Gloucestersh. Hæ Berwicæ pertinent ad Berchley, & sit recitat plus quam viginti Villas.* Co. 1. Inst. 116, a.

Bordarii, (1) says *Sir Edward Coke,* is derived of the French word *Borde,* a cottage : and signifyeth the same with *Cotarii,* that is *Bores* holding a little house with some land of husbandry, bigger than a cottage. And *Coterelli* are meer cottagers *qui Cotagia & Curtalagia tenent.* These *Bordarii* were ever named after the *Villani* in *Domesday-Book* Co. Lit. fo. 5. b.

Bovata terræ, a *Bovate* or *Oxgange* of land, is as much as an ox can till, and may contain, meadow, pasture, and wood, necessary for such tillage, *Co. Lit. fo.* 5. *a. Octo Bovatæ faciunt Carucatam terræ, &* 18. *acræ faciunt Bovatam terræ.*

Carucata, a *Carucate* or *Carve* of land, otherwise called a *Plowland,* may contain houses, mills, pasture, meadow, wood &c. *Co. Lit. fo.* 86. *b.* and it is *Sir Edward Coke's* opinion, that a carucate, or plowland, is not of any certain content, but as much as one plow can by course of husbandry plow in a year, which in some countries is more than in other, and therefore a plowland may contain less in one place than in another; yet says the same author, of antient time every plowland was of the yealy value of 5 nobles *per an.* and this was the living of a plowman or yeoman, *Et ex duodecim Carucatis constabat unum feodum militis.* Co. Lit. fo. 69. a.

Demesne, or *Demain, (Dominicum)* hath divers significations, but the most common acceptation of Demesne lands is to signify the lords chief seat or mansion with the lands thereunto belonging, which he and his ancestors have from time to time kept in their own manual occupation. Yet in law all the parts of a manor except what is in the hands of freeholders, are said to be Demains. *Co. Lit. fo.* 17. *a.*

Geldum, in Domesday-book is generally written for the *Danegeld,* and so to be understood. Which was a Tax or tribute imposed by a certain law in the Saxons time, upon every town and village in *England, Spelm. Gloss. verb Geldum.* The Rate was at first 12 d. and afterwards rais'd to 2 s. per an. for every hide of land. This imposition began *Anno Domini* 1007, in the time of *King Etheldred,* who was forced by vast sums of money to buy a peace with the *Danes,* tho' it lasted but for a time. However this tax being once set on foot was continued, till released in part by *King Edward the Confessor,* and totally by *King Stephen,* in the beginning of his reign. After which the word was never more used, but the like impositions were in after ages called *Tallages* and *Taxes, vid. spelm. Gloss. verb. Danegeldus. Selden, Mare Clausum lib.* 2. *ca.* 11.

Hida, Some hold a *hide* of land to contain four yard land, some one hundred acres. But *Sir Edward Coke* is of opinion, that a hide is all one with a carucate or plowland : and that neither is of any certain content, but as much as a plow can till in a year, with good husbandry. *Co. Lit. f.* 69. *a.*

Knight's

(1) They were to supply their Lord's table with small provisions, to perform domestic work, or even any lower offices that he might require. *L.*

Knights fee. (1) It is agreed by all good authors that a Knight's fee ought to be eftimated not according to the quantity of land; but the value of the eftate : and that 20 *l. per an.* was antiently called a knight's fee be the number of acres held more or lefs. *Mr. Seiden* cites the ancient record called *Modus tenendi Parliamentum,* and fhews that the knight's fee is there *computed ad viginti Libratas terræ.* Seld. Tit hon. part. 2. ch. 7. which is the land worth 20 l. *per an.* vide *Low's* cafe. *Co. Rep. lib.* 9. *f.* 124. thefe knights' fees at fome time were liable to a kind of tax called *Efcuage,* affeft by parliament higher or lower : and the tenants in chivalry paid the fame proportionally as they held their eftates, fome for one knights fee fome for half, and fome for the 20th. and fome for the 100th. part of a knight's fee. I have feen a record in the Exchequer ; It is *Pafch.* 29 *E.* 3. *Inter communia, ex parte Rememoratoris Thefaurarii, Tit. Fines &c. Rotulo quarto in dorfo.* In which it appears that John fon of *Richard le Wright de Hornefburton* ; in *Hornefburton* in *Holderneffe* in the county of *York,* which he held of the King, as of his honour of *Albermarle,* by the fervice of the one thoufand one hundred and fiftieth part of a knights fee. And the relief of chivalry being always a fourth part, his eftate was it feems valued at 4 *d. per an.* now according to this computation the whole knights fee did amount to 19 l. 3 s. 4 d. Yet hath the value of thefe knights fees been very differently eftimated in feveral king's reigns fometimes at 20 l. *per an.* fometimes at 40 l. fometimes at 15 l. and fometimes at 10 l. *per an.* as may be feen in the *Second Inftitutes, p.* 596.

Leuca or *Leuga.* Signifies in Doomfday-Book, a mile as then computed ; and did contain twelve *Quarantenes,* or furlongs. *Monaf. Ang.* 1. *Vol. f.* 313. which according to our prefent meafure, makes a mile and a half.

Librata terræ. Is land of 20 s. *per an.* value. In old time lands were granted according to their value, as *Centum Libratas terræ,* a hundred pound of land ; or *centum Solidatas terræ,* a hundred fhillings of land as may be feen in the *Firft Inftitutes* fo. 5. *b.* and in *Fitzh. N.B.* fo. 87. f. where we read of *viginti Libratas terræ, vel reditus,* as two things of the fame fignification.

Quarantena, is a furlong of land, containing 40 perches, each perch 16 foot. Twelve of thefe *Quarantenæ* or furlongs at the time of the *Norman* furvey, were accounted a mile ; tho' at this day but eight. *Spelm-Glofs. verb. Quarantena.*

Saca & Soca. Sac or *Sak* is an old word fignifying conifans of pleas in a court belonging to a Manor, with a liberty of amercing the tenants for offences, and levying the faid Amerciaments to his own ufe. *Seld. Tit. hon. part.* 2. *c.* 7. The word *Sac* (fays *Sir Henry Spelman* in his *Glofs.*) fignifies in the *Saxon* as much as *Caufa, Lis, Certamen,* in the *Latin.* And I cannot, find any different fignification of the word Soca.

Sockmen, Socmanni, fo often mention'd in *Domefday-book,* were tenants of freehold of inheritance, who held their lands of the Lord in free foccage, and not by knights fervice, paying yearly to their Lords a certain free rent. *Co. Lit. fol.* 5. *b.* Yet did thefe *Socmanni* or freeholders perform certain fervices befide their Rents. As for inftance in the manor of *Stonely* in the county of *Warwick,* the cuftom was, that each of them at his death fhould give to the Lord an intire *Heriot, i. e.* his horfe and Arms, if he had any, otherwife his beft beaft. That his heir fhould be admitted to the inheritance at 15 years of age paying his rent doubled for a relief. That in harveft they fhould upon notice and requeft come to help the Lord, with every of their tenants, themfelves to ride up and down on horfeback to fee that the others work well, and both they and their tenants to have at noon meat and drink provided by the lord, &c. *Antiquities of Warwickfhire, p.* 170. The fucceffors of thefe *Sockmen,* in fuch manors where the king was lord at the time of *Domefday* furvey, are now called *Tenants in Antient Demefne,* and capable of feveral privileges and immunities, *Co.* 4. *Inft. p.* 169. which privileges and the original caufe of them, you may read of, *Co.* 2. *Inft. fol.* 542.

Villains, were of two forts : *Villains of Blood,* and *Villains of Tenure.* The firft of thefe were themfelves and their iffue bondmen, and bound to fuch fervices as the lord fhould command, *ubi fciri non potuerit vefperi quale fervitium fieri debet mané.* Thefe had no property in any eftate, they could purchafe but the lord might enter and hold it to his own ufe. Yet were thefe Villains free againft all men but only their lords: Neither could the lord himfelf kill or maim his villain, for that would be an infranchifement to him and his pofterity: the other villains were only by tenure ; and they were freemen themfelves, but only they were obliged to do certain cuftomary fervices yearly, as to plow and manure the lords land, or bring in his harveft, &c. The firft fort of thefe are now quite worn out, and in procefs of time become free like other men. The fecond fort are now called *Copyholders,* which fays *Fitzh. N. B. fol.* 12. *c.* is but a new invented name, for of old time they were called tenants in villainage, or bafe tenure. Thefe fort of tenants in villainage were before the Conqueft, tenants of freehold and held by free fervices ; but when they were ejected from their eftates by the conquering *Normans,* they afterwards obtain'd back again their old lands to hold at the will of their new lords in *Villainage,* by fervile offices, but certain and exprefs ; yet did their perfons remain free tho' their tenure was fervile. *Co. Lit. fol.* 172. *b.* *Villani,* in *Domefday-book,* as Sir *Edward Coke*

---

(1) When *William* I. came into the poffeffion of *England,* he divided it into 60,000 knights' fees, the land conftituting a fingle fee being 20 l. per annum, the pound containing thrice the weight of filver that it does at prefent.

Thefe fees he divided among 250 of his Barons, temporal and fpiritual, on condition that for each fee they fhould fupply him in his wars with a man at arms for forty days every year, fo that he had always 60,000 men at his command, being the whole militia of the kingdom, to be raifed by thefe Barons, who were not neceffarily knights themfelves, but only to provide knights or horfemen.

Thefe nobles again let their lands to tenants, not only for a rent, but on condition of the fame perfonal fervice befides when required; fuch tenant as poffeffed a whole fee was to ferve forty days, he who rented only half a fee twenty days, and fo in proportion.

The demefne lands, which belonged folely to the crown, were about the tenth part of the lands of *England,* but, all the remaining nine were held of the crown, either immediately or mediately, fo that *William* and his fucceffours, for many ages, were the grand landlords of the kingdom, there being one continued chain of vaffalage from the king to the flave, he being the only abfolute freeholder.

A Barony or Baron's eftate was thirteen knights' fees and two thirds, or 266 l. 13 s. 4 d. per annum.

An Earl's or Count's eftate was twenty fuch fees, or 400 l. per annum.

Perfonal attendance on the king at length growing troublefome to thefe great men, they compounded for it, by fending others in their ftead firft, and then by money, which was affeffed at fo much a fee under the name of fcutage.

It is computed that *William* had for his revenue 1061 l. 10 s. a day, equal now to four millions a year. *I.*

thinks

thinks, are not taken for bondmen ; but such are there called *Servi. Co. Lit. fol. 5. b.* This we ought to understand of the *Villains of Blood*, and that the word *Villani* is applicable in that old record to the Villains by tenure only ; so call'd *de Villis*, where they inhabited farms of husbandry, and did their lords work. (1)

Virgata Terræ, a yard land ; Is a quantity of land of different computation in divers places, in some Countries 10, in some 20, in some 24, in some 30 acres. *Co. Lit. fol. 5. a.*

(1) Villains under the *Saxons*, says *Blackstone*, were only slaves belonging, together with their children and effects, to the lord of the soil, like the rest of the cattle.

They were of two sorts regardant and grofs, the former belonging to the manor or land, the latter to the lord and transferrable but the lord might not kill or maim either ; they were a little raised by the *Normans*, who by admitting them to the oath of fealty conferred a right of protection to them, their children were called *nativi* because natives of the manor, hence *neifs* and knaves.

In 1206 the abbot of *Waltham* claimed *John le Tanur* as his villain, having been purchased for 60s. by *Walter* his predecessor.

When Sir *Philip Sidney* was slain at the battle of *Zutphen* in 1536, the *Spanish* minister, in his letter, regrets that so brave a knight should fall by the hands of villains, meaning private soldiers, who were chiefly raised from that class of people. *L.*

[Here Mr. Wright finishes his Preface, not forgetting to return his best Thanks to the Nobility, Gentry, and Clergy, having Possessions in the County, for the PLATES which ornament his Work. The Publisher hereof hopes that he shall not be less fortunate than his Predecessor; and can assure the Public that should be meet with the same Favour --- not less grateful.]

WRIGHT's

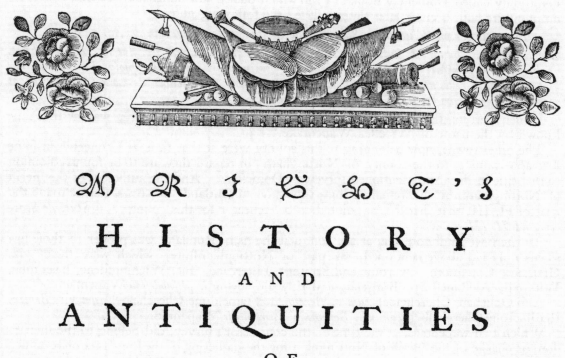

WRIGHT'S
HISTORY
AND
ANTIQUITIES
OF
RUTLAND,
With Additions.

THE county of Rutland, or (as it is latinized) *Rotelandia*, is sufficiently known to be the leaft county in this kingdom : it's form round,
it's dimenfions not above fome twelve miles over in any place, it's
fituation is on the north parts of Northamptonfhire, (from which it
is divided by the River Welland,) on the eaft of Leicefterfhire, and
fouth of Lincolnfhire : by which three counties, this is enclofed from
the reft of England.

Concerning the Etymology of the name; there goes a tale of one *Rut*, who rid round
this county in a day : in memorial of which act, the fpace of ground fo encircled, was from
him called Rutland. Another opinion (a little, and but a little more probable) is, that
it took that name from the ruddy complexion of the foil, (1) which notwithftanding I
never perceived, but in one part of the county, and that about Glaifton. And no doubt
there are few fhires in England, but produce a Mould of the fame colour in fome parts or
other. To thefe therefore let me add one Etymology more, which is that *Rotelandia* may
poffibly be fo named from it's circular form, *quafi Rotunda-landia*, or *Rotundlandia*, which
by contraction, leaving out the confonants, *n* and *d*, for the more eafy pronunciation,
makes *Rotulandia*.

And this the rather becaufe the word *Rotunda*, fignifying not only round, but well fafh-
ioned, handfome, and perfect, may in all it's fignifications be juftly applied to this county.

Touching the original of this county, it is to be noted, that Rutland, as it is now limited, was not a county of it felf at the time of the Norman conqueft, and that a great part of
the towns, thofe efpecially, which lie on the fouth limits of this fhire, did at that time belong

(1) *Camden* fays that in many parts of *Rutland* the fleeces of fheep are of a reddifh hue, owing to the
earth being of that colour ; but *Plot* writes that in fome parts of *Staffordfhire* horfes will become dappled
whatfoever colour they were of before. *L.*

long to the county of Northampton; and as part of that county, they are to be found under the title of Northamptonshire, in the general survey taken in the reign of K. William I. commonly called Domesday Book; (1) in which book, and under the said title of Northamptonshire hath been of later times inserted the following note.

Inquisitio coram Wilielmo de Saham et Sociis suis, inter Rageman de An. 4. E. 1.

Com. Northant. hundr. de Sutton (juratores inquisit.) quot hundred &c. sint in com. Northant. dicunt quod comitat. Roteland. quondam fuit pertinens ad com. istum quosq. dominus H. rex pater domini regis nunc illum dedit domino regi Alman. sed nesciunt de modo (huic concordat hundred de Spelho & plura alia hundreda ibidem.)

Which part of this county, then belonging to Northamptonshire, was at that time known by the name of Wicelsea Wapentake.

The other towns, now belonging to this county were at that time as I conceive in some sort appertaining to the county of Nottingham, in regard they are to be found adjoining to that title in the abovementioned survey of Domesday. And the authority of the sheriff of Nottinghamshire did remain a long time after in Rutland; for by a statute made the 51st of H. III. that sheriff is appointed to be escheator for this country. --- *Stat. de Scaccerio 51 H. III.*

And here we must note that at the conquest the name Roteland was proper to those few towns only last abovementioned, as part of Nottinghamshire, which were these, viz. Gretham, Cotesmore, Overtune and Straton, Tistertune, Tie, Wichingsdene, Exentune, Witewell, Alestanestorp, Burgelai, and Exwelle, being in *Alfnodestou* Wapentac.

Also Ocheham Cherchesoch *cum* v. *Berewicis.* Hameldune Cherchesoch *cum* vii. *Berew.* Redlinctune Cherchesoch *cum* vii. *Berew.* in *Martineslie* Wapentac.

Which two wapentacs, at the time of the conqueror's survey, did belong to the sheriffdom or charge of the sheriff of Nottingham for the gathering of the king's tax or revenue, which in those days did amount to a hundred and fifty pouuds of silver *per annum* from Roteland: the words of the record are, " *Hæc duo Wapent. adjacent Vicecomitatui Snotingham ad geld. Regis. Roteland reddit regi C L. libras albas.*"

However though Roteland was formerly no county of itself, yet it was even at that time an entire parcel of land or soak, as appears by Domesday book, where speaking of the estate which Gislebert de Gant held in Empingham, we may read these words, " *Ipse ten. in ead. villa* vii. *hid. & dim. & unam bovatam terre de soca regis de Roteland, et dicit regem suum advocatum esse.*" To this may be added what we read in Camden, viz. That king Edward the Confessor by his last will and testament bequeathed so much of this county as then bore the name of Roteland to his wife Eadith for her life, and after her death to St. Peter's at Westminster, in these words, *Volo quod post mortem Eadgithæ Reginæ conjugis meæ Roteland cum omnibus ad se pertinentibus detur monasterio meo beatissimi Petri, et reddatur sine tardatione abbati et monachis ibidem Deo servientibus in perpetuum.*

Besides this will mentioned by Camden, there is a large charter of the said king Edward's to be seen in Dugdale's Monasticon, whereby that pious king confirming to the said church divers lands formerly given by other kings his predecessors: it follows,

—— *Postremo ego ipse pro spe retributionis eternæ & pro remissione delictorum meorum & pro animabus patris mei, & matris meæ, et omnium parentum meorum, & ad laudem omnipotentis Dei, posui in dotalitium, & in perpetuam heræditatem super altare, varia ornamentorum genera quibus eclesiæ serviretur, vel in quotidianis vel solemnibus ministeriis: & ad usus fratrum inibi Deo servientium, de meo jure, quod mihi soli competebat absque ullius reclamatione vel contradictione, ista (inter alia) Roteland cum omnibus ad se pertinentibus, post mortem Edgithæ Reginæ.*

Which charter was dated at Westminster on the day of the Holy Innocents, 1064, in the 25th year of his reign.

---

(1) This curious book was composed in imitation of the roll of *Winton*, made by order of *Alfred* called *Domboc*, and is one of the most antient manuscript records in the kingdom; it is written on vellum, in two volumes, and took seven years in compiling: vol. I. is in *Folio*, consisting of 382 double pages and double columns, and written in a small, but plain character: vol. II. is in 4to and contains 450 such pages in single columns, and written in a large fair hand; these books are kept at the chapter house at *Westminster* under three locks and keys, and were not to be searched under 6s. 8d. nor transcribed under 4d. a line, but they have been lately printed in a type cast on purpose to express the abbreviations.

All the lands in *England* are described in these volumes, excepting *Cumberland, Northumberland, Westmoreland,* the bishopric of *Durham, Wales,* and part of *Lancashire,* for this last county was carved out of *Yorkshire* and *Cheshire* after the composing of it; the other northern counties were then in the hands of the *Scots,* and *Wales* was governed by monarchs of it's own.

It received it's name from the word Doom signifying judgement, because from it judgement was given in tenures of estates; the word Day, says *Hammond*, had formerly the same meaning: in the north of *England* arbitrators are called Daysmen.

But *Cleland* will have it that it was so called from *Dom's* judge's, *D'ey* law and book, meaning the judge's law book. *L.*

But

But this donation was foon after cancelled and made void by William the Conqueror upon his arrival in this nation, allowing only to the church of Weftminfter the tithes of Roteland, which tithes in procefs of time were alfo diminifhed to thofe only of the church of Okeham and parcels thereunto appertaining; but as to the lands he referving a great part of them to himfelf, divided the reft among Robert Mallet a Norman, lord chamberlain of England; Gilbert de Gant who came into England in his army, and was his wife's brother's fon; earl Hugh; Albertus or Aubrey, the clerk; and divers others: but in a more fpecial manner, he expreft his bounty to his niece Judith daughter of Lambert de Leins, and Maud countefs of Albemarle, the conqueror's fifter by the mother's fide: to which Judith, her faid uncle gave eighty fix lordfhips in Northamptonfhire and Rutland. She became the wife of Waltheof earl of Northumberland, a Saxon of great account, whom the conqueror made alfo earl of Northampton and Huntingdon(1)but the faid Waltheof being afterwards beheaded in 1073 for confpiring againft the king; and this countefs Judith, being fufpected of promoting her hufband's death, fhe lived a penitent widow all the reft of her life. She founded the priory of Helenftow in Berkfhire, and procured from king William a charter of divers immunities for the monks of Saltry in Huntingtonfhire, which religious houfe fhe much frequented in her time.

But to return from this digreffion, it feems that Rutland was a county before Henry the third's time: for in the fifth of king John, Ifabel his new queen had, at her coronation, affigned her in parliament, for her dower, among other lands, *Com. Roteland. & villam de Rokingham, in Com. Northampt. de communi affenfu & concordi voluntante Archiepifcoporum, Epifcoporum, Comitum, Baronum, Cleri, & populi totius Regni.*

Alfo in the twelfth year of the faid king John, Robert de Braibroc, as cuftos or fheriff of this county, did account for the profits of the fame, in the excequer. Of which Cuftodes, being, I fuppofe, neither more nor lefs in effect than fheriffs, there is to be found a large catalogue, even from the tenth year of Henry the fecond: fome of which held the office for life, as may appear by the lift hereafter inferted. By all which it appears, that Rutland, tho' not a county at the time of the Norman Conqueft, yet was made fuch long before the time of king Henry the third. (2)

ADDITIONS.

THE county of Rutland is often called Rutland*fhire*, but improperly. Thofe counties which end in *land* have not fhire added to them, as Cumberland, Northumberland, and Weftmoreland. A fhire is that which takes it's name from the county town as Yorkfhire; if therefore Rutland were a fhire at all it fhould be Oakhamfhire: there are feveral other counties which are not fhires as Effex, Middlefex, and Suffex, which are the Eaft Saxons, the Middle Saxons, and the South Saxons. Norfolk and Suffolk are the Northern folk and the Southern folk; Northumberland is the country North of Humber: Weftmoreland is the weft Morelands. The duke of the county is always called Duke of Rutland. Of the feveral etymologies of the county no one knows which is the true one, or whether any of them at all.

Since then all that has, or, I doubt, can be faid in difcovering the Etymology of the name of the county, would amount to nothing more than conjecture, it were lofs of time to purfue the fubject any farther. Dean Swift attempts to expofe the folly of fpending too much time in fruitlefs refearches of this kind, one inftance of which is as follows:

'ALEXANDER THE GREAT. This hero derived his name from his being particularly fond of eggs done under the grate, and on his return home he would cry out *All Eggs under the Grate*; this being often repeated, his fervants would fay on perceiving him coming from the fields --- Here comes *All Eggs under the Grate*.'

There are variety of foils in this county, 1ft. The Red Land is in all parts of it, but chiefly on the fouth-weft fide bordering on Northamptonfhire, but is neither peculiar to this county nor univerfal in it: it is in many parts of Northamptonfhire quite acrofs it, and

---

(1) According to *Stukely* he fometime refided at *Rihall*; *Barnak* belonging to him he gave it's church to *Croyland* abbey in which abbey he was buried, he was the firft nobleman that was beheaded in *England*.

(2) *Henry* III. gave the county to his brother *Richard* king of the *Romans*; but *Henry* II. firft made it a county. *L.*

as far as to Benfington, (commonly called Benfon) twelve miles Eaft of Oxford. It is a kind of fandy land full of red ftones here called Cale, and in fome places a red, blue, or greenifh ftone for building is dug in it : the red cale, (Keal, Moreton calls it,) that is the Red Land is judged to be iron ftone, for in fpring time the drains in the red cale ditches have the fame ochery look as fteel waters, and turn purple with galls.

2d. Rich clay is in all parts, but chiefly in the north-weft againft Leicefterfhire.

3d. White Limeftone is in great quantities in the eaftern parts againft Lincolnfhire and Northamptonfhire, among which are beds of a harder ftone with a bluifh caft, which is very good for building as no froft will hurt it : thefe are the principal foils, but there is alfo what they call White Clay, a burning foil, not fruitful either for grafs or corn, and is feldom found either at the top of the hill or the bottom, but very frequently on the fides of hills. About Woolfox and that part of the county there is a cold moift clay, which in fome countries is called Woodland Clay; and at Ketton and Ingthorpe there are pits of very good white freeftone which has been fent as far as Woburn in Bedford-fhire, and there is freeftone, though of fomething a different kind, at Clipfham.

The Rivers of this county are 1. The Welland, which rifes above Harborough, parts Leicefterfhire and Rutland from Northamptonfhire, and is navigable up to Stamford.

2. The Guafh, which comes out of Leicefterfhire, runs quite acrofs the middle of the county and into the Welland a mile below Stamford.

3. The Chater, which juft comes out of Leicefterfhire, croffes the county by Ridling-lon and Lyndon, and lofes it's name in the Welland above Tinwell.

4. The little Eye anciently the Lytelee parts Leicefterfhire from the fouth-weft part of Rutland, and runs into the Welland at Caldecot, it is generally a fmall Brook but fubjeft to very great floods.

5. The Ey a very fmall Brook, runs by Langham and Afhwell into the Wreke in Lei-cefterfhire, this has nearly if not quite loft it's name, perhaps the Catmofe.

The county fouth of the Guafh is generally hill and valley, chiefly running pretty re-gular eaft and weft; but the north-weft part is a fruitful valley call'd Catmofe, (perhaps from Coet maes, which in the Britifh tongue fignifies a woody field or ground,) bounded by the high lands of Market-Overton, Burley, Hambleton, Manton, Brook, Flitteris, and Whiffendine; and the north part of the county is in good meafure a higher flat, from Market-Overton to Pickworth.

Dr. Fuller tells us, in his 'Worthies' that there were a fort of poor men called Raddle-men, or Reddlemen, peculiar to this county, who went up and down the neighbouring parts, carrying packs of red-ftones, or oker, which they fold to the country farmers and jobbers for the marking their fheep; and as it would be well nigh difcernable and lafting as pitch brands, and lefs hurtful to the fleeces, it is more than probable, that the red-lands in this county, at leaft in fome parts of it, were of a clear different nature from thofe in o-ther counties, partaking fomething of the oker-rednefs, and fo might make the fheeps fleeces reddifh, efpecial in folding upon lands broken up by the plough, which might touch the oker-mines. Upon Whichley-heath, between Ketton and Tinwell in Eaft Hundred, we find fome marks or pits in our maps, called the quarries, which we fup-pofe were holes in the earth, out of which formerly fome fort of building-ftone hath been dug; but the vein being long fince exhaufted, we have no account of any fuch quarries here either by Mr. Wright or any other hiftorians, who treat of this county.

The author of Magna Britannia does not think, with Wright, that Rutland was not made a county before the tenth of Henry II. and afks, why then doth Doomfday-book place towns in Rutland as a diftinct county ? adding that it is probable this county might be before under the jurifdiction of the fheriffs of Nottingham or Northampton fhires and yet be a diftinct county, having no fheriffs of it's own till Henry II. appointed one.

Our anceftors had many Dome or Doomfday Books. That made by order of Alfred is faid to have been extant fo late as the reign of Edward IV. but is now unfortunately loft. It probably contained the principal maxims of common law, the penalties for mifdemeanors, and the forms of judicial proceedings. It is next to impoffible that pofte-rity can be deprived of the benefit of the Conqueror's furvey it having been printed by order of government and copies thereof diftributed among our nobility.

Befides the Doomfday-book beforementioned in two volumes folio, there is a third in quarto, differing from the other in folio rather in form than matter : it was made by order of the fame Conqueror and feems to be the more ancient of the two.

A fourth book there is in the exchequer called Domefday, which, though a very large volume, is only an abridgment of the other two. It has abundance of pictures and gilt letters at the beginning, which refer to the time of Edward the Confeffor. There is alfo a fifth book, called Domefday, and the fame with the fourth now mentioned.

Berewick

Berewic, or Berewica, in our old writers, denotes a village or hamlet belonging to some town or manor, situate at a distance therefrom. The word frequently occurs in Doomsday-book: *Istæ sunt berewichæ ejusdem manerii.*

It is recorded in the Conqueror's survey, that Morcar, earl of Northumberland, was in the reign of Edward the Confessor, possessed of Casterton in the county of Rutland, which shews, that then it was esteemed a distinct county, and the rather, because that town is in neither of those wapentakes, which are found belonging either to Northamptonshire or Nottinghamshire; as likewise were Barrowden and Seyton, the estate of Robert de Todinai in this county, when the said survey was taken.

The dimensions of this county are not above eighteen miles long and fifteen wide.

Of the WAPENTAKES or HUNDREDS

AT THE CONQUEST.

T the time of the survey made by William the Conqueror, commonly called Domesday Book; there were in Roteland, (I mean so much of the present county, as then bore that name) only two Wapentakes; Alfnodestow, and Martinsleie.

In Alfnodestou wapontac were two hundreds, in each of which were reckon'd twelve carucates, as they were taxed or rated to the geld, but in each of the said two hundreds there was really twenty and four carucates. This wapentac (saith the record) is half in Turgastune wapentac, and half in Brochelou wapentac. That is, it was at that day accounted as part of those two wapentakes in Nottinghamshire.

In Martinesleie wapentac was one hundred, in which was reckon'd twelve carucates, as taxed or rated to the geld; and forty eight plows might possibly be going therein, besides the three demesne manors of the king, in which there might be fourteen plows.

These two wapentacs (as I observed before) did in those days belong to the vice county or sheriffdom of Snottingham for the collection of the king's tax or geld.

Thus far out of the Ancient Record called Domesday *Book.*

Of the Hundreds 9th E. II.

IT was found by inquisition taken at Okeham on Tuesday next before the feast of S S. Tiburtius and Valerian (which is April 14.) in 9 E. 2. before Gilbert Holme the sheriff (or under sheriff) of Rutland, that there were at that time in this county four hundreds, viz. Martinesle, Alnestowe, Est Hundred, Wrondedyke.

Of the three first of which, the king was lord, and received the profits of the same, (as in the sheriffs turns, and suit of courts) except in certain liberties; all which profits of the said hundreds were at that time assigned to the lady Margeret de Gaveston countess of Cornwall to hold at the king's will.

The Fourth, viz. Wrondedyke was found to be late the estate of Guy de Bellocampo earl of Warwick, and was at that time in the king's hands by reason of the nonage of Thomas son and heir of the said earl: in which hundred the bishop of Lincoln had his liberty in the soke of Lydington.

And note, that then the present hundred of Okeham soke was included in that of Martinesle, which are now two distinct hundreds.

Of the Hundreds at this Day.

THE county of Rutland is at this day divided into five hundreds, viz. Okeham soke, Alstoe, East hundred, Wrandyke, and Martinsly.

1. Okeham soke lies on the edge of Leicestershire, and contains chiefly the west parts of this shire, except one town call'd Clipsham, lying in the utmost limits northwards on the borders of Lincolnshire, the whole hundred of Alstoe being interposed. In this hundred are contain'd about nine towns, among which one market, Okeham.

2. Alstoe hundred takes up the north parts, and borders on part of Leicester and Lincoln shires, and contains in it's division twelve towns.

The

3. The Eaft hundred lies (as it's name imports) on the eaft limits of this county, towards Stamford; and hath in it's divifion about thirteen towns and villages.

4. Wrangedyke or Barrowden hundred takes up the fouth parts of this county, and is bounded by the river Welland, parting this and Northamptonfhire, this hundred contains about fourteen towns and villages.

5. The hundred of Martinfley lies in the middle of the county, enclofed with the other four, and has formerly contain'd in it's divifion twelve towns and villages, among which one market, Uppingham.

There is alfo another hundred (tho' not commonly fo accounted in the ordinary computation) and that is the hundred of Cafterton parva, lying wholly within the Eaft hundred, and contains eight towns and villages, part of Eaft hundred, as commonly reputed: viz. Little Cafterton, Ryal, Belmifthorp, Efenden, Tinwel, Ingthorp, Tickencote, and Tolethorp. Which faid hundred of Little Cafterton together with many large privileges and liberties to the fame belonging, king Henry the feventh, on the fourteenth day of May, in the nineteenth year of his reign, granted to Chriftopher Brown, efq; whofe heir of the fame name, enjoys the fame at this day. --- *Ex Autogr. penes Chr. Brown Armig.*

ADDITIONS.

THE Wapentakes or Hundreds remain the fame as they did at the time of the publication of Mr. Wright's Hiftory. A Table of the towns under their refpective hundreds may be feen facing page 1.

Wapentake is a divifion of certain northern counties, particularly thofe beyond the Trent, anfwering to what in other places is called a hundred, or a cantred.

Authors differ as to the origin of the word. Brompton brings it from the Saxon *waepen*, and *taecan*, *to deliver*, by reafon the tenants anciently delivered their arms to every new lord as a token of their homage.

Sir Thomas Smith gives a different account. Mufters, he obferves, were anciently taken of the armour and weapons of the feveral inhabitants of every hundred; and from fuch as could not find fufficient pledges for their good abearing, their *weapons* were taken *away*, and delivered to other.

Others give a different account of its rife; viz. that when firft the kingdom was divided into *wapentakes*, he who was the chief of the divifion, and whom we now call *high-conftable*, as foon as he entered upon his office, appeared in the field, on a certain day, on horfeback, with a pike in his hand; and all the chief men of the hundred met him with their lances; who, alighting, touched his pike with their lances, as a fignal they were firmly united to each other, by the touching of their weapons. Whence the denomination *wapentake*, from the Saxon *waepen*, and *tac*, *touching*. (1)

Our Anceftors the Saxons, expreffed their meaning in a manner which appears very fingular, or ridiculous, to us; but when it is confidered that they had not even names in their own tongue for feveral things, they ought to be looked upon as people of fome ingenuity, --- they had GRAPES; but, having no name for them, they were obliged to call them *Wine-berries:* they likewife had GLOVES; but, having no name for them, were obliged to call them *Hand-fhoes*; as the High Dutch do to this day: and, to mention only one more, they had the article of BUTTER among their delicacies; but having no name for it, they politely called it *Kuofmeer*, i. e. *Cow-fmeer*, or that unguent, which the *cow* afforded, and which they *fmeered* on their bread.

(1) When the *Saxons* conquered *England* they introduced the following mode of government.

Every Chief was allowed a Share in proportion to the number of his tribe, which was afterwards called a Shire, over this Share or Shire was fet a ruler or Earl, in whofe place was afterwards fubftituted a Shire-reeve or Sheriff.—The Shire was divided into three parts, thence called Trythings, now corruptly Ridings, thefe Trythings were divided into Wapentakes or Hundreds, the latter fo called becaufe confifting of a hundred families; over this divifion they placed a governor called a conftable.

The Wapentakes or Hundreds were again divided into Tythings or ten families, called alfo Boroughs, over thefe ten was fet a Tything-man or Head-borough, and, fays *Whitaker*, in this Tything every mafter of a family had nine other mafters of families to be fureties for his behaviour, fo that ten fuch families or Free-holders compofed one; but then fuch a Freeholder, continues he, muft have been mafter of a Townfhip, who with nine others his equals were refponfible for thofe below them.

All thefe Governors were chofen annually and the Tything, Hundred, and Shire, had each a court of Juftice from whence appeals lay to the next fuperior, and fo up to the kings.

Thefe annual governors or prefiding judges of the Courts were alfo the people's Reprefentatives, for when their parliament, called *Wittenagemote*, met they attended it and were members of it, fo that it was fcarcely poffible for human wifdom to devife a jufter mode of government for a nation fo large as that of *Britain*, but this fair form was fadly defaced at the *Norman* Conqueft, for then thefe governors inftead of being elective and annual, became hereditary, which was the very bane of liberty.

Yet admirable as the above fyftem of our rude *Saxon* anceftors was among themfelves, it muft be confeffed that they were cruel conquerors, for they took two thirds of the conquered lands into their own poffeffion, whereas the *Romans* fcarcely received the fifth part of theirs, fo that the poor *Britons*, who were infinitely more numerous than their victors, were little better than flaves, nor fuffered to live in their mafters families, but tilled their lands, and performed other fervile offices for a wretched fubfiftance, having a paltry cot, and a piece of land affigned them, which they held only at the will of their landlords. *L.*

ECCLESIASTICAL GOVERNMENT.

 ONCERNING the Ecclesiastical Government, this county was always under the archdeacon of Northampton, and part of the diocese of Lincoln, till the year 1541, at which time king Henry VIII. erecting a new bishoprick at Peterborough, made John Chambers (the last abbot there) the first bishop of that see, and assigned to his jurisdiction, the archdeaconry of Northampton and Rutland, which last is now one of the rural deaneries of that diocese, having within it's limits forty-nine parish churches, or chapels parochial; five of which, viz. Empingham; Ketton cum Tixover; and Lyddington cum Caldecot, being three prebends belonging to the church of Lincoln, are of peculiar jurisdiction, and exempt from the ordinary.

In the kings book of valuations. There are 31 Rectories, and 12 Vicarages.

In 45 E. 3. (1371.) this county did contain forty-four parishes, out of all which, was paid to the aid then granted in parliament for the wars in France the sum of 255*l.* 4*s.* viz. the sum of 5*l.* 16*s.* from every parish one with another. --- *Stow's Annals Fol.* 268.

I Will now proceed to give an account of the general officers which have been belonging to this county, so far as I can recover their names. And first for the noble earls of Rutland.

But before I mention the history of their persons, I conceive it not improper to say something of their title, and office, or jurisdiction.

Earls, in Latin, Comites, were so called (as all good authors do agree) *à Comitatu sive à Societate Principis qui etiam dici possunt Consules à consulendo.* These were persons of the greatest eminency, and were in continual attendance upon their princes, for matters of council and authority. Some think the name and office came to us as also to the French, from the Roman Emperors, who when that empire was grown to the full strength, begun to have about them a certain privy council, which was called Cæsaris Comitatus, and then those whose counsel they used in war and peace were termed Comites: or rather, (as I find it in another author) those emperors stiled them in war Commilitones, in the court Comites.

By the Saxons they are called Eoldormen, or Eorles, from whence cometh our word Earls, in whose disposition and government (saith Mr. Selden) upon delegation from the king, the county was; the title of earl being then officiary and not hereditary, except in some particular shires. These earls sat in the Scyre mote with the bishop of the diocese twice every year, where charge was given touching God's right and the world's right. . (Or as in another author, *Agantur itaque primo debita veræ Christianitatis jura; secundo Regis placita; postremo causæ singulorum dignis satisfactionibus expleantur.*) But by the conqueror this medling of the bishop in Turnes was prohibited.

These earls were the chief governors or justices of the respective counties under the king, and they received the third part of the profits of the county to themselves, the other two parts going to the king. (I speak not of those earldomes that were palatinate, as Chester after, and Mercland before the conquest; for they had the whole profit.) These earls, who were the king's officers, did exercise in old time very great power, in granting, releasing, and imposing liberties and exactions, which since only the crown hath as inseparably annexed unto it.

But this power, whatsoever it was, together with their third part of the profit of the county is now ceas'd and by time quite worn away. The sheriff being now the king's immediate officer in the several counties, who in former times was only a deputy to the earl; as the name imports, vice comes, or vicount, (of latter times made a title of honour, tho' formerly officiary only) subordinate to the earl, as the earl was to the king. (1)

One remarkable instance of the ancient power of these earls is given by the learned Selden in these words, " I have seen original letters of protection (a perfect and uncommunicable power royal) by that great prince Richard earl of Poiters and Cornwall, brother to Henry 3. sent to the sheriff of Rutland, for and in behalf of a Nunnery about Stamford."

From this authority of Mr. Selden, I think, I may safely make this farther observation; that tho' this county of Rutland, did not give title to any earl before the thirteenth of Richard the second, yet it had virtually an earl long before, who was superior to the

---

(1) The Sheriffs were substituted instead of the Earls, but were totally independant of them, nor does their *Latin* title necessarily imply dependance. *L.*

sheriff

sheriff in Rutland, as the earls were in other counties: and that those whose names we find in the following list of sheriffs during the latter part of the reign of H. 3. and the beginning of E. 1. were but his deputies.

And this seems the more probable, in regard that king H. 3. in the thirty sixth year of his reign, granted the manor and castle of Okeham in this county to the said Richard earl of Cornwall, (who was also king of the Romans) in tail, whose son and successor Edmund earl of Cornwall, in 28 E. 1. died seised of the said castle and manor with several members thereunto belonging, as also of the bailywick or sheriffalty of the county of Rutland, without issue.

EARLS OF RUTLAND.

THE first earl, entitled from this county that I read of, was Edward eldest son to Edmund surnamed of Langley earl of Cambridge, and duke of York, fifth son of king Edward the third. Which Edward was created earl of Rutland, Feb. 25. in the thirteenth year of king Richard the second, but to enjoy that title no longer than his father's life. In the fourteenth year of Richard the second, he was constituted lord admiral, in the next year he was made justice of all the king's forests south of Trent. In the twentieth year of Richard the second he was constituted governor of the isles of Guernsey, Jersey, and Wight, warden of Newforest, constable of Dover castle, and warden of the cinque ports: and in the one and twentieth year of Richard the second, constable of England, and in the same year advanced to the title of duke of Albemarle. Soon after which, upon king Richard's disposal in parliament, held the first year of Henry the fourth, his title of duke was taken from him. Yet afterwards he obtain'd such favour with the king, that in the parliament held the seventh year of Henry the fourth he was restored to his hereditary title of duke of York. This Edward built and endowed the college of Fotheringhay, in which church he was buried, being killed in the battle of Agincourt, the third year of Henry the fifth. He dying without issue, his nephew Richard, eldest son of his younger brother Richard of Coningsborough earl of Cambridge, was found to be his next heir. This Richard was also heir on his mother's side to Edmund Mortimer earl of March, viz. son of Ann daughter of Roger de Mortimer, earl of March, and sister of the said Edmund, who died without issue, the third year of Henry the fifth. This great prince, great by his father, but greater by his mother's side, as being descended from Lionel duke of Clarence, third son of king Edward the third, marryed Cecyly daughter of Ralph Nevil earl of Westmorland, and by her had several sons; among others, Edward earl of March, (afterwards king by the name of Edward the fourth) and Edmund;

Which Edmund was created earl of Rutland; but little enjoy'd that title, being barbarously stabbed by the lord Clifford, presently after the battle of Wakefield, (in which battle his father lost his life) this Edmund being then but twelve years of age, Anno Dom. 1460.

The title of earl of Rutland being thus determined in the males of this royal family, we shall find it however continued to the present possessor by a female. For the abovesaid Richard duke of York, father to king Edward the fourth, had several daughters; of which Ann, the eldest, was married first to Henry Holland duke of Exeter, from whom being divorced (the twelfth year of Edward the fourth) and having no issue by him, she afterwards became the wife of sir Thomas St. Leger, knight, by whom she had one sole daughter and heir, Ann, married to George Manners, lord Roos in right of his mother, sister and coheir to Edmund lord Roos; which George lord Roos dying in the fifth year of Henry VIII. left issue by the said Ann, Thomas Manners lord Roos, who in consideration of his high descent, as above specified, was on the twenty-eighth of June in the seventeenth year of king Henry VIII. advanced to the title and dignity of earl of Rutland, intail to him and his heirs males of his body.

Which said earl Thomas married Alianore daughter of sir William Paston, knight, by whom he had issue Henry his next successor, John who took to wife one of the daughters and coheirs of sir George Vernon of Haddon in com. Derby, Roger, Thomas, and Oliver: and departed this life, September the twentieth, in the five and thirtieth year of Henry the eight.

Henry earl of Rutland, son and heir of the said earl Thomas, was in the second year of Edward the sixth, made constable of Nottingham castle, and chief justice of the forest of Sherwood. In the third and fourth of Philip and Mary, he was made captain general of all the forces then designed against France. In the first of Elizabeth he was constituted lieutenant of the counties of Nottingham and Rutland; and in the third year of that queen, lord president of the council in the north, and installed knight of the most noble order of the garter, and died the seventeenth of September 1563. (5. Eliz.)

Edward

Edward, son and heir of the said Henry, succeeded; who among divers other honours, was in the year 1582, constituted lieutenant of the county of Lincoln, and in the year 1584, installed knight of the garter; and departed this life the fourteenth of April, 1587, without issue male.

Whereupon John his brother, as heir male succeeded to the honour and dignity of earl of Rutland, who, in the nine and twentieth of Elizabeth, was made constable of Nottingham castle, and soon after lieutenant of Nottinghamshire, and died 21 February, 1587, leaving issue Roger, Francis, and George.

Which Roger, succeeding his father, was in the first year of king James made lord lieutenant of Lincolnshire, and sent embassador into Denmark with the order of the garter to that king, and dying without issue the 26 June, 1612

Francis his brother and heir, succeeded, who among divers other honours, was justice in Eire of all the forests north of Trent, and knight of the most noble order of the garter, buried without issue male, the 17 December, 1632. (8. Car 1.)

To whom succeeded sir George Manners, his brother and next heir male, but he dying without issue the nine and twentieth of March, 1641, the title of earl of Rutland did thereupon resort to

John Maners esquire, then seated at Haddon in the county of Derby, as next heir male, viz. son and heir of sir George Maners, son of John Maners, esquire, second son of Thomas first earl of Rutland of this family. Which said earl John departed this life the nine and twentieth of September 1679, full of years and honour.

His only son, John, then commonly called lord Ros (who had been summon'd by special writ to the house of lords in his father's life time, by the title of John lord Maners of Haddon) succeeded: and is the present earl of Rutland, [1684] and lord lieut. of Leicestershire. Which noble lord hath been thrice married, first to the lady Ann Pierpont eldest daughter to Henry marquis of Dorchester; but from her being lawfully divorced by sentence of the court christian, and her issue disabled by act of parliament to inherit to any of his lands or honours, and he also inabled to marry again, he next wedded the lady Diana daughter to Robert earl of Aylesbury, widow of sir Seamour Shirley, baronet, and surviving her, took to wife Catherine daughter to Bapist viscount Campden, by whom he hath issue.

The lineal descent of which noble family from Robert de Todeni, a noble Norman, who built Belvoir castle, com. Leicest. and seated himself there, in the reign of king William the Conqueror, I have here inserted, as follows. *See the Genealogy, here mentioned, facing this page.*

ADDITIONS.

BY the above lady Catharine his grace had two sons and two daughters. The sons were, John lord Roos, born September 18, 1676, who succeeded to his estate and honours; and lord Thomas Baptist Manners, born the 12th of February 1678, but died unmarried in 1705. The daughters were lady Catharine, born May 19, 1675, and married in September 1692 to sir John Leveson Gower, bart. afterwards lord Gower; and Dorothy, born September 13, 1681, wife to Baptist Noel earl of Gainsborough.

He was succeeded by his son John, the second duke of Rutland. He married his first wife, 1693, Catharine, second daughter to the celebrated and unfortunate William lord Russel, by whom he had four sons and four daughters.

The sons were, First, lord John, marquis of Granby, his successor. Second, lord William, born in 1697. Third, lord Thomas, who died in 1723, aged 20. Fourth, lord Edward, who died young. The daughters were, First, lady Catharine, married in 1726 to the right hon. Henry Pelham esq. Second, lady Rachael, who died in 1720-1. Third, lady Frances, married in 1732 to Richard Arundel esq. Fourth, lady Elizabeth wife to John Monckton, viscount Galway, who died in 1729-30. Their mother the duchess died in childbed in 1711.

His second wife was Lucy, sister to Bennet Sherard earl of Harborough, by whom he had five sons and two daughters. The sons were, First, lord Sherard Manners, who died in 1741-2. Second, lord Robert. Third, lord Henry, who died in 1745, twin-brother to fourth lord Charles. Fifth, lord James. The daughters were, First, lady Carolina, married to Henry Harpur esq. and secondly to sir Robert Burdet bart. Second, lady Lucy married to William, duke of Montrose in Scotland, and earl of Belford in England.

His grace, the second duke of Rutland, died the 22d of February, 1720-1, and was buried at Botsford. He was succeeded by his son

John, third duke of Rutland, who was born in 1696. In 1717 he married Bridget, only daughter and heir to Robert Sutton, lord Lexington, by whom he had seven sons and six daughters, First, John marquis of Granby, born in 1720-1, who, when the rebellion broke out in 1745, raised a regiment of foot. In 1759 he was commander in

chief

chief of all his majesty's forces in Germany, where he diftinguifhed himfelf with the greateft honour, judgment, and intrepidity, and no commander in chief, perhaps, ever had a greater fhare than his lordfhip of the love and affection of the troops he commanded. In 1750 he married the lady Frances Seymour, who died in 1760, and his lordfhip by her had a fon John lord Roos, lord Charles, lady Frances, Catharine, another daughter who died very young, and another fon Robert, of whom below. He died univerfally lamented in 1770. The fecond fon of this third duke of Rutland was lord Robert, who took the name of Sutton, on the failure of the former branch, from his uncle lord Lexington, who bequeathed him his eftate. Third, lord George, married, in 1749, to Diana, daughter of Thomas Chaplin of Blankney, in the county of Lincoln, efq. by whom he had iffue George, John, Robert, Charles, &c.; he married, fecondly, Mifs Peart of Lincoln.

The daughters of this third duke all died unmarried.

The prefent fourth duke of Rutland is Charles Manners, who was born March 15, 1754. His grace, when lord lieutenant of Ireland, gained great merit in clofing the unhappy divifions between that nation and England.

He married Dec. 26, 1775, Ifabella Somerfet, fifter to the prefent duke of Beaufort, by whom he has two daughters and three fons; the eldeft is John, the prefent marquis of Granby, born January 3, 1778.

We have to lament the death of the gallant lord Robert Manners, brother to the prefent duke, and fon of the renowned marquis of Granby, who was unfortunately killed, on the twelfth of April 1782, on board his own fhip the Refolution, in that moft defperate engagement in the Weft Indies between the Englifh fleet commanded by fir George Brydges Rodney, and the French fleet under count de Graffe, in which we had two hundred and thirty killed, and feven hundred and fifty-nine wounded. He received feveral fhots in his body while fighting with the utmoft intrepidity, till at laft he nobly fell, lamented by all.

The origin of the furname of this family, is thought by fome to be derived from the village of Manner, in Chefter hundred, in the bifhopric of Durham; others are of opinion it had it's rife from the great number of manors (*maneria*) poffeffed by the family, nothing being more cuftomary, before furnames were general, than for the head of a family to borrow the etymology of his name from ftriking events or circumftances in his life or fituation. There is not the leaft doubt, however, that the family is very ancient, and well known in the northern part of England.

The duke of Rutland has, nor ever had, any manor in this county, excepting that of Byfbrook.

Originally, the title *earl* always died with the man. William the Conqueror firft made it hereditary; giving it in fee to his nobles, and annexing it to fhires or counties; for the fupport of the ftate thereof, he allotted the third penny out of the fheriff's court, iffuing out of all pleas of the fhire from which the *earl* took his title. But, of later days, the matter is much altered.

If Mr. Wright had looked into the firft vol. of the Monafticon Anglicanum, p. 411, he would have difcovered this name and title, *Ego Robertus Com. Roteland*, among the witneffes fubfcribing to the charter of king Henry I. granted to Herebert bifhop of Norwich, and to the monks of the Holy Trinity, A. D. 1101, which is a proof that there were earls of this county before thofe he mentions.

SHERIFFS

SHERIFFS of RUTLAND.

HE firſt Sheriff of this County, of whom I find any mention, is Richard de Humet, Conſtable of Normandy, in the time of King Henry II. to whom that King granted the Cuſtody of this County, in the tenth year of his reign, and therefore it is to be preſumed that Rutland was made a County of it ſelf about that year.

☞ 1168 Richard de Humet, al. Wil. Baſſet. ——— 1188 Willielm. Molduit, al. Almericus Diſpenſer. 1191 Will. Albeney & Will. Freſney, al. Almericus Diſpenſer.

HENRY II.

| 1164 TO 1179 | } Richard de Humet |
| 1180 TO 1888 | } Willielm. Molduit. |

RICH. I.

1190 Anna Brigg.

| 1191 TO 1197 | } Will. Albeney & Will. Freſney: |

1198 Williel. Albeuine, vel Albini.

JOHN.

1200 Benedic. de Haverſam.

1201 TO 1203	} Robertus Malduit.
1204 TO 1210	} Radulp. Normanvil.
1211 TO 1216	} Rober. & Hen. de Brabo.

HENRY III.

1217 Rober. & Hen. de Brabo.

1218 TO 1227	} Allan. Baſſet
1228 TO 1253	} Galfrid. de Rockingham
1254 TO 1258	} Radulph. de Greneham
1259 TO 1272	} Anketyn de Markinal

EDWARD I.

1273 TO 1280	} Pet. Wakervil, & Wil. Bouile
1281 TO 1288	} Alberic. de Whitleler
1289 TO 1301	} Edmund Comes Cornubiæ
1302 TO 1306	} Marg. Vidua Edm. Com. Corn.

EDWARD II.

| 1308 TO 1312 | } Marg. Vid. Edm. Com. Corn. |

1313 TO 1315	} Marg. Vidua Pierce Gaveſton
1316 TO 1321	} Hugo de Audeley, qui duxit in uxorem prædictam Marga.
1322 1323	} John de Aldeburgh
1324 TO 1326	} Edmund Comes Cantii

EDWARD III.

1327 TO 1347	} Hugo de Audely Comes Glouc:
1348 TO 1358	} Wil. de Bohun Com. Northam.
1359 TO 1363	} Willielmus Wade
1364 TO 1372	} Humph. de Bohun
1373 1374	} Johannes de Whitleſborough
1375 1376	} Simon Ward

RICH. II.

1378 Johannes Whittlebury
1379 Thomas de Burton
1380 Johannes Baſings
1381 Willielmus Morwood
1382 Johannes de Whittleſbury
1383 Willielmus Flore
1384 Walterus Scarle
1385 Johannes de Calverley

| 1386 1387 | } Robertus de Veer |

1388 Johannes Whittebury
1389 Walterus Skarles

| 1390 TO 1397 | } Edwardus Com. Rutland |
| 1398 1399 | } Thomas Ondeley |

HENRY IV.

Recorda manca per totum hujus Regnum.

HENRY V.

1413 Thomas Ondeby
1414 Jacobus Bellers
1415 Johannes Boyvill
1416 Thomas Burton, Mil.
1417 Robertus Brown
1418 Robertus Chiſleden
1419 Johannes Penſax

Thomas

In Dugdale's Baron. vol. 1, p. 744, 1218, al. Fulk de Brent. In the ſame vol. p. 384, Baſſet, from 1222 to 1226.

1420 } Thomas Burton, Mil.
1421 }

HENRY VI.

1422 Thomas Burton
1423 Johannes Ondeby
1424 Johannes Davis, Mil.
1425 Johannes Colepeper
1426 Henr. Pleſſington, Mil.
1427 Thomas Burton, Mil.
1428 Johannes Denys
1429 Johannes Colepeper
1430 Thomas Flore
1431 Henr. Pleſſington, Mil.
1432 Johannes Boyvile
1433 Willielmus Beaufo
1434 Rob. Davis & Joha. Pilton
1435 Johannes Branſpath
1436 Hugo Boyvile
1437 Laurentius Sherard
1438 Willielmus Beaufo
1439 Thomas Burton
1440 Henr. Pleſſington, Mil.
1441 Thomas Flore
1442 Willielmus Beaufo
1443 Thomas Barkeley
1444 Johannes Baſings, Mil.
1445 Willielmus Walker
1446 Johannes Boyvile
1447 Willielmus Haſelden
1448 Hugo Boyvile
1449 Robertus Fenne
1450 Thomas Floure
1451 Willielmus Heton
1452 Robertus Sherard
1453 Robertus Fenne
1454 Willielmus Beaufo
1455 Willielmus Haſelden
1456 Thomas Flore
1457 Thomas Dale
1458 Robertus Fenne
1459 Everardus Digby
1460

EDWARD IV.

1461 Johannes Francis
1462 } Thomas Palmer
1463 }
1464 Willielmus Greenham
1465 Thomas Flore
1466 Richardus Sapcots, Mil.
1467 Willielmus Brown
1468 Galfridus Sherard
1469 Johannes Dale
1470 Thomas Flore
1471 Brian Talbot
1472 Thomas Barkley, Mil.
1473 Willielmus Haſelden
1474 Johannes Pilton
1475 Willielmus Brown
1476 Johannes Sapcote
1477 David Malpas
1478 Henry Mackworth
1479 Johannes Pilton
1480 Galfredus Sherard
1481 Willielmus Palmer
1482 David Malpas

EDWARD V.

1483 Willielmus Brown

RICHARD III.

1484 Galfredus Sherard
1485 Johannes Pilton

HENRY VII.

1486 Everardus Digby
1487 Willielmus Brown
1488 David Malpas
1489 Maurice Barkley
1490 Thomas Sapcots

1491 Johannes Digby, Mil.
1492 Robertus Harington
1493 Chriſtopher Brown
1494 Johannes Pilton
1495 Thomas Sherard
1496 Thomas Sapcots
1497 George Mackworth
1498 Robertus Harington
1499 Everardus Digby
1500 Johannes Chiſleden
1501 Chriſtopher Brown
1502 Johannes Digby
1503 Johannes Harington
1504 Mauritius Berkeley
1505 Willielmus Pole
1506 Thomas Sherard
1507 Richard Flowr
1508 Johannes Coly
1509 Everardus Fielding, Mil.

HENRY VIII.

1509 Chriſtopher Brown
1510 Edward Sapcote
1511 George Mackworth
1512 Johannes Harington
1513 Everardus Digby
1514 Thomas Brookeſby
1515 Johannes Caldecot
1516 Johannes Harington
1517 Johannes Digby, M.
1518 Everardus Digby
1519 Willielmus Fielding
1520 Johannes Harrington, Jun.
1521 Johannes Harrington, Sen.
1522 George Mackworth
1523 Johannes Digby, M.
1524 Franciſcus Brown
1525 Johannes Caldecot
1526 Willielmus Fielding
1527 Edwardus Sapcots
1528 Everardus Digby, M.
1529 Edwardus Cateſby
1530 Georgius Mackworth
1531 Edwardus Sapcots
1532 Everardus Digby, M.
1533 Johannes Harington, M.
1534 Georgius Mackworth
1535 Edwardus Sapcots
1536 Andreas Noel, Ar.
1537 Thomas Brudnel, Ar.
1538 Franciſcus Mackworth, Ar.
1539 Richardus Cecil, Ar.
1540 Johannes Harington, M.
1541 Kenelmus Digby, Ar.
1542 Edwardus Sapcots, Ar.
1543 Franciſcus Mackworth, Ar.
1544 Georgius Sherard, Ar.
1545 Anthonius Brown
1546

EDWARD VI.

1547 Anthonius Colly, Ar.
1548 Simon Digby, Ar.
1549 Kenelmus Digby, Ar.
1550 Andreas Noel, Ar.
1551 Anthonius Colly, Ar.
1552 Johannes Harington, M.
1553

MARY.

1554 Kenelmus Digby, Ar.
1555 Simon Digby, Ar.
1556 Franciſcus Mackworth, Ar.
1557 Andreas Noel, Ar.
1558 Anthonius Brown, Ar.

ELIZABETH.

1559 Anthonius Colly, Ar.
1560 Jacobus Harington, M.
1561 Kenelmus Digby, Ar.

Georgius

1562 Georgius Sherard, Ar:
1563 Willielmus Caldecot, Ar.
1564 Georgius Mackworth, Ar.
1565 Johannes Floure, Ar.
1566 Jacobus Harrington, M:
1567 Kenelmus Digby, Ar.
1568 Anthon. Colly, Ar.
1569 Johannes Floure, Ar.
1570 Maurice Berkley, Ar.
1571 Anthon. Brown, Ar.
1572 George Mackworth, Ar.
1573 Thomas Cony, Ar.
1574 Robertus Sapcots, Ar.
1575 Willielmus Caldecot, Ar.
1576 Anthon. Colly, Ar.
1577 Johannes Floure, Ar.
1578 Jacobus Harrington, Mil.
1579 Michael Catesby, Ar.
1580 George Mackworth, Ar.
1581 Willielmus Fielding, Ar.
1582 Rogerus Smith, Ar.
1583 Anthon. Colly, Ar.
1584 Thomas Cony, Ar.
1585 Kenelmus Digby, Ar.
1586 Jacobus Harrington, Mil.
1587 Andreas Noel, Mil,
1588 George Sheffield, Ar.
1589 Robertus Sapcots, Ar.
1590 Henry Herenden, Ar.
1591 Willielmus Fielding, Ar.
1592 Rogerus Smith, Ar.
1593 Jacobus Harrington, Mil.
1594 Johannes Harrington, Mil.
1595 Andreas Noel, Mil.
1596 Willielmus Fielding, Ar.
1597 Henry Ferrers, Ar.
1598 Johannes Harrington, Mil.
1599 Thomas Mackworth, Ar.
1600 Andreas Noel, Mil.
1601 Jacobus Harrington, Mil.
1602 Johannes Harrington, Mil.

JACOBUS.

1603 Willielmus Bodendine, Ar.
1604 Willielmus Bulstred, Mil.
1605 Basil Fielding, Ar.
1606 Henry Berkley, Ar.
1607 Guido Palmes, Ar.
1608 Edwardus Noel, Mil.
1609 Thomas Mackworth, Ar
1610 Willielmus Halford, Ar.
1611 Johannes Elmes, Ar.
1612 Robertus Lane, Mil.
1613 Anthon. Andrews, Ar.
1614 Franciscus Bodinden, Ar.
1615 Edwardus Noel, Mil. & Bar:
1616 Richardus Cony, Mil.
1617 Guido Palmes, Mil.
1618 Abraham. Johnson, Ar.
1619 Richardus Halford, Ar.
1620 Anthon. Colly, Ar.
1621 Edwar. Harington, Mil. & B.

1622 Robertus Lane, Mil.
1623 Robertus Tredway, Ar:
1624 Johannes Osborne, Ar.

CAROLUS I.

1625 Guido Palmes, Mil.
1626 Willielmus Gibson, Ar.
1627 Henr. Mackworth, Ar.
1628 Everardus Falkner, Ar.
1629 Johannes Huggeford, Ar.
1630 Johannes Wingfield, Mil.
1631 Richardus Halford, Ar.
1632 Anthon. Colly, Mil.
1633 Richardus Hickson, Ar.
1634 Franciscus Bodington, Mil.
1625 Henr. Mynne, Mil.
1636 Edwar. Harrington, Mil. & B
1637 Edwardus Andrews, Ar.
1638 Johannes Barker, Ar.
1639 Thomas Leuit, Ar.
1640 Robertus Horsman, Ar.
1641 Thomas Wait, Ar.
1642
1643
1644
1645
1646 Abel Barker, Ar.
1647 Cristoph. Brown, Ar.
1648

CAROLUS II.

1649 ⎫
TO ⎬ *Temporis hoc spatium detur*
1659 ⎭   *Oblivioni*
1660 Eusebius Pelsant, Mil:
1661 Thomas Hartop, Mil.
1662 Richardus Wingfield, Mil:
1663 { Hug. Ducy, Mil. Baln.
   { Willielmus Palms, Ar.
1664 Thomas Mackworth, Bar.
1665 Richardus Rouse, Ar.
1666 Carolus Halford, Ar.
1667 Beaumont Bodenham, Ar.
1668 Walter Moore, Ar.
1669 Edwardus Horsman, Ar.
1670 Andreas Broughton, Ar.
1671 Thomas Pilkington, Ar.
1672 Thomas Barker, Ar.
1673 Johannes Newland, Ar.
1674 Willielmus Atkins, Ar.
1675 Richardus Fancourt, Ar.
1676 Johannes Wallet, Ar.
1677 Samuel Brown, Ar.
1678 Anthonius Palmer, Ar.
1679 Johannes Wingfield, Ar.
1680 Cristopher Brown, Ar.
1681 Thomas Barker, Bar.
1682 Richard Verney, Ar.
1683 Andreas Noel, Mil.
1684 Edwardus Coney, Ar.

     ADDITIONS

ADDITIONS.

SHERIFFS CONTINUED.

1685 Johannes Bullingham, Arm.
1686 Eusebius Buswell, alias, Pelsant, Arm.
1687 Clement Breton, Arm.
1688 William Stafford, Esq.
1689 John Flavell, Esq.
John Flavell, Esq.
1690 John Allen, of Wing, Esq.
1691
1692 William Collins, of Belton, Esq.
1693 William Johnson, Esq.
Richard Halford, Esq.
1694 John Brown, Esq.
Samuel Hunt, Esq.
1695 Armine Bullingham, Esq.
1696 Edward Harrison, Esq.
1697 Sir Thomas Mackworth, Bart.
1698 William Stafford, Esq.
1699 Christopher Clithero, Esq.
1700 Nehemia Tookey, Esq.
1701 Bartholomew Burton, Esq.
1702 John Wingfield, Esq.
1703 Nicholas Bullingham, Esq.
1704 Thomas Burrell, Esq.
1705 Henry Hubbard, Esq.
1706 William Edgson, Esq.
1707 Thomas Cox, Esq.
1708 Henry Smith, Esq. *altered to* William Fancourt, Esq.
1709 Samuel Barker, Esq.
1710 William Fancourt, Esq.
1711 John Sharp, of Wing, Esq.
1712 William Roberts, of Glaiston, Esq.
1713 John Neabond, Esq.
1714 Charles Roberts, Esq.
1715 John Boyal, Esq.
1716 Robert Ridlington, Esq.
1717 John Sismey, Esq.
1718 Thomas Johnson, of Tinwell, Esq.
1719 John Whiteing, Esq.
1720 Francis Wotton, Esq.
1721 Orlando Brown, Esq.
1722 Thomas Roberts, of Wardley, Esq.
1723 Francis Browne, Esq.
1724 George Brushfield, Esq.
1725 William Scott, Esq.
1726 William Algar, of Tixover, Esq.
1727 Charles Tryon Esq.
1728 Edward Wright Esq.
1729 Kenelm Digby, Esq.
1730 William Tampion, Esq.
1731 George Marston, Esq.
1732 Lycester Barrowden, Esq.
1733 William Goding, Esq.
1734 William Fowler, Esq.
1735 Thomas Tomlyn, Esq.
1736 George Cooke, Esq.
1737 Redenhall Pearse, Esq.
1738 Thomas Bradgate, of Uppingham, Esq.

1739 Richard Sharpe, of Wing, Esq.
1740 Edmund Sismey, Esq.
1741 Kenelm Johnson, Esq.
1742 John Brown, Esq.
1743 John Cook, Esq.
1744 Henry Shield, Esq.
1745 Anthony Lucas, Esq.
1746 John Mitchell, Esq.
1747 Thomas Wotton, Esq.
1748 William Chisseldine, of Ridlington, Esq.
1749 Charles Smith, Esq.
1750 Robert Hotchkin, of Uppingham, Esq.
1751 Thomas Wotton, of Ketton, Esq.
1752 Richard Marston, of Belton, Esq.
1753 William Brushfield, Esq.
1754 James Sismey, of Liddington, Esq.
1755 John Maydwell, of Barr Gates, Oakham, Esq.
1756 Robert Tomblin, of Edithweston, Esq.
1757 John Digby, of North Luffenham, Esq.
1758 Thomas Trollop Brown, of Tolthorp, Esq. *altered to* Thomas Hotchkins, of Preston, Esq.
1759 Edward Warden, of Preston, Esq.
1760 Charles Roberts, of Belton, Esq.
1761 Henry Dove, of Tinwell, Esq.
1762 Thomas Sharp, of Langham, Esq.
1763 John Batson, of Empingham, Esq.
1764 Edward Hunt, of Glaston, Esq.
1765 William Lawrence, of Preston, Esq.
1766 James Tiptaft, of Braunston, Esq.
1767 John Ridlington, of Edithweston, Esq.
1768 Henry Shield, of Preston, Esq.
1769 Edmund Sismey, of Liddington, Esq.
1770 John Boyal, of Belmisthorpe, Esq.
1771 Thomas Bullivant, of Ashwell, Esq. *altered to* Sir Gilbert Heathcote, of Normanton, Bart.
1772 Francis Cheselden, Esq.
1773 John Palmer, of Seaton, Esq.
1774 Robert Walker, of Uppingham, Esq.
1775 John Cooke, of Uppingham, Esq.
1776 Henry Sharpe, of Wing, Esq.
1777 Robert Hotchkin, of South Luffenham, Esq.
1778 George Godfrey, of Wardley, Esq.
1779 John Freer, of Oakham, the younger, Esq.
1780 Nedham Cheselden, of Manton, Esq.
1781 Thomas Saunders, of Morcot, Esq.
1782 Tobias Hippisley, of Hambleton, Esq.
1783 John Bellars, of Seaton, Esq.
1784 John Hawkins, of Brook, Esq.
1785 Thomas Falkner, of Morcot, Esq.
1786 Thomas Baines, of Uppingham, Esq.
1787 George Belgrave, of Ridlington, Esq.
1788 William Belgrave, of Uppingham, Esq.

KNIGHTS

SUBSCRIBERS.

The Right Honourable the Earl of Exeter.
Sir John Smith, Baronet.
T. Barker, Efq. Lyndon.
R. I. Sulivan, M. P. for Thames Ditton, Surry.
The Rev. T. Rennel, Prebend of Winchefter.
The Rev. Dr. White, Lavington, Lincolnfhire.
R. Henfon, Efq.
Mr. Everard Digby.
The Rev. C. Johnfon.
The Rev. B. N. Turner.
The Rev. Mr. Fofter.
The Rev. Mr. Healey,
Mr. John Nichols, London.
Mr. Gough, ditto.
Mr. Robert Hunt.
Mr. Robert Weft.

☞ No. II. of this Work, which is in great forwardnefs, will be ornamented with an exact Reprefentation of the Eaft End of that ancient Fabric Tickencoat Church, together with the curious Arch between the Church and Chancel, alfo the wooden figure of the Warrior lying in the Chancel.

It will alfo contain a compleat Lift of the Members of Parliament from the earlieft accounts to the prefent Time.

Any Drawings, or Articles of Information, refpecting this Work, will be thankfully received. --- The Publifher returns his beft Thanks to thofe Gentlemen who have already affifted him, and begs a continuance of their Favours.

Thofe Notes, which have an (L.) for their Signature, were given by Mr. Lowe, of Stamford, Surgeon.

The Genealogical Tables will be given in the laft Numbers, in order to give the different Families an Opportunity of improving them.

Of the Publifher her of may had in 2 vol. with Plates, price 7s.

THE ANTIQUITIES of STAMFORD and St. MARTIN's; with NOTES: To which is added their PRESENT STATE, including a Defcription of BURGHLEY, the Seat of the Earl of Exeter.

The Monthly Review gives the following Account of the Work.

Four reafons are affigned for this publication; The firft is 'The fcarcity of the prefent Hiftories of Stamford. 2d. 'The length of time elapfed fince their publication.' 3d. 'That by methodizing and pruning the redundances of former writers, a Hiftory lefs exceptionable than the preceding might be obtained.' The laft, though, fays our chearful Editor, not the leaft, is --- 'my own private emolument.' Yet he adds, 'as egotifm is a figure of fpeech which no reader is fond of and myfelf being as little fond of it as any reader, I fhall not dwell on this, but infift on the three former heads only.'

It fufficiently appears that a work of this kind was wanting. Mr. Peck, an induftrious antiquary brought down his annals no lower than 1461, and though collected with great care, they will afford but little pleafure except to the profefsed antiquary. Other books of the kind are fhort, defective and yet very fcarce. On fuch accounts taking *Peck* for his ground, and ufing what other helps he could obtain; Mr. Harrod brings down his work to the prefent time. He acknowledges obligation to feveral who have contributed to his affiftance and in particular to the Earl of Exeter, 'for the privilege of confulting his libraries, and for enabling him to give a correct account of his moft valuable pictures; He affigns as a reafon for the fmall fize of his volumes, his opinion, *that a great book is a great evil*. Should any fay that this is arguing againft his own intereft, fince he has fome *Folios* to difpofe of; he replies, he has fome little reafon to lament, with *Fulmer* in the Weft Indian, '*that when I fet up bookfelling the people left off reading.*' * He has beftowed attention and labour on his work, which, though it will admit no doubt of emendations and improvement, is entertaining and informing; and will be particularly acceptable to thofe who have connections with Stamford and it's environs.'

* The Friends of the Publifher will, no doubt, be glad to hear that he has no further reafon to lament, his Hiftory of Stamford having met with a Sale beyond his expectation.

This day is published, Price One Shilling, containing a compleat List of the Sheriffs from the earliest Accounts to the present time, and ornamented with an Engraving of Burley Hall, executed by PAGE,

No. II of

WRIGHT's

ANTIQUITIES

OF

RUTLAND,

With Additions ;

Bringing it down to the present Time,

By W. HARROD.

☞ The Publisher did not intend to have printed this Work by Subscription, having observed that Applications to the Public on this business are too often treated with indifference and inattention --- the Advice of his Friends, however, added to the unsolicited number of respectable Names, have set aside this objection, and he now humbly solicits the Patronage of the Public, hoping that the List of Subscribers on the cover of each succeeding Number will be ornamented with the addition of kind Encouragers, the perusal of which cannot fail of inspiring him with GRATITUDE.

Stamford: Printed by W. HARROD, 1788.

THIS Noble Mansion is built of fine freestone which was fetched with great labour and expence from Clipsham and Ketton. The north and south fronts are exactly similar, being 196 feet in length; the east and west fronts are also similar, and in length 96 feet. The grand terrace to the south commands a fine prospect of rich country, fine vales and hanging woods, and this grand terrace, it is thought, exceeds every thing of the kind in the kingdom, being nearly 300 yards long and 30 wide, from whence you descend by several flights of steps into an extensive vale of fine hanging woods, &c.

To the north is the grand entrance to this elegant house, which is singular and grand, surpassing every thing of the kind in this kingdom, and perhaps in Europe. You enter a noble court, by two handsome lodges, which is spacious and striking, being 800 feet from these lodges in a straight line to the hall door : to the left is a handsome line of stables, and to the right are other offices answerable --- from these offices you enter a beautiful circular colonade of great length supported by Doric columns, which carries you to the house.

This Noble Palace has lain in a neglected state many years during the present Earl's minority, who has already done considerable repairs, having fitted up a new dining room, drawing room, &c. with great taste, and new sashed the lower part of the house which gives great life to the building.

There is a fine painted room on the first floor called the Salloon, which is more admired for it's magnificent and fine proportion than for the value of it's paintings which represent the History and Wars of Julius Cæsar : the length of this fine room, which extends the whole depth of the house from north to south, is 65 feet long, 36 wide, 28 high, and was painted by Lanscroon, pupil of Verrio, who painted many excellent rooms and compositions the work of many years at Burghley near Stamford.

The Library is of great length, and contains, besides a valuable collection of Books, some curious subjects in Anatomy and Natural History, and many valuable Portraits of this ancient family.

....

* *The above Account is the best that can be procured at present — it is intended to speak more largely on the subject in it's proper place. The publisher will be very thankful for further information.*

ERRATUM. In page IV. line 26, dele the words, *this has nearly if not quite lost it's name, perhaps the Catmose.*

East End of *TICKENCOTE CHURCH*.

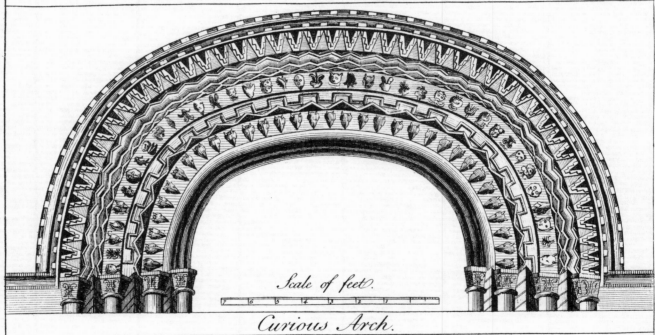

Scale of feet.

Curious Arch.

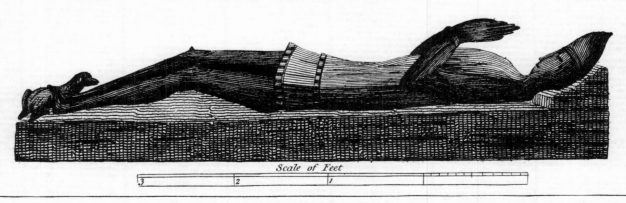

Scale of Feet

Figure of a MAN in WOOD.

T. Espin delt. 1788.

Publifh'd June 1ft. 1789, by W. Harrod, of Stamford.

Regn. HEN. IV.

1 Rogerus Flore, Johan. Durant
2 Johan. Durante, Williel. Onteby
4 Tho. Ondeby, Rogerus Flore
5 Tho. Thorp, Joh. Penfax
6 Tho. Ondeby, Johan. Flore
8 Johan. Penfax, Rober. Scarle
9 Rober. Brewe, Williel. Sheffield

The records are wanting during the refidue of this king's reign, and in like manner are they imperfect as to feveral years in the reigns of H. 5. H. 6. and E. 4.

Regn. HEN. V.

1 Johan. Penfax, Johan. de Burgh. *Weft.*
2 Rogerus Flore, Rober. Brewe. *Leic.*

This Roger Flore efq. was fpeaker in the houfe of commons in the 4th, fifth, and 7th years of this king.

3 *Roger Flore, —— Playnell*
3 Rober. Brewe, Williel. Sheffield
8 *Tho. Burton, Hen. Plefington, knights*
9 Johan. Culpepir, ar. Tho. Grenham, ar.

Regn. Hen. VI.

1 Hen. Plefington, mil. Roger. Flore, ar.
3 Tho. Burton, Henr. Plefington, *knights*
5 Tho. Burton, mil. Johan. Colepepir, ar.
7 Rober. Browe, Johan. Boyvile
13 Johan. Browe, Williel. Beaufo
20 Joha. Braunfpath, ar. Will. Heyton, ar.
25 Hugo Boyvile, Everard Digby
27 Everard Digby, Joh. *Browarm*
28 Everardus Digby de Stokedri, Robertus Frene de Exton
29 Tho. Palmer, Everardus Digby, arm.
32 —— *Thorpe, ar.*
38 Johan. Browe, Johan. Boyvile
38 Everardus Digby, ar. Radu Beaufo, ar.

Regn. EDW. IV.

7 Johan. Browe ar. Joha. —— ar.
12 Brian Talbot ar. Joha. Pilton

The writs, returns and indentures from the 12th of Ed. 4. to the firft of queen Mary are all thought to be loft. *Prin. Bre. Parl. rediviva, p.* 203.

The following names I have collected from the records remaining in the chapel of the rolls, but the returns for feveral parliaments are wanting; fuch as are to be found are

33 HEN. 8th, *Joh. Harrington, Sim. Digby, efqrs.*

Regn. EDW. VI.

1 Kenelm Digby ar. Anthon. Colly, ar.
7 *The fame.*

Regn. MARY.

1 Andre. Noel, ar. Kenelm Digby, ar. *Weft.*
1 Anthon. Colly, ar. Johan. Hunt. ar. *Oxon.*

Regn. PH. & MA.

1,2 Jaco. Harrington, ar. Anthon. Colly, ar.
2,3 Jaco. Harrington, ar. Kenel. Digby, ar.
4,5 Idem.

Regn. ELIZ.

1 Idem.
5 *Anthony Colly, John Flore, efqrs.*
13 *Kenelm Digby, Joh. Harrington, efqrs.*
14 Jaco. Harrington, mil. Kenel. Digby, ar.
27 *Kenelm Digby, And. Noel*
28 *J. Harrington, And. Noel*
31 Jaco. Harrington, mil. And. Noel, mil.
35 *The fame.*
39 *The fame.*
43 Joh. Harrington, mil. And. Noel, mil.

The returns for the whole reign of king James are wanting.

JAMES.

1 *J. Harrington, knight of the Bath. W. Bulftrode*
12 *W. Bulftrode, knight, Guido Palmes knight*
18 *The fame.*
21 *The fame.*

Regn. CAR. I.

1 *The fame.*
1 Will. Bulftrode mil. Fran. Bodenham, mil.
3 Guido Palmes, mil. Will. Bulftrode, mil.
15 Baptifta Noel, ar. Guido Palmes, mil.
16 Idem. *(both expelled for their loyalty, and in their places James Harrington knight, and col. Tho. Wayte, both regicides.)*

Regn. CAR. II.

12 Phil. Sherard ar. Sam. Brown, ar.
13 Edward. Noel, ar. Phil. Sherard ar.
30 Phil. Sherard, ar. Tho. Mackworth bart.
31 Phil. Sherard, ar. Abellus Barker, bart.
32 Tho. Mackworth bart. in loco Abelli Barker, defunct.
33 Phil. Sherard, ar. Edward Fawkener, ar. *Oxon.*

Regn. JAC. II.

1 Baptifta Noel ar. Tho. Mackworth bart.

WILL. & MARY.

1 *Thomas Mackworth bart. Bennet Sherard efq.*

N. B. *Thofe Words which are printed in Italics in the above Lift are Additions and Corrections extracted by the Publifher from a Copy of Wright's Antiquities having M. S. Notes.*

ADDITIONS.

ADDITIONS

1681 Hon. Philip Sherard, Edward Faukener
1685 Baptift Noel, Sir Thomas Mackworth, bart.
1688 Sir Thomas Mackworth, bart, Bennet Sherrard.
1690 Sir Thomas Mackworth, bart. *dead.* Bennet Sherrard.
     Sir Thomas Mackworth, bart.
1695 John lord Burghley, Bennet Sherrard.
1698 John lord Burghley, Richard Halford.
1700 Sir Thomas Mackworth, bart. Richard Halford.
1701 The fame.
1702 The fame.
1705 The fame.
1707 The fame.
1708 Philip Sherrard, Richard Halford.
1710 Hon. John Noel, *not duly elected,* Daniel lord Finch.
     Richard Halford
1713 Daniel lord Finch, Bennet lord Sherrard.
1714 Daniel lord Finch, *an Off. and re.* Hon. John Noel, *dead.*
                              John marquis of Granby, *a peer.*
                              Sir Thomas Mackworth, bart.
1722 Sir Thomas Mackworth, bart. Daniel lord Finch.
1727 Daniel lord Finch, *a peer,* John Noel, *dead.*
     William Burton, Thomas Noel.
1734 Hon. James Noel, Thomas Noel.
1741 Hon. John Finch, Hon. James Noel.
1747 Brownlow lord Burghley, Hon. James Noel, *dead.*
                     Thomas Noel.
1754 Brownlow lord Burghley, *a peer,* Thomas Noel.
     George Bridges Brudenell
1761 Thomas Noel, Hon. Thomas Chambers Cecil.
1768 Thomas Noel, George Bridges Brudenel.
1775 Thomas Noel, George Bridges Brudenell.
1780 Thomas Noel, *dead,* George Bridges Brudenell.
     G. N. Edwards.

Lord Lieutenants of this County.

IN the firft year of queen Elizabeth Henry earl of Rutland was conftituted lord lieutenant for the counties of Nottingham and Rutland.

In the twelfth of the faid queen Henry earl of Huntingdon was conftituted lieutenant of the counties of Leicefter and Rutland: and again in the 17th of the faid queen.

In the 38th year of the faid queen George earl of Huntingdon fecond brother and heir to the former earl was conftituted lieutenant of the faid counties; and again in the firft year of king James.

In the 12th year of king James Henry earl of Huntingdon, grandfon and heir to the aforefaid earl George, was conftituted lieutenant of the faid counties; fo alfo in the firft of king Charles I.

In the 14th of Car. I. Ferdinando lord Haftings, eldeft fon to the laft mentioned earl Henry, was joined with his father in the lieutenancy of the faid counties.

In the 12th year of our now fovereign king Charles II. Baptift lord vifcount Campden was conftituted lord lieutenant of the county of Rutland, being the firft lord lieutenant of this county apart by itfelf.

In the 34th year of our now fovereign, upon the death of the faid lord, his fon and heir the right honourable Edward then vifcount Campden, and foon after created earl of Gainfborough, was conftituted lord lieutenant of this county of Rutland and Cuftos Rotulorum of the fame.

Thus far of the county in general; I come now to treat of the feveral towns, villages, and places of note, particularly. [Thus far Mr. WRIGHT.]

ADDITIONAL LIST OF LORD LIEUTENANTS.

Bennet, Earl of Harborough, who died in 1732.
Baptift, Earl of Gainfborough, who died in 1751.
Brownlow, Lord Burghley, now Earl of Exeter, [1789]
And the prefent is George Earl of Winchilfea and Nottingham.

The

The Names of the Gentry of this County returned by the Commiſſioners in the twelfth year of King Henry VI.

William Biſhop of Lincoln,
William de Souche de Harringworth, *chiv.*
Thomas Grenham,
William Beaufo, } *Knights for the ſhire.* } Commiſſioners to take the Oaths.

Johannes Baſinges de Empyngham, mil.
Johannes Colepepar, de Exton, mil.
Henricus Pleſington de Burley, mil.
Robertus Browne de Wodehead, ar.
Robertus Davis de Tykencoat, ar.
Johannes Browne de Tygh, ar.
Johannes Pleſington de Wiſſenden, *ar.*
Thomas Flore de Oakham, *ar.*
Franciſcus Clerke de Stoke-dry, ar.
Johannes Chycelden de Brameſton, ar.
Johannes Sapcoat de Ketton, merchant.
Robertus Whitwell de eadem, gentleman.
Johannes Clerk de Wiſſenden, merchant.
Willielmus Lewis de Oakham, merchant.

Johannes Brigge de eadem, merchant.
Joh. Baſſet de North Luffenham, gent.
Jacobus Palmer de eadem, gent.
Johannes Palmer de eadem, gent.
Willielmi Sheffeild de Seyton, gent.
Johannes Sadington de eadem, gent.
Rob. Souſex de Market Overton, gent.
Johannes Vowe de Whitwell, gent.
Willielmus Pochon de Wiſſenden, gent.
Willielmus Swafeld de Braunſton, gent.
Henricus Breton de Keton, gent.
Willielmus Uffington de Pilton, gent.
Thomas Luffenham de Winge.

The Diſtances of ſeveral Places in Rutland meaſured by a Wheel.

	M.	F.	P.
ASHWELL to Whiſſendine,	2	3	4
Brook to Egleton,	2	2	0
Caldecote to Liddington,	2	2	24
Stoke dry,	2	7	32
Great Caſterton to Tickencote,	0	7	23
Scotgate,	1	7	13
Clipſham to Stretton,	1	4	0
Cotteſmore to Aſhwell,	2	3	20
Barrow,	1	4	14
Hall to Burley,	2	5	16
Clipſham,	5	0	32
Greetham,	1	5	9
Market Overton,	2	4	0
Oakham,	4	2	17
Stretton by Greetham,	3	6	16
Thiſtleton,	3	2	4
Empingham to North Luffenham,	3	7	32
Whitwell,	1	6	20
Exton court yard gate to Burley,	3	0	0
Cotteſmore,	2	1	30
Egleton,	4	0	22
Empingham,	2	6	36
Church to Burley court yard, eaſt gate,	2	4	1
Empingham church,	2	7	0
Greetham,	2	3	0
Manton,	5	1	32
Okeham,	4	1	1
Tickencote,	4	6	23
Tinwell,	6	4	28
Whiſſendine,	7	1	0
Whitwell,	1	5	0
Wing,	6	1	3
Langham to Barleythorpe,	1	0	0
Whiſſendine,	2	4	15
Morcot to Glaiſton,	1	1	30
North Luffenham,	1	6	20
Okeham to Barleythorpe,	1	0	26
Peter's gate to Tinwell,	1	2	4
Preſton to Manton,	2	1	0
Riddlington to Aiſton,	1	4	16
Brook,	2	1	0
Stoke dry to Beaumont Lodge,	2	0	24
Teigh to Barrow,	2	2	12
Market Overton,	1	6	26
Thiſtleton to Greetham,	2	4	0
Market Overton,	1	7	32
Uppingham to Aiſton,	1	0	20
Beaumont Lodge,	1	4	8
Glaiſton,	2	1	14
Liddington,	1	7	16
Preſton,	2	0	8
Wing,	3	0	0

As ſeveral lordſhips have been incloſed ſince the above meaſurement was taken, alterations may have been made in ſome of the diſtances, particularly between Preſton and Manton, and north of the town of Greetham.

Meaſurement of the turnpike road from the ſouth-eaſt corner of Kettering bowling Green near the 75th mile ſtone, to the Crown inn Oakham.

	M.	F.	P.
Guide poſt in Glen lane,	1	7	4
Barford bridge,	3	0	22
Oakley guide poſt,	4	5	20
Single inn,	4	6	26
Pond at the entrance of the Leap,	5	7	0
The Swallow hole,	6	2	1
Jones's Lodge,	6	4	0
Cottage pond and guide poſt.	7	1	3
Rockingham caſtle gate to the ſhyre,	8	3	16
Rockingham croſs,	9	0	30
Rockingham bridge,	9	3	30
Caldecot nether croſs,	10	3	11
Caldecot church,	10	4	36
Liddington church,	12	6	24
Liddington croſs,	12	7	14
Uppingham church,	14	4	3
Preſton town pond,	16	5	0
Preſton bridge,	17	3	24
Manton bridge,	18	6	20
Entrance of Oakham lordſhip,	20	4	26
The Crown Inn,	21	2	4

Alterations have been made on Rockingham Shyre and in Great Eaſton meadow ; the road now goes by Stoke park wall (not by Liddington) and is turned much ſtraighter between Preſton and Manton.

Meaſurement of the Turnpike Road from Leiceſter to Wanſford.

Humberſton bridge,	1 mile
Saltersford bridge,	2 and a quarter
Buſhby,	4
Houghton,	5 and an half
Billeſdon,	8 and an half
Skeffington,	10
Tugby,	11 and an half
Eaſt Norton,	13
Fincet bridge,	14
Alexton,	15
Wardley,	16
Beaumont chace,	18
Uppingham,	19
Glaiſton,	21
Morcot,	22 and an half
Barrowden,	24
Tixover,	26
Duddington,	27
Badgates,	29
Sipperton,	31 and an half
North road at Wanſford,	32 and an half

RYALL.

R Y A L

IES in the Eaſt Hundred. Before the conqueſt Godive, a widow, who became the ſecond wife of Siward earl of Northumberland, gave for the health of her ſoul (by conſent of king Edward the confeſſor) Righale and Boelmeſthorpe, to the abbey of Peterborough; but after her death the ſaid Siward obtained the lordſhip of Righale, by agreement with the ſaid monks, to hold for his life, and after to return to the abby.

At the conqueror's ſurvey, Judith counteſs of Huntington (who married Waltheof ſon of the abovementioned Siward earl of Northumberland) held of the king one hide and a half in Ryal, of arable land, eight carucates *cum appendicis*, in demeſne one carucate, four ſervants, ten villains, and four ſockmen poſſeſſing four carucates. Here were alſo at that time two mills of 26s. and a wood of four furlongs in length and two in breadth. To this manor did then appertain Belmeſthorpe, both being at that time valued at 6l. --- *Domeſd. Nort n.* 56.

This eſtate did once belong to Reginald earl of Bollen, who dying, king Henry III. by his charter dated at Abingdon Auguſt 22d in the eleventh year of his reign *(donec illud hæredi ipſius Reginaldi redidderimus)* gave the manor of Ryal to Hugh Deſpenſer an eminent baron in thoſe days, whoſe grandſon, a ſecond Hugh, held the ſaid lordſhip of that king in free farm, and in the fortieth year of the ſaid king Henry III. was made governor of Hareſton caſtle in the county of Derby. This laſt mentioned Hugh was father to Hugh Deſpenſer ſenior, who with his ſon Hugh Deſpenſer junior, were the two great favorites of that unfortunate prince king Edward II. but for ill uſing their power with him were both baniſhed in parliament, 15 E. 2. Notwithſtanding this the younger Spencer obtained the next year a formal revocation of that ſentence under the king's great ſeal, as alſo a ſpecial protection from any diſturbance whatſoever by reaſon thereof, and became more in favour than ever, with the grants of many new honours and eſtates, among which a new grant of this manor of Ryal, though not long after they both ſuffered the ignominious death of traitors. --- *Baron Eng. Vol. I.* 389. 392.

In the firſt of Edward III. Edmund earl of Kent, ſurnamed of Woodſtock, ſecond ſon to king Edward I. obtained a grant of this manor, of which lordſhip he died ſeiſed, being executed for treaſon in the fourth year of Edward III. leaving iſſue Edmund and John his ſons, both which departing this life without iſſue, Joan their ſiſter, then wife of ſir Thomas Holland knight, was found to be the next heir, which ſir Thomas died ſeiſed of this manor in right of his wife in the thirty-fifth of Edward III. but the ſaid Joan ſurviving became ſoon after the wife to Edward the Black Prince.(1) The forementioned ſir Thomas Holland having in his life time aſſumed the title of earl of Kent in his wife's right, left iſſue Thomas earl of Kent his ſon and heir, who after his mother's death in the ninth of R. II. obtained a ſpecial livery of all the lands of his mother's inheritance, among which were Ryal and Whiſſendine both in this county, and of both died ſeiſed in the twentieth of R. II. leaving iſſue Thomas Holland his ſon and heir, which Thomas was afterwards in the twenty-firſt of R. II. created duke of Surry, though from that great title again depoſed in the firſt of Henry IV. and ſoon after, viz. on Wedneſday after the feaſt of the Epiphany in the ſame year endeavouring a rebellion againſt that king he loſt his life; after whom Edmund his brother ſucceeded in the honour and moſt part of thee ſtate, by reaſon of an ancient entail; which Edmund was killed at the ſiege of Briack in Normandy in the ninth of H. IV. being at that time ſeiſed of this manor. His eſtate was afterwards divided among ſeveral heirs general, he leaving no iſſue of his own.

(1) Sir *Thomas Holland* with his wife *Joan*, the fair maid of *Kent* were buried in the Grey Friary at *Stamford*, ſhe not chuſing to be buried near her laſt huſband, although a prince and a man of great fame. *L.*

A   Mr.

The prefent lord of this manor is the right hon. John Earl of Exeter.

Mr. Camden tells us that in former ages one Tibba, whom he calls *Minorum gentium Sancta*, was here at Ryal, like a fecond Diana, worfhipped by falconers, as the patronefs of hawking. But upon what authority he delivers this he expreffes not. Certain it is that this St. Tibba was a virgin-anchoreffe at Godmanchefter, a kinfwoman of Penda king of Mercia, and lived in or about the year of Chrift 696, of fo great reputation for piety that our hiftorical poet Michael Drayton, enumerating all the holy women among our anceftors the Englifh Saxons, wrote thus,

> —— And to thefe Saint Tibba let us call,
> In folitude to Chrift that paft her whole delight,
> In Godmanchefter made a conftant anchorite;
> Amongft which of that houfe for faints that reckoned be,
> Yet never any one more graced the fame than fhe.

How this character agrees with a fecond Diana, or how St. Tibba came from Godmanchefter to be worfhipped in Rutland, I know not.(1)

The family of the *Bodenhams* have, for feveral defcents enjoyed a fair eftate of freehold in this town, the pedigree of which worfhipful family may be feen facing this page.

Of the ADVOWSON.

IN the fifth of E. III. John bifhop of Lincoln did certify the vicarage of the church of Ryal, (which church was at that time appropriated to the priory of St. Andrew's of Northampton) to confift in the tithes of wool, milk, lambs, poultry, fwine, geefe, calves, fheep, &c. two yard land, tithes of hay and mills, and in a penfion of two marks.

IN THE CHURCH.

On two handfome Monuments erected in the Eaft end of the Chancel, are engraved the following Infcriptions.

Ultimum Chrifti adventum hic expectat *Gulielmus Bodenham* eques auratus. Duas habuit uxores, *Sence* filiam *Francifci Harington* de *South Witham* in com. *Lincol.* armigeri unam ex hæredibus matris fuæ *Barbaræ Sutton* de *Aram* in com. *Nott.* & *Ifabellam* filiam *Jacobi Quarlis* de *Ufford* in com. *Northam.* armigeri. Ultimam hujus lucis ufuram amifit, An. Dom. 1613.

Ultimum Chrifti adventum hic expectant *Francifcus Bodenham* alias *Bodenden* eques auratus & duæ ejus uxores quarum prima fuit *Penelope* filia *Edwardi Wingfield* de *Kimbolton Caftle* equitis aurati, fecunda *Theodocia* filia prænobilis *Francifci* domini *Haftings* de *Afhby de la Zouch.* Ultimam hujus lucis ufuram amiferunt annis 1625, 1645, 1671.

(1) *Howgrave* thought that the Hunting found *Tantivy* originated from her name; and *Stukeley* writes that her cell was in the north-weft corner of *Rihall* church. *L.*

ADDITIONS.

ADDITIONS

RYAL is a pleafant village about two miles north-eaft of Stamford, through which runs the river Guafh, and is alfo feated very near the turnpike road which leads from Stamford to Lincoln through Bourn, Fokingham, Sleaford, and Branfwell.

The lordfhip, which is not enclofed, confifts more of arable than pafturage, the foil of which is chiefly light. The feat of the Earl of Exeter would be feen to great advantage from this village if it were not in part hidden by thofe venerable trees which furround it.

A feaft or wake is held here yearly on the Sunday after *St. Luke*.

The number of fouls in Ryal, with Belmifthorpe, (a member of the parifh) amounted, in the year 1785, to three hundred and feventy three; of which two hundred and twenty five were above fourteen years of age, and one hundred and forty eight were under that age: eleven perfons then received collection; now there are not fo many paupers.

The name of this village was formerly fpelt *Royal*, and as the manor feveral times came into the hands of our kings, it might probably take it's name from being a *Royal Manor, &c.*

THOMAS BURREL Efq. had an eftate here which is now defcended to the Reverend THOMAS FOSTER the prefent Incumbent.

At the weft end of the church is a fpire built of ftone in which are five bells, on which are the following infcriptions.

I. *Thos. Norris made me*, 1633.
II. *Omnia fiant ad Gloriam Dei*, 1627.
III. *Non Clamor fed Amor cantat in Aure Dei*, 1626.
IV. *Gloria Deo Soli*, 1729.
V. *Thos. Norris made me*, 1633.

The following is copied from BACON's LIBER REGIS, 4to, pub. in 1786.

Clear Yearly Value.	King's Books.
31l. 10s. 0d.	13l. 17s 0d.

Royal alias Ryhall, V. (St. John the Evangelift) with
Effenden Cap. (St. Mary.) Prox. Epifc. 3s. 6d.
Pri. Sancti And. Northamp. Propr. Lord Exeter,
1711. Earl of Exeter, 1773. Difcharged.

THOMAS HARRISON, Clerk, was prefented to the living by the late EARL of EXETER in the year 1777, and refigned it in July 1773.

THOMAS FOSTER, Clerk, was prefented by the prefent EARL in the year 1773.

PRESENT LORD OF THE MANOR,
The Right Honourable BROWNLOW EARL OF EXETER.

It appears from the poll-book of the High Sheriff, that at the contefted election of Knights of a fhire for this county, between Lord Finch, Mr. Halford, Mr. Noel, and Mr. Sherrard, taken October 16, 1710, that eleven freeholders polled from this parifh; and again, at the conteft in 1722, between Lord Finch, Sir Thomas Mackworth and Mr. Sherrard, that fourteen freeholders polled.

ANNUAL ACCOUNT OF MARRIAGES, BIRTHS, AND BURIALS IN THIS PARISH.

A.D.	Mar.	Bir.	Bur.	A.D.	Mar.	Bir.	Bur.	A.D.	Mar.	Bir.	Bur.
1784	2	13	16	1794				1804			
1785	7	12	8	1795				1805			
1786	—	13	5	1796				1806			
1787				1797				1807			
1788				1798				1808			
1789				1799				1809			
1790				1800				1810			
1791				1801				1811			
1792				1802				1812			
1793				1803				1813			

RYAL.

MONUMENTAL INSCRIPTIONS.

IN THE CHURCH.

IN THE CHANCEL.*

On a mural Monument.

Memoriæ facrum Bellomontius Bodenhamus armiger, Equeftris Familia oriundus, vir fummi candoris, integritatis fidei, cum per quadraginta, plus minus, annos omnia Vitæ Chriftianæ ac civilis officia quantum fert humana imbecilitas compleviffet heic tandem placide in Domino requiefcens, fecundum Salvatoris fui adventum beatæ eternitatis canditatis expectat heu prifca fides, fanctaque veritas quando ullum habetis parem? Cui pietatis et amoris ergo, coniux meftiffima Elizabetha Bodenhama præfens monumentum poni curavit: ter lector benevole poft defletas huius copulæ partes, tam fuperftitem quam ereptum, abi profpere in rem tuam. Obiit i die viibris. anno Chrifti MDCLXXXI.

On a neat Monument. --- Sacred to the Memory of THOMAS HARRISON, D. D. Rector of Cafterton Magna and Market Overton, and late vicar of this place, all in this county. He departed this life on the 10th day of Auguft 1782, aged 87. He married Mary relict of the late Wm. Byott; fhe was only daughter and heirefs of Thomas Luck efq. of Kennet-Hall in Cambridgefhire. His fecond wife was Margaret fecond daughter of John Wingfield efq. of Tickencote in this county. He was a man of a moft amiable difpofition, a good Chriftian, a tender hufband, one of found learning and ftrict integrity.

> When on the borders of the gloomy grave,
> Beyond all power of human art to fave,
> Calm and collected he refigned his breath,
> Put off mortality and fmiled in death.

Near to the laft mentioned,

To the happy memory of SAMUEL the fon of EDM. BARKER Vicar of this Church, of the family of Edmund Barker of Otley in the county of York gent. and of Frances the daughter of Samuel Brown of Stockin-Hall of this county efq; and Ann his wife. He was a child of admirable fweetnefs of temper, of an erect and comely body, of a moft pregnant wit, even beyond what could be imagined at the age of two years and fifteen days, at which time he departed this life October 30, 1696.

On a flab in the floor. --- Here repofe the remains of MARY BADDELY, daughter of Robert and Mary Tipping, who died the 21ft of June 1780, aged 70.

On a flab in the floor. --- Here lieth the body of ROBERT COPE who died May 24, 1777, aged 59.

On a flab in the floor. --- Here lie the remains of SUSANNAH COPE who departed this life the 13th of July 1776, aged 51

On a flab in the floor. --- Here lies the body of ELIZBETH HARRISON, daughter of John Templar, D. D. and wife of Willm. Harrifon rector of Snailwell, Cambridgefhire. Ob. May 1, 1729, Æt. 64.

On a brafs plate within the altar rails. --- JANE FOSTER died Sep. 15, 1783, aged 73.

On a flab within the altar rails. --- In Memory of MARY relict of the Rev. ROBERT TIPPING, who departed this life Feb. 5, 1744, in the 67th year of her age.

Near to it, on a flab. --- Here lieth interred the Body of Robert Tipping, vicar of this church, who departed this life May 4th 1727, aged 44.

Near to it, on a flab. --- MARGARET TIPPING died Aug. 3, 1760, aged 56.

On a flab which formerly had a brafs plate upon it. Here lieth the body of Mr. Edward Mallory, who departed April 6, 1703.

Here lieth the body of Francis Thirkill gent. who was here interred Nov. 29, 1678.

Thomas Harrifon, D. D. 1782.

---

* In the chancel are feveral Monuments of the very antient Family of the *Bodenhams*, (of which only the above is legible,) defcendants of *Hugo de Bodham* in tne county of *Hereford*, the Pedigree of which Family, from the year 1154 to the year 1621, is in the poffeffion of the prefent Vicar of this place.

IN THE BODY OF THE CHURCH.

On a square stone against the wall at the west end. --- Beneath here lie interred the Remains of Sarah Moisey, who departed this life September 24, 1781, in her 76th year.

ON THE FLOOR.

Here lieth interred the body of John Lowth who departed this life October 3, 1784, in the 40th year of his age.

Here lieth interred the body of Susannah Lowth, who departed this life Jan. 4, 1783, aged 42.

In Memory of Paul Lowth who died July 2, 1777, aged 73.

Also Susanna, Wife of Paul Lowth, who died March 24, 1785, aged 75.

In Memory of Mary Moisey who departed this life Dec. 20, 1775, in her 77th year.

In Memory of Sarah, the wife of Richard Moysey, who departed this life Jan. 2, 1761, in the 85th year of her age.

In Memory of Richard Moysey who departed this life Dec. 27, 1738, in his 61st year.

Here lieth interred the Body of Rebecca Moysey who departed this life Feb. 19, 1786 aged 72.

Here lieth interred the Body of John Moysey who died Nov. 2, 1782, in his 73d year.

IN THE CHURCH YARD.

On an angular stone over the grave. -- In Memory of Priscilla, wife of John Measure, who died June 19, 1760, aged 53.

ON HEAD STONES.

Mary Clarke died April 20th 1779, aged 55.

Thomas Clark died December 17th 1775, aged 52.

James Thistilton died September 18th 1761, aged 46.

Alice the wife of Edwd. Owen died July 26 1750, aged 65.

Edwd. Owen Gent. died Nov. 22d 1767, aged 71.

Eliz. the wife of Edwd. Clark late of Southwark London died May 28, 1762, aged 74.

Amy, the wife of John Flowers, died April 29, 1746, aged 36.

John Flowers died June 4, 1762, aged 56.

Mary the wife of Thomas Hunt died Dec. 16, 1767, aged 58.

John Hunt died Nov. 6, 1755, aged 67.

John Turlington died Feb. 20, 1773, aged 52.

Johannah wife of John Turlington died Jan, 20, 1783 aged 82.

Wm. Watson died May 10, 1741, aged 29.

Anthony Watson senior died May 20, 1743, aged 63.

Eleanor the wife of Anthony Watson died Sep. 11, 1748, aged 70.

Anthony Watson Junior died May 10, 1778, aged 55.

Wm. Watson died June 6, 1751, aged 60.

Also Elizabeth his wife died Oct, 4, 1765, aged 56. Likewise 4 Sons and 3 Daughters who died in their Infancy.

Ann the wife of Thomas Beecham died June 21, 1778, aged 34.

Also John the son of Thomas and Ann Beecham died June 22, 1778, aged 6 months.

Wm. Stafford died Jan, 4, 1775, aged 36.

Also Sarah daughter of Wm. and Ann Stafford died Dec 29, 1774 aged 2 months.

John the son of William and Elizabeth Stafford died April 22, 1772, aged 28.

Elizabeth wife of William Stafford, died April 20, 1780, aged 74. Also William Stafford died Oct. 18, 1780, aged 74.

Ralph Verney Cope, son of Robert and Jane Cope, died Aug. 26, 1784, aged 10.

Robert Cope died Oct. 16, 1727, aged 47.

Elizabeth, his wife, died Dec. 8, 1761, aged 84.

John, the son of William and Dorothy Reddish, by fatal accident died May 4, 1779, aged 13.

William Reddish died May 24, 1783, aged 48.

Sarah, daughter of William and Dorothy Reddish, died Nov. 13, 1783, aged 20.

ON HEAD STONES, CONTINUED.

Elizabeth, the wife of John Christian died Sep. 13, 1778, aged 36.

Francis Mishael died Sep. 14, 1781, aged 56.

Anne Goforth died June 29, 1773, aged 29.

William Goforth died Octr. 3, 1745, aged 55.

Thomas Broom died Jan. 13, 1786, aged 26.

Rebecca wife of Saml. Ward died Nov. 5, 1762, aged 70.

Sarah, daughter of Wm. and Rebecca Lenton, died Feb. 14, 1752, aged 9.

Matthew Ringham died Jan. 24, 1766, aged 65.

Eleanor, wife of John Ringham died June 24, 1763, aged 45.

Daniel Crook died Jan. 21 1782, aged 79.

Ann wife of Daniel Crook died April 15, 1763, aged 58.

Christopher Thompson died July 1, 1776, aged 85.

Mary Wife of Wm. Lusing died Oct. 19, 1756, aged 73.

Robert Christian died Feb. 9 1785, aged 80.

Sarah Wife of Robt. Christian died April 25, 1780,

Ann Gann died Aug. 27, 1747, aged 15.

John Gann died Apl. 19, 1742, aged 49.

Jane the wife of John Gann died March 31, 1773, aged 77.

John Gann died Oct. 8, 1775, aged 52.

Thomas Gann died Oct. 10, 1780, aged 55.

Abigail wife of Thomas Gann died Sep. 19, 1780, aged 49.

Thomas Podom died April 12, 1769, aged 82.

Alice the wife of Thomas Podom died Jan. 27, 1764, aged 73.

Richard Sharp died March 4, 1741, aged 61.

John Sharp Junior died May 26, 1778, aged 22.

Mary wife of Richd. Sharp died Jan. 20, 1763, aged 84.

Ann wife of John Francis died Nov. 12, 1777, aged 46.

Eleanor wife of John Francis died July 4, 1763, aged 29.

John Hare died Feb. 15, 1761, aged 24.

George Bedford died March 7, 1754, aged 74.

Anthony Shepherd died Jan. 26, 1777. aged 64.

Anthony Shepherd died July 10, 1782, aged 76.

Richard Brumhead died June 9, 1785, aged 63.

John Skeath died June 12, 1775, aged 63.

John Skeath died June 23, 1752, aged 78.

Thomas Holmes buried Sep. 22, 1707, aged 88.

Francis Holmes died Dec. 21, 1768, aged 77.

Also Mary his wife died March 12, 1782, aged 84.

Elizabeth 3d. wife of Wm. Holmes died Mar. 18, 1705.

Jane wife of John Lupton died April. 6, 1761, aged 48.

Edward Lenton brother to Jane Lupton died Nov. 19 1767, aged 58.

Sarah wife of John Oldham died Aug. 8, 1754, aged 70.

TINWELL.

T I N W E L L.

TINWELL lies in the Eaſt hundred, and did formerly belong to the church of St. Peter's de Burg, or Peterborough, for at the conqueror's ſurvey it was found that that church held Tedinwelle, where were five hides and one yard land, of arable eight carucates, in demeſne two; twenty four villains and eleven bordarii poſſeſſing ſeven carucates. Here were alſo two mills of 24s. and twenty acres of meadow, formerly valued at 10s. but at the time of that ſurvey at 7l.

And in the poſſeſſion of that abby did this town continue till the diſſolution; after which king Edward VI. in the ſeventh year of his reign granted his letters patent of confirmation of the manor of Tinwell in this county, and Worthorp in eom. Northamp. (formerly granted to Richard Cecyl and his heirs) to William Cecyl knight, afterwards lord Burley, to hold of the king in capite, by knight's ſervice, reſerving the yearly rent of 65s. 7d. for a tenth payable at Michaelmas; from whom is lineally deſcended the right honourable John earl of Exeter the preſent lord of this manor, and of Intharp a ſmall village within this pariſh.

MONUMENTS IN THE CHURCH.

On a Plate of Braſs fixed upon a plain Grave-ſtone near the weſt end of the chancel.

En (Hoſpes) Sepulchrum *Gulielmi Robinſon* Armigeri, viri doɕti, prudentis, pii : Sapientiam & gravitatem multa leɕtio conciliavit : virorum nobilium amicitiis cognitus, quos ſine adulatione coluit : duas filias reliquit quas pie educaverat : interim mors oppreſſit anno ætatis 48, & Redemptoris, 1640.

On two plain Grave-ſtones placed in the ſouth eaſt angle of the chancel.

Here lieth the Body of *Elizabeth Cecil* daughter of *David* Earl of *Exeter* by *Elizabeth* his Counteſs, daughter of *John* Earl of *Bridgwater*. Buried November 13, Anno Domini 1638.

Here lieth *Thomas Cecil* ſixth ſon of *David* Earl of *Exeter* by *Elizabeth* his Counteſs, daughter of *John* earl of *Bridgwater* : buried May 28, Anno Domini 1641.

In the south wall of the Chancel is erected a handsome Monument (but without date) to the Memory of Elizabeth *daughter of* Richard Cecil *esq. and Sister of* William lord *Burley, who was first married to* Richard Wingfield *esq. and after his death to* . . . . . . *on which monument are the following inscriptions,*

Deo æterno opt. max. & Memoriæ sacrum.
   Fide   *Charitate*
  Certaque Spe   *Resurgendi.*
Ut viret occato denatum semen in agro,
Mortua sic vivent Corpora nostra Deo.

On this Monument are these three Escutcheons representing a Feme and her two husbands, *viz.*

In the middle *Cecil* with the distinction of the younger house, and over the coat *E L I Z A B E T H.*

On the Dexter, *arg. on a Bend. gu. Cottised Sab. 3 pair of Wings conjoined, of the first, and over the Coat, R. W.*

On the Sinister, *S. a Bend engraled between 6 Billets ar.* Over the coat *H. A.*

OF THE ADVOWSON.

In the 4 H. 3. the abbot of Peterborough presented Roger de Welles to the church of Tinewell.

The Rectory of Tinwell is valued in the King's Books at 12l. 10s. 5d.

The present Patron is the right honorable the earl of Exeter.

ADDITIONS.

L Y N D O N,

Alias, LINDON, LYNDEN, LINDEN,

IS in the hundred of Martinſley. Of this town I find no mention in Domeſday book; it being no doubt ſurveyed under the title of Hameldune Cherchefock.

In the 9, Ed. II. the King was lord of this manor. --- *Nom. Vill.*

In the 18, Ed. II. Matthew Bron did account in the exchequer the ſum of 14s. 4d. for the iſſues of one yard land in Lyndon in com. Roteland. then in the king's hands on the death of Simon de Lindon. --- *Pip. Vet. Eſch.*

King Edward III. by his letters patents dated the twenty-third of June in the twenty-ſecond year of his reign, granted to Robert de Corby, and to Joan his wife, and the heirs of the ſaid Robert for ever, the manor of Lyndon *cum pertinen.* to the value of ten pounds a year, or even if it be more, and the advowſon of the church there, formerly granted to Hugh de Montgomeri for life, and which the aforeſaid Hugh has now of his own accord reſtored. And this was in conſideration of the ſervice which he performed to his dear mother Iſabel the queen, and alſo in exchange for certain lands which the ſaid Robert held in Eltham and Mandevil. --- *Rot. Pat.* 22d. *Ed. III. n.* 12.

It was found by office taken in the tenth year of Henry IV. that John Daneys, ſon and heir of John Daneys, held of the king in capite, the manor of Lindon in the county of Rutland by the ſervice of one knight's fee. --- *Ex parte Rem. Theſ. H.* 10. *H.* 4.

In the thirteenth of Henry VI. it was found that Robert Daneys, ſon and heir of John Daneys knight held the ſaid manor by the ſervice of one third part of a knight's fee. --- *Ib. P.* 13th *Hen. VI. Rot.* 1.

Edward VI. in the ſixth year of his reign granted licence to Franciſce Peyton widow of ſir Robert Peyton, to Robert Peyton eſq. his ſon, and Elizabeth his wife, to John Peyton ſon of Robert and Frances, and to Richard Peyton ſon of John, to alienate the manor of Lyndon with the appurtenances, view of frank pledge, and advowſon of the living, to John Hunt gentleman and his heirs.

This John Hunt, (as appears by the following pedigree,) was the father of Remigius Hunt, who in the thirty-ninth of Eliz. borrowing 110l. of Tobias Loveday of Stamford in the county of Lincoln, gent. did join in a leaſe with Elizabeth his wife, Thomas and Francis his ſons, whereby they demiſed certain farms in this town to the ſaid Loveday for twenty one years by way of mortgage for the ſecurity of the ſaid ſum; the rent of which farms being received by Loveday, and amounting to thirty pounds per annum clear, one William Cook of Normanton in this county exhibited an information againſt the ſaid Loveday in the exchequer, upon the ſtatute of uſury, but became nonſuit. The particulars of which caſe, being too prolix to be here inſerted, may be ſeen at large in Co. Entries, Tit. Inform. fol. 393, b.

The preſent lord of this manor is ſir Thomas Barker bart. ſon and heir of ſir Abel Barker, bart. and nephew and heir of Thomas Barker eſq. brother of the ſaid ſir Abel; which two brothers, not many years ſince, purchaſed this lordſhip and advowſon.

[*Here follows a Genealogical Account of the Family of the BARKERS, but having been favoured with a correct Copy brought down to the preſent time, I have therefore given it in the ADDITIONS.*]

Of the ADVOWSON.

In the nineteenth of Henry III. Alanus de Lindon preſented John de Tyes to the church of Lindon, at that time vacant by the reſignation of Steven de Sandwic.

The Rectory of Lindon is valued in the king's books at 6l. 17s.

The preſent patron is ſir Thomas Barker bart.

ADDITIONS.

ADDITIONS.

Rotel. **I**N Trinity term an. 13, Ed. I. *Rot.* 36. Mafter Henry Sampfon knowledges in the court of common pleas that he had by his deed remifed and quit claimed for himfelf and his heirs to Edward king of England, and queen Alianor his confort, all the right and claim which he had or might have in, or to, the manor of Lyndone with it's appurtenances, under the demife of Simon de Lyndon.

By a fine levied in the court of common pleas at Weftminfter in Trinity term an. 13, Ed. I. *Inter ipfum dominum regem & dominam Alionoram reginam confortem fuam querentes, et Simonem de Lyndon deforciantem de maneriis de Afton in com. Northt. et de manerio de Lyndon in com. Rotel.* --- The faid manors are granted to the king and queen, by Simon of Lyndon, and they regrant them to the faid Simon of Lyndon for term of his life, to be held of the faid king and queen and their heirs by the rent of one penny a year payable at Eafter, *Pro omni fervitio, confuetudine et exactione,* and with warranty of the faid manors to the faid Simon during his life, the reverfion after his deceafe to the faid king and queen and their heirs for ever.

Edward III. in his thirty-fecond year gave licence to Robert de Corby and Johanne his wife to alienate the manor of Lyndon with the appurtenances to Rolland Deneys.

In the thirty-fecond of Edward III. Robert de Corby granted to fir Rollande Daneys the manor of Lyndon and advowfon of the church, to be held of the king and the chief lord of the fee by the accuftomed fervices.

By a fine levied in the court of common pleas at Weftminfter in Michaelmas term, in the thirty-fecond year of Edward III. between Rowland Deneys plaintiff, and Robert de Corby and Joanna his wife deforciants, the manor of Lyndon *cum pertinen. in com. Roteland.* is affured to the faid Rowland Deneys and his heirs in fee. The faid fine was levied *per præceptum domini regis.*

In Hillary term, in the fixth of Henry VII. *Rot.* 312, *dorfo Rotel.* John Hafvlden fuffered a common recovery of the manor of Lyndon in the court of common pleas to fir Thomas Cheyne, fir Henry Heydon, fir William Findern, knights; Philip Calthorp, Thomas Cotton, William Gurnay, Robert Drury, William Cheyne, Robert Parys, and Francis Calthorp, in which the faid demandants alledge that the faid Hafylden came to the faid manor by a deffeifin made by Brian Neweton.

Book of Surveys ab anno 1, ad 33, Henry VIII. fol. 86, dorfo. In the 13th of Henry VIII. Robert Payton efq. and Frances his wife, daughter and heir of Francis Hafilden efq. fued livery of the manor of Cheftirford in Effex, valued at 22*l.* 17*s.* 8*d.* the manor of Brianfpedil in Dorfet at 7*l.* 16*s.* 8*d.* and of Okeford fkilling, in the fame county, at 33*l.* 7*s.* and of the manor of Lyndon alias Hornsfield in Rutland, valued at 16*l.* 10*s.* in all 80*l.* 11*s.* 4*d.* and as to the manors of Pitchards, Foxleis, and Bonefbury, and Litelington valued at 55*l.* 13*s.* 4*d.* they did not fue livery, being then held by Elizabeth widow of the faid Francis Hafilden for term of her life, with reverfion to the faid Frances. The faid Francis died the fixth of April anno 12, leaving his daughter eighteen years old and upwards.

The following is extracted from a Book of Views and Mufters taken before John Haryngton the elder, and other the king's commiffioners of the county of Rutland, for taking of views and mufters within the faid county, in the fourteenth of Henry VIII.

MERTYNSLEY Hundred.

LYNDON.

Habilitas perfonarum.

Nomina perfonarum, cum Qualitatibus et cujus tenens.	Valor terrarum.	Valor bonorum.	Armatur et equi.
Robert Peyton efquier is chieff lord of the feid manor, - - - - - - - -	In Lond xviij *li.*	In goods nil. *quia extra* (*manet.*)	nil.
Ambrofe Barker yoman, and tenant to the feid lord, - - - - - - - -	In Lond xxs.	In goods xx *li.*	nil.

William

William Barker Preſt is perſon of the ſeid town, - - - - - - - - -	Perſonage vi marks.	In goods 111 *li*. nil.
John Harbar huſbondman, and tenant o the ſeid lord, - - - - - - -	In Lond nil.	In goods xx*li*. nil.
Gregory Barker huſb. and tenant to the ſeid lord, - - - - - - - -	In Lond nil.	In goods xx *li*. nil.
Edmond Stondelond huſb. and tenant to the ſeid Robert Peyton, - - - -	In Lond nil.	In goods xvi *li*. nil.
(*Archer*) William Diccons huſb. and tenant to the ſeid Robert Peyton, - - -	In Lond nil.	In goods xviii*li*. nil.
(*Archer*) Thomas Thornham huſb. and tenant to the ſeid chieff lord, - - - -	In Lond nil.	In goods v *li*. nil.
John Rawlyn huſbond. and tenant to the ſeid chieff lord, - - - - - -	In Lond nil.	In goods vi *li*. nil.
John Miller huſb. and tenant to the ſeid chieff lord, - - - - - - - -	In Lond nil.	In goods iii*li*. nil.
Robt. Grene laborer, and tenant to the ſeid lord.	In Lond nil.	In goods xx *s*. nil.
Edward Savell laborer, and tenant to the ſeid lord, - - - - - - - -	In Lond nil.	In goods xx*s*. nil.

The Church ſtoke, nil.

Pedes Fin. Mich. 27th of Henry VIII. No. 1.

By a fine made in Eaſter term, and recorded in Michaelmas term in the twenty-ſeventh of Henry VIII. between Robert Hawke clerk, and Richard Spencer chaplain, plainants, and ſir Robert Peyton knight and Frances his wife deforciants, the manor of Lyndon and ſixteen meſſuages, ſix hundred acres of land, two hundred of meadow, one hundred of paſture, forty of wood, two hundred of heath and furze, and a rent of ten pounds in Lyndon and Tykyncote, and the advowſon of the church of Lyndon, are limited to the ſaid ſir Robert and Frances, and the ſurvivor of them without impeachment of waſte; remainder to Robert Peyton eſq. their ſon and heir apparent, and the heirs of his body; remainder to John Peyton his brother, and the heirs of his body; remainder to Richard Peyton his brother and the heirs of his body; remainder to the heirs of the joint bodies of the ſaid ſir Robert and Frances his wife; remainder to the right heirs of the ſaid Frances in fee.

In the ſixth of Edward VI. dame Francys Peyton widow of ſir Robert Peyton, and Robert Peyton her ſon, conveyed the manor of Lyndon with the appurtenances, the advowſon of the living and courtes letes to John Hunte of Morecote gentilman.

In the ſixth of Edward VI. Franciſca Peyton, of Iſelham in Cambridgeſhire, widow of ſir Robert Peyton knight, gave a letter of attorney to Robert Watſon to take poſſeſſion of the manor of Lyndon with the appurtenances, and give poſſeſſion to John Hunt of Morcot.

Fine Paſch. 7 Ed. VI. No. 204.

By a fine made in Hillary term, and recorded in Eaſter term the ſeventh of Edward VI. between John Hunt plaintiff, and Frances Peyton widow of ſir Robert Peyton, Robert Peyton eſq. their ſon and heir and Elizabeth his wife, John Peyton and Richard Peyton gent. brothers of Robert Peyton junr. deforciants; the manor of Lyndon and ſixteen meſſuages, ſix hundred acres of land and three hundred of meadow, five hundred of paſture, twenty of wood, two hundred of heath and furz, a rent of ten pounds, and view of frank pledge (*i. e.* a court leet) in Lyndon and Ty kyngcote *alias* Tykyncote, and the advowſon of the church of Lyndon, are conveyed by the ſaid deforciants to the ſaid John Hunt gent. and his heirs in fee.

By an inquiſition taken the thirtieth of Eliz. after the death of John Hunt, it appears that he died poſſeſſed, among many other things, of the manor of Lindon, view of frank pledge, and advowſon of the church, and that Remigius Hunt his eldeſt ſon and heir was then forty years old.

Book of Decrees of the Court of Wards from the 21ſt of James I. to 3d of Charles I. incluſive, Fol. 556 --- 558.

Thomas Hunt eſq. died Jan. 7th in the twenty-firſt of *Jac.* (leaving Anne Hunt his widow and Edward Hunt eſq. his ſon and heir a minor) ſeized in fee of the manor of Lynden in Rutl. holden of the king in chief by knight's ſervice. The wardſhip of the body and lands of the ſaid Edward was committed to his ſaid mother Anne, and ſhe and

Q

her

her said son Edward the eighth day of April in the the third of Charles, he being then nineteen years old, by articles of agreement between them and fir John Wingefielde of Tyckencoate in the county of Rutland knight, reciting, that in order to perfect the inclosure of some part of the lands lying within the manor of Linden, and to enable her to pay for certain land in Linden purchased by her of Richard Hallforde of Edith Weston in the said county esq. for the use and on the account of her said son Edward for 600 *l*. The said sir John was willing to lend her the sum of 500 *l*. in consideration of which they covenant, if they can obtain the licence of the master and court of wards to demise two closes or pasture grounds in Lynden aforesaid lying next Luffenham Gapp towards Pilton, for six years from Lady-day then last past, to the said sir John at the rent of a pepper-corn per annum, and in case at, or before, the expiration of the said six years the said Anne or Edward &c. shall not pay to the said sir John the sum of 250 *l*. then the said sir John to hold the said premises for a term of seven years more at the rent of the pepper corn &c. And the court of wards, by their decree of the thirteenth of April in the third of Charles, ratify and confirm the said articles, and order that they make leases accordingly, and that the said Edward the ward shall not sue his livery until he shall, after he hath come of age, have confirmed the said leases and agreements by the said articles.

In 1634 Edward Hunt sold the manor and lordship of Lyndon to Valentine Saunders, who not having money sufficient to pay for it, gave Hunt a mortgage for 3000*l*. which mortgage transferred to other persons, was in being when Valentine grandson of this Valentine Saunders sold the estate again.

In 1654 Valentine Saunders the grandson sold the freehold in Lyndon to Hugh Audeley esq. of the Temple, and in 1662 Abel, (afterward sir Abel Barker baronet) and his brother Thomas Barker purchased both the freehold and Lincoln hold land in Lyndon, but Thomas Barker not marrying, and the male line of sir Abel failing in his son, sir Thomas Barker left it by will to Samuel son of Augustin Barker the only male heir then remaining in the family, whose son Thomas is now lord of this manor.

The dean and chapter of Lincoln have an estate in this parish, but when and how they came possessed of it I have not found.

There were two other little estates in Lyndon, one of which passed from Wymarke to Noel, to Halford, and so to Hunt then owner of Lyndon; and the other from Allen to Orme, and so to Saunders while he possessed Lyndon.

ADVOWSON.

In the thirty-sixth of Edward III. Richard Godard was rector of Lyndon.

Sir Robert Payton seazed in fee of the advowson of Lindon presented Anthony Smith to the rectory who was instituted the first of Edward VI. 1547, Dec. 31st, on the resignation of Thomas Sisson.

It appears by the abstracts above quoted that the advowson of the living has all along gone with the manor of Lyndon.

The following is copied from BACON's LIBER REGIS, *4to. published in* 1786.

King's Books.		Yearly Tenths.
6*l*. 17*s*. 1*d*.	Linden, alias Lynden, R. (St. Martin.) Prox. Episc. 1*s*. 8*d*. Sir Thomas Barker, Bart. 1687. Samuel Barker, Esq. 1731. Thomas Barker, Esq. 1765. 63*l*. 13*s*. 11*d*. 2*q*. certified value.	0*l*. 13*s*. 8*d*. 2*q*.

The present Incumbent is the Rev. JOHN FREEMAN, M. A. who was presented by THOMAS BARKER Esq. in 1765.

BENEFACTIONS.

Baldwin Barker of Hambleton d. 1603, 2d. Eliz. Taylor, d. 1619.
m. 1ſt.

Thomas Rector of All Saints, Stamford.

Clement

Mary m. Tookey.

Agnes m. Taylor.

Dorothy m. Tampion.

Suſan m. Cooke.

Abel Barker of Hambleton, d. 1637. m. Eliz. Wright of Uppingham.

Samuel of S. Luffenham, b. 1586, d. 1658, m. Dorothy Dixey of Barnwell, Northampſh.

Thomaſin, b. 1583 m. Muſſon.

John of Hambleton, b. 1608, d. 1639. Ext.

Sir Abel, bart. of Hambleton, b. 1618 d. 1679. (bought Lyndon between them.) b. 1622, d. 1580. Ext.

Thomas of Lyndon,

Eliz. m. Goodman, Blaſton, Leiceſterſh. Ext.

Thomaſin, m. Collin, Gr. Eaſton, Leiceſterſh. Ext.

Mary m. Greene, of Rolleſton, Leiceſterſh.

Samuel of S. Luffenham, b. 1616, d. 1676 m. E. Wildbore Lyndon

Abel Rector of Lancaſter, m. E. Wildbore Lyndon of Lancaſter, widow of Challoner of Duffield, Derbyſh. Ext.

Nathaniel Ext.

Jonathan both of N. Luffenham Ext.

John Ext.

Thomas Ext.

Eliz. Ext.

Bridget Ext.

Dorothy m. Sill. b. 1639 d. 1711 Ext.

1ſt Anne Burton Stockerſton, Leiceſterſh. mar. 2d Mary Noel Whitwell.

Sir Thomas Barker of Lyndon, b. 1647, d. 1708. Ext.

Mary m. Dighton, Ext.

Eliz. m. Leigh, Ext.

Thomaſin m. Parſon, Ext.

Samuel of Gray's Inn and S. Luffenham d. 1682, Ext.

Auguſtin of S. Luffenham m. Thomaſin Tryſt of Maldford, d. 1689.

Elizabeth d. 1681, Ext.

Dorothy d. 1686. Ext.

Samuel Barker of Lyndon b. 1686, d. 1759. m. Sarah Whiſton.

Elizabeth m. Dawes of Seyton b. 1688. d. 1749.

Thomas Barker of Lyndon, b. 1722, m. Anne White of Selbourn, Hampſh.

Sarah Elizabeth

Anne d. 1780.

Samuel Barker b. 1757. m. Mary Haggit, of Ruſhton, Northamptonſhire.

Sarah m. E. Brown, eſq.

Anne

Mary

Elizabeth

SUBSCRIBERS.

The Right Honourable the Earl of Exeter.
Sir John Smith, Baronet.
T. Barker, Efq. Lyndon.
R. I. Sulivan, M. P. for Thames Ditten, Surry.
The Rev. J. Rennel, Prebend of Winchefter.
The Rev. Dr. White, Lavington, Lincolnfhire.
R. Henfon, Efq.
Mr. Everard Digby.
The Rev. C. Johnfon.
The Rev. B. N. Turner.
The Rev. Mr. Fofter.
The Rev. Mr. Healey,
Mr. John Nichols, London.
Mr. Gough, ditto.
Mr. Robert Hunt.
Mr. Robert Weft.

Lord Sherard.
Rev. Mr. Twopenny.
Honourable J. Monckton, Efq.
W. Gery, Efq. Bufhmead Priory.
J. Wingfield, Efq.
Edward Muxloe, Efq.
Major Chefelden, Somerby.
J. W. Reed, Efq.

Mr. Swann.
Mrs. Pauncefort.
Mr. Fryer, jun.
Mr. Howgrave.
Mr. Thomas Wilfon.
Mr. Newcomb.
Mr. Richard Wilfon.

ERRATA — In the Lift of Sheriffs, For the year 1759 read Edward Ward, not Warden.

Any Drawings or Articles of Information, refpecting this Work, will be thankfully received. --- The Publifher returns his beft Thanks to thofe Gentlemen who have already affifted him, and begs a continuance of their Favours.

Thofe Notes, which have an (L.) for their Signature, were given by Mr. Lowe, of Stamford, Surgeon.

The Genealogical Tables will be given in the laft Numbers, in order to give the different Families an Opportunity of improving them.

Of the Publifher her of may had in 2 vol. with Plates, price 7s.

THE ANTIQUITIES of STAMFORD and St. MARTIN's; with NOTES: To which is added their PRESENT STATE, including a Defcription of BURGHLEY, the Seat of the Earl of Exeter.

The Monthly Review gives the following Account of the Work.

Four reafons are affigned for this publication; The firft is 'The fcarcity of the prefent Hiftories of Stamford. 2d. 'The length of time elapfed fince their publication.' 3d. 'That by methodizing and pruning the redundances of former writers, a Hiftory lefs exceptionable than the preceding might be obtained.' The laft, though, fays our chearful Editor, not the leaft, is --- 'my own private emolument.' Yet he adds, 'as egotifm is a figure of fpeech which no reader is fond of and myfelf being as little fond of it as any reader, I fhall not dwell on this, but infift on the three former heads only.'

It fufficiently appears that a work of this kind was wanting. Mr. Peck, an induftrious antiquary brought down his annals no lower than 1461, and though collected with great care, they will afford but little pleafure except to the profefsed antiquary. Other books of the kind are fhort, defective and yet very fcarce. On fuch accounts taking Peck for his ground, and ufing what other helps he could obtain; Mr. Harrod brings down his work to the prefent time. He acknowledges obligation to feveral who have contributed to his affiftance and in particular to the Earl of Exeter, 'for the privilege of confulting his libraries, and for enabling him to give a correct account of his moft valuable pictures; He affigns as a reafon for the fmall fize of his volumes, his opinion, *that a great book is a great evil.* Should any fay that this is arguing againft his own intereft, fince he has fome *Folios* to difpofe of; he replies, he has fome little reafon to lament, with *Fulmer* in the Weft Indian, 'that when I fet up bookfelling the people left off reading.' * He has beftowed attention and labour on his work, which, though it will admit no doubt of emendations and improvement, is entertaining and informing; and will be particularly acceptable to thofe who have connections with Stamford and it's environs.'

* The Friends of the Publifher will, no doubt, be glad to hear that he has no further reafon to lament, his Hiftory of Stamford having met with a Sale beyond his expectation.

This Day is publifhed, in Folio, Price only *One Shilling.*

EMBELLISHED: firft, with an elegant South Weft View of Burley, *the Palace of the Right Honourable the* Earl of Winchelfea, *engraved by* Page, *at the expence of* NINE GUINEAS.

Second. A View of the Eaft-End of Tickencote Church, *the figure of* a Warrior, *and a curious* Arch *in the Chancel, at the expence of* FIVE GUINEAS.

Third. The Arms of the Nobility and Gentry in the faid County.

The following Particulars relating to R U T L A N D.

1 DESCRIPTION of Burley Houfe.
2 Preface to Wright's Hiftory of Rutland, with Notes, now firft added.
3 General account of the County both Ancient and Modern, with Notes.
4 Of the Wapentakes or Hundreds.
5 Ecclefiaftical Government.
6 Of the Earls of Rutland.
7 Lift of the Sheriffs, from 1164 to 1788, procured at the expence of *Four Guineas* from the proper office in London.
8 Lift of knights of the Shire, from the 23d of Edward I. to this prefent time.
9 Of the Lord Lieutenants.
10 Names of the Gentry returned by the Commiffioners in the reign of Henry VI.
11 Upwards of 50 diftances of feveral places meafured by a wheel.
12 Meafurement of the turnpike Road from the fouth eaft corner of Kettering Bowling-Green, near the 75th mile-ftone to the Crown Inn, Oakham.
13 Meafurement of the turnpike road from Leicefter to Wansford.
14 Antient and prefent ftate of the Parifh of Ryhal.
15 Ancient account of Tinwell.
16 Antient ftate of Lyndon.
17 Genealogy of the Family of BARKER, of LYNDON, from 1603 to the prefent time.

N. B. The above mentioned was fold to Subfcribers for 2s, and is part of a Work which was intended to contain Wright's Hiftory of Rutland, entirely, with Additions, bringing it down to the prefent time, which Work is now difcontinued for want of a little more encouragement.

The Engravings, which are really worth double the purchafe-money, when framed and glazed, will form no mean ornamental furniture.

Printed and Sold by W. HARROD, *Stamford.* 1790.

Knights of the Shire in Parliament.

THIS little county having never had any city, borough or corporation within it's limits sends only two knights for the shire to the house of commons in parliament. A list of whom I have here collected from the 23d Ed. I. to this day: so far as any records are extant.

Regn. EDW. I.

23 Ro. de Flikesthorp, & Sim. de Bokminster.
26 Johan de Foleville, Williel. de Berks. *Lond.*
28 Williel de Blunt, Joha. de Foleville, *Linc.*
29 Idem.
30 Joha. de *Seyton*, Rober. de *Flixthorp.*
33 Theobaldus de Nevil. *Rob. de Flixthorpe, chevs.*
34 Rob. de Flixthorpe, Tho. de Buckland.
35 Williel. le Blunt, Bernardus de Brus.

Regn. Ed. II.

2 Williel. de *Basings*, Symon de Lyndon.
4 Radulf. de Bellafago, *Beaufoe* Nicol. de Burton.
5 Richardus de Bouton. *Lond.*
5 Bernardus de Brus, Rober. de la Sale. *Westm.*
6 Willi. de Sancto *Lizcio*, Bricius le *Dancys. West.*
6 Willi. de Helewell, Alanus de Frankton. *West.*
6 Johan de *Wyvele*, Walterus Poul. *West.*
7 *Will. le Blount, Rob. Rebuz.*
8 Reginaldus de Warley, Husculphus de Whitewell.
8 *Idem. York.*
9 Nich. de Burton, Rogerus Pucost. *Lincoln.*
9 Hasculphus de Whitewell, Joh. Basset. *West.*
10 Joha. Basset, Hasculphus de Whitwell. *Linc.*
15 Johan. de Hakelyne, Rober. Birom.
16 Rober. de *Lufwyke*, Rich. de Seyton. *York.*
17 Willi. Haward, Williel. de Alesbury. *West.*
18 *John Bouet, Robert Bynouh.*
19 Hasculphus de Whitewell, Stephanus de Wytleford.

Regn. EDW. III.

1 Johan de Boivyle, Steph. de Wytleford. *West.*
1 Johan. de Wittelisbur. Johan. de Bellafago. *Linc.*
2. Rich. de Sancto Licio, Willi. de Aylesbury, *Sarum.*
2 Rich. de Sancto Licio, Johan. de Bellafago. *Ebor.*
2 Johan. de Wittlebury, Rich. de Sancto Licio, *Northamp.*
2 Johan. de *Beaufon*, Johan. de *Wevyvile. Ebor.*
4 Johannes de Weyvile, Walterus Poul. *West.*
4 Rich. de Sancto Licio, Tho. de Grenham. *Winton.*
5 Clem. de Casterton, Johan. de Wevyl.
6 Johan. de Wyvil, Walterus Poul.
6 Rogerus de Denford, Rich. de Seyton.
7 Johan. le Hunt, Thomas de *Winge*, *York.*
8 Johan. de Wittilbury, Johan. Hakeluit, *West.*
8 Johan. Hakeluit, Johan. de Weyvile. *Ebor.*
9 Rich. de Sancto Licio, Hasculph. de Whitewell.
10 Rich. de Sancto Licio, Thomas de Wympton, *Notting.*
10 Idem.
11 Johan de Seyton, Johan. Basset.
11 Tho. de Wympton, Sim. de Lyndon.
11 Johan. Hakeluit, Thomas de Grenham, *West.*
12 Joha. Hakeluit, Reginaldus de la More, *Northamp.*
12 Rich. de Burton, Will. de Ayelsbury

13 Joha. de Hakeluit, Rogerus de Bellofago.
13 Joha. de Hakeluit, Walterus Poul.
14 Tho. de Grenham, Rogerus de Deneford. *Westm.*
14 *Walter de   , Simon de Lyndon.*
14 *Bernard le Bras, Hugo Nottingham.*
14 *John de Wyville, Walter Poul.*
15 Willi. Wade, Rogerus de Beafo.
17 Hasculphus de Whitewell, Wil. Wade.
18 Idem.
20 Wil. Wade, Reginaldus de Tykesovere.
21 Joha. Hakeluit, Willi. Wade.
22 Idem.
25 Will. Wade, Reginaldus de Tykesovere.
26 Galfridus de la Mare, Rolandus Daveys.
26 Rolandus Daveys. *(one only summoned)*
27 Willielmus de Burton. *ditto.*
28 Will. de Burton, Rolandus Daveys.
29 Will. Beaufen, Rob. de Luffenham.
31 *Will. de Burton, Rolan. Daveys.*
34 *Will. de Wade, Rob. de Luffenham.*
34 *Rol. Daveys, Will. Wade.*
35 Rolan. Daveys, Wil. Wade de Stokefaston.
36 Joha. de Boyvil, Rober. de Luffenham.
37 Williel. Beaufou, Williel. Wade.
39 Rob. de Luffenham, Will. Beaufo.
42 Will. Beaufo, Walterus de Scayle.
43 Joha. Boyvile, Will. Beaufo.
45 Laurentius Hauberk, Nichol. Grene, *West.*
45 Laurentius Hauberk. *Winton.*
46 Nichol. Grene, Johan. Wittlesbury.
47 Ric. Nevylle, Joha. Knotte de Gretham.
50 Joh. Basyngs, Tho. de Burton, chivalers.
51 Nichol. Grene, Lurentius Hauberk.

Regn. RIC. II.

1 Thomas de Burton, chivaler.
2 Walterus Scarle, Nichol. Morwood. *Glouc.*
2 Joh. Hellewell, chiv. Lauren. Hauberk *West.*
3 Tho. de Burton, chiv. Walterus Scarle
4 Johan. Wittelbury, Will. Morewood
5 Tho. de Burton, Johan. Wittelbury
5 Joh. Daveys, Will. Morewood.
6 Joh. Daveys, Will. Flore.
6 Joha. Helwell, Williel. Morewood.
7 Joh. de Calverly, Joh. Wittlebury, chiva. *West.*
7 Rober. de Haryngton, Nichol. Grenham. *Sarum*
8 Williel. Flore. Williel. Morewoode.
9 Hugo de Calveley, Johan. Knot.
10 Johan. Wittelbury, Walterus Scarle.
11 Hugo Browe, Oliverus Maleverer, chiva.
12 Joh. Daveys, chivaler, Walterus Scarle.
13 Hugo de Calveley, Oliverus de Maleverer.
14 Hugo Browe, Johan. de Calveley.
15 Hugo Grenham, Johan. Bushe.
16 Walterus Scarle, Johan. Elme.
17 Johan. Daveys, chiv. Johan. Elme.
18 Joh. Wittelbury sen. Walterus Scarle.
20 Rob. Fleffington, Rogerus de Flore.
21 Oliver Maleverer, chiva. Tho. de Onteby

Regn.